Elmer A. Martens and Howard H. Charles, Editors

Believers Church Bible Commentary

Matthew

Richard B. Gardner

HERALD PRESS
Scottdale, Pennsylvania
Waterloo, Ontario

Library of Congress Cataloging-in-Publication Data
Gardner, Richard B., 1940-
Matthew / Richard B. Gardner.
p. cm. — (Believers church Bible commentary)
Includes bibliographical references.
ISBN 0-8361-3555-5 (alk. paper)
1. Bible. N.T. Matthew—Commentaries. I. Title. II. Series.
BS2575.3.G375 1991
226.2'07—dc20 91-12048
CIP

The paper used in this publication is recycled and meets the minimum requirements of American National Standard for Information Sciences—Permanence of Paper for Printed Library Materials, ANSI Z39.48-1984.

Library of Congress Catalog Card Number: 91-12048
International Standard Book Number: 0-8361-3555-5
Printed in the United States of America
Cover by Merrill R. Miller

99 98 97 96 95 94 93 92 91 10 9 8 7 6 5 4 3 2 1

To my family
Carol, Eric, and Mark

Contents

Series Foreword

The Believers Church Bible Commentary Series makes available a new tool for basic Bible study. It is published for all who seek to understand more fully the original message of Scripture and its meaning for today—Sunday school teachers, members of Bible study groups, students, pastors, or other seekers. The series is based on the conviction that God is still speaking to all who will hear him, and that the Holy Spirit makes the Word a living and authoritative guide for all who want to know and do God's will.

The desire to be of help to as wide a range of readers as possible has determined the approach of the writers. Since no blocks of biblical text are provided, readers may continue to use the translation with which they are most familiar. The writers of the series use the *New Revised Standard Version,* the *Revised Standard Version*, the *New International Version*, and the *New American Standard Bible* on a comparative basis. They indicate which of these texts they follow most closely, as well as where they make their own translations. The writers have not worked alone, but in consultation with select counselors, the series' editors, and with the Editorial Council.

To further encourage use of the series by a wide range of readers, the focus is on illumination of the Scriptures, providing historical and cultural background, sharing necessary theological, sociological, and ethical meanings and, in general, making "the rough places plain." Critical issues are not avoided, but neither are they moved into the foreground as debates among scholars. The series will aid in the interpretive process, but not attempt to provide the final meaning as authority above Word and Spirit discerned in the gathered church.

The term *believers church* has often been used in the history of the church. Since the sixteenth century, it has frequently been applied to the Anabaptists and later the Mennonites, as well as to the Church of the Brethren and similar groups. As a descriptive term it includes more than Mennonites and Brethren. *Believers church* now represents specific theological understandings, such as believers baptism, commitment to the Rule of Christ in Matthew 18:15-18 as part of the meaning of church membership, belief in the power of love in all relationships, and a willingness to follow the way of the cross of Christ. The writers chosen for the series stand in this tradition.

Believers church people have always been known for their emphasis on obedience to the simple meaning of Scripture. Because of this, they do not have a long history of deep historical-critical biblical scholarship. This series attempts to be faithful to the Scriptures while also taking archaeology and current biblical studies seriously. Doing this means that at many points the writers will not differ greatly from interpretations which can be found in many other good commentaries. Yet basic presuppositions about Christ, the church and its mission, God and history, human nature, the Christian life, and other doctrines do shape a writer's interpretation of Scripture. Thus this series, like all other commentaries, stands within a specific historical church tradition.

Many in this stream of the church have expressed a need for help in Bible study. This is justification enough to produce the Believers Church Bible Commentary. Nevertheless, the Holy Spirit is not bound to any tradition. May this series be an instrument in breaking down walls between Christians in North America and around the world, bringing new joy in obedience through a fuller understanding of the Word.

The Editorial Council

Author's Preface

The Gospel of Matthew is a resource both written *for* the church and highly prized *by* the church. It established itself early as the first book in the church's canon, and it has played a pivotal role in shaping the church's life and practice. Nowhere is this more true than in the believers church tradition. When we speak of making disciples, when we call for church discipline, when we advocate nonresistance, when we talk of serving *the least of these,* in each instance we have been shaped by the Gospel of Matthew.

To write a commentary on Matthew is thus to undertake a venture that is both inviting and intimidating. It is intimidating in the sense that it is treading on holy ground, holy ground that we may not wish to have disturbed. And yet because the First Gospel has so much to offer to the church, it keeps luring interpreters to reflect afresh on its contents. As I have responded to that lure, allowing myself to be drawn into Matthew's story, I have grown increasingly appreciative of its structure and power. My hope in writing the commentary is that it will assist other readers to feel the lure of this Gospel, to be drawn into its story, and to respond to its summons.

Many persons have "fed" this undertaking in one fashion or another. Among the teachers of Scripture from whom I have learned, I am especially grateful to my doctoral adviser, Rudolf Schnackenburg. With probing questions, friendly encouragement, and obvious enthusiasm for the text, he modeled an approach to biblical study which could not help but be contagious. In more recent years, as teaching and writing assignments have tended to focus on the First Gospel, I have been nourished by the work of others for whom Matthew is a special interest. Among those whose studies have proven especially helpful are Jack Dean Kingsbury, Ulrich Luz, John Meier, Eduard Schweizer, and Donald Senior.

No less important, however, have been opportunities to explore Matthew with inquisitive groups of students. In addition to regular classes at Bethany Theological Seminary, several special events took place while the commentary was underway which provided stimulating occasions to test material in process. These included a summer extension school for Church of the Brethren leaders at Juniata College (Huntingdon, Pennsylvania, July 1986); a professional growth event for Mennonite pastors held at Associated Mennonite Biblical Seminaries (Elkhart, Indiana, January 1987); and the Sebring Bible Conference at the Sebring (Florida) Church of the Brethren (January 1988). It is in gatherings such as these, where communities of learners grapple together with the text, that we discover most fully what Scripture has to offer.

The translation I have used as the basis for discussion in this commentary is the *New Revised Standard Version Bible.* Except where otherwise noted, biblical and apocryphal texts are quoted from this version. Quotations from the Qumran texts come from Geza Vermes, *The Dead Sea Scrolls in English*. James H. Charlesworth, *Old Testament Pseudepigrapha*, is the source for quotations from that body of Jewish literature. Sources for other texts cited are noted in the Bibliography. To help decode some of the references to literature outside the Bible, readers may want to consult the first entry in the Glossary and Essays, "Abbreviations/Citations." A further entry, "Jewish Writings," supplies additional information on this material.

The most important work to use alongside this commentary is obviously the Bible. In addition, many readers will find it useful to have a synopsis of the Gospels close by, so that they can look up parallels to Matthew's material in other Gospels. Two excellent editions of this type of resource are Robert W. Funk, *New Gospel Parallels* (Polebridge Press), and Kurt Aland, *Synopsis of the Four Gospels* (United Bible Societies).

As the manuscript for the commentary was taking shape, a number of persons read the material at one stage or another and offered helpful counsel and critique. Heading the list of such persons is the New Testament Editor of the series, Howard H. Charles, who oversaw the project from the beginning and was supportive in many ways. Others who reviewed all or parts of the manuscript, and whose contributions are likewise valued, included René Calderón, Estella Horning, Sharon Hutchison, Robert Ives, Walter Klaassen, Elmer Martens, Gordon Matties, Henry Poettcker, Donald Senior, Willard Swartley, Hugh Whitten, and Paul Zehr.

On the technical side, I am indebted to my secretary, Marilyn Nelson. It was she who helped initiate me to the brave new world of computers and word processing, and it was she who assisted in preparing the material in its final form.

Last of all, I want to thank the two bodies with whom I currently serve—Bethany Theological Seminary and the Church of the Brethren General Board. Both institutions made it possible for me to use professional as well as personal time to pursue this project. In addition, knowingly or unknowingly, faculty and staff colleagues became partners in the venture, both through nudging words of encouragement and through countless conversations about the church's vision and mission. It is that vision and mission, which belongs to all the people of God, that keeps calling us to study the Bible—and to write commentaries *on* the Bible!

Rick Gardner
Bethany Theological Seminary
Oak Brook, Illinois

August 1990

Matthew

Entering the World of Matthew

Getting Our Bearings

The purpose of a commentary on a text is to help the reader enter into and explore the world of that text. But how do we do that? In the case of Matthew, there are at least three *worlds* to explore. And for each of these worlds, there are certain questions to raise or procedures to follow to discover what is going on.

The *world* of Matthew is, first of all, *the world we find within the story Matthew tells*. Like contemporary books, dramas, and filmscripts, the First Gospel plunges us into a miniature universe of speech and action. Certain characters play prominent roles in this literary world, characters such as Jesus, the disciples, Jewish leaders, and the crowds. Together with other characters, these persons take part in a developing plot, a plot marked by a growing conflict that eventually leads to Jesus' death.

Along the way, many lines are spoken, some of them important because of the way they contribute to the plot, others simply because they come from the mouth of Jesus—who speaks for God in this story. To appreciate this narrative world of Matthew, we need to be attentive to questions of plot, structure, form, and rhetoric. We need to subject each piece of the story to close literary scrutiny—and ask how the pieces fit together into a larger whole.

The second *world* of Matthew is *the historical setting in which this Gospel was composed*. The story Matthew tells is not simply a piece of art for art's sake, but a text with vital connections to the real-life story of Christian groups in the first century. To begin with, the sources on which Matthew draws to construct his story came *from* the developing church. In a similar manner, Matthew writes *for* a community in time and space, readers shaped by a particular cultural heritage and facing critical issues in their social and religious context.

A second task of a commentary, therefore, is to clarify the connections between the literary world within the Gospel and the historical world of the author and the first readers. To do this, we pay close attention to phenomena such as the way Matthew uses his sources, points of contact with Jewish tradition, recurring issues and emphases, and episodes that seem to reflect or speak to a later time.

A still broader *world* which the First Gospel inhabits is *the story of the people of God from the days of Abraham and Sarah right down to our own time*. Although Matthew wrote to Christians in a particular time and place, his text is part of an ongoing conversation between God and the faith community. Earlier moments in this dialogue helped to shape Matthew's own script, and Matthew's script has played a key role in the conversation ever since.

Yet another piece of our exploration, therefore, is to ask how Matthew does in fact relate to this broader world of speech and story. How does Matthew draw from the earlier story of God and Israel? How does Matthew's agenda relate to that of other New Testament writers? How has Matthew been heard and used in the life of the church? And how does Matthew contribute to the conversation between God and the community of faith today? Such questions receive attention in the sections of the commentary entitled The Text in Biblical Context and The Text in the Life of the Church.

Author and Setting

Unlike the letters of Paul, the Gospels do not name their authors. The titles currently affixed to the Gospels, such as *The Gospel According to Matthew,* were likely added to manuscript copies early in the second century. The question of who wrote the First Gospel is thus an open question. One approach to answering the question is simply to take church tradition from the second century and later at face value. In the case of Matthew, that tradition is supported by a statement attributed to an early bishop named Papias, cited by the church historian Eusebius. According to Papias, Matthew assembled a Hebrew or Aramaic version of "the oracles" of Jesus, and other

Gospel writers translated or interpreted them as each was able. Papias' words are usually taken to mean that the apostle Matthew wrote the First Gospel.

Another approach to the question of authorship is to ask what clues the Gospel itself provides to the identity of the writer. If we go this more inductive route, we discover data that suggest a different answer. First, the existing Greek text of the Gospel of Matthew shows no signs of being a translation. On the contrary, there is evidence that it was composed from the outset for a Greek-speaking readership. Second, the author appears to draw most if not all of his knowledge of Jesus from other sources and traditions. There is nothing to suggest that the author brings the fresh eyewitness testimony of an apostle. His vocation is rather that of interpreting the earlier witness of others (cf. 13:52). Finally, the plot and language of the First Gospel suggest that its author wrote in the aftermath of a final break between church and synagogue. This likely did not occur until A.D. 80 or later, by which time the apostle Matthew may well have been dead.

The most plausible way to bridge the tension between these two approaches to authorship is to posit an *indirect* link between the apostle Matthew and the Gospel. It is conceivable that this apostle had a hand in an Aramaic collection of Jesus' sayings which circulated at an earlier time in the church from which the Gospel came. Or it is possible that the apostle played a role in founding this church, likely in Syria, and that the Gospel is ascribed to Matthew as a patron saint of the community (cf. commentary notes on 9:9).

Whatever the circumstances, the apostle Matthew was likely a contributor to the gospel tradition rather than the author of the First Gospel. The latter was an unknown Jewish-Christian, a second- or third-generation leader who built on the work of his predecessors. For convenience' sake, and in deference to long-standing tradition, we will continue to designate this unknown figure as "Matthew" in the pages that follow.

As hinted above, the church for whom this Matthew wrote was clearly a community in transition. In the early decades of the Christian era, Jewish-Christians maintained active ties to the larger Jewish community. The controversies that occurred were *intramural* disputes, between siblings who belonged to a common family. All that changed, however, after the Romans destroyed Jerusalem in A.D. 70. The structure of Judaism was altered forever. As the larger Jewish community rebuilt itself under Pharisaic leadership, it defined boundaries between itself and groups it viewed as heretical. Consequently,

Jewish-Christians found themselves no longer welcome in the synagogue.

The implications of this division for the church were at least twofold: (1) The church had to redefine its own identity as a community with a Jewish heritage but cut off from Jewish institutions. (2) The church's mission from this point on would be almost exclusively a mission to the Gentiles. Realities such as these helped to shape the agenda Matthew pursues in his Gospel. Unfortunately, these realities also contributed to the bitter tone Matthew reflects and the caustic language he sometimes uses when he describes Jewish leaders. *[Anti-Semitism, in Glossary and Essays, p. 417.]*

How Is It Put Together?

It is clear that Matthew organizes material systematically at the level of literary units and the sections to which they belong. But what about the Gospel as a whole? Does it also exhibit a well-ordered design or structure? There is no lack of proposals concerning such a structure.

According to some scholars, the five major discourses of Jesus in the Gospel (found in chapters 5—7, 10, 13, 18, and 24—25) supply the backbone of the structure, with the surrounding stories setting the stage for Jesus' authoritative teaching. Other interpreters believe they can discern a chiastic arrangement of materials, where the last section of the Gospel corresponds to the first, the next to the last corresponds to the second, etc. (*a b c c' b' a';* cf. the discussion of *chiasmus* under "Matthew, Literary Characteristics" in Glossary and Essays). Still others argue that the structure lies in the plot of the story, and that Matthew uses the phrase *from that time* to introduce new major sections of the story at 4:17 and 16:21. According to this proposal, Matthew develops his narrative in three stages, one focusing on who Jesus is, a second on Jesus' word and deeds, and a third on Jesus' death and resurrection.

While each of these proposals has a certain attraction, no one of them commands consensus. It may be, therefore, that Matthew did *not* launch his work with a single, overarching design in mind. More likely, the situation can be compared to a homeowner who takes a fairly simple house and decides to expand it. In Matthew's case, the simple structure with which he begins is the narrative of Mark's Gospel. The story line of Mark becomes the foundation of Matthew's story line as well.

Within that plot, however, Matthew decides to construct a number of topical collections of material, including the discourses of Jesus noted above. These collections incorporate material from sources other than Mark, among them a written source that Matthew and Luke both used. In addition, Matthew develops a lengthier prologue to the story with the material on Jesus' origins in the opening chapters of the Gospel.

Out of such a process a mixed or composite structure evolves, not unlike that in a present-day musical. A story with a plot determines the basic contours of this structure. Like the songs in a musical, however, Matthew's topical exhibits also occupy a prominent place in the structure. In addition to furthering the plot, they expand on themes that have significance beyond the story, and that engage the audience in terms of its own life experience. How to outline the composite structure of this Gospel is still debated. The outline developed in this commentary identifies six larger blocks of material, within which Matthew combines story and teaching in a variety of ways:

1:1—4:16	Jesus' Origins and Calling
4:17—10:42	Jesus' Messianic Mission
11:1—16:20	Israel Responds to Jesus
16:21—20:34	Jesus' Final Journey
21:1—25:46	Jesus in Jerusalem
26:1—28:20	Jesus' Death and Resurrection

Further discussion of the origin and shape of the First Gospel can be found in several entries in the Glossary and Essays. Readers interested in Matthew's editorial style may want to consult the entry "Matthew, Literary Characteristics" *[p. 425]*. Another entry, "Matthew's Sources" *[p. 426]*, reflects on the question of where Matthew obtained some of the material he incorporates in his story. Finally, there is an essay that explores the theological dimension of Matthew's story, entitled "Matthew, Distinctive Themes" *[p. 423]*.

So much, then, by way of introduction. It is time to move on, time to enter the world of Matthew.

Part 1

Jesus' Origins and Calling

Matthew 1:1—4:16

PREVIEW

Each of the four Gospels begins with an account of the roots or antecedents of Jesus' ministry. Mark relates Jesus' work to the earlier activity of John the Baptist in the wilderness. The other Gospels also refer to John but push the question of Jesus' roots even further back. In both Matthew and Luke, we find records of Jesus' ancestry and stories related to his birth. In the Fourth Gospel, the author traces Jesus' origins all the way back to the Word of God which was active in the world from creation on. Common to these introductory accounts is an attempt to link the story of Jesus with the story of God's prior activity in the life of the people of Israel.

The account of Jesus' roots in the Gospel of Matthew runs from 1:1 to 4:16. In this section we find a number of different types of material: a genealogy, stories about Jesus' infancy (modeled in part after popular stories about Moses' infancy), quotations of OT (Old Testament) texts which are *fulfilled* in the story of Jesus, sayings attributed to John the Baptist, and narratives of Jesus' baptism and temptation. Some of this content Matthew found in earlier written sources (see "Matthew's Sources" in Glossary and Essays). Other material is peculiar to Matthew and may come either from Matthew's community or from his own Spirit-guided reflection on Jesus' origins.

Whatever his sources, Matthew has taken this diverse material and developed a coherent narrative which sets the stage for Jesus' public ministry. Throughout this section Matthew focuses on Jesus' identity and calling, making certain that readers know *who* Jesus is. Along the way he emphasizes some of the places *where* Jesus appears: Bethlehem, Egypt, Galilee, the wilderness, the river Jordan. The association of these places with earlier biblical events and promises confirms, for Matthew, the messianic character of Jesus' coming and calling.

OUTLINE

Jesus' Family History, 1:1-17

Jesus' Birth and Infancy, 1:18—2:23

1:18-25	A Child Conceived by the Spirit
2:1-12	A Child Acclaimed as King
2:13-23	A Child Delivered From Destruction

Jesus' Preparation for Ministry, 3:1—4:16

3:1-12	John's Work as the Forerunner
3:13-17	Jesus' Baptism by John
4:1-11	Jesus' Temptation in the Wilderness
4:12-16	Jesus' Return to Galilee

Matthew 1:1-17

Jesus' Family History

PREVIEW

The Gospel of Matthew opens with a genealogy, a long list of names tracing Jesus' ancestry through David back to Abraham. This strikes many modern readers as a rather tedious and uninspiring way to begin a narrative. For ancient peoples such as Israel, however, genealogies held great interest and functioned in a variety of ways. Some simply show the extent of kinship. Others support an individual's claim to a hereditary political or religious office. Still others serve as the framework for relating the history of a particular group. Rarely, if ever, were genealogies compiled with the concern for biological precision and completeness that we look for in a family tree today.

Since Jesus was born into a world in which genealogies were important, it is not surprising that Matthew begins his work in the way he does. He wants the reader to know *how* Jesus belongs to the story of Israel—and how that story belongs to him! For the names in his genealogy, Matthew is indebted both to biblical genealogies (cf. 1 Chron. 1—3; Ruth 4:13-22) and to lists of descendants of David born after the time when the biblical records end. The genealogy which he constructs is intended to show how Jesus' family is connected to the important forebears named in earlier lists. More specifically, Matthew attempts to make the following points:

(1) Jesus is a descendant of both David and Abraham, and so a legitimate heir to the promises of God associated with both.

(2) The number and pattern of the generations leading up to Je-

sus confirm that he is the Messiah, the one through whom God will fulfill the promises.

(3) There are certain irregularities in the origins of Jesus' ancestors which anticipate an even greater irregularity in his own origins.

OUTLINE

Heading, 1:1

From Abraham to David, 1:2-6a

From David to the Exile, 1:6b-11

From the Exile to Jesus, 1:12-16

Summary, 1:17

EXPLANATORY NOTES

Heading 1:1

The first verse of Matthew describes the contents to follow as *an account of the genealogy of Jesus the Messiah.* Some scholars interpret the underlying Greek phrase more freely as "a history of Jesus the Messiah" and regard the phrase as a title for the Gospel of Matthew as a whole. However, in two passages from the Septuagint (LXX) where we find similar phrases (Gen. 2:4a; 5:1), the words in question clearly refer to an account of *origins*. One of those passages includes a long genealogy, not unlike Matthew's. The more likely meaning of the phrase in Matthew 1:1, therefore, is that of a record of Jesus' ancestry or origins. The phrase serves as a heading for the genealogy—and perhaps for the entire opening section of the Gospel.

Verse 1 goes on to speak of Jesus as *the son of David* and *the son of Abraham.* Both phrases are significant. As an heir of Israel's great king, David, Jesus is a candidate to fulfill all the royal promises associated with David. As an heir of Israel's great patriarch, Abraham, Jesus is a candidate to fulfill the even wider promises made to Abraham. The latter speak of blessings which will extend beyond Israel and bring life to Gentile nations as well (Gen. 12:1-3). At the outset, then, Matthew introduces themes important to the larger story, the motifs of Jesus' messianic rule and of a gospel for *all nations* (cf. 28:19).

From Abraham to David 1:2-6a

In verses 2-6a Matthew enumerates the generations from Abraham to David. The list of names follows closely the list we find in 1 Chronicles 1:34 and 2:1-15. Here and throughout the genealogy, Matthew uses the formula: "*A* was the father of *B*, *B* the father of *C*, etc." A more literal translation would read: "*A* fathered (or begat) *B*, *B* fathered *C*, etc."

One surprise in the list of names is the inclusion of several women, not the usual practice in Jewish genealogies. Nor are the women named some of the illustrious matriarchs of Israel's history, such as Sarah, Rebekah, and Rachel. Instead, Matthew names such women as Tamar (who seduced her father-in-law), Rahab (the famed harlot of Jericho), and Ruth (who took unusual steps to pursue Boaz). In the next group of names, Matthew introduces yet another woman, Bathsheba, referring to her in a way that underscores her role as an adulteress (*the wife of Uriah*, v. 6b). How shall we explain the presence of these names in the genealogy of the Messiah?

Raymond Brown expresses the consensus of many interpreters in his analysis of the matter. With each of the four women mentioned, Brown observes, "there is something extraordinary or irregular in their union with their partners." In spite of this, these women "played an important role in God's plan and so came to be considered the instrument of God's providence or of His Holy Spirit" (Brown, 1977:73). The role of the four women in the origins of some of Jesus' ancestors, therefore, foreshadows the role of Mary in Jesus' own extraordinary origins (cf. 1:18-25).

Further, the four women named by Matthew were either Gentiles or associated with Gentiles: Tamar and Rahab were Canaanites, Ruth a Moabite, and Bathsheba the wife of a Hittite. The inclusion of these women in Jesus' genealogy, therefore, may foreshadow the inclusion of Gentiles in Jesus' community later on. In several ways, then, the women named in the genealogy signify something important in the story of Jesus about to unfold.

From David to the Exile 1:6b-11

Verses 6b-11 enumerate the generations from the reign of David to the Babylonian exile. The names we find were likely drawn from the list in 1 Chronicles 3:1-16. Comparison of Matthew's list with that of the Chronicler, however, discloses that Matthew's account omits the names of several kings. In verse 11 Josiah is named as the father of

Jechoniah, while in fact he was the father of Jehoiakim, and the latter the father of Jechoniah. A more major omission occurs in verse 8, where three generations are missing. Between the reigns of Joram and Uzziah (whom the Chronicler calls Azariah) were the reigns of Ahaziah, Joash, and Amaziah. All this confirms our earlier observation that ancient genealogists were guided by concerns other than precision and completeness (see Preview for 1:1-17, above).

The most important thing to note in the list of names in this section is that it is a list of *kings*. Unlike Luke (cf. Luke 3:23-38), Matthew traces Jesus' descent from David through a line of royalty. The list begins with the greatest of Israel's rulers and concludes with the last free king before the exile. Such a lineage serves to underscore the messianic role which Matthew ascribes to Jesus and invites the reader to think of Jesus as one destined for kingship.

From the Exile to Jesus 1:12-16

In verses 12-16 Matthew lists the generations from the exile in Babylon to the birth of Jesus. The first three names are found in the genealogies in 1 Chronicles (3:17-19), and the names of Joseph, Mary, and Jesus were part of the tradition of the early church. For the names from Abiud to Jacob, however, we have no record apart from Matthew's. They may derive from one or more popular lists of royal descendants of David which were circulating in the NT (New Testament) era.

The genealogy reaches its climax in verse 16 when it states that Jesus *who is called the Messiah* is the end product of all the preceding generations. Note how the language used to describe Jesus' origins breaks with the formula used to describe the begetting of earlier generations: No longer does Matthew speak of a father begetting a son, but of a husband of a wife *from whom* a son is born. The very structure of the sentence hints at the irregular or extraordinary manner of Jesus' origins. Since Joseph is Mary's husband, Mary's child is legally Joseph's son, and thus heir to the long lineage recorded in the genealogy. Jesus' ultimate identity, however, will not be determined by Joseph, but by a source which Matthew will reveal in an episode to follow.

Summary 1:17

In verse 17 Matthew summarizes the material in his genealogy, stressing the number and pattern of the generations leading up to Jesus. He indicates that there were three distinct periods between Abraham and Jesus, with fourteen generations in each era. Two questions arise in this connection.

First, *do* the three groups of names in the genealogy each contain the required number of *fourteen* generations? For the first and second groups of names, there are no major problems. The third group, however, appears to represent only *thirteen* generations. Among the solutions proposed is that somewhere along the way a name was accidentally dropped from the list, or that the names of Jesus and Christ are to be counted separately (Christ signifying the new generation of the exalted Messiah). A more likely suggestion is that Matthew intends us to count Joseph and Mary as separate generations. The structure of verse 16 points in this direction, emphasizing that Jesus is begotten from Mary (apart from Joseph), even though Joseph is reckoned as Jesus' legal father. If this analysis is correct, then the group of names in verses 12-16 does represent fourteen generations.

A more major question is why Matthew attaches importance to the pattern of three periods of history with fourteen generations in each. Perhaps we find a clue in several Jewish writings which reflect on history in a similar fashion. So, for example, Daniel 9:24-27 refers to seventy weeks of years between the exile and the coming of God's kingdom. And the pseudepigraphical work known as Second Baruch divides world history from Adam to the Messiah into twelve distinct periods (cf. 2 Bar. 53—74). Both works reflect the apocalyptic conviction that God is moving history toward a clearly defined goal according to a carefully structured plan. In the framework which he uses for his genealogy, Matthew shows that he shares that conviction.

We find a further clue to Matthew's thinking in the symbolical meaning of the numbers he uses: Fourteen is a multiple of seven, and in Hebrew thought the numbers seven and three both signify completeness or perfection. Moreover, fourteen is the numerical value of the Hebrew letters for David, and Jesus is the son of David! Through his genealogy, therefore, Matthew is communicating his belief that when Jesus was born the time was right for God to fulfill the promises. Considered in the light of the Gospel as a whole, the number and pattern of the generations which lead up to Jesus confirm that he is the son of David who will rule history as the Messiah.

THE TEXT IN BIBLICAL CONTEXT

The genealogy which we find in Matthew 1:1-17 is one of a number of genealogies in the Bible. We have already alluded to the lists in the early chapters of 1 Chronicles and to the account of human origins in Genesis 5. Other OT lists include the record of the line from Shem to Abraham in Genesis 11:10-26, a list of Jacob's offspring in Genesis 46:8-27, and an account of Ezra's ancestry in Ezra 7:1-6. When we compare these and other genealogies, we see that they are addressing a variety of questions: Where did it all begin? Who is connected to whom? Who has the right credentials? Through whom does God fulfill the promise? The genealogy in Matthew 1:1-17 reflects an interest in all these questions.

The genealogy most directly related to Matthew 1:1-17 is the record of Jesus' forebears in Luke 3:23-38. For some persons, the differences between the two lists are both puzzling and troubling. And in spite of some noble attempts to harmonize the two accounts, we probably never will know who was Jesus' paternal grandfather. We need to remind ourselves again that compilers of genealogies in the ancient world were less concerned than we are about an exact and complete record of ancestry. Rather, they sought to make a particular statement about the roots and destiny of their subjects and used the data at their disposal to achieve that end.

Therefore, we study Matthew's and Luke's genealogies not to determine who is correct, but to discover what each is saying about Jesus. The latter is quite clear: Matthew wishes to make the point that Jesus is heir to all the promises of God which shaped the story of Israel. Luke wishes to make the point that Jesus catches up the *entire* human story, beginning with God's creation of the first ancestor. Both affirmations are important to NT faith—and to faith today.

One particular issue that Matthew's genealogy raises which is important for the larger story is the issue of how God works in history. Are God's ways orderly and predictable, or are they full of surprises? The genealogy in 1:1-17 suggests that both answers are partly right. On one hand, the scheme of three eras with fourteen generations in each, suggests that God pursues an orderly plan. Moreover, the underlying premise of the genealogy is that God will remain faithful to earlier promises to Abraham and David.

On the other hand, the genealogy speaks of irregularities in the family history, revealing that at times God worked through unlikely and unexpected relationships. In addition, Matthew identifies the exile in Babylon—a major *disruption* in Israel's story—as the dividing line between two eras in the genealogy. All of this prepares the way for the story Matthew has yet to tell about Jesus and the church. That too will be an account marked by both expected and unexpected developments. Through Jesus and his community, Matthew will argue, God is acting on the basis of long-standing purposes and promises, but fulfilling them in a way which results in another major disruption in the story of Israel.

THE TEXT IN THE LIFE OF THE CHURCH

At first glance, ancient genealogies such as Matthew 1:1-17 seem to have little to say to us. But is this the case? It is clear that some cultures continue to prize the sense of connectedness reflected in a genealogy. It is equally clear that many persons in Western culture are seeking to recover that sense of belonging to a larger context. When author Alex Haley shared his research into the history of his black ancestry in the classic work, *Roots*, it encouraged countless others to reclaim their own family history. Not to have some sense of corporate belonging such as this is to experience life as orphans in the midst of history.

At this point the text in Matthew offers us something of the highest importance. As it unfolds the story of Jesus' ancestry, it provides us with the possibility of finding roots for *ourselves* that we never knew about. Those who belong to Jesus' community become heirs with him to all the promises of God to Abraham and David. And the family history which shaped his identity becomes our family history as well.

Another point at which the genealogy has something important to say is the issue of the way God moves in the life of the church. No less than the community of Israel, the community of Jesus wrestles with the question of how orderly or how disruptively God works in history. In the believers church tradition, we have good reason to affirm God's freedom to move in new ways. We know that our own origins in church history involved a radical break with existing structures. What is not so clear is whether we *remain* open to God's irregular and extraordinary activity in our story, and whether we can affirm those who (like the women in the genealogy) become God's unconventional channels for fulfilling the promises. Matthew 1:1-17 challenges us to recognize a God who guides history in both orderly and disruptive ways.

Matthew 1:18—2:23

Jesus' Birth and Infancy

PREVIEW

Matthew continues his account of Jesus' origins with several stories related to Jesus' birth and infancy. As we read the materials in 1:18—2:23, we find all kinds of connections with the story of Israel. Most obvious are the quotations from the OT which Matthew introduces with a special literary formula: *This was to fulfill what the Lord had spoken by the prophet* (cf. 1:22; 2:15). These fulfillment quotations attempt to show how a particular event in Jesus' life embodies or reflects a specific text in Israel's Scripture.

For Matthew's Jewish-Christian readers, however, the stories of Jesus' birth and infancy would have had a biblical flavor even *without* these quotations. The story of the angel announcing the impending birth of Jesus recalls similar stories announcing the births of Ishmael, Isaac, and Samson. The role of Joseph as *a righteous man* guided through dreams to protect the life of the helpless and so further God's purposes is not unlike the role of the patriarch Joseph in Genesis. The description of Herod's frustrated attempt to destroy the infant Jesus contains several parallels to the biblical account of Pharaoh's attempt to destroy the Hebrew children and later Moses himself. Finally, the episode of the magi from the east who were guided by a star catches up features in the story of Balaam, a soothsayer from the east who predicted that a star would come forth out of Jacob. Like the magi he foiled the plans of a wicked king.

Later we will look at some of these OT parallels in greater detail.

For now it is enough to get an overall sense of the way Matthew's story of the infant Jesus gathers up numerous strands of the story of Israel.

Much of the material in 1:18—2:23 was likely familiar to the churches in Matthew's world prior to the writing of his Gospel, though we can only guess at the form in which it circulated. One of the traditions on which Matthew drew was clearly a story of the angel's announcement of Jesus' conception through the Holy Spirit, a tradition reflected in Luke's Gospel as well. In Matthew's community this story may have been linked with the materials we find in 2:13-23, which also focus on Joseph and his dreams. The story of the magi was perhaps a separate account at one time, which Matthew then incorporated into his narrative. Matthew himself was probably responsible for inserting OT quotations into the narrative, though he likely built on earlier Christian efforts to find texts that related to the story of Jesus.

The narrative which Matthew constructed from the material at his disposal consists of three parts. In 1:18-25, Matthew spells out the "holy irregularity" in Jesus' origins: He is conceived by the power of the Holy Spirit, an event which signifies his future role as a divine deliverer. In the story of the magi in 2:1-12, Matthew tells of differing reactions to Jesus' birth which give a preview of things yet to come: Gentiles acclaim Jesus as king with joy and adoration, while Jewish officialdom fears and rejects him. In the account of Jesus' flight from Herod's wrath in 2:13-23, Matthew highlights God's protection of the infant Jesus.

Here again the episodes prefigure the future, depicting Jesus as a wandering, unwanted ruler who is destined finally to suffer. In 1:18—2:23, therefore, is a narrative which looks forward as well as backward. The stories of Jesus' birth and infancy both catch up the past story of Israel and point ahead to the story of Jesus' messianic mission.

A final question to consider in relation to the birth and infancy stories is the literary genre or form of this material. As others have noted, Matthew's narrative contains features similar to those found in Jewish Midrash. *Midrash* is the name for interpretation of Scripture or commentary on Scripture. Among the techniques used in Jewish Midrash were comparing related texts, applying texts to contemporary events, and composing stories (*Haggadah*) which enhance or illustrate the text.

Of special interest as we look at Matthew 1—2 are some first-century stories dealing with Moses' birth and infancy (cf. Josephus, *Antiquities* 2.205-237). One such story speaks of Pharaoh's alarm when one of his sacred scribes told him that a Hebrew deliverer was about to be born. The story goes on to say that God appeared in a dream to Moses' father, telling him that the child to be born to him would deliver the Hebrew people from bondage.

Just as the Jewish community developed Haggadah to enhance the biblical account of Moses' birth, so Jewish-Christians may have developed similar stories to interpret Jesus' birth. (An example of Christian haggadah on Jesus' nativity in our own time is *The Story of the Other Wise Man*, by Henry van Dyke.) If Matthew's stories of Jesus' birth and infancy do in fact reflect Jewish-Christian midrash, then we should read them not so much to discover historical information about Jesus' early years, but rather to discover the *meaning* of Jesus' advent for our faith.

A Child Conceived by the Spirit

Matthew 1:18-25

PREVIEW

As indicated above, the story in 1:18-25 contains an announcement of Jesus' conception and birth. Similar annunciation stories are found in Genesis 16:7-14; 17:15—18:15; Judges 13:2-25; Luke 1:18-23; and Luke 1:26-38 (cf. Isa. 7:10-17). If we compare these narratives, we find a number of common elements: (1) An appearance of the Lord or the angel of the Lord. (2) A greeting by the one who appears, sometimes addressing the recipient by name. (3) A message that a child has been or soon will be conceived. (4) The giving of a name for the child and an explanation of the name. (5) Information on the future role or destiny of the child. Sometimes (though not in Matthew's account), the recipient questions how all this can happen and receives a sign of reassurance.

Central to the *good news* in annunciation stories is the word that God has intervened or will intervene to make possible the birth of someone important for God's purposes. In several cases (cf. also 1 Sam. 1), God grants fertility to a woman who is barren or beyond child-bearing age, and the woman then conceives in the usual manner. In the case of Jesus' conception and birth, however, God has intervened in an even more radical fashion. The child growing in

Mary's womb has been conceived wholly through God's initiative and so clearly signifies God's presence among us. What we have then in the announcement of Jesus' conception and birth is a powerful heightening of the theme of divine intervention in the parallel OT accounts. If the births of Isaac, Samson, and Samuel manifest God's redemptive purposes, how much more so does the birth of Jesus!

OUTLINE

Joseph's Dilemma, 1:18-19

The Angel's Message, 1:20-21

A Supporting Prophecy, 1:22-23

Joseph's Response, 1:24-25

EXPLANATORY NOTES

Joseph's Dilemma 1:18-19

The word translated *birth* in verse 18 is the same word (*genesis*) translated *genealogy* in verse 1. In this way Matthew links the narrative which follows to the genealogy and again focuses attention on the question of Jesus' origins. As in verses 1 and 16, *the Messiah* of verse 17 is identified with *Jesus*.

Verse 18 informs us that Mary became pregnant after she *had been engaged* to Joseph but before *they lived together*. The phrases quoted represent the two steps involved in Jewish marriage practice at the time. A formal exchange of consent before witnesses was the first step, and this constituted a legally ratified marriage. From this point on the man and woman were regarded as husband and wife, and any severing of their relationship required a certificate of divorce. The second step occurred when the groom took the bride to his family home, and the two began living together as husband and wife. Until the second step took place—often a year later than step one—the bride continued to live in her family home. This apparently is Mary's situation when she discovers her pregnancy.

According to verse 19, Joseph responds to the situation on the basis of two considerations. Being *a righteous man*, Joseph cannot overlook an apparent breach in Mary's fidelity. At the same time, Joseph does not wish to expose Mary to the disgrace which would result from a public trial for adultery. Seeking to act in a way that is both honorable and compassionate, Joseph resolves to divorce Mary in as private a manner as possible.

The Angel's Message 1:20-21

Before Joseph can carry out his resolve, *an angel of the Lord* appears and instructs him to alter his plans. As noted above, an appearance by God or an angel (messenger) of God is a regular feature in birth announcement stories. In the story at hand, the angel's message comes to Joseph in a dream. Further references to dreams as a channel of God's revelation occur in 2:12; 2:13; 2:19; and 2:22. Elsewhere in the biblical story, the divine message is sometimes found in the symbols which dreams contain (cf. the dreams of Pharaoh and his officials in Gen. 40—41). Here, however, dreams merely provide the setting in which God's messenger speaks.

The angel bids Joseph to *take Mary as your wife,* to take Mary to his home and live together as husband and wife. Mary has not conceived through an act of adultery, the angel reassures Joseph, but through an act of the Holy Spirit. Matthew has already informed the reader of the reason for Mary's pregnancy in verse 18, but only now does Joseph become aware of this. When the text indicates that the child conceived by Mary *is from the Holy Spirit,* the idea is not that the Holy Spirit carried out the husband's role in fathering Jesus. Rather, the Holy Spirit acts as that life-giving power which is the source of all life (cf. Gen. 1:2; Ps. 104:30; Ezek. 37:1-14) and thus capable of creating life apart from the usual means of conception.

The angel also instructs Joseph to name the son whom Mary will bear. In Jewish culture either parent could name a child (cf. Gen. 4:25-26; 16:11; 17:19), and Luke 1:31 designates Mary as the one who will name Jesus. For Matthew, however, it is important that Joseph carry out this responsibility. Naming the child will signify that Joseph accepts the child as his own, and this in turn will secure Jesus' claim to Davidic ancestry.

The name *Jesus* is a transliteration of the Greek *Iēsous*, which in turn translates the Hebrew name *Yešua'*, a shortened version of *Yehošua'* (Joshua). The longer form *Yehošua'* probably meant *Yahweh (the Lord) helps* or *Yahweh is salvation.* In the first century the form of the name likely to be used was *Yešua'*, which popular etymology associated with words meaning *save* or *salvation.* The angel's message reflects this understanding of the name: Mary's child is to be called Jesus because *he will save his people.* It is not from the Romans that Jesus will deliver his people, however, but *from their sins.* Although the births of both Moses and Jesus signal God's intention to deliver, Jesus will deliver the people from a bondage even more critical than political oppression (cf. Ps. 130:8; Matt. 26:28).

A Supporting Prophecy 1:22-23

At this point in the text Matthew interrupts the story to introduce one of the fulfillment quotations we mentioned earlier. There are a dozen such quotations in the first Gospel, including four or five in the infancy narratives. In the case at hand, Matthew quotes from the LXX, and the passage quoted is Isaiah 7:14. This passage speaks of the conception and birth of a child who will somehow signify God's presence in the life of the people. While the Hebrew text of Isaiah 7:14 refers to the mother of the child as a *young woman,* the LXX translates the underlying Hebrew word with a more specific Greek term meaning *virgin* (1:23). According to Matthew, the promise of Isaiah finds its deepest fulfillment when Mary conceives Jesus through the power of the Holy Spirit.

More important than the process of conception is the fact that the one conceived will be *Emmanuel*, God with us (cf. Isa. 7:14; 8:8, 10). Interestingly, Matthew does not say that Jesus' *father* will call him Emmanuel. Rather, using wording which differs both from the Hebrew text and the LXX, Matthew states that *they shall name him Emmanuel.* Who do *they* refer to? Most likely Matthew is thinking of the *people* whom he mentions in verse 21, the true Israel which acknowledges Jesus.

Joseph will call Mary's child *Jesus,* because *he will save his people from their sins.* The people whom Jesus saves from sin, however, will hail him as *Emmanuel*—for only someone in whom God is present can deliver from sin! At the end of his Gospel, Matthew will return to this theme of divine presence and reaffirm it in a new way: As God is with us in Jesus, so Jesus promises to be *with his community* at all times until the very end (28:20).

Joseph's Response 1:24-25

The birth announcement story concludes with a brief statement on Joseph's response to the angel's message. Several times in the infancy narrative we find a pattern of obedient response to a divine command (cf. 2:13-15; 2:19-23). So here Joseph *did as the angel of the Lord commanded him.* (1) He took Mary to his home, thereby assuming public responsibility for both Mary and her child. (2) He exercised a father's right to name the child, thereby acknowledging Jesus as his legal heir. Through these actions, the child conceived by the Spirit acquired Joseph's Davidic ancestry, making him *the son of David* (1:1, 20) as well as *the Son of God* (4:3).

Matthew also informs us that Joseph *had no marital relations with* his wife prior to Jesus' birth. The Greek text actually says that Joseph *did not know* (NKJV) his wife, a common Semitic idiom for sexual relations (cf. Gen. 4:1; 1 Sam. 1:19). The language of the text leaves open the question of how Joseph and Mary related to each other *after* Jesus' birth. Later in the Gospel, however (12:46; 13:55-56), Matthew refers both to sisters and brothers of Jesus, who apparently were conceived in the usual manner. It is unlikely, therefore, that Matthew was aware of the later tradition that Mary remained a virgin forever. Matthew's own interest does not lie in Mary's virginity as such but in confirming the message that Jesus' conception is the work of the Holy Spirit.

THE TEXT IN BIBLICAL CONTEXT

In the genealogy of 1:1-17, Matthew calls attention to some irregular relationships or unusual circumstances in the origins of Jesus' ancestors. All of this prepares the reader for an even greater irregularity in Jesus' origins. Having thus prepared us, Matthew goes on in 1:18-25 to spell out the unparalleled nature of Jesus' entry into the family of Israel: Jesus is not conceived in the conventional way, but through a special act of the Holy Spirit.

Matthew's description of Joseph's dilemma serves to highlight the issue of the unusual and unexpected. At first Joseph can only interpret Mary's pregnancy in conventional terms (adultery) and seeks to handle the situation through a conventional solution (divorce). It takes an unusual revelation of God through a dream to convince Joseph that Mary has conceived in an unconventional way, and that the child to be born will have an extraordinary mission! To be sure, Matthew tells the reader, all this is in keeping with a promise of God found in Scripture. But in no way does this take away from the element of surprise when God acts on that promise (cf. Minear: 35-37).

Matthew's motivation in sharing this episode, of course, goes beyond a storyteller's delight in surprise for its own sake. Matthew uses this account to tell us something important about Jesus' unique relationship with God. Although Matthew has not yet introduced the title *Son of God* (4:3), the story of Jesus' conception by the Holy Spirit certainly invites us to think of Jesus in this way. Elsewhere in the NT, Jesus' role as God's Son is sometimes linked with his resurrection (Rom. 1:3) or with his baptism (Mark 1:9-11). Both Matthew and Luke make it clear, however, that Jesus enjoyed a special relationship with God from the very beginning. Stories of God's activity in Jesus' conception and birth serve to underscore that point. *[Christ/Christology, p. 418.]*

As noted earlier, there are partial parallels to the story of Jesus' conception and birth in the OT. There too God plays an active role in the birth of offspring who will later carry out God's purposes. For Matthew, however, God's role in Jesus' advent exceeds anything in the past. Both the manner of Jesus' conception and the name signifying his mission attest that Jesus will manifest God's presence in a way that is unique and incomparable.

A further question is whether the story of Jesus' conception has anything to do with our own "conception" as a community of believers. Although Matthew himself does not pursue this question, other NT texts provide some intriguing parallels. In the book of Acts, the author clearly depicts the life of the earliest Christians as a life which derives from the power of the Holy Spirit. The apostle Paul speaks of the Spirit as the source of our identity as children of God (Rom. 8:9-17) and affirms that those who are in Christ experience a new creation (2 Cor. 5:17).

Most striking of all is the language we find in the Fourth Gospel. There the author describes believers as those who are "born from above" or "born of the Spirit" (John 3:3, 6). In another place he refers to those whom Jesus has given "power to become children of God," asserting that they have been born "not of blood or of the will of the flesh or of the will of man, but of God" (John 1:12-13). If we consider Matthew 1:18-25 alongside texts such as these, we see that the theme of conception by the Spirit applies to believers' origins as well as Jesus' origins. In a somewhat different but real sense, we too are "conceived by the Holy Ghost."

THE TEXT IN THE LIFE OF THE CHURCH

The Gospel accounts of Jesus' conception by the Holy Spirit have not suffered from neglect in the history of the church. The church has drawn on this material as a resource for both worship and theological discussion. Not all of the attention which Matthew 1 and Luke 1 have received, however, has proven helpful. At times the church has gotten sidetracked with questions which the text neither answers nor asks: Was a virgin birth necessary to keep Jesus from acquiring our sinful nature? Did Jesus receive his human identity from Mary or from the Holy Spirit? Was Jesus born of a virgin because virginity is somehow holier than normal marital relations? At other times the church has gotten sidetracked with attempts to prove or disprove the virgin birth: Is such an event a scientific possibility? Can we verify the historicity of the gospel accounts?

In the midst of this history of use and misuse of the text, we need to ask the fundamental question: What does it mean to believe in Jesus' virgin birth or virginal conception? Or to put it another way: What does Matthew invite us to affirm in his story of Jesus' birth? Eduard Schweizer puts it well in his commentary on the text:

> The focus of the story . . . is not the physical, biological process, but the theological watershed. . . . What the text asks is therefore not whether we can consider a virgin birth physically possible, but . . . whether in this birth we can see God's own and unique intervention for [our] salvation. And if this is the case, then we can also say what this story of the virgin birth is further meant to say: that this birth stands not merely as one among many in the long series of millions of births, that it took place not merely through the creative will or drive of a man, but through God's own will as creator. (35)

To believe in the virgin birth is to believe that Jesus receives his life from God, that God is with us in Jesus' life from the very beginning, and that Jesus therefore manifests God's power to save.

To believe in the virgin birth is also to understand our own life in a different way. First, we will acknowledge our radical dependence on the Spirit for our Christian identity. As the texts cited above reveal, the Spirit which created Jesus' life now creates the life of Jesus' community. If this is so, then we will look to the Spirit rather than to our culture for our fundamental sense of who we are.

Second, we will recognize the freedom of God's Spirit to act in powerful and unpredictable ways. A virgin birth attests a God who is interested in something much more than business as usual in our lives. It attests a God who is not reluctant to do a new thing, and who in fact seeks to make all things new.

Third, we will remain open to demands of the Spirit which alter old perceptions of God's will. No less than Joseph, we may discover that God's actions call for responses which run contrary to conventional religious behavior. To believe in the virgin birth is to respond as Joseph did, becoming partners with God in a new creation.

A Child Acclaimed as King

Matthew 2:1-12

PREVIEW

Unlike Luke, Matthew does not tell us a story about the night of Jesus' birth. He does, however, tell us about a delegation that comes looking for Jesus some time thereafter. According to Matthew 2:1-12, this delegation consisted of several magi or astrologers, whom we usually refer to as *wise men.* It was commonly believed in the ancient world that signs in the heavens accompanied the births of great figures, including rulers such as Alexander and Augustus. The magi in Matthew 2 claim to have seen just such a sign. Having observed the rising star of a newborn Jewish king, they make a pilgrimage to Judea to find him and pay him homage.

Listening to such a story, Matthew's readers may have recalled a similar (and widely publicized) pilgrimage which took place in A.D. 66 (cf. Dio Cassius, *Roman History* 63.1-7; Suetonius, *Nero* 13; Pliny, *Natural History* 30.6.16-17). In that year a delegation arrived in Rome, consisting of Tiridates, king of Armenia, and the sons of three neighboring Parthian rulers. This royal party from the East (described as magi by Pliny) had come to Rome to honor the emperor, Nero, and Rome was decorated with lights and garlands to receive them. Upon meeting Nero, Tiridates proclaimed: "I have come to you, my god, to pay homage, as I do to Mithras." After Nero confirmed Tiridates as king of Armenia, the party returned home, but by a different route than the way they had come (cf. Matt. 2:12).

While the story of Tiridates provides a fascinating parallel to our text, the roots of Matthew's story lie in biblical history rather than Roman history. Matthew 2:1-12 exhibits several similarities to the story of Balak and Balaam in Numbers 22—24. In that story we learn of a wicked king (Balak) who wants to destroy God's people, of the king's attempt to use a pagan soothsayer from the East (Balaam) to carry out his plan, and of a revelation from God which prevents the soothsayer from assisting the king.

Each of these features surfaces in Matthew's description of Herod and the magi. Further, Balaam utters a prophecy in Numbers 24:17 which uses the image of a *star* to describe the appearance of a future ruler of God's people: "A star shall come out of Jacob, and a scepter shall rise out of Israel" (cf. T. Levi 18:3; CD 7:18-20). What is a metaphor in Numbers 24 becomes a sign in Matthew 2: A star appears in the heavens which signifies the birth of the "star ruler" of the Jewish people.

Matthew 2:1-12, then, offers another episode in which the story of Jesus catches up and carries on the plot of earlier moments in Israel's story. As Matthew develops the narrative before us, we find him pursuing two major themes: (1) Jesus is destined to kingship over his own people and all nations. (2) Jesus will be rejected by his own nation but acclaimed by Gentiles. *[Gentile, p. 420.]* From a literary standpoint, the story of the magi falls into four dramatic scenes, as indicated below:

OUTLINE

The Magi Seek a New King, 2:1-2

Herod Confers with His Advisers, 2:3-6

Herod Confers with the Magi, 2:7-8

The Magi Find a New King, 2:9-12

EXPLANATORY NOTES

The Magi Seek a New King 2:1-2

The story of the magi begins with a brief historical reference to the time of Jesus' birth. Matthew dates this event *in the time of King Herod* (literally: *in the days of* (KJV), a common biblical idiom to refer to a period of time; cf. Ruth 1:1; Neh. 12:46). The Herod mentioned here is Herod the Great. An Idumean by birth, Herod ruled Palestine as a vassal of Rome from 37 B.C. till his death in 4 B.C. Acclaimed by some for his massive building projects (including Caesarea and the Jewish temple), he was at the same time feared and despised for his ruthless treatment of rivals and opponents. Matthew 2 confirms Herod's reputation as a wily and vicious politician, ever anxious about his status as king.

While Herod was still king, Matthew tells us, the delegation of *wise men* or *magi* (NIV) arrived in Jerusalem. *Magi* is a Latin rendering of the word *magoi* in the Greek text. Referring originally to a priestly caste among the Medes and Persians, the term *magoi* became an umbrella word to refer to a wide range of persons who exercised special religious or occult powers: astrologers, fortune-tellers, dream-interpreters, sorcerers, magicians, and others (cf. Daniel 1:20; 2:2; Acts 8:9-24; 13:6-11). Interestingly, the first-century Jewish author Philo refers to Balaam as a *magos*. In Matthew 2:1 it is clear from the context that *magoi* means *astrologers* (REB).

We are told that these astrologers have come *from the East*, which could mean either Arabia, Babylonia, or Parthia (Persia). In any case, Matthew depicts the magi as *Gentiles*: They come seeking a *king of the Jews*, which is the way non-Jews would speak of a Jewish ruler (cf. Matt. 27:37). Further, they do not yet possess the knowledge of Scripture which will point them to Bethlehem. They are not just ordinary Gentiles, however. As others have observed, the magi represent the spiritual elite of the Gentile world, those who have taken pagan wisdom as far as it can go.

The magi report that they have seen the star of a newborn Jewish king *at its rising* (or less likely, *in the East*, KJV), and thus have come to the Jewish capital to find him. From the second century on, interpreters have tried to identify this star, proposing such phenomena as a supernova, a comet, or a planetary conjunction, appearing in a constellation of the zodiac (Pisces, the Fishes) associated with the Jews. None of the theories proposed, however, fits all the data in the text. Moreover, Matthew himself is clearly less interested in the physical properties of the star than he is in its theological significance. Against the backdrop of Balaam's prophecies, as understood by Matthew, the star signifies the appearing of the messianic king who will rule many nations (cf. Num. 24:7 LXX; 24:17). When the magi come looking for this king, *they* embody the promise of Isaiah 60:3: "Nations shall come to your light, and kings to the brightness of your dawn."

Verse 2 notes that the magi seek the newborn king in order *to pay him homage*. The verb translated *pay homage* is the Greek word *proskuneō*. Matthew uses this word thirteen times in his Gospel, in most instances to describe the way persons respond to Jesus (cf. *knelt before* in 9:18; 15:25; and *worshiped* in 14:33; 28:9; 28:17). In the story before us, Matthew uses *proskuneō* no less than three times, in verses 2, 8, and 11. The word itself can indicate either homage paid to a person of authority or the special homage known as worship which we offer to a deity. Here the two meanings appear to blend or merge. The magi come to pay homage to royalty, but we the readers know that Jesus is no ordinary king, and that his rule will be indistinguishable from God's rule. When the magi pay *homage* to Jesus in Matthew 2, therefore, they foreshadow the *worship* of Jesus as the risen Lord in Matthew 28 (vv. 9, 17).

Herod Confers with His Advisers 2:3-6

In verses 3-6 the focus shifts to Herod and how he reacts to the quest of the magi. Matthew tells us that Herod was *frightened,* using a word that indicates great agitation or anxiety. The same word describes the disciples' terror when they behold Jesus walking on the sea and think it is a ghost (14:26). Given Herod's fear of rivals, his reaction to those who seek a new king in his kingdom is not surprising. We learn, however, that Herod was not alone in his reaction, but that *all Jerusalem* was shaken up with him. Here Matthew echoes the Jewish Midrash on Moses which stated that the news of the impending birth of a Hebrew deliverer alarmed the Pharaoh and filled the Egyptians with dread (Josephus, *Antiquities* 2.205-206, 215). Now the roles are reversed, however: It is the Jewish people and their king who are upset by the birth of a Hebrew deliverer, while representatives of a foreign nation seek to honor him! The irony is profound.

To discover where the newborn king is likely to be found, Herod calls together some of the leaders of Jewish officialdom (v. 4). The Greek verb for *call together* is the same word Matthew uses to describe sinister gatherings of Jewish leaders in his account of Jesus' trial and crucifixion (cf. 26:3, 57; 27:17, 27, 62; 28:12). It is also the word used in the LXX in Psalm 2:2, which speaks of rulers who take counsel together against the Lord and his anointed. Using a vocabulary with associations such as these, Matthew makes it clear that this gathering is no innocent theological consultation. It is a meeting which anticipates more ominous gatherings yet to come.

In verses 5 and 6 Herod receives an answer to his question about the Messiah's birthplace. Reflecting common Jewish tradition, the leaders indicate that the Messiah is to be born *in Bethlehem of Judea* (cf. John 7:40-44). The phrase *of Judea* or *of Judah* (cf. Judg. 17:7, 9; Ruth 1:1-2) served to distinguish this Bethlehem from another Bethlehem in Galilee. As the town of David's origins (cf. 1 Sam. 16:1: 17:12; 20:6), Bethlehem readily became the focus of speculation about the Messiah's origins. Micah 5:2-4 (5:1-3 in the Hebrew text) supports the view that the Messiah will come from Bethlehem and so is quoted (in part) in verse 6.

Actually, Matthew has combined parts of two passages here, Micah 5:2 and 2 Samuel 5:2. While the latter text is cited verbatim, the form of the Micah passage differs from both the Hebrew text and the LXX. Much like modern-day students who pick and choose from several different Bible translations, Matthew felt free to draw on different renditions of the text and even to make his own independent scribal judgments on the correct form of the text. While Matthew's methods may seem arbitrary to us at points, they reflect an approach to studying Scripture which was quite common at that time in both Jewish and Christian circles.

Herod Confers with the Magi 2:7-8

The scene changes again in verse 7. Having conferred with his advisers, Herod now confers *secretly* with the magi. No one else is to know his plans, and even the magi will not know his real intent. Herod's inquiry about the time when the star appeared likely refers to the rising of the star mentioned in verse 2: What is the precise day, month, and year when the star first came up over the horizon? Matthew is preparing us here for the following narrative, when Herod will make use of this astronomical information: It will indicate the age of the newborn king who must be eliminated (2:16). But that will come later. For now it is sufficient to dispatch the magi to Bethlehem to search for the child, with instructions to report back on their findings: "I too would like to *pay homage* to this newborn king," Herod professes. While Herod's hypocrisy is hidden from the magi, it is fully apparent to the reader who knows Herod's lust for power.

The Magi Find a New King 2:9-12

In verses 9-12 the magi again become the main actors. As they set out on the five-mile trip to Bethlehem, the star which they saw *at its rising* reappears. Up to this point, there is no suggestion in the story that the magi actually *followed* the star. Both Jerusalem and Bethlehem could be found without assistance of this sort. Now, however, the star leads the magi on (like the pillar of fire in Exod. 13:21-22) and pinpoints the exact place where the child is to be found. Matthew calls attention here to the incomparable joy which the magi experienced when the star *stopped.* Joy such as this is regularly associated with the messianic age (cf. Isa. 35), and so is also a key theme in Luke's birth narrative (cf. Luke 1:44; 2:10).

Verse 11 tells us that the magi find Jesus in a *house* in Bethlehem. Whereas Luke depicts Mary and Joseph as visitors to Bethlehem, Matthew apparently thinks of Jesus' family as residents of the town, who only later make Nazareth their home (cf. 2:19-23). Entering the house, the magi find Jesus *with Mary his mother.* Matthew may be describing the scene in this manner to evoke memories of the royal household in ancient Judah, in which the queen mother had a seat of honor beside the king (cf. 1 Kings 2:19; Jer. 13:18).

In any case, the homage or worship which the magi offer to Jesus leaves no doubt about his regal status. The *gold, frankincense, and myrrh* which the magi take from their treasure coffers and give to Jesus were in fact gifts "fit for a king!" (cf. 1 Kings 10:1-2, 10; Ps. 72:8-11, 15; Isa. 60:6; Song of Sol. 3:6-7). For Matthew, the scene which unfolds here proclaims Jesus to be that king whom all the nations will honor and serve (cf. Ps. 72:11).

The episode concludes in verse 12 with a last-minute shift in the plot. At this point the magi are supposed to report their discovery to Herod. It is not God's will, however, that the magi should contribute unwittingly to the demise of the child they have just acclaimed as king. Like Joseph, therefore, they receive special instructions from God through a dream to alter their plans. This they do, exiting from the story as they return to their own country.

THE TEXT IN BIBLICAL CONTEXT

Matthew and Luke both report a disclosure of Jesus' birth to a select group of persons, who then come to Bethlehem to find the child. In Luke 2 it is a group of shepherds, who respond to an angelic announcement of the good news. In Matthew 2 it is a group of astrologers, who respond to the message they deduce from a star in the heavens. At first glance the two groups seem totally unrelated. What have Palestinian shepherds to do with gift-bearing magi from the East? To be sure, there is no literary connection between the Matthean and Lukan accounts. In both cases, however, the news of Jesus' birth is revealed to a group of "outsiders" rather than to the faithful core of the Jewish people.

Shepherds were a lowly group on the margin of Jewish society, viewed by many as persons of questionable integrity. The magi were Gentiles from a foreign country, with no real link to Jewish faith and life. In both Matthew and Luke, therefore, the visitors who come looking for Jesus serve to underscore the *universal significance* of his birth. As outsiders in one sense or another, the magi and the shepherds represent the many separated or excluded groups who will be *included* in the salvation which Jesus brings.

For Matthew, of course, the quest of the outsiders stands in sharp contrast to the attitude of the insiders. Whereas word of a new king's birth leads the Gentile magi to seek and worship Jesus, that word evokes consternation in Jerusalem and leads Herod to seek to destroy Jesus. Both features amount to a preview of what will happen later in the story of Jesus. The leaders of Jesus' own nation will refuse to acknowledge his lordship and will in fact seek his death. Other nations, however, will receive the one whom Israel rejects and will acknowledge his reign and rule. To a certain extent this theme of Jewish rejection and Gentile acceptance runs throughout the NT. It is greatly accentuated in Matthew, however, reflecting the intense rivalry between the synagogue and the church in Matthew's own time. *[Entering the World of Matthew, pp. 19-23.]*

As noted already, the story of the magi gives special prominence to the theme of Jesus' *kingship*. Jesus is at one and the same time the *king of the Jews* and the long-awaited world ruler whom all the nations will honor and serve. Only after his resurrection will Jesus really be able to claim that *all authority in heaven and on earth has been given to me* (28:18). The adoration of the magi, however, confirms and celebrates Jesus' royal destiny in advance.

Interest in Jesus' kingly role is not confined to Matthew's Gospel, but pervades the NT. It is true that the early church did not understand Jesus' messiahship in traditional political terms (cf. John 18:33-36). Neither, however, did it "spiritualize" the concept of Jesus' lordship. The NT writers speak freely of Jesus as heir to David's throne (Luke 1:32-33), as "Lord of lords and King of kings" (Rev. 17:14), and as one who "must reign until he has put all his enemies under his feet" (1 Cor. 15:25). As God rules history and creation as the almighty King (cf. Ps. 24:7-10; 99:1-5), so Jesus now shares in that sovereignty. The story of the magi contributes substantially to this way of thinking about Jesus.

THE TEXT IN THE LIFE OF THE CHURCH

The role of the magi in Christian piety across the centuries has been enormous. Already in the second century they became the subject of early Christian art. On the basis of texts like Psalm 72 and Isaiah 60, the church soon determined that the magi must have been kings.

From the fact that three gifts are mentioned in the text, it was deduced that the magi were three in number. So it is that we sing the carol: "We Three Kings of Orient Are."

A symbolic interpretation of the gifts goes back as far as Irenaeus, according to which gold relates to Jesus' kingship, incense to his divinity, and myrrh to his suffering. Eventually more specific identities were ascribed to the magi. In the Western church (which recognizes the magi at Epiphany), the best-known tradition names the magi as Melchior (an old man with white hair), Caspar (a young and ruddy-complexioned man), and Balthasar (a heavily bearded black man).

In the church today, the magi play leading roles in the typical annual Christmas pageant. It is debatable, however, whether those pageants let us perceive the full significance of the visit of the magi. What we usually miss is the powerful impact of the contrasting reactions to Jesus' birth which Matthew portrays. A more faithful script might include a scene focusing on the anxiety of the authorities over the birth of a new leader who would upset the current establishment. Herod would be cast as a present-day ruler, surrounded by advisers in three-piece suits and clerical garb. The magi in turn might consist of persons today who come from the "outside" and who are looking for a new order—perhaps an ardent feminist, a human rights advocate, maybe even a new age mystic. In such a pageant, the cutting edge of Matthew's story would again become evident.

However portrayed, the story of the magi invites us to wrestle with the question of Jesus' *kingship*. In texts yet to be studied, we will learn what that kingship means for particular areas of our faith and life. Here the issue is the more fundamental question of whether we can think of Jesus as our *king*. For many, talk of kings and kingdoms belongs to other eras or other cultures. For still other persons, talk of kingship is problematic because it reinforces a hierarchical view of life.

Whatever limitations talk of royalty may possess, it directs our attention to a fact of life which applies to us as much as it did to ancient monarchies. We live in a world in which various powers or structures exert sovereignty over our lives and clamor for our loyalty. We in turn must make decisions about what powers we will recognize and how much loyalty to offer them. To acclaim Jesus as king is to affirm that his sovereignty is ultimate, and that he has the first and final claim on our loyalties. That is what the homage of the magi is all about.

A Child Delivered from Destruction

Matthew 2:13-23

PREVIEW

In the third and final part of Matthew's infancy narrative, the life of the newborn king hangs in the balance. Herod the Great finds no cause for joy in Jesus' birth. Threatened by the prospect of a rival to his power and enraged by the failure of the magi to cooperate in his scheme, Herod moves to destroy the infant child. His plans, however, cannot thwart the divine plan. God reveals Herod's designs to Joseph, who once again becomes a central figure in the story. Responding to the message he receives in a dream, Joseph averts danger by fleeing with Jesus and his mother to another country. Subsequent revelation after the threat has passed finally allows the holy family to return to the land of promise. There the story will continue in chapters 3–4 with an account of Jesus' preparation for ministry.

The overarching theme of this section of material is clearly God's protection of the infant Jesus from the threat posed by Herod and his cohorts. As Matthew develops the story, he seems to be making at least three subpoints along the way: (1) Jesus' escape from destruction at the hands of Herod parallels Moses' escape from destruction at the hands of Pharaoh. (2) The trials of the infant Jesus catch up some of the holy events and holy geography of Israel's story in earlier days. (3) Jesus' experience as a child prefigures the homeless wandering and hostile reactions that will characterize his messianic mission. We will have more to say on each of these points a little later.

The outline or structure of 2:13-23 is fairly clear. The material consists of three literary units, each of which concludes with one of the fulfillment quotations mentioned earlier.

OUTLINE

The Flight to Egypt, 2:13-15

The Massacre at Bethlehem, 2:16-18

The Return to Israel, 2:19-23

EXPLANATORY NOTES

The Flight To Egypt 2:13-15

In verses 13-15 a motif recurs which we noted earlier in 1:18-25, and which will appear two more times in the account before us (cf. 2:19-23): God uses a dream to reveal critical information to Joseph, who then acts on that information in the way God instructs. When the angel warns that Herod *is about to search for the child, to destroy him,* the language used conveys the sense of an imminent danger. Wasting no time, therefore, Joseph and his family leave town by night and head for Egypt.

Matthew reports the escape to Egypt succinctly, showing no interest in the details of the journey. In later Christian legends, however, the experiences of the holy family are described at great length. One such account tells of leopards and lions worshiping the infant child and of palm trees responding to Jesus' command to provide food and water for the travelers (Gospel of Pseudo-Matthew 19-20).

Egypt is one of several geographical locations which Matthew highlights in 2:13-23. As a classic land of refuge for those fleeing political danger in Palestine (cf. 1 Kings 11:40; Jer. 26:21), Egypt was a likely destination for the family in our story. For Matthew, however, Egypt is important not only as an appropriate asylum for refugees but as a land which figured prominently in Israel's early history. It was in Egypt that Jacob's family found refuge under the protection of another Joseph. And it was *out of Egypt* that the children of Israel came when God delivered them from bondage and called them to be his people.

It is this connection which Matthew has in mind when he introduces the fulfillment quotation from Hosea 11:1 in verse 15: *Out of Egypt I have called my son* (cf. Num. 23:22; 24:8). Like Israel at the time of the exodus, Jesus enjoys a special relationship with God and will emerge from Egypt to carry out God's purposes. As Raymond Brown puts it:

> Matthew sees that the filial relationship of God's people is now summed up in Jesus who relives in his own life the life of that people. If the whole people was God's "son," how much more is that title applicable to him who "will save his people from their sins." (1977:215)

The Massacre at Bethlehem 2:16-18

With Jesus safely out of the country, the story shifts now to the massacre of the children at Bethlehem. Herod is determined to destroy the newborn king whose star appeared two years earlier, even though he has failed to learn his identity. In an action reminiscent of Pharaoh's edict in Exodus 1:15-22, Herod dispatches officers to kill *all the children in and around Bethlehem* born after the star appeared (cf. 2:7, 16). The story before us reflects Herod's well-known rage and brutality in the face of real or imagined threats. From Josephus' writings we know that he had several of his own children killed, as well as countless others. A pun attributed to the emperor Augustus, alluding to the Jewish avoidance of pork, noted that "it is better to be Herod's swine (*hus*) than Herod's son (*huios*)!"

In verses 17-18 Matthew comments on the episode at Bethlehem with a quotation from Jeremiah 31:15. This time Matthew speaks more guardedly about the matter of fulfillment. He states that the passage from Jeremiah *was fulfilled* at the time of Herod's massacre. He refrains, however, from saying that the tragedy took place *in order to* fulfill Scripture—which might imply that God willed the massacre.

In the passage which is quoted, we hear of the matriarch Rachel crying out from her grave to mourn a nearby tragedy. In the original setting of the text in Jeremiah, Rachel is lamenting the tragic deportation of God's people to other lands. It is assumed that Rachel is buried north of Jerusalem in the territory of Benjamin, near Ramah (cf. 1 Sam. 10:2), where the people are gathering for their march into exile.

In Matthew, however, Jeremiah's words acquire a new meaning. Here the assumption is that Rachel is buried in the vicinity of Bethlehem (cf. Gen. 35:19; 48:7), making her a witness to the slaughter carried out by Herod's officers. Weeping over the loss of her latter-day children, she cries out with a voice that is heard as far away as Ramah!

The Return to Israel 2:19-23

In verses 19-23 Matthew returns to the situation of the family hiding out in Egypt. After some time has elapsed, Joseph learns that Herod has died and that it is now safe for the family to return to *the land of Israel.* The language used in the angel's message confirms that Matthew is drawing on Moses' story to tell Jesus' story. In the Exodus account, Moses had to flee from Pharaoh because Pharaoh "sought to kill Moses" (Exod. 2:15). Later, however, Moses received a command to "go back" to his people, because "all those who were seeking your life are dead" (Exod. 4:19).

The parallels with this story are obvious. Earlier God had warned

Joseph to flee, since Herod was seeking *to destroy* Jesus (v. 13). Here Joseph is instructed to take Jesus and his mother back to their country, *for those who were seeking the child's life are dead* (v. 20).

As in previous episodes, Joseph responds obediently to God's command and takes his family back to Israel. Joseph assumes, initially, that he is returning to the home he left in Judea. Further revelation, however, convinces him that the political climate in Judea is still too risky.

At Herod's death, his kingdom was divided between three of his sons: Herod Antipas, Philip, and Archelaus. As the text indicates, Judea was one of the areas that came under the rule of Archelaus. Archelaus apparently inherited his father's violent tendencies, for he was reputed to have murdered 3,000 people at the beginning of his reign. His brutality and dictatorial ways finally became so intolerable that he was deposed by Rome in A.D. 6 and exiled to Gaul. All of this helps to explain why Joseph is afraid to go back to Judea and heads instead for Galilee. Although Galilee was also ruled by a son of Herod, Herod Antipas, the circumstances there were relatively less threatening.

As the story of Jesus' return continues, his destination becomes increasingly more specific. It is defined first as *the land of Israel* (vv. 20, 21), then as *the district of Galilee* (v. 22), and finally as *a town called Nazareth* (v. 23). Because he resides in Nazareth, Jesus will be known as a Nazarene or *Nazorean*. For Matthew, however, the designation of Jesus as a Nazorean not only points to the place where he lives, but in some way fulfills *what had been spoken through the prophets*.

The difficulty here is that the OT nowhere mentions the city of Nazareth or its residents. There are several texts, however, which use words similar in form to Nazorean, and which Matthew may be citing in a more general way. For example: Judges 13:5, 7 (cf. 16:17) speaks of one who will deliver God's people as a *nazir* or Nazirite, a leader consecrated to God from birth. Isaiah 11:1 speaks of the messianic king as a *neṣer*, a branch which will grow out of David's roots. Texts such as these are fulfilled, Matthew contends, when God's deliverer appears in Nazareth and is hailed as a Nazorean.

THE TEXT IN BIBLICAL CONTEXT

Matthew 2:13-23 is a story which, in many respects, revolves around the places it names. As noted earlier, we cover a lot of holy geography in the account of Jesus' flight and return. The story begins in Bethlehem, which evokes memories of David and his kingdom. From there we move to Egypt, which is connected with the exodus and Israel's birth as a nation. Then our attention is drawn to Ramah, which is linked with the tragedy of the exile. Finally we come to Galilee, which is associated with the trauma and hopes of the northern tribes (cf. Isa. 9:1ff.; Matt. 4:14-16).

In chapters yet to come, still other special places become part of the story: Jesus will go down into the Jordan, spend time in the wilderness, and teach the people from a mountain. All this is hardly coincidental. By connecting Jesus' infancy with places such as these, Matthew makes it clear that Jesus' story is rooted in and gathers up the larger story of Israel.

The travelogue which we find in 2:13-23 is connected, of course, with a plot of pursuit and flight. Jesus and his family do not leave Judea on a pleasant sabbatical excursion to see the biblical world. Instead, they leave because hostile forces are closing in on them, forcing them to seek a place of refuge elsewhere. Like Luke in his story of the inn with no vacancy, Matthew wants us to understand that Jesus' world did not receive him with hospitality. Jesus must begin his life as a homeless wanderer, threatened by the very world he comes to save.

For the biblical interpreter, such a portrayal of Jesus' infancy is doubly significant: (1) It links Jesus once again with the larger biblical drama. As Jesus must flee from Herod, so Moses had to flee from Pharaoh, David from Saul, and Elijah from Jezebel. Jesus' plight is typical of the plight of God's servants in every age. (2) It gives us a preview of what Jesus will experience later in his ministry. *Foxes have holes, and birds of the air have nests; but the Son of Man has nowhere to lay his head* (8:20). To put it another way: The hostility which threatens Jesus at Bethlehem is a foretaste of the hostility which will manifest itself at Calvary.

In spite of the threat which Jesus faces, it is finally God's purpose rather than Herod's purpose which prevails. Here too Matthew reflects a theme which recurs again and again in the biblical story. "The human mind may devise many plans, but it is the purpose of the Lord that will be established" (Prov. 19:21). When Joseph's brothers and Pharaoh's wife try to destroy Joseph, God manages to encompass their evil designs in his own design to save a starving people (cf. Gen. 50:20). When a later Pharaoh attempts to destroy the Hebrew population in Egypt, God foils his schemes and preserves the life of a child who will one day lead the Hebrews to freedom (Exod. 1—2).

Because God's purposes prevail, moreover, those who live at the center of God's purpose enjoy God's protection in one form or another: "We know that God makes all things work together for good for those who love him, who are called according to his purpose" (Rom. 8:28, NRSV footnotes). So it is with the infant Jesus in Matthew 2. God delivers his child from destruction, for it is God's purpose to save others through his life.

THE TEXT IN THE LIFE OF THE CHURCH

To view Jesus as a fugitive or refugee, caught in the conflict between God's agenda and Herod's agenda, raises a number of questions. Chief among them is the calling and destiny of Jesus' community: Does Jesus' fate say something about our own fate as his disciples? Matthew himself leaves little doubt on this matter. To follow Jesus is to choose a course of homeless wandering (8:18-22) and to face persecution which forces one to flee from one town to the next (10:16-23). Such was the experience of the Anabaptists of the sixteenth century and countless groups and individuals across the centuries.

In summarizing some ordeals of his contemporaries, Menno Simons (599-600) speaks of God's people as a refugee people:

> How many pious children of God have we not seen during the space of a few years deprived of their homes and possessions for the testimony of God and their conscience . . . driven out of city and country. . . . [They] wander aimlessly hither and yon in want, misery, and discomfort, in the mountains, in deserts, holes, and clefts of the earth, as Paul says. They must take to their heels and flee away with their wives and little children, from one country to another, from one city to another—hated by all men, abused, slandered, mocked, defamed, trampled upon, styled "heretics."

Where Christian believers still must flee the terror of hostile powers, the force of Matthew's story will be readily felt. For them it brings the assurance that God's deliverer knows their uprooted condition and runs with them in their flight. For others of us, however, it is difficult to identify with the way of the refugee. We have never had to seek a more hospitable city or country. How does Matthew's story speak to us? At least, it is a reminder that the comfortable, settled life we now live is a precarious blessing, subject to disruption at any moment. Beyond that, it is an invitation to express our solidarity with those who *are* refugees—and to welcome them into our midst. When we do so, we confirm our kinship with the refugee of Bethlehem, Jesus the Christ.

Matthew 3:1—4:16

Jesus' Preparation for Ministry

PREVIEW

On leaving Matthew 2 and moving into Matthew 3, we soon discover that the story has taken a sudden leap forward. No longer does the account present scenes of Jesus' infancy. Rather, we are dealing with events about thirty years later, events which bring us to the threshold of Jesus' messianic work. Matthew's agenda in chapters 3—4 remains that of clarifying the roots or antecedents of Jesus' work. The focus shifts, however, from the question of Jesus' entry into the world to that of Jesus' entry into his *ministry*: Who or what sets the stage for Jesus' appearance? How are Jesus and his people prepared for the mission he will carry out?

Matthew pursues these questions through four vignettes of varying length, all of which reflect the interest in "holy geography" mentioned earlier. In the first of these vignettes (3:1-12), Matthew tells of a fiery preacher named John the Baptist, who paves the way for Jesus with his campaign for repentance in the wilderness of Judea. In the next episode (3:13-17), we learn that Jesus is among those who come to be baptized in the Jordan—and that this event confirms his messianic calling. In the sequel which follows (4:1-11), Matthew reports an ordeal which Jesus faces immediately after his baptism, a time of testing in the wilderness. Finally, in the brief account which concludes this section (4:12-16), we hear of Jesus' return to Galilee, where his ministry will unfold according to prophecy.

For this section of his Gospel, Matthew is indebted to the narrative we find in Mark 1:1-15. He has expanded this narrative, however, with sayings and dialogue taken from another source, one that Luke also uses (cf. Matt. 3:7-10 and Luke 3:7-9). Similar use and enrichment of a basic gospel outline derived from Mark are evident throughout the First Gospel. *[Matthew's Sources, p. 426.]*

Matthew was apparently guided by at least three special interests as he put together and shaped the material from his sources: (1) He wanted to underscore the conviction that John and Jesus represented a common cause, the coming of the kingdom, and that both alike urged the people to repent. (2) He wanted to clarify the respective roles of John and Jesus—and to establish John's subordinate status in relation to Jesus. (3) He wanted to highlight the theological significance of Galilee as a part of the holy geography of the gospel: The place where Jesus' mission will begin says something important about where it will end. We will see how Matthew works at these three concerns in our commentary on the text.

John's Work as the Forerunner

Matthew 3:1-12

PREVIEW

According to Mark 1:1-8, "the good news of Jesus Christ" begins with John the Baptist. Matthew shares Mark's estimate of the significance of Jesus' predecessor and so directs our attention to John and his ministry. From a historical point of view, John the Baptist and his followers belong to a wider movement of separatist groups which flourished in Palestine and Syria, especially in and around the Jordan valley, in the centuries before and after the time of Jesus. Each of these groups tended to pursue an ascetic style of life, apart from the religious mainstream, and to practice some rite of washing with water.

The best-known such group is the Essene community at Qumran, which left behind the so-called Dead Sea Scrolls. Some scholars like to imagine that John the Baptist had a connection with the Qumran group at some point. While that remains uncertain, it is clear that John shared many of the convictions of those calling for a more radical expression of the Jewish faith, including the conviction that the endtime was close at hand. *[Jewish Groups and Parties, p. 421.]*

For Matthew, of course, John the Baptist is much more than an illustration of a wider movement: John has a singular and distinctive role in relation to Jesus' messianic ministry, a role in keeping with the biblical promises. In chapter 3, the author is content to tell us that John's activity as a forerunner fulfills a prophecy from Isaiah, and to drop a few hints about John's true identity. Later on, Matthew will be more explicit about who John is: *For all the prophets and the law prophesied until John came; and if you are willing to accept it, he is Elijah who is to come* (11:13-14; cf. 17:9-13). For Matthew, John the Baptist is none other than the great prophet who was taken up in a whirlwind, returning to prepare people for the coming of the Lord (cf. Mal. 3:1-2; 4:5-6; Sir. 48:9-10).

OUTLINE

John's Mission in the Wilderness, 3:1-6

John's Appeal for Repentance, 3:7-10

John's Promise of a Mightier "Baptist," 3:11-12

EXPLANATORY NOTES

John's Mission in the Wilderness 3:1-6

Matthew begins his account of John's activity by telling us when and where John appeared. Although the baptism John administers takes place in the river Jordan, Matthew identifies the larger area of John's work as *the wilderness of Judea*. The phrase refers to the regions sloping down from the Judean highlands to the Dead Sea. In using this phrase, however, Matthew is doing more than giving us a geography lesson. To speak of the *wilderness* is to recall Israel's time in the wilderness following the exodus—and to catch up hopes for a new act of deliverance which would commence in the wilderness.

Lest anyone miss the point, Matthew cites Isaiah 40:3 (as punctuated in the LXX), affirming that John the Baptist is the *one crying out in the wilderness* who starts things rolling. We should also keep in mind that the prophet Elijah is associated with the wilderness (1 Kings 19:4ff.). And interestingly enough, John wears the same kind of haircloth garment and leather girdle that Elijah once did (cf. Matt. 3:4 and 2 Kings 1:8). All of these associations are important.

In verse 2 we find a summary of the message which John proclaims: *Repent, for the kingdom of heaven has come near.* It is noteworthy that the First Gospel is the only one to suggest that John preached about the *kingdom*, and that Matthew summarizes Jesus' message in 4:17 with exactly the same words we find here. As noted earlier, Matthew wants the reader to see John and Jesus as allies in a common cause, joint heralds of the imminent reign of God which makes repentance so urgent.

We will say more about *the kingdom of heaven* in our comments on 4:17. Here the term which calls for further comment is the verb translated *repent, metanoeō*, and the related noun, *metanoia, repentance*. These words are used three times in the account of John the Baptist (3:2, 8, 11) and four times in material dealing with Jesus (4:17; 11:20-21; 12:41). While *metanoeō* can refer somewhat generally to a change of mind, most scholars agree that it carries a much richer meaning in the gospels. It likely reflects the Hebrew verb *šub*, which means *turn around* or *return*. This verb was used frequently by the prophets to urge Israel to return to a right relationship with God (cf. Deut. 30:2; Jer. 4:1; Ezek. 18:30-32; Hos. 14:1). When John appealed for repentance, therefore, he was inviting his hearers to make a radical break with their sinful past and to turn afresh to the God who would soon come in judgment.

According to verse 6, John *baptized* those who responded to his preaching (hence his nickname, *the Baptist*). This washing in the Jordan was a symbolic action, confirming one's desire to turn away from sin, and in some way preparing one for the endtime baptism of judgment (cf. vv. 11-12). The Essenes at Qumran also practiced a rite of washing; those willing to submit to all the precepts of God were "sprinkled with purifying water and sanctified by cleansing water" (1QS 3:8-9). Whereas the rite at Qumran was frequently repeated, however, baptism by John was apparently a one-time event.

In his description of John's baptism, Matthew departs from Mark 1:4 in one important respect: Mark tells us that John's baptism of repentance was "for the forgiveness of sins" (cf. Luke 3:3). Since only Jesus can truly forgive sin, however, Matthew deletes the words about forgiveness from the description of John's rite and inserts them later on in a saying of Jesus about his death (cf. Matt. 26:28)!

John's Appeal for Repentance 3:7-10

Verses 7-10 preserve a sample of John's preaching about repentance, full of vigorous and colorful language. In the parallel account of Luke 3:7-9, John delivers these stinging words to the multitude as a whole. Matthew, however, points to the Pharisees and Sadducees (who function as official representatives of Israel in the First Gospel) as the hearers whom John rebukes. In verse 7, it is not clear whether the leaders named were really *coming* for *baptism* (NRSV, emphasis added) or simply *coming to the* place of *baptism* (cf. NIV).

In any case, John addresses the group in most unflattering terms as a *brood of vipers*, a bunch of snakes, the very epitome of evil (cf. 12:33-34; 23:33). The sarcastic tone continues in the question which follows: "What leads you—of all people—to show up here?" John implies that his hearers are in fact prime candidates for *the wrath to come* which they seek to escape, God's final judgment (Eph. 5:6; 1 Thess. 1:10).

To come through God's fiery judgment, John goes on, one must have more to stand on than claims of Abrahamic ancestry (cf. John 8:31-40; Rom. 9:6-9; Wisd. of Sol. 12:20-22). Here John challenges the popular assumption that descent from Abraham guaranteed one a share in the blessings promised to Abraham. If necessary, the God who "hewed" Israel from the rock of Abraham (Isa. 51:1-2) can make lifeless stones give birth to *new* children of Abraham who will replace the original heirs. (John's pronouncement likely carried even more punch in Aramaic or Hebrew, where the words for *children* and *stones* are almost identical.) Instead of appealing to Abraham, those wishing to escape judgment need to exhibit concrete evidence of God's righteousness in their lives, *fruit worthy of repentance* (v. 8, cf. 7:15-20; Luke 13:6-9; Phil. 1:11; Gal. 5:22ff.).

John's Promise of a Mightier "Baptist" 3:11-12

The sample of John's preaching continues in verses 11-12, but with a new theme: John's work will soon give way to the work of another "baptist," in relation to whom John clearly plays a lesser role. Matthew establishes this point through three related arguments: (1) The one who comes after John will in fact be *more powerful* than John (cf. John 1:30; 3:31). (2) John is unworthy to *carry* or *remove* (REB) the sandals of the one to come, suggesting the relationship of a slave to a master. (3) The one who is coming will carry out a baptism that far exceeds John's in power and effect.

The identity of this mightier one has been interpreted in different ways. Some have proposed that John is speaking in OT terms of God's own coming (cf. Isa. 40:10; 59:20; Zech. 14:5; Mal. 3:1). Were this the case, however, John likely would have refrained from making *any* comparison between himself and the one to come. It is more likely that John is thinking of a messianic figure who acts on God's behalf, the sort of figure we find in Jewish apocalyptic writings (cf. 1 Enoch 38; 46; 48; Ps. Sol. 17). For Matthew, of course, this messianic figure is none other than Jesus.

We are told that the *more powerful* one will baptize persons *with the Holy Spirit and fire.* In the early church, the first part of this promise was sometimes connected with the powerful presence of the Spirit in the church's life (Acts 1:5, 8; 2:1-4), while the reference to fire was connected with the last judgment. John himself, however, likely envisioned a single event in which God's Spirit would purge and purify the people of Israel, a fiery process in which every unworthy object is destroyed (cf. Zech. 13:9; Mal. 3:2-3; 4:1; 1QS 4:20-21).

Verse 12 supports this interpretation. Earlier John had spoken of judgment in terms of the chopping down and burning of trees failing to yield *good fruit* (v. 10). Now he introduces another metaphor, that of a *threshing floor* which must be cleansed. God's judgment will be like a *winnowing fork* which lifts grain and chaff into the air, where the wind separates them. To underscore the finality of judgment, John notes that the chaff will be burned *with unquenchable fire.* Here John is drawing on the language of the prophets (cf. Isa. 34:10; 66:24; Jer. 7:20), using an image for judgment which Jesus and his followers will also adopt (Matt. 13:40; 18:8; 25:41; 2 Thess. 1:5-10; Rev. 20:14-15).

THE TEXT IN BIBLICAL CONTEXT

When we observe the attention which Matthew and the other Gospels devote to John the Baptist, we may rightly ask: Why is John so important? Why is his story linked so closely to the story of Jesus? Why does his work mark the beginning of the gospel? Part of the answer is that Jesus' movement was in some sense an outgrowth and continuation of the movement which John began. Jesus himself was baptized by John, acclaimed John as a prophet *and more than a prophet* (Matt. 11:9), and was viewed by many as John's successor (14:1ff.). Furthermore, it is likely that many of the disciples whom Jesus attracted came from the circle of John's followers (cf. Acts 1:21-22). For the early church, then, it was not a matter of inventing a relationship with John the Baptist. That relationship was there from the beginning.

What the early church *did* have to do was *define* or *interpret* the relationship between John and Jesus. Was Jesus merely a disciple of John, following in his teacher's footsteps? Or is the relationship to be interpreted in a different manner? To a certain extent Jesus himself began the process of interpretation, through sayings such as we find in Matthew 11:7-19. That process continued as early Christian witnesses passed on the stories of both John and Jesus. Central to their testimony is the conviction that John prepared the way for Jesus. As Jesus is the promised Messiah, so John is the promised forerunner who sets things in motion (cf. Isa. 40:3; Mal. 3:1; 4:5-6; Luke 1:16-17, 76-79).

Each of the four gospels builds on this basic conviction—but in different ways. In Matthew's case, as noted earlier, there is an effort to sharpen or pinpoint the role which John carries out. Building on clues already present in Mark's Gospel, Matthew identifies John the Baptist as the great prophet Elijah, whom God has sent to call the people of Israel to repentance.

At one level, therefore, Matthew is interested in John as a figure "back then" who played a pivotal role in the developing history of salvation. However, Matthew's fascination with John does not stop at the point of John's *past* significance. The call to repentance which paves the way for Jesus is a call which must continue to be heard in Jesus' community. There too the true people of God will be known *by their fruits,* apart from which no one will enter the kingdom (7:15-23; 21:43). For Matthew, therefore, John the Baptist is a preacher with *present* significance, who speaks to the church as well as to Israel. He warns against the complacency and hypocrisy that can befall *any* religious community. And he challenges the church in every generation to examine its life afresh.

THE TEXT IN THE LIFE OF THE CHURCH

What does it mean to *repent*? That is the question which the message of John puts before us—and a question with which the church has struggled across the centuries. At times repentance has been understood primarily as a feeling, a feeling of sorrow or regret about one's sins. At other times repentance has been equated with "doing penance" for one's sins through such penitential actions as fasting, self-mortification, special prayers, and pilgrimages. The repentance of which John and Jesus spoke, however, goes beyond feeling sorry or doing penance. As suggested above, repentance involves a radical reorientation of life, a total turnaround in our priorities and values. To repent is to turn *away* from a life controlled by sin and to turn *toward* a life under God's lordship and direction. To put it another way: Repentance means conversion.

If this is what repentance is all about, then we need to go on to ask a second question: What does it mean for *the church* to define its identity in terms of repentance? It means, fundamentally, that the church will be a *converted* people (cf. Menno Simons' comments on "genuine penitence," 110-115). Just as claims to descent from Abraham did not suffice for John's hearers, so claims to spiritual descent from the church fathers, the Reformers, or the Anabaptists do not suffice to make *us* the people of God. Instead, each generation must respond anew to the appeal to repent—and reorder its life accordingly. Where that happens, where the church becomes the arena of a continuing moral revolution, where captivity to culture gives way to loyalty to God's reign, where people turn from the ways of death to the way of life, there the true church emerges again.

Jesus' Baptism by John

Matthew 3:13-17

PREVIEW

Among the many who came to the Jordan to be baptized was Jesus of Nazareth. Each of the gospels reports this event, which is the subject of Matthew 3:13-17. As we read Matthew's account, we soon discover that Jesus' baptism means something different than the baptism John administered to countless others. For them, baptism was connected with confession of sin. For Jesus, baptism is a rite of entry into his messianic calling. This becomes evident in the theophany which takes place as Jesus comes up from the water. A voice from heaven confirms that he is the one who will carry out God's purposes. In form and theme, therefore, the story of Jesus' baptism is similar to the stories of the burning bush in Exodus 3, the temple vision in Isaiah 6, and the Damascus road experience in Acts 26.

The primary source of Matthew's account of Jesus' baptism is Mark 1:9-11. However, Matthew has expanded Mark's brief narrative by adding a conversation which takes place between John and Jesus just prior to the baptism (Matt. 3:14-15). Through the objection which John raises in verse 14, Matthew poses a question which apparently troubled many persons in the early church: Why was *Jesus* baptized by *John*? Jesus' reply to John in verse 15 offers a rationale for his baptism which guards against any misunderstandings.

OUTLINE

A Fitting Act, 3:13-15

A Chosen Son, 3:16-17

EXPLANATORY NOTES

A Fitting Act 3:13-15

Matthew begins his story of Jesus' visit to the Jordan by telling us that Jesus came to John *to be baptized.* We know at once, therefore, that Jesus is acting on his own initiative in this matter, not simply giving in to evangelistic pressure. He has *chosen* to be baptized. When John learns of Jesus' intention, however, he is reluctant to go along with it. Somehow, Matthew implies, John already knows that Jesus is the Messiah, not the typical candidate for baptism.

The objection which John raises in verse 14 presupposes John's preaching about the coming one in verses 11-12: Why should one who baptizes with the Holy Spirit and fire submit to one who merely baptizes with water? Should it not be the other way around? Jesus' reply in verse 15 assumes that John's appraisal of their respective roles is ultimately correct. For the time being, however (*let it be so now*), *it is proper* for Jesus to undergo baptism. In some way this act will *fulfill all righteousness.*

Righteousness translates the Greek word *dikaiosunē*, which is a key term in Matthew's vocabulary. *Fulfill* is also an important word in the First Gospel, used in conjunction with quotations from the OT. What does it mean, however, when Matthew combines the two words in one expression? How do John and Jesus *fulfill all righteousness* through the act of Jesus' baptism? At least three interpretations are possible:

(1) Baptism is a practice which God ordains or commands; hence, the baptism of Jesus will fulfill God's righteous requirements.

(2) Baptism is the first step in Jesus' identification with sinners, by which they in turn will become righteous through him (cf. 2 Cor. 5:21).

(3) Baptism is the way Jesus assumes his role in God's plan, which

has righteousness as its goal in the community which Jesus gathers (cf. Matt. 5:6, 17-20; 6:33). By baptizing Jesus, John will enable *the way of righteousness* which his own work initiated (21:32) to move toward fulfillment in the work of his successor. Although each of these interpretations has some validity, Matthew most likely was thinking along the lines of the third option.

A Chosen Son 3:16-17

With John's objection now overcome, the story moves on and Jesus' baptism takes place. It is not the baptism itself which the text describes, however, but the theophany which follows it. *[Epiphany, p. 419.]* We read of three different symbolic actions which attest God's presence: (1) The heavens are opened. (2) God's Spirit descends like a dove and rests on Jesus. (3) A voice speaks from heaven. Since phenomena such as these are regularly associated with vi sions and revelation (cf. Ezek. 1:1, 28; 2:1-2; 2 Bar. 13:1-3; Acts 10:11; Rev. 4:1; 19:11), we know at once that an important disclosure is about to take place.

The reference to the Spirit which alights on Jesus is especially significant. Although this story is the only biblical narrative to use the dove as a symbol for God's Spirit, a number of texts speak of the Spirit coming upon God's chosen servant to anoint or equip him for his calling (cf. Isa. 11:2; 42:1; 61:1; 1 Enoch 49:3; T. Levi 18:6-7). When the Spirit comes upon Jesus, therefore, we know he is ready to begin his messianic ministry.

The voice from heaven confirms Jesus' identity as God's *Son,* which is the first time Matthew uses *Son* as an official title for Jesus. *[Christ/Christology, p. 418.]* In Mark's account of the theophany (Mark 1:11), the words which come from heaven are a private disclosure to Jesus himself: "*You* are my Son, the Beloved; with *you* I am well pleased." In Matthew 3:17, however, the words are a public declaration for the benefit of everyone: *This is my Son, the Beloved, with whom I am well pleased.*

The phrase *my Son, the Beloved* may suggest one who is prized as an *only* son (cf. Gen. 22:2) or, alternately, one who is *chosen* for a special task. The idea of chosenness is definitely present in the phrase which follows, which is better translated *on whom my favor rests* (cf. JB, NEB). As others have noted, the language of 3:17 seems to echo both Psalm 2:7 and Isaiah 42:1. One of these texts deals with a king who will rule the nations, the other with a servant figure who will bring salvation to the nations. The beloved Son baptized by John will fulfill both roles in his messianic ministry.

THE TEXT IN BIBLICAL CONTEXT

The story of Jesus' baptism serves at least two purposes in the larger narrative of the Gospels. First, it creates a transition from the work of the forerunner to the work of the Messiah. Once Jesus has been baptized, the plot can center on *his* activity, while John the Baptist fades into the background. Second, it is the first of several stories which provide the reader with divine confirmation of who Jesus is. The sonship of Jesus which is proclaimed at his baptism will be attested later by the demons at Gadara (8:28-34) and once again by a voice from heaven at Jesus' transfiguration (17:1-8). Closely related are those stories in which various human figures acknowledge Jesus as God's Son, including the disciples (14:28-33; 16:13-20) and a Roman centurion (27:51-54). Narratives such as these keep focusing our attention on Jesus' very special relationship with God.

A more disputed question is whether the Gospel writers intended the story of *Jesus'* baptism to provide a way of looking at *Christian* baptism. To be sure, neither Matthew nor any other NT author points explicitly to Jesus' baptism as a model or example for our own. In addition, the baptism which Jesus receives is in fact John's baptism rather than a Christian rite.

Nevertheless, there are features in the story before us which suggest an *indirect* interest in Christian baptism. For example, Matthew depicts Jesus as one who asks to be baptized, who declares his intention in seeking this act, and who enters into baptism in a spirit of humbleness and obedience. In this way, Jesus exemplifies the ideal candidate for baptism. Further, the story focuses on the themes of *identity* and *calling*, which are also central to the significance of Christian baptism (cf. Gal. 3:23-29; Rom. 6:1-11). It would appear, therefore, that the story of Jesus' baptism looks forward to the practice of baptism in the church.

THE TEXT IN THE LIFE OF THE CHURCH

Whatever Matthew's intentions, the story of Jesus' baptism has in fact informed the church's understanding of baptism, both in earlier periods and in our own time. This is definitely the case with writers in the believers church tradition, who have frequently pointed to Jesus' action as the beginning of Christian baptism, as an example of humility and obedience, and as evidence that baptism and commitment go hand in hand.

Typical is a statement by Alexander Mack in his "Rights and Ordinances" (Durnbaugh, 1958:350):

> The Son of God knew well the plan and will of His Father. For this reason He said to John, "For thus it is fitting for us to fulfill all righteousness" [Matthew 3:15]. The Son of God wished to found and ordain a water bath for His entire church, that it should be an efficacious seal and outward symbol of all those who would believe in Him. Thus, the Son of God, in the first place, fulfilled the will of His Father (because the baptism by John was commanded by God), and at the same time made a beginning of water baptism. . . . He has left this to us and all of His followers as a mighty example in which we should follow him.

More recently, attention has focused on the way Jesus' baptism supports an understanding of baptism as ordination. As the text makes clear, Jesus' baptism was closely linked with entry into his messianic ministry. So likewise, our baptism is linked with a calling to serve or minister in Christ's name. Whether or not we see the heavens bursting open, the Spirit of God descends upon believers today, just as it did upon Jesus at the Jordan. And that Spirit equips us to carry out our particular calling within the larger mission of God's people in the world. For some who are eventually called to make ministry a set-apart vocation, there may be a subsequent service of commissioning which we designate as *ordination.* In baptism, however, every believer enters into Christ's ministry.

Jesus' Temptation in the Wilderness

Matthew 4:1-11

PREVIEW

The sequel to the story of Jesus' baptism is the account of his temptation in the wilderness. Like Israel of old after crossing the Red Sea (Deut. 8:2), Jesus must be *tested* after he comes out of the water: Will he or won't he remain true to his calling as God's chosen one? Once again, the setting of the test is the wilderness, the occasion for the test is hunger, and the issue at stake is loyalty. What is different in Jesus' case is the outcome. To paraphrase the author of Hebrews 4:15, Jesus is "tested as Israel was, yet without sin." That outcome, however, is not a foregone conclusion. Jesus' test is a real test, a test in which he might have turned away from God's will.

In constructing the story before us, Matthew has drawn on two earlier reports of Jesus' ordeal. Some of the language used to introduce and conclude the story appears to come from Mark 1:12-13. There the emphasis falls on the wilderness itself as a place of wild beasts and evil spirits, which Jesus survives with the help of angels. Mark says nothing in his brief account, however, about a conversation between Jesus and Satan. For the latter Matthew is indebted to a fuller version of Jesus' temptation found in another source he shares with Luke (cf. Luke 4:1-13). Here the struggle centers on fidelity to God's will, a theme of utmost significance to Matthew.

The form of the story as we find it in Matthew 4:1-11 can be viewed in several ways. As the dialogue between Jesus and Satan takes shape, with each party appealing to Scripture at one point, it sounds much like a rabbinic debate. In the midst of this debate, however, lines are spoken which call to mind stories of another type, stories concerned with the legitimacy of one who claims divine authority. When Satan challenges Jesus to validate his sonship by turning stones into bread or by jumping off the temple, the taunts are similar to the *demand for signs* which we encounter later on (Matt. 12:38-39; 16:1-4; 27:40; John 6:30ff.). In each case Jesus is invited to "prove" that he acts with divine authority. And in each case Jesus refuses to jump to the tune of those who pose the challenge.

Matthew 4:1-11 reads like the script of a drama. It begins with a brief prologue, then develops the plot through three scenes of mounting intensity, and concludes finally with an appropriate epilogue.

OUTLINE

Into the Wilderness, 4:1-2

A Test of Priorities, 4:3-4

A Test of Confidence, 4:5-7

A Test of Allegiance, 4:8-10

Over at Last, 4:11

EXPLANATORY NOTES

Into the Wilderness 4:1-2

Immediately after his baptism, Jesus is *led up* by the Spirit into the wilderness. Taken literally, the phrase describes a normal journey from the Jordan valley to the rugged slopes of the Judean wilderness. The text could mean, however, that Jesus is *taken up* by the Spirit and transported to the wilderness in a rapture or vision (cf. Rev. 17:3; Ezek. 8:3; 37:1; 1 Enoch 17:1ff.; 2 Cor. 12:1-4). Whatever the manner of Jesus' entry into the wilderness, the reason the Spirit takes him there is quite clear: He is to be *tempted,* tested by the devil.

According to Matthew, Jesus fasts for *forty days and forty nights* prior to the test. The duration of Jesus' ordeal confirms that he is reliving Israel's experience of long ago. Forty years the people of Israel wandered in the wilderness, dependent on God for sustenance (Exod. 16:35; Deut. 2:7; 8:2). And for "forty days and forty nights" Moses fasted on Mt. Sinai before he received the tablets of the covenant from God (Exod. 34:28; Deut. 9:9-11). After the fast, Matthew tells us, Jesus was hungry—and vulnerable. Now the test can begin.

A Test of Priorities 4:3-4

In verse 3 (and again in v. 5) the devil appeals to Jesus with the words, *If you are the Son of God. . . .* The phrase *assumes* rather than questions Jesus' sonship and refers back to the revelation of Jesus' identity at his baptism. In each of the tests which Jesus faces, then, the tempter is proposing ways for Jesus to claim and demonstrate his messianic role. Jesus responds by quoting texts from the OT which challenge these propositions. All of the texts come from Deuteronomy and, appropriately, all deal with Israel's wilderness experience.

The first of the devil's three propositions is that Jesus command stones to become loaves of bread. At one level the appeal relates to the immediate situation of Jesus' hunger after forty days of fasting. At another level the story poses the question of how Jesus will exercise his messianic power throughout his ministry. Jesus "is asked to become a self-serving wonder-worker, flexing his power for his own ends" (Senior, 1977:49). The reply of Jesus in verse 4 makes clear that he is not about to act independently of God and use his power to gratify his own desires. In his reply Jesus quotes Deuteronomy 8:3, which interprets Israel's dependence on manna as a lesson on feeding on God's will for our lives. That is the food for which Jesus hungers above all else.

A Test of Confidence 4:5-7

For the second test (the order differs in Luke's account), the actors move in some manner from the wilderness to *the holy city,* Jerusalem (cf. 27:53). The pinnacle of the temple to which the devil takes Jesus has been variously interpreted as a corner of the outer court wall, a balcony, the lintel of a high gate, or the peak of the temple proper. In any event, Jesus is invited to throw himself down from this lofty place. Once again the test may have more than one meaning. From one perspective, it is a subtle attempt to get Jesus to destroy himself (through false confidence). From another perspective, it is an appeal to Jesus to seek public acclaim for his work through miracle and magic.

This time the devil himself quotes Scripture (Ps. 91:11-12), bolstering his challenge with the promise that God will protect those who trust him against all harm. But Jesus is not deceived and shows himself to be a more faithful interpreter of biblical texts. Quoting Deuteronomy 6:16, he reminds his adversary that it is a mistake for us to try to force God's hand. At Massah in the wilderness (see Exod. 17:1-8), the people of Israel did just this when they "tested the Lord" by demanding water. Such demands reveal unfaith rather than faith. Jesus, however, neither needs nor seeks miraculous proof that God is with him.

A Test of Allegiance 4:8-10

Again the scenery changes as the devil takes Jesus *to a very high mountain* for the third test. Mountains provide the setting for several narratives in Matthew (4:8; 5:1; 15:29; 17:1; 28:16), all of them dealing with power and authority. Here the mountain is unusually majestic, and clearly figurative, for from it Jesus can survey *all the kingdoms of the world* (cf. 2 Bar. 76). We are reminded of the story in Deuteronomy 34:1-4 where Moses ascends Mount Nebo and God shows him "all the land" which Israel one day will possess. We are also reminded of God's offer to the king in Psalm 2:8: "Ask of me, and I will make the nations your heritage, and the ends of the earth your possession." Only here it is the devil who makes the offer—and the price he demands is Jesus' allegiance.

To appreciate this offer, we need to remember that the NT itself speaks of the devil as the present world ruler (cf. John 12:31; 16:11; Eph. 2:2; 6:12). It would seem that he is in a strategic position to grant dominion to Jesus, at least the dominion that a conventional Messiah might seek. Once again, however, Jesus refuses to succumb. He commands Satan to depart, in much the same way that he does when Peter tries to divert him from the way of the cross (cf. 4:10; 16:21-23). And he reminds Satan of the basic tenet of Israel's faith that only God deserves our worship and allegiance (Deut. 6:13).

All along the reader knows, of course, that Jesus *will* receive dominion over the nations (cf. 28:18-20). This dominion, however, will not come from an opportunistic alliance with the present evil order. Instead, it will come from the triumph of God's reign through Jesus' death and resurrection.

Over at Last 4:11

When the third and final test is over, there is really little left to say. Jesus has rejected each of the ploys of the tempter, and the latter has no choice but to obey Jesus' order to leave (v. 10). Further testing, to be sure, awaits Jesus later in the story (cf. 16:1; 16:23; 26:36-46; 27:39-44). For now, however, there is a moment of respite. As the devil exits, angels arrive and *wait on* Jesus. Here the text recalls the wilderness experience of the prophet Elijah, who was fed by the angels before undertaking a journey of "forty days and forty nights" to Mount Horeb (1 Kings 19:1-8). In both episodes the angels represent the comfort and strength which God provides to those who are tested. And on that note the story of Jesus' temptation concludes.

THE TEXT IN BIBLICAL CONTEXT

The report of Jesus' ordeal in the wilderness is by no means the only place the Bible looks at temptation or testing. As noted earlier, Matthew's account alludes in various ways to the story of Israel's test in the wilderness. Elsewhere we find accounts of the testing faced by ancient patriarchs such as Abraham (Gen. 22:1-14) and Job (Job 1—2), the tests posed by Jesus' adversaries (Matt. 22:18), the testing which comes with persecution (1 Pet. 4:12), and the trials related to the endtime (Rev. 3:10). Sometimes testing comes from our own evil desires (James 1:14) or from the powers of darkness which seek our downfall (1 Thess. 3:5). At other times God conducts the test (Deut.

8:2), not to entice or entrap us but to probe the depth and genuineness of our loyalty. Whatever the source, testing comes again and again to God's servants in the biblical story.

Matthew 4:1-11 links Jesus with this larger biblical context. It lets the reader know that Jesus too had to prove his faithfulness in the midst of testing (cf. Heb. 2:17-18; 4:14-16; 5:7-10). To be sure, Jesus' test has its own distinctive character. In this particular struggle we are dealing with a cosmic conflict, a collision of divine and demonic authority which will characterize Jesus' ministry from beginning to end. Further, the test does not deal with faithfulness in a generic sense but with faithfulness in the context of a messianic calling: How will Jesus act as the Son of God?

At this point the story serves at least three purposes: (1) It gives a preview of the way Jesus will approach his mission in the stories to follow. (2) It suggests that any discrepancy between the shape of Jesus' ministry and traditional views of the Messiah's role results not from a lack of credentials on Jesus' part but from his adherence to God's will. (3) It provides clues on what it means for the church to be faithful as the messianic community which acts in Jesus' name.

THE TEXT IN THE LIFE OF THE CHURCH

As we have already noted, Jesus' *temptation* by Satan was in fact a *test*. Here the meaning of *tempt* goes beyond our everyday use of the term. Sometimes we use the word in a neutral way to describe anything we find appealing: That's very tempting, we may remark. At other times we connect temptation with the urge to do something wrong, especially misconduct in the areas of money and sex. One thinks of the classic line: "The devil made me do it!" Jesus, however, was facing neither a neutral appeal nor a lure to misbehave. *His* temptation went to the core of who he was and what he was about. As in well-known later stories of persons persuaded to sell their souls to the devil (tales indebted to the biblical account), Jesus is tempted to trade his true calling for instant power and glory. It is at this point that the story invites us to reflect on temptation in the life of the church.

All too often, the record shows, the church has succumbed to temptation, coveting the power which Jesus rejected and betraying the loyalty which Jesus modeled. The sharpest commentary on all this is Dostoyevski's story of "The Grand Inquisitor" in *The Brothers Karamazov*. As the Inquisitor speaks to Christ (who has returned to earth), he boasts that the church has "corrected Thy work and founded it upon miracle, mystery, and authority." He describes how the church has achieved control and dominion, accepting the very options rejected by Jesus in the wilderness.

Much has changed in the church since the time described in Dostoyevski's story, particularly in our perceptions of the power appropriate to Jesus' community. Nevertheless, the church today still confronts the temptations of Jesus, whether as a temptation to serve its own institutional needs, or to esteem charismatic gifts above the weakness of the cross, or to make success the criterion of the church's mission, or to give allegiance to alien ideologies and causes.

Similar tests come to us in our individual experience. For some, the test may occur as they make decisions about life vocations. For others, the occasion is a position of leadership, where the abuse or misuse of power is an ever-present possibility. For still others, faithfulness is tested in everyday moral choices, where conflicting values compete for our attention and loyalty. Whenever and however the temptation comes, we need to listen afresh to Matthew 4:1-11.

Jesus' Return to Galilee

Matthew 4:12-16

PREVIEW

The final unit of material in Matthew 1:1—4:16 tells of Jesus' return to Galilee after his test in the wilderness. In constructing this section, Matthew takes the brief statement found in Mark 1:14a and expands it in two ways: (1) He reports Jesus' change of residence from Nazareth to Capernaum, a prominent city of Galilee. (2) He quotes a passage from Isaiah to show how Galilee fits into God's redemptive purposes. All of this lets us know that the period of preparation is over. The time and the place are now right for Jesus to launch his messianic program.

OUTLINE

Capernaum by the Sea, 4:12-13

Galilee of the Gentiles, 4:14-16

EXPLANATORY NOTES

Capernaum by the Sea 4:12-13

Matthew and Mark agree that Jesus emerges as a leader in Galilee *after* John is arrested in Judea. In Mark's account it is a simple matter of chronological sequence (cf. Mark 1:14a). Matthew's wording, however, suggests that hostile action toward John actually *prompts* Jesus to turn to Galilee. This *withdrawal* to Galilee is not simply a move to evade evil powers. Instead, Jesus interprets John's arrest as a signal to begin his own work and so *returns* to the place where that work must take shape. Nevertheless, the *way* in which Jesus' return to Galilee is introduced sounds ominous: The reference to John's arrest points forward to the time when Jesus too will be delivered to the authorities (cf. Matt. 17:22; 26:2).

Once in Galilee, Jesus passes through his hometown of Nazareth, but moves on immediately and settles in Capernaum. Located on the northwest shore of the Sea of Galilee at the site now known as Tell Hum, Capernaum was a busy and prosperous community with a population of 15–20,000 people. Because it lay near a political border, it had a tax office or customs station (cf. 9:9) and also served as an outpost for a detachment of Herod's troops (cf. 8:5-13).

The Gospels agree that Capernaum was a major center of Jesus' activity (cf. 11:23), referring to the city some sixteen times. Only Matthew, however, explicitly identifies Capernaum as the place of Jesus' residence, *his own town* (9:1). As Matthew describes Capernaum in verse 13, he uses language which connects the city with the quotation from Isaiah in verses 14-16: It is a city *by the sea* (cf. v. 15), in the area which once belonged to the tribes *of Zebulun and Naphtali.*

Galilee of the Gentiles 4:14-16

The passage from Isaiah which Matthew cites is yet another fulfillment quotation, one of several drawn from the book of Isaiah (cf. 2:23; 8:17; 12:18-21). The passage comes from Isaiah 9:1-2 (8:23—9:1 in the Hebrew text), which Matthew has edited in his own distinctive way. In their original context, the words of Isaiah 9:1 about "the way of the sea, the land beyond the Jordan, Galilee of the nations" may refer to the three provinces which the Assyrians set up when they conquered Israel: Dor, Gilead, and Megiddo. As quoted by Matthew, however, the phrases all seem to deal with one area, i.e., Galilee (cf. 1 Macc. 5:14-15). The phrase *Galilee of the Gentiles* may allude to the large numbers of non-Jews who resided in Galilee. Or it may simply designate Galilee as the place from which God launches a program of salvation that eventually will encompass Gentiles. [Gentile, p. 420.]

The quotation continues in verse 16, which depicts Galilee as a land of darkness. For those who first heard Isaiah's words, *darkness* referred to a political climate marked by gloom and anxiety. For Matthew the metaphor takes on a broader meaning, describing a people who have yet to discover a right relationship with God. Life in Galilee, however, is about to change. With Jesus poised to begin his messianic work, *light has dawned* on those who live in darkness (note Matthew's use of *dawn* instead of *shine* in the last line of the quote; cf. Luke 1:78-79). Here the recipients of light are first and foremost the Jewish crowds who flock to Jesus during his ministry (cf. 4:23-25). The fact that Galilee, however, is a land *of the Gentiles,* hints at a wider circle of darkness to which Jesus will bring light through the work of his followers.

THE TEXT IN BIBLICAL CONTEXT

As noted earlier, Matthew 4:12-16 concludes the section of the First Gospel on Jesus' origins and calling. Several features are characteristic of this section, including (1) scriptural quotations which link Jesus' story to God's promises, (2) travelogues which connect Jesus with the holy landscape of God's people, and (3) subtle signs of God's intention to include the Gentiles in his design. By incorporating all of these features in the text before us, Matthew succeeds in tying together various strands of the preceding story.

In addition to catching up what has gone before, 4:12-16 sets the stage for what is to follow. With Jesus settled in Capernaum by the Sea of Galilee, the story is ready to move on to Jesus' public ministry. It is clear, therefore, that 4:12-16 is a well-constructed unit, creating a transition from one section of Matthew's Gospel to another.

One of the features mentioned above which relates to a wider biblical context is Matthew's interest in *the land*. When Matthew traces Jesus' journeys within and beyond Israel, he assumes a linkage of faith and geography reflected elsewhere in Scripture. Salvation does not occur in some ethereal realm, but in places which can be located on a map of the ancient world—the rivers Jabbok and Jordan, Mt. Sinai and Mt. Carmel, Jericho and Jerusalem. Because this is so, the land of Israel is regarded as a holy land, a land at the center of God's purposes, intimately related to Israel's existence as a people.

At the same time, the biblical record makes clear that God's salvation is not confined to one particular geographical arena. It can manifest itself in new and unlikely locations, places like Nineveh, Babylon, Antioch, and Rome. Matthew's treatment of Galilee works at both points simultaneously. Inasmuch as Galilee is a part of the area of Zebulun and Naphtali, it represents God's fidelity to the old land of promise. Inasmuch, however, as Galilee is a land *of the Gentiles,* a gateway as it were to other nations, it represents God's freedom to expand the boundaries of holy geography and claim new lands for his purposes.

THE TEXT IN THE LIFE OF THE CHURCH

Faith and geography continue to be intermeshed in the story of God's people. In spite of the fact that the church is not linked to one particular holy land, we too look on certain places as sacred landmarks in our story. It may be Rome or Constantinople, Wittenburg or Geneva, Schleitheim or Schwarzenau. Closer home, our faith may connect with the ground of the church we attend, or with a camp or retreat center, or with a river or lake used for baptisms. Whatever the places which we ourselves associate with God's activity, we are following Matthew's example when we recount our holy geography.

As Matthew reminds us, however, God's redemptive action is not confined by old boundaries and landmarks. New chapters of the saga of faith and geography may find God working in places far removed from the landscape of the past—in developing nations which did not exist when we were born, or in areas where cultural patterns differ widely from our own, or in urban settings having little in common with the village life of an earlier day. If we appreciate the significance of *Galilee* in Matthew 4:12-16, we will look for signs of God's activity in the "Gentile" areas of our own world, even as we cherish the holy places already associated with God's salvation.

Part 2

Jesus' Messianic Mission

Matthew 4:17—10:42

PREVIEW

In the section of the Gospel which begins at 4:17, Matthew sketches the shape of Jesus' mission in Galilee. It is clear from the opening account in 4:17-25 that this mission consists of both *words* and *deeds*. Matthew illustrates these two facets of Jesus' work in the two collections of material which follow. First comes the discourse called the Sermon on the Mount (5:1—7:29), the first of five such discourses in Matthew's Gospel. There the reader discovers that Jesus teaches with authority that far exceeds that of other teachers. Then, with hardly a break at all, we move into a collection of stories featuring Jesus' miracles (8:1—9:34). Here it is evident that Jesus *acts* with special authority as well, restoring life and health in accord with God's purposes. In short, Jesus exhibits his messianic power both in the message he proclaims and in the wonders he performs. Both are integral to his mission and to the story about that mission.

No less significant is the way Matthew weaves the theme of discipleship into his picture of Jesus' mission. In the middle of his opening account of Jesus' work, we find a story of the calling of the first disciples (4:18-22). This allows disciples to be present when Jesus teaches on the mountain (5:1-2), the core of the community that will remember and observe his teaching (5:13-16; 7:24-27).

Especially striking is the way Matthew organizes the material on Jesus' messianic deeds, dividing the three groups of miracle stories with interludes on discipleship (8:18-22; 9:9-17). All this leads up to the commissioning of *the twelve* (9:35—10:42), who will extend Jesus' mission throughout all of Israel. From beginning to end, therefore, 4:17—10:42 is an account both of Jesus' messianic mission and of the preparation of disciples to share in that mission.

OUTLINE

Jesus Launches His Ministry, 4:17-25

Jesus Teaches with Authority, 5:1—7:29

5:1-16	Heirs of the Kingdom
5:17-48	A Greater Righteousness
6:1-18	True Piety and False
6:19—7:12	A Focused Life
7:13-29	A Critical Choice

Jesus Acts with Authority, 8:1—9:34

8:1-17	Mighty Works, Cycle 1
8:18-22	Following Jesus, Interlude 1
8:23—9:8	Mighty Works, Cycle 2
9:9-17	Following Jesus, Interlude 2
9:18-34	Mighty Works, Cycle 3

Jesus Commissions His Disciples, 9:35—10:42

9:35—10:4	Laborers for the Harvest
10:5-15	The Mission of the Twelve
10:16-42	The Cost of Discipleship

Matthew 4:17-25

Jesus Launches His Ministry

PREVIEW

As indicated above, Matthew highlights Jesus' *disciples* as he portrays Jesus' *mission*. This is illustrated clearly in the unit before us. The unit opens with a brief summary of the message Jesus preached (v. 17) and ends with an overview of the scope and impact of Jesus' work (vv. 23-25). Right in the middle of the narrative, however, the author relates a story about the calling of four disciples and the new vocation they will assume (vv. 18-22). Here and throughout the Gospel, the prominence given to the disciples is much more than a literary phenomenon. The disciples, for Matthew, are the charter members of the church. Through the disciples, therefore, the church can find itself in the story of Jesus. And Jesus speaks to the church as he speaks to his disciples.

Matthew's source for the material in 4:17-25 is once again the Gospel of Mark. Verse 17 is based on the synopsis of Jesus' preaching in Mark 1:14b-15. In like manner, the account of the four fishers in verses 18-22 comes from Mark 1:16-20. In verses 23-25, Matthew departs from the order of Mark's narrative, moving instead into the overview of Jesus' work mentioned above. Here too, however, Matthew is indebted to Mark. When we look at the language of verses 23-25, we see that Matthew has blended phrases from several different statements in Mark (cf. 1:28, 34, 39; 3:7-8). This composite description prepares us for the story about to unfold and allows us to sense the awe that accompanies Jesus from the outset.

OUTLINE

Jesus' Proclamation of the Kingdom, 4:17

Jesus' Invitation to Discipleship, 4:18-22

Jesus' Ministry of Word and Deed, 4:23-25

EXPLANATORY NOTES

Jesus' Proclamation of the Kingdom 4:17

In 4:12-16 we learned of Jesus' return to Galilee and his decision to dwell in Capernaum. *From that time,* Matthew tells us in verse 17, Jesus began to preach to the people of Galilee. Later on in the Gospel, when Jesus begins to talk of his death, Matthew will again use the phrase *from that time* (16:21). In both instances the words signal a major turning point in the story. Here it marks the shift from preparation to proclamation. The message Jesus proclaims is identical to the message Matthew ascribes to John the Baptist in 3:1. Only now, however, does that message reach a wider audience, bringing light to Galilee and thus fulfilling the promise quoted in 4:15-16.

Matthew summarizes Jesus' message in words adapted from the summary found in Mark 1:15: *Repent, for the kingdom of heaven has come near.* At least two things are noteworthy in the formulation Matthew offers: (1) It accents the ethical character of the response Jesus seeks, focusing the reader's attention on the single word *repent.* (2) It grounds the call to repent in the coming of the kingdom, which is presented as the overarching theme of Jesus' preaching.

The *kingdom of heaven* (or kingdom of God) of which Jesus and Matthew speak refers to God's eschatological *reign* or *rule.* *[Eschatology, p. 420; Matthew, Distinctive Themes, p. 423.]* Central to Jesus' teaching about this coming administration is the conviction that it now is at hand or upon us. Although the kingdom in its fullness still lies in the future, "its powers are in operation in, with, and around Jesus" (Stendahl, 1962:774). It is this that gives urgency to Jesus' summons to repent.

Jesus' Invitation to Discipleship 4:18-22

While Jesus calls all to repent, a smaller circle of persons receive the call, *Follow me!* Verses 18-22 tell of one such invitation, which comes to two sets of brothers who are fishers by trade, and who are busy at work in or by the Sea of Galilee. Similar stories are found in Luke 5:1-11 and John 21:1-19. The immediate parallel, however, is Mark 1:16-20, which Matthew follows closely. One feature worth noting in Matthew's version of the story is the way he reports the reactions to Jesus' call. When he describes the response of James and John in verse 22, he uses the same construction found earlier in verse 20:

Verse 20: *Immediately they left their nets and followed him.*

Verse 22: *Immediately they left the boat and their father, and followed him.*

Together these statements create a vivid impression of the immediacy and completeness of the decision to follow Jesus (cf. 8:18-22).

To *follow* someone means literally to walk behind or follow after. This is the sense in which the crowds *follow* Jesus in the Gospels. In other instances, however, to *follow* someone means to be a disciple of that person. The story at hand likely implies both meanings: When Jesus calls the four Galilean fishers, he invites them both to come along on a journey *and* to take up a new vocation as his disciples.

Many religious figures in the first century, among them Jewish rabbis, were accompanied by followers or disciples. Whereas rabbinic students, however, chose the teacher they wanted to follow, here *Jesus* takes the initiative in calling the persons he wants as followers. The closest parallel to Jesus' action is found in 1 Kings 19:19-21, where Elijah casts his mantle on Elisha, and Elisha begins to "follow" Elijah. There, as in the Gospels, discipleship involves sharing in the mission and power of God's servant.

The new vocation of those who are called is not unrelated to their old one. They will continue to be fishers. Only now, Jesus tells them, they will cast their nets *for people*. Some interpreters see an allusion here to Jeremiah 16:16. It is more likely, however, that the metaphor grows out of the actual work of Simon and the others.

In any case, it provides a provocative way to talk about mission, in keeping with material later in the Gospel. In a chapter of parables on the kingdom of heaven, Jesus compares the kingdom to *a net that was thrown into the sea and caught fish of every kind* (13:47-50). Jesus uses a related metaphor before he sends out *the twelve*, appealing for laborers to go out and gather in the harvest (9:35-38). Both texts envision a far-reaching venture of drawing people into the sphere of God's reign. That is the calling of those Jesus summons.

Jesus' Ministry of Word and Deed 4:23-25

As noted earlier, these verses give an overview of the scope and impact of Jesus' work. Some scholars refer to this passage as a summary, while others would see it more as an extended topic sentence, providing a basis or context for the material to follow. Whatever label we choose to assign, we find a number of such passages in the Gospels and Acts (cf. Mark 3:7-8; Luke 6:17-19; Acts 2:43-47; 9:31).

The passage before us begins in verse 23 with a threefold description of Jesus' activity: He teaches in the synagogue, preaches good news of the kingdom, and heals diseases of every sort. This description is repeated in 9:35 (creating what is known as a literary inclusion), reinforcing the thematic framework of the story. Verses 24-25 report the reaction to Jesus' work—and again the description includes three elements: Jesus' fame spreads far and wide, the sick are brought to Jesus for healing, and great crowds follow Jesus.

Several details in this overview call for further comment: (1) The phrase *good news of the kingdom* is peculiar to Matthew and confirms the centrality of the kingdom in his thinking. In addition, it shows that Matthew views the coming of God's reign as a joyous event, bringing hope to those who receive it. (2) The text abounds in hyperbole: Jesus goes *throughout Galilee,* and *all Syria* hears of his deeds; the people bring *all the sick,* and Jesus heals *every* illness; *great crowds* follow Jesus, from every quarter of Israel. With language such as this, Matthew paints a picture of a major undertaking. (3) Among the evangelists, only Matthew informs us of Jesus' fame throughout *Syria*, which was the name of the Roman province to which Palestine belonged. This may be a clue that Matthew is writing for a Syrian church, giving his readers a heightened sense of connection with Jesus' story.

THE TEXT IN BIBLICAL CONTEXT

Two themes surface in 4:17-25 which are basic to the message of the synoptic Gospels. One of those themes is *the kingdom of God*, which Matthew prefers to call *the kingdom of heaven* (probably to guard against overuse of the name *God*; cf. Exod. 20:7; Dan. 4:34-37). In each of the Synoptics, the kingdom of God is the primary metaphor for God's saving activity.

The kingdom comes as God's gift (Luke 12:32), fully establishing God's sovereignty over human life (Matt. 12:28), and offering blessing to the poor and others crushed by life (Luke 6:20-23). It brings fulfillment to history (Mark 1:14) and inaugurates a new era (Luke 16:16), opening the doors even now to participation in the endtime banquet of life with God and God's people (Matt. 22:1-14). A NT theology of salvation, therefore, does not begin with Paul's doctrine of justification by faith. It begins, as Matthew tells us, with the good news of God's reign and the blessing it brings.

The second theme which 4:17-25 introduces is following Jesus or *discipleship* (cf. "Matthew, Distinctive Themes" in Glossary and Essays). Outside the four Gospels and Acts, there are no references to disciples and only scattered references to following Jesus (see Rev. 14:4; 1 Pet. 2:21; cf. Heb. 13:13). Within the Gospels, however, and in Luke's account in Acts, we find scores of such references. Some are simply part of the narrative structure, while others delve into the nature of discipleship (cf. Matt. 10:16-39; Mark 8:34-38; Luke 9:57-62).

In the First Gospel, the author works with a two-track approach to discipleship. For the duration of Jesus' ministry, Matthew restricts the term *disciples* to the limited circle of *the twelve* (cf. 10:1-5; 11:1; 19:28). All this changes, however, at the end of the Gospel. There Jesus commissions *the eleven* (Judas is now out of the story) to *make disciples* throughout the world (28:16-20)! All those who hear the gospel will now be invited to follow Jesus as disciples. At that point the reader realizes that the disciples in the preceding chapters have much more than historical significance. Jesus' training of the twelve was a backdrop all along for instructing future disciples in every age to come.

THE TEXT IN THE LIFE OF THE CHURCH

Texts yet to be studied will provide a number of opportunities to reflect further on the theme of discipleship. Here we observe the way the church has appropriated Jesus' teaching about *the kingdom*. Unfortunately, misconceptions of the kingdom have been all too common in every age of the church. Some have equated the kingdom with the institution of the church or with a theocratic state in which the saints hold the power. Others have viewed the kingdom as a wholly future reality, whether in terms of a millennial reign or in terms of a heavenly realm. Still others have spiritualized the image of the kingdom, restricting its meaning to an inward reign in the heart. Finally, there are those who speak of Christians *building* the kingdom, losing sight of the fact that God's reign is *God's* doing. While each of these views contains an element of truth, each distorts or truncates the NT message.

Fortunately, there are voices in our own time which are helping us to reclaim Jesus' vision of God's reign. From one direction we hear the voices of scholars, who have analyzed the kingdom texts and worked to clarify their meaning. From another direction we hear the voices of Christians in oppressive societies, who attest the power of Jesus' vision in their ongoing struggle against violence and injustice. The word we hear from both sources is that the metaphor of the kingdom is a *potent* image, challenging old ways of looking at life. It speaks of God's mighty presence and power to save, the power of the future at work in the present, reaching into our world to reshape and reorder it. That is what we ask for when we pray, *Your kingdom come* (6:10). And that is the cause for joy when we hear Jesus say: *The kingdom of heaven has come near!"*

Matthew 5:1—7:29

Jesus Teaches with Authority

PREVIEW

For countless Christians across the centuries, the primary source for Jesus' teaching has been the collection of Jesus' sayings which we find in Matthew 5—7. It contains such classic texts as the Lord's Prayer and the Beatitudes, and it portrays Jesus as one who speaks with unparalleled authority. Numerous titles have been proposed for this collection of sayings. Because of its link to Jesus' message of God's reign, some have labeled it a charter or manifesto of the kingdom. Others have called it a design or pattern for life, calling attention to its significance as a resource for Christian ethics. The title by which it is known to most readers, however, derives from its setting in the Matthean narrative, and is first attested in a commentary by Augustine. That title is *the Sermon on the Mount.*

In one sense the label *sermon* is somewhat of a misnomer. The body of material in Matthew 5—7 is not a transcript of a single presentation by Jesus. Rather, it is a compendium of words spoken on a number of different occasions. In another sense, however, the name *sermon* is appropriate. Whatever the original setting of the various sayings in the text, the literary setting in which they now appear is clearly that of a *speech* or *discourse.*

Classical scholar George Kennedy notes some striking parallels between the structure of this speech and that of other ancient speeches of the type known as "deliberative rhetoric" (cf. Kennedy: 39-63). Such a speech often begins with a carefully crafted proem or prologue, then states a proposition which is explored under several headings, and concludes with an epilogue designed to move the hearers to action. In the case of Jesus' teaching in Matthew 5—7, the three sections of the speech can be identified as follows:

Proem, 5:3-16 (the Beatitudes and related sayings)

Proposition and elaboration, 5:17—7:12 (Jesus' teaching as fulfillment of the law and the prophets)

Epilogue, 7:13-27 (admonitions to hearers to act on Jesus' words)

If this analysis of the form of Matthew 5—7 is correct, it confirms the author's skill in literary composition.

A counterpart to Matthew's Sermon on the Mount is found in Luke 6:17-49. There Jesus speaks as he stands "on a level place," leading scholars to call the passage the Sermon on the Plain. Although the sermon in Luke is much briefer than Matthew's, the two passages exhibit the same sequence of material: Both begin with Beatitudes, then proceed to moral instruction, and conclude with the story of the wise and foolish builders. This suggests that the two evangelists are indebted to the same sermon in the common source they use elsewhere.

The expanded version of this sermon in Matthew 5—7 may have begun to take shape long before Matthew wrote, as the church in which he was active adapted the earlier text for use in teaching and in worship. Matthew himself found it natural to continue this process, enlarging the sermon with other sayings from his sources, clarifying the relation of Jesus' teaching to Jewish tradition, and adapting the form and content to address his readers more effectively.

The Sermon as we now have it makes an important contribution to the development of Matthew's story. As noted earlier, it depicts the teaching side of Jesus' messianic mission. Early in his Gospel, the writer of Mark also speaks of Jesus' new and powerful teaching (Mark 1:21-22, 27). For Matthew, however, it is not enough to simply tell us *that* Jesus taught with authority. Instead, he presents the Sermon as an exhibit of Jesus' teaching, allowing readers to *experience* the breadth and power of Jesus' word.

Heirs of the Kingdom

Matthew 5:1-16

PREVIEW

As already suggested, 5:1-16 functions as a proem or prologue for the Sermon on the Mount. This prologue consists of three elements, each of which exhibits a distinct literary form: (1) A narrative introduction in verses 1-2 (the sequel to which is the narrative conclusion in 7:28-29). (2) A series of sayings known as Beatitudes or *macarisms* (from the Greek word for *blessed*) in verses 3-12. Each begins with the key word *blessed*, thereby designating the favorable or fortunate status of a particular group of people. (3) A pair of *you are* sayings in verses 13-16. Like the *I am* sayings of Jesus in the Fourth Gospel (cf. John 6:35; 8:12), these *you are* statements describe a special role or calling. Together these three elements provide a context for understanding the ethical instruction Jesus will offer in 5:17—7:12.

The sayings known as Beatitudes call for further comment. As a literary form, the beatitude was widely used in the ancient world. Greek literature, for example, speaks of the happy state of the gods, of parents with fine children, of finding love and its bliss, of those with knowledge or piety. In Jewish writings we find two different types of beatitudes. The earliest type occurs frequently in the Psalms and wisdom literature: "Happy are those who do not follow the advice of the wicked" (Ps. 1:1). "Happy is the one who finds a friend, and the one who speaks to attentive listeners" (Sir. 25:9). Here the emphasis might be called *this-worldly*: Life turns out well for those who live as indicated.

The second type of beatitude emerges somewhat later in texts that reflect an apocalyptic view of history: "Blessed are you, righteous and elect ones, for glorious is your portion" (1 Enoch 58:2). "Blessed are those who are invited to the marriage supper of the Lamb" (Rev. 19:9). Here the well-being of those whom the text declares blessed relates not to this age but to the age to come. Instead of defining the "good life" in the present scheme of things, these Beatitudes bring a promise of a new order yet to appear. Blessedness consists in knowing that one will be part of the new order. *[Apocalyptic, p. 418; Eschatology, p. 420.]*

The Beatitudes of Matthew 5 clearly belong to the second of these two types. They do not describe a way of life that is guaranteed to bring success and well-being in the world, nor do they appeal to luck or chance. Instead, they congratulate those to whom God promises the future. Those designated as blessed seem at first to be several distinct categories of people, to each of whom Jesus promises an appropriate reward: The meek will inherit the earth; mourners will receive comfort; the pure in heart will see God. . . .

Upon closer analysis, however, we discover that the various statements are really dealing with *one* group and *one* promise. Each of the phrases describing the *blessed* calls attention to some aspect of the life and conduct of Jesus' community. And each of the descriptions of the age to come calls attention to some facet of the kingdom of heaven. Taken together, the Beatitudes in Matthew 5:3-12 set forth a single message: *Blessed are those who hear and live by Jesus' word, for they will enter into the reign of God which Jesus proclaims.*

For four of the Beatitudes in Matthew 5, we find parallel sayings in Luke's Sermon on the Plain (cf. Luke 6:20-23). In the course of transmission, these core sayings were supplemented in different ways. In Luke 6 we find a counterpart to the four Beatitudes in the four "woe" sayings of verses 24-26. Matthew 5 contains no such woes. Instead, Matthew gives us an enlarged group of Beatitudes, nine sayings in all. These appear to be arranged in two stanzas containing four Beatitudes each (verses 3-6 and 7-10), followed by the longer and more complex beatitude in verses 11-12.

Another noteworthy feature in Matthew's Beatitudes is that most are cast in the third person: "Blessed are the so and so." Luke's Beatitudes, however, are all cast in the second person: "Blessed are *you* so and so." Although the Matthean form is more common in Jewish tradition, it is difficult to determine which form is more original in the tradition of Jesus' sayings. In any case, the form Matthew uses tends to underline the fact that the Beatitudes are valid for hearers in every age, not just Jesus' immediate audience.

OUTLINE

Jesus and His Hearers, 5:1-2

The Fortunate Faithful, 5:3-12

5:3-6	Promise and Need
5:7-10	Promise and Righteousness
5:11-12	Promise and Persecution

The Visible Community, 5:13-16

EXPLANATORY NOTES

Jesus and His Hearers 5:1-2

The narrative introduction in verses 1-2 sets the stage for what follows. Among other things, we learn that Jesus will be speaking from *the mountain.* Mountains, as noted earlier (cf. p. 72), are important for Matthew. A mountain was the setting for Jesus' third temptation as he began his ministry (4:8-10), and a mountain will be the setting for Jesus' great commission at the end of his ministry (28:16-20)! It is not surprising, therefore, that Jesus' first major discourse should be delivered from a mountain.

As Matthew develops this scene, he may have two particular mountains in mind that relate to Israel's story. One is Mount Sinai, the mount from which Moses brought God's word to the people (Exod. 19—20). The other is Mount Zion (Jerusalem), which Isaiah depicts as the site to which all nations will stream in the endtime to be taught by God (Isa. 2:1-4, cf. Mic. 4:1-4). If these are the associations Matthew wants to evoke, then Jesus' message on the mountain is no ordinary sermon. It is a moment of revelation that signals Jesus' authority to inaugurate God's reign and to gather and teach God's people.

As well as telling us the location, Matthew notes the audience that is present for the occasion. There are two groups of people, each important in its own way. The larger group is *the crowds,* the same crowds just mentioned in 4:25, who come from every corner of Israel. Closer in is the smaller group, the cluster of Jesus' disciples, the calling of whom was the topic in 4:18-22. This smaller group is apparently sitting in a semicircle in front of Jesus, while the larger group forms a deep concentric semicircle behind them, down the slope of the mountain.

According to verse 1, Jesus himself is also seated, the customary posture for teaching in Jewish circles (cf. Matt. 13:2; 23:2; Luke 4:20-21). And then *he opened his mouth and taught them* (RSV). The phrase has a lofty and poetic ring, and similar language is used elsewhere to introduce important teaching (cf. Ps. 78:1-2; Job 33:1-2; Acts 8:35).

To whom, however, is Jesus speaking? Is his teaching for the disciples, the crowds, or both? When the text says in verse 2 that he *taught them,* the closest antecedent is *his disciples* in verse 1. Furthermore, it is clear that the discourses in Matthew contain instruction for disciples. At the same time, it is striking to observe at the end of the Sermon that *the crowds were astounded at his teaching* (7:28).

From all this it appears that Matthew wants us to think of the crowds as more than a scenic backdrop. When Jesus teaches about the claims of God's kingdom, he is addressing all of Israel, whom the crowds represent. It is conceivable that all the people will respond as the disciples have, and it is important that they have the opportunity to do so. That opportunity is there in the Sermon on the Mount, as Jesus speaks a word *for disciples*, but a word *that all can hear*.

The Fortunate Faithful 5:3-12

5:3-6 Promise and Need

Jesus begins his discourse with the Beatitudes, the first set or stanza of which is found in verses 3-6 (cf. Luke 6:20-21). Several things are noteworthy in this group of sayings: (1) The words describing the blessed in the underlying Greek text all begin with *p* (*ptōchoi*, *penthountes*, *praeis*, and *peinōntes*). The alliteration enhances the poetic power of the sayings. (2) The wording in Matthew's version differs from Luke's at several points. Most significantly, Matthew highlights the religious stance or disposition of the blessed, while Luke focuses more on their circumstances in society. (3) The language Matthew uses draws on OT texts, notably Isaiah 61. To understand the Matthean Beatitudes, we need to be attentive to this biblical background.

The first of the Beatitudes lifts up *the poor in spirit.* (In Luke 6:20 the designation is "you who are poor.") As a quick review of the listings in a concordance reveals, the OT is replete with references to the poor (cf. Deut. 15:11; Pss. 37:14; 72:1-4; Amos 8:4). The vocabulary used to speak of the poor calls attention not only to their economic deprivation but to the lowly situation that accompanies poverty, often as a result of oppression. In such circumstances, God champions the cause of the poor and takes action to deliver them (cf. Pss. 34:6; 35:10; 1 Sam. 2:8; Isa. 41:17). Thus it is that *the poor* eventually comes to signify the whole community of those in need who look to God for help. Matthew builds on this context of meaning when he renders *the poor* as *the poor in spirit.*

The phrase *poor in spirit* does not occur in the OT, although it does appear once in the Dead Sea Scrolls (1QM 14:7). The precise meaning of the phrase has been the subject of much discussion, and interpreters tend to go in one of two directions. According to some, the phrase refers to those who cultivate a humble spirit, who empty themselves and relate to others in the unpretentious way of the poor. Others suggest that the phrase describes those who like the poor have a needy condition, but whose poverty is more an affliction of the spirit.

In this case the *poor in spirit* might be those who feel weak and vulnerable in the face of persecution (cf. vv.10-12), or those who sense a lack of righteousness in their relationship to God (cf. v.6). Similar nuances are present in the reference to the poor or afflicted in Isaiah 61:1, which likely was in Matthew's mind as he reflected on this beatitude. Robert Guelich puts it well when he writes that " 'the poor in spirit,' now as then, are ultimately those standing without pretense before God, stripped of all self-sufficiency, self-security, and self-righteousness" (98).

To such as these, the poor in spirit, God will give *the kingdom of heaven.* We noted earlier that the kingdom of heaven is the all-encompassing point of reference for all the good things Jesus promises. God's reign is the source of the comfort promised in verse 4, the inheritance promised in verse 5, the satisfaction promised in verse 6, and all the rest. For this reason the kingdom is mentioned both here at the beginning of the first set of Beatitudes and again in verse 10 at the end of the second set.

As used in these sayings, the language of the kingdom looks forward to a gift that still lies in the future. In Jesus' ministry, however, God's reign is already being manifested in Israel. The blessedness of those to whom the promise is given is thus twofold: They are assured that they will be part of God's future for God's people. And they sense the *power* of the age to come in the very word Jesus speaks!

The second beatitude promises comfort to *those who mourn.* In the parallel saying in Luke 6:21, the contrast is expressed in terms of weeping and laughing. There the language recalls Psalm 126:5-6. Matthew's version, however, uses the vocabulary of Isaiah 61:2-3, which speaks of comfort for those who mourn the plight of Israel following the exile. This gives us some clues as to the grief of the mourners whom Jesus calls blessed. Their grief is not merely bereavement at the grave, nor is it limited to sorrow over personal sin. What they mourn is the condition of the world as it now exists—and all the loss and suffering they have experienced in this world. Like Simeon (cf. Luke 2:25), they are "looking forward to the consolation of Israel," for a new age in which sorrow no longer reigns.

Such persons, Jesus says, *will be comforted.* Here the passive voice points to the action of God, who will transform the world and turn mourning into joy (cf. Isa. 49:13; 66:13; Jer. 31:13; 2 Cor. 1:4; Rev. 21:4). This "comforting" reversal of the present scheme of things is once again a matter of hope. It is a hope, however, which begins to be fulfilled as Jesus speaks. His *assurance* of comfort is itself a foretaste of the comfort yet to come.

In the third beatitude, found only in Matthew, Jesus congratulates *the meek.* The language reflects the promise of Psalm 37:11 that "the meek shall inherit the land, and delight themselves in abundant prosperity" (cf. Isa. 61:7). There the meek are those powerless to defend their own claims, but who trust God to intervene and break the grip of oppressors. Matthew himself sheds further light on the meek in our text, when he uses the same word to describe the manner in which Jesus exercises his authority (cf. *gentle,* 11:29; *humble,* 21:5). Here the word points to a style of relating to others, a style in which we eschew the proud and violent ways of the mighty.

Whether as those who lack power, or as those who treat their power lightly, the meek receive the assurance that they will *inherit the earth.* In the OT texts which lie behind our saying, the land or earth to be possessed is the land of Canaan (cf. Gen. 17:8). In Jesus' beatitude, however, land or earth has a broader meaning. It is a way of depicting a place to dwell without fear in the new realm of God's kingdom. Such will be the lot of the meek who follow Jesus, who look to God to shape and to guarantee their destiny.

The final saying in the first stanza of Matthew's Beatitudes expands the shorter saying we find in Luke 6:21a. Where Luke speaks only of "you who are hungry now," Matthew speaks of *those who hunger and thirst for righteousness.* This wording reflects OT themes: God as the one who satisfies our hunger and thirst (Ps. 107:9), eating and drinking as a metaphor for relationship with God (Isa. 55:1-3), and righteousness as a gift which God bestows on the people (Isa. 61:3, 10-11). The hungry and thirsty whom Jesus pronounces blessed, therefore, are those who yearn for a deeper and right relationship with God (cf. Matt. 6:33). They are the same persons identified as *the poor in spirit* in verse 3, who have needs that they know only God can fulfill. And they are the ones who respond to *the way of righteousness* revealed by John the Baptist and Jesus (cf. 21:32).

Such persons will not be disappointed, the text tells us, for God will satisfy their longings. Already they have access to a right relationship with God through the word Jesus brings. And they will take part in the banquet of the kingdom yet to come, in which communion with God will be full and complete.

5:7-10 Promise and Righteousness

Verses 7-10 contain four more Beatitudes, the second of the two sets or stanzas mentioned earlier. All four of these sayings are unique to Matthew, and all touch on themes that are important to Matthew's agenda. To put it another way, the blessed whom Jesus singles out in these sayings exhibit the qualities which Jesus will call for in teaching soon to follow. The merciful, for example, model the forgiveness lifted up in the Lord's Prayer and elsewhere (cf. 6:12, 14-15; 7:1-5; 18:21-35). In a similar way the pure in heart reflect the focused and genuine faith that is free from all duplicity (cf. 5:33-37; 6:1-8, 16-18; 6:19-34). And the peacemakers, finally, embody Jesus' striking call to break the cycle of human violence and pursue the way of love (cf. 5:21-26, 38-48; 26:52). In all of this it becomes clear that the heirs of the kingdom not only *hunger and thirst for righteousness,* but also *practice* the way of righteousness in the way they conduct themselves with one another and in the world.

The trait or quality lifted up in verse 7 is *mercy*. It is *the merciful,* Jesus says, who will experience *God's* mercy. This emphasis on the reciprocity of human and divine mercy is attested elsewhere. In the Talmud a saying states that "those who have mercy on others, heaven will have mercy on them" (bShab. 151b). Clement of Rome cites a collection of Jesus' sayings in this area, including the words "Show mercy, that you may be shown mercy" (1 Clem. 13:2; cf. James 2:13).

At first glance such statements seem to suggest that the process of showing mercy begins with us. That, however, is not the case. It is God who is merciful and gracious, first of all (Exod. 34:6; Ps. 86:15-16), and the people of God are who they are because they have received God's mercy (Isa. 63:7-9; 1 Pet. 2:10). As Matthew himself makes clear in a parable about forgiveness (18:23-35, especially v. 33), it is God's prior mercy which supplies the model and basis for showing mercy to one another. The *merciful* of whom we hear in the beatitude, therefore, are those who offer to others the same pardon and compassion they have experienced from God. All who do so, we are told, can look forward to finding mercy at the end as well.

In the next beatitude the blessed are described as *the pure in heart.* The language used here likely comes from Psalm 24:3-6, which poses the question of who is ready to seek God in the temple. According to the psalmist, it is those "who have clean hands and pure hearts, who do not lift up their souls to what is false, and do not swear deceitfully." As is apparent from the psalmist's words, purity of heart refers not so much to what we usually think of as "clean thoughts" as it does to a lack of guile in the way we relate to God and others (cf. James 4:8). The pure in heart are those persons whose vision is clear and focused, whose commitments are always genuine, and whose dealings have integrity.

The promise given to the pure in heart is that *they will see God.* To see God is to experience God's presence in an intimate way, the way we experience fellow humans in face-to-face encounters. This is the kind of experience attested by the psalmist, when he reports that he has looked upon God in the temple (Ps. 63:1-2; cf. 24:3-6). Although encounter with God can be both fearful and overwhelming (Isa. 6:5; Gen. 32:22-31), it is also the source of transformation and blessing (Isa. 6:6-7; Gen. 32:26-30). For later writers it was thus natural to speak of seeing or beholding God when they envisioned the age to come (2 Esd. 7:98; 1 John 3:2). That is the hope picked up in Jesus' promise to the pure in heart: Having already looked to God in singleminded trust, they can await a future day when faith will truly become sight!

The beatitude in verse 9 adds *peacemaking* to the list of things that mark the life of the blessed (cf. 2 Enoch 52:11-14; Aboth 1:12). Although within the NT the word translated *peacemakers* occurs only here, related terms are found elsewhere. James 3:18 commends believers who make peace, while Ephesians and Colossians refer to peacemaking on God's part (cf. Eph. 2:13-16; Col. 1:19-20). Outside the NT the term peacemakers is used to describe Greek and Roman rulers who establish peace in their domain.

From all of this it is evident that the peacemakers Jesus blesses are not merely peaceful persons. Instead, they are those who work actively to bring peace or make peace. Taking their cue from God, whose love extends to friend and enemy (Matt. 5:45), they pursue peace with all persons. They work to restore wholeness in their relationships with others, whether with members of the church (5:23-24; 18:10ff.), or with hostile parties on the outside (5:38-48). Because those who make peace are acting as God acts, they show themselves to be the true children of God. Thus, Jesus says, God will claim them as his own in the age to come.

The beatitude which concludes the second stanza of sayings speaks of *those who are persecuted for righteousness sake* (cf. 1 Pet. 3:14). The Greek word for *persecuted* is a perfect passive participle, a clue that Matthew's readers are well acquainted with persecution (cf. comments below on verses 11-12, on which verse 10 seems to draw). With its carefully chosen language, the saying in verse 10 recapitulates and ties together the Beatitudes as a whole.

First, it identifies the social plight of the blessed which verses 3 and 4 presuppose: Persecution is one of the reasons for the needy condition and state of mourning in which the blessed find themselves. Second, the saying picks up the theme of righteousness introduced in verse 6 (the saying which concludes the first set of Beatitudes). The persecution the blessed face results from opposition to *the way of righteousness.* Finally, the saying repeats the core promise which Jesus gives to the blessed in verse 3: Whatever deprivation they may experience here and now, the persecuted are assured that they will receive *God's kingdom.*

5:11-12 Promise and Persecution

Persecution remains the topic in the longer beatitude in verses 11-12. For this saying we find a parallel in Luke 6:22-23, as well as related sayings in 1 Peter 4:13-16. Several things stand out in the wording of verse 11. Note the shift from third-person to second-person language, and note further the way Jesus speaks of trouble *on my account.* Both features confirm that the Beatitudes in Matthew are directed to a specific group. They are sayings for and about those who give their allegiance to Jesus and his word. Also noteworthy in the text is the description of three forms that opposition may assume—ridicule, persecution, and slander.

Persecution is a broad term, covering a wide range of hostile actions, while ridicule and slander both deal with verbal abuse. In Luke the language is somewhat more pointed, referring to the exclusion of Jesus' followers from the synagogue. That may well have been an earlier focus of the saying. Matthew knows, however, that the threat to *his* community comes from *many* quarters, both Jewish and Gentile (cf. 10:17-18), and so describes that threat in more general categories.

In the face of persecution, Jesus' followers have two reasons to *rejoice and be glad.* First, they know that God rewards those who suffer for their faith, and that their reward will indeed be *great in heaven.* The topic of rewards is typically Jewish and widely attested in the NT era (cf. Matt. 6:1-4; 10:42; 20:1-16; 2 Esd. 7:83; 13:56; 1 Enoch 108:10). When such language is used, the idea is not that *we earn* future reward, but that God is just and faithful to those who suffer and endure.

The second reason Jesus' followers can rejoice in tribulation is that they stand in good company: *In the same way they persecuted the prophets who were before you,* Jesus says (cf. 23:29-39; Acts 7:51-52; 1 Thess. 2:14-16; Heb. 11:35-38). There are two ways to read the words just quoted. Jesus could mean only that prophets and disciples share a common fate. As punctuated in the NRSV, however,

Jesus' words say something more. They imply that disciples are themselves prophets, persecuted in the same manner as prophets of an earlier day. This is likely the meaning that Matthew intends, and it fits with the prophetic role ascribed to Jesus' followers elsewhere (5:13-16; 10:26-33; 10:40-41).

The Visible Community 5:13-16

Having described the joys awaiting the faithful, Jesus goes on in verses 13-16 to describe their *calling* in the world. He uses two vivid metaphors for his followers, naming them first *the salt of the earth* and then *the light of the world.* For the basic content of these verses, Matthew apparently drew on several sayings dealing with salt and light (cf. Mark 4:21; 9:49-50; Luke 8:16; 11:33; 14:34-35; G. Thom. 32, 33). The *you are* formulation, however, is found only in Matthew. It is this phrase which gives the verses their distinctive character, underlining the vocation of Jesus' community.

Salt was and is used in a number of ways—as a seasoning, as a preservative, or as a purifying agent. Which if any of these meanings was foremost in Matthew's mind is hard to say. What is certain is that salt plays a vital role in everyday life, and that disciples have a similar role to play in the world. Not to fulfill that role, which is defined more clearly in verse 16, is to become like salt that *has lost its taste* (literally, *become foolish or insipid*). Jesus may have been thinking of salt like that from the Dead Sea, which due to chemical impurities can in fact decompose and lose its savor. Such salt, says Jesus, serves no useful purpose and can only be *thrown out.* Here the metaphor hints at judgment for those neglecting their call, reminding the reader of other texts in which Jesus speaks of persons *thrown out* of God's kingdom (cf. 8:12; 22:13; 25:30).

In the second metaphor, Matthew takes the image of light and develops it in several ways. He begins by emphasizing that it is the nature of light to be seen or visible: Lamps are placed on stands where they can illumine large areas, and a city atop a hill will be visible at a great distance. In the saying about a city, Matthew may be alluding to Jerusalem or Zion, the hilly city of God's temple. From this city, it was believed, the glory or word of God would one day command the attention of every people on earth (Isa. 2:1-4; 60:1-3). In any case, the light-bearing role of Jesus' community has important antecedents: It reflects Israel's call to be "a light to the nations" (Isa. 42:6), and it extends Jesus' role of bringing light to Galilee (Matt. 4:12-16; cf. John 8:12).

Matthew proceeds then in verse 16 to spell out the obvious: If we are the light of the world, and if light is meant to be seen, then we should let our light shine in ways that evoke praise of the One who has called us. This we do, the text says, through *good works.* Later we will learn that our light-bearing mission includes witness through words (cf. 10:26-33; 28:20). Here, however, the emphasis falls on the witness of our lives through righteous deeds of love.

THE TEXT IN BIBLICAL CONTEXT

In the NT writings, and especially in Matthew's Gospel, eschatology and ethics are closely linked to one another. There are at least three dimensions to this linkage: (1) The advent of God's kingdom creates a new and urgent possibility for right relationships with God and others. (2) The dawning kingdom introduces a new framework for ethical thinking, redefining the shape of God's will for our lives. (3) Participation in the kingdom hinges on a moral decision, on a readiness to follow the way of life the kingdom entails. All of this is presupposed in the Beatitudes of Matthew 5. As Jesus names the blessed who will receive the kingdom, he speaks of those who yearn for righteousness and pursue the kind of life the kingdom envisions.

If the kingdom points to a certain way of life, so also it envisions a certain corporate calling. Those who respond to the claims of the kingdom have a role to fulfill in the world in which they live. This is the topic of the salt and light statements in 5:13-16. Through works of love that are visible for all to see, Jesus' followers are to bear witness to the power of God in their lives.

The *you are* statements in Matthew 5 recall a similar type of pronouncement in 1 Peter 2:9. "But you are a chosen race, a royal priesthood, a holy nation, God's own people, in order that you may proclaim the mighty acts of him who called you out of darkness into his marvelous light" (cf. Exod. 19:5-6; Isa. 49:6; Phil. 2:15). Such declarations perform at least two functions. They assure us, on the one hand, that we are "somebody" in God's plan. But they remind us at the same time that our special identity is linked to mission.

What we find then in the prologue to the Sermon on the Mount is the convergence of a number of important themes—kingdom, ethics, community, and mission. To expand an earlier statement: *The reign of God that Jesus proclaims creates a new possibility for the life and mission of God's people.* That is the context in which Matthew invites us to listen to Jesus' teaching in the Sermon.

THE TEXT IN THE LIFE OF THE CHURCH

The Beatitudes in Matthew 5 are widely known and widely quoted, not only in Christian circles but throughout the Western world. Many persons view these sayings as a counterpart to the Ten Commandments. Needless to say, the popularity of a text is no guarantee that it will be understood correctly. In the case of the Beatitudes, at least two misconceptions have been prevalent among interpreters.

Some have treated the Beatitudes as a list of Christian virtues, whether as counsels of perfection for clergy or saints, or as signposts to maturity for believers at large. The problem here is that the sayings are really promises, not commands, and that they aim more at validating the way of discipleship as a whole than at spelling out certain steps to achieve perfection.

Other interpreters have treated the sayings as a design for human happiness, a prescription for well-being like the beatitudes of Psalms and Proverbs. Here the problem is one of misconstruing the nature of Jesus' promise. The good things promised to the faithful have their basis in *God's reign*, not on the way life works in the present scheme of things. To hear the Beatitudes rightly, then, we must hear them on their own terms.

The sayings about salt and light have received considerably less attention than have the Beatitudes. In discussions about the nature of the true church, however, they have played a significant and sometimes controversial role (cf. Menno Simons: 734-759, especially 747). The sayings clearly call for such a presence of the church in the world that the world can look at the church and see something different.

Thus, in his commentary on the text in *The Cost of Discipleship*, Dietrich Bonhoeffer opposes those content with an invisible church. Jesus' followers, he writes, "are a visible community, their discipleship visible in action which lifts them out of the world" (106). This distinctness from the world, notes Gerhard Lohfink, is essential to the mission Jesus gives to his community: "The radiant city on the hill is a symbol for the church as a contrast-society, which precisely as *contrast-society* transforms the world. If the church loses its contrast character, if its salt becomes flat and its light is gently extinguished . . . it loses its meaning" (66).

A Greater Righteousness

Matthew 5:17-48

PREVIEW

The central section of Matthew's Sermon, as outlined earlier, runs from 5:17 to 7:12. There Jesus sets forth a definitive statement of God's will, addressing various questions of ethics and piety. Governing this section is an issue of great interest to Matthew and his readers: How does Jesus' message relate to Jewish Torah—and to its observance in the life of the Jewish community? So it is that 5:17 begins with an announcement concerning the law and the prophets. And 7:12 concludes with the observation that Jesus' message as expressed in the Golden Rule *sums up the law and the prophets.* (Note the inclusion formed by 5:17 and 7:12.)

The central section begins with the unit we find in 5:17-48. Here Matthew develops his basic proposition concerning Jesus and Torah: Jesus has come not to abolish what the law and prophets teach but to fulfill it. In verses 17-20, a group of four shorter sayings, the understanding of fulfillment sounds rather conservative. Jesus seems to be calling for strict adherence to every precept laid down in the law. The statements that follow in verses 21-48, however, force us to think about fulfillment in a different manner. Here we find six sets of sayings usually labeled "antitheses," in which Jesus *contrasts* his teaching with the Torah of old. Here Jesus defines God's will in radical and surprising ways, fulfilling the law by going *beyond* the law.

Matthew's interest in the law was shared by many of his contemporaries. From the time of Ezra onward, a strong devotion to the law was one of the marks of Judaism. References to keeping the law abound in Jewish writings in the centuries preceding the Christian era (cf. the listings in a concordance to the Apocrypha). One group in which concern to keep the law was especially intense, and which revered the instruction of its Teacher of Righteousness, was the Qumran community by the Dead Sea (cf. 1QS 1:1-5; 5:7-9; 8:14; 1QpHab 7:1-5; 8:1-3).

In Matthew's own world, at least two developments may have heightened interest in the issue of law. One of these involved Jewish scholars assembled at Jamnia, under the leadership of Johanan ben Zakkai. In the wake of the destruction of Jerusalem in A.D. 70, these persons were attempting to reorganize the Jewish community around authoritative rabbinic teaching. The other development was a debate going on within Christian circles: How obligated were Jesus' followers, and especially those of Gentile background, to keep the law of Moses and observe Jewish practices? Jesus' comments on the law in 5:17-48 speak to both of these matters.

OUTLINE

Jesus Comes to Fulfill, 5:17-20

Jesus Seeks a Greater Righteousness, 5:21-48

5:21-26	Love That Makes Peace
5:27-30	Love That Honors Boundaries
5:31-32	Love That Keeps Commitments
5:33-37	Love That Speaks the Truth
5:38-42	Love That Endures Evil
5:43-48	Love That Includes All

EXPLANATORY NOTES

Jesus Comes to Fulfill 5:17-20

The common theme of the four sayings in verses 17-20 is clearly that of *the law.* How and when these sayings arose and were linked together is not so clear. Matthew may have adapted the loose chain of sayings found in Luke 16:14-18, or he may have built on another collection of unknown origin. In any case, Matthew uses these sayings to introduce the subject of Jesus and Torah. The *I have come* saying in verse 17 (cf. 9:13; 10:34) supplies the framework for understanding everything that Jesus says in chapter 5: Jesus' purpose is not to abolish or set aside what is taught in the law and the prophets (the Scripture, cf. 7:12; 22:40; Luke 16:16; 2 Macc. 15:9). Instead, Jesus comes to *fulfill* the word spoken in earlier times. But how?

Fulfill as used here can be interpreted in several ways: (1) Jesus comes to fulfill God's promise of salvation. While that is certainly true, the moral agenda of the text seems to point in a different direction. (2) Jesus comes as one who lives in complete obedience to God's will, fulfilling the law and the prophets in the way he embodies their teaching. While this too is valid, the text is interested not only in *Jesus'* life but in the life of his followers as well. (3) Jesus comes to reveal the perfect will of God to which the law and prophets point—and to create a community that hears and does God's will. When this happens, when righteousness takes shape in Israel and the world, then the purpose of the law and prophets is truly fulfilled.

Verse 18 shifts the focus to the status of the law itself. In the saying as Matthew found it (cf. Luke 16:17), the sole concern was likely that of the validity of the law throughout the present age: So long as heaven and earth endure, the law remains in force right down to the last detail. Verse 18, however, does not end on this note but qualifies the saying with a final *until* phrase: The law in its entirety remains in force *until all is accomplished.* Although this phrase could allude in a general way to endtime happenings, it most likely picks up the theme of fulfillment in verse 17. For Matthew, *the law remains valid until all that the law intends is fully revealed in Jesus' teaching and fully reflected in Jesus' community.*

The subject in verse 19 is that of teachers in the church (cf. James 3:1) and what they do with the law. If Jesus did not come to abolish the law, then those who teach in his name should not set aside its precepts or encourage others to do so. Instead, they should teach and practice even *the least* of the law's commandments (a formulation reminiscent of the rabbinic distinction between heavy and light commandments).

Implicit here, of course, is the assumption that the law will be taught *as redefined by Jesus.* Even so, the correlation of keeping the law with *great* stature *in the kingdom* is somewhat striking. Those who disregard the law in *the least of these commandments* will find that they themselves are *the least in the kingdom!* The latter phrase may suggest low esteem or low rank, or it may in fact hint at exclusion from the kingdom (cf. v. 20 and 18:1-4). In any case, verse 19 upholds the law as a basis for Christian teaching and firmly opposes those who neglect or discredit the law.

Verse 20 concludes the brief collection of law-sayings in 5:17-20. In this saying Matthew underscores Jesus' expectations for his followers. Their righteousness, Jesus says, must *greatly exceed* that of *the scribes and the Pharisees* (cf. 23:2-12). The scribes (sometimes called rabbis) were teachers and interpreters of the law, while the Pharisees were a religious party concerned with keeping the law scrupulously. How could one possibly surpass leaders such as these in the quest for righteousness? Jesus, however, calls for something more in his community and makes it a prerequisite for entry into the kingdom. What that something greater *is* becomes evident in the antitheses of verses 21-48.

Jesus Seeks a Greater Righteousness 5:21-48

5:21-26 Love That Makes Peace

The six sets of antitheses in verses 21-48 are all introduced by a similar formula. In the longer version found in the first and fourth antitheses, the formula reads: *You have heard that it was said to those of ancient times. . . .* Some scholars interpret the phrase in the light of partial rabbinic parallels and understand it to mean "according to earlier tradition." In that case, Jesus would simply be contrasting his understanding of the law with that of other Jewish teachers.

More likely, however, the words *it was said* are a "divine passive" construction, referring to what *God* said. In this case, we could paraphrase the full formula as follows: "You have heard in the synagogue, as the law has been expounded, that God said to those of old who received the law at Sinai. . . ." When Jesus then goes on to say, *But I say to you,* he is not simply giving his commentary on the law. He is placing his word on a par with God's word, claiming divine authority to redefine the law's demands.

In the first antithesis, the *old word* cited is the sixth commandment: *You shall not murder* (Exod. 20:13; Deut. 5:17), along with a brief summary of related legislation: Those who commit homicides are *liable to judgment,* i.e., subject to a court-proceeding and the penalty that follows (cf. Exod. 21:12; Lev. 24:17; Num. 35:16-17; Deut. 17:8-13).

Jesus' counterword, *But I say,* begins in verse 22. There he expands the sixth commandment to cover hostile words and feelings that readily lead to acts of violence. Anger, no less than murder, makes one *liable to judgment,* and anger expressed in harsh invectives merits judgment in the highest quarters. (The Sanhedrin in Jerusalem was the "supreme court" of Judaism, and *hell* or Gehenna represents the *final* judgment of all history!) In all of this, Jesus' point is not that his hearers should revise the legal code to punish hate and anger. His intent is, instead, to show that every act or emotion that threatens life in one's community violates God's will. (Cf. Eccles. 7:9; Sir. 28:1-12; Eph. 4:26; James 1:19-20; 1 John 3:15.)

Two related sayings pursue the theme of anger as a problem in the church (verses 23-24 and 25-26). Here the issue is what to do when offense on *our* part *causes* enmity and brokenness. The first saying reflects a setting of worship in the temple and states a precondition for offering sacrifice: Before we can find peace with God in worship, we must first make peace with our brother or sister (cf. Mark 11:25; Did. 14:1-2; Yoma 8:9). The second saying is a parable about the wisdom of settling a lawsuit before it gets to court. In the Lukan parallel (Luke 12:57-59), the story urges hearers to settle things with God while time remains to do so. Matthew, however, uses the parable with its note of imminent judgment to deal with human relations. Act with haste, Matthew says, to reconcile your differences with one another!

5:27-30 Love That Honors Boundaries

The second antithesis takes up the issue addressed in the seventh commandment, the issue of adultery (cf. Exod. 20:14; Lev. 20:10; Deut. 22:22). As understood in the OT, adultery was an act in which a man had sexual relations with another man's wife. The law prohibited adultery to protect marital rights and to preserve the stability of marriage itself. Jesus' own word on the subject (vv. 28-32) once again expands the law. Adultery does not begin in the neighbor's bedroom, Jesus says, but in the *craving* in one's heart to *possess* the neighbor's spouse.

What Jesus does here is include the tenth commandment within the scope of the seventh (*look . . . with lust* translates the word the LXX uses for *covet* in Exod. 20:17). At this point Jesus' teaching is not without parallel. A number of Jewish writings note that one can commit adultery with the eyes and/or heart (cf. Ps. Sol. 4:4; T. Iss. 7:2; Kalla 1; Lev. R. 23:122b). The original feature in the antitheses is not always the position taken—but the authority Jesus claims as he articulates that position.

Verses 29-30 contain sayings Matthew uses in two different contexts (cf. 18:8-9/Mark 9:43-48). We can only guess at the setting in which Jesus himself might have used such material. Here, however, Jesus' words exhort the hearer on the need to avoid adultery at all costs. The saying about plucking out the *eye* comes first, since the eye *looks at* others with lustful intent. Note also that the *right* eye and *right* hand are involved, the loss of which would be perceived as especially severe. On the surface these sayings seem to call for self-mutilation. That, however, is not the case. The harsh statements are a sample of Jesus' use of hyperbole, extravagant language that forces one to seek a meaning beyond the literal. The point made is that Jesus' followers should take whatever steps are needed to nip adultery in the bud. In this way, the text says, we can avoid the destructive end to which desire so often leads.

5:31-32 Love That Keeps Commitments

The third antithesis, on divorce, consists of only two verses. For interpreters, however, it raises numerous questions. The law cited on divorce comes from Deuteronomy 24:1-4. There permission is given for a man to divorce his wife if "she does not please him because he finds something objectionable about her." Instructions are given for writing a "bill of divorce," which both dissolved the marriage and freed the woman to remarry.

Because of the somewhat vague language in the text in Deuteronomy, rabbinic teachers held differing views on valid grounds for divorce. The school of Hillel took a somewhat broad approach to the law, permitting divorce at any time a wife offended her husband (even for burning his supper!). The school of Shammai, on the other hand, limited divorce to situations in which the wife was unchaste (or at least immodest). What no one questioned was the basic assumption of the law—that marriage can be dissolved by an appropriate legal procedure.

Jesus challenges this assumption in his statement on divorce in 5:32 (cf. Luke 16:18; Mark 10:2-12/Matt. 19:3-9; 1 Cor. 7:10-11). According to Jesus, divorcing a wife does not alter the fact of marriage. What it does is put the woman in a situation where economic need will almost compel her to commit adultery by entering into a new relationship. Likewise, the man who marries this divorcée ends up an adulterer. In the related texts in Mark and Luke, Jesus opposes divorce without qualification. In Matthew 5, however (cf. also 19:9), we find the modifying phrase *except on the ground of unchastity.*

Some scholars relate this exception phrase to the words *causes her to commit adultery* rather than to the words *divorces his wife.* In this case, the phrase is not giving a possible ground for divorce, but simply saying that the husband divorcing his wife is not responsible for her subsequent adultery if she has already been unchaste while married. This is a somewhat forced interpretation of the language, however, and one that is not an option in the best-supported text for the parallel exception clause in Matthew 19:9. In short, 5:32 does appear to sanction divorce in the case of *unchastity.*

The Greek word translated *unchastity* (*porneia*) can have one of several meanings, of which the two most likely are adultery and incest. Incest would refer to marriages of Gentile converts in which the partners were related in a way forbidden by Jewish law (cf. Lev. 18:6-18; 1 Cor. 5:1; Acts 15:20). Whether the issue is adultery or incestuous marriage, the exception clause was added to deal with marital situations that Jewish Christians found offensive. In situations such as these, Matthew advises his community, one may (or perhaps *should?*) dissolve the marriage.

5:33-37 Love That Speaks the Truth

Taking oaths is the subject of the fourth antithesis, a subject Jewish teachers discussed at great length (the Mishnah devotes a whole tractate to the topic). The *old word* on the subject echoes several passages (Lev. 19:12; Num. 30:2; Deut. 23:21-23) and picks up a concern of the third commandment (Exod. 20:7). In these texts the twofold issue is honesty in taking oaths and faithfulness in keeping oaths. Later texts begin to question the frequency with which oaths apparently were being used. "Do not accustom your mouth to oaths," the writer of Sirach warns, "nor habitually utter the name of the Holy One" (Sir. 23:9-11). What the author of Sirach (and others) tried to curb, Jesus prohibits altogether in verse 34: *Do not swear at all,* Jesus urges his followers—and then goes on to state the case for refusing to take oaths.

Jesus' case against oaths makes two basic points. First of all, Jesus says, the attempt to find "harmless" oaths that do not use God's name is clearly bound to fail (vv. 34-36; cf. 23:16-22). Every oath one takes will implicate God in one way or another: Heaven is God's throne, the earth is God's footstool, and Jerusalem is God's city (cf. Isa. 66:1; Ps. 48:2). Even to swear by one's life involves God in the matter, for life is *God's* to determine, down to the color of one's hair!

The second argument is found in verse 37. There Jesus condemns the double standard for truth which taking oaths implies. If oaths are needed to guarantee that our assertions are true and our promises genuine, it is a sign that the power of evil holds sway in our lives. The righteous community, by contrast, is a place where truthful discourse is the norm at all times. There a *yes* will mean yes and a *no* will mean no (cf. James 5:12). This, Jesus says, is how it should be among you.

5:38-42 Love That Endures Evil

In the final two antitheses, Matthew draws on sayings that also appear in Luke's version of Jesus' sermon (cf. Luke 6:27-36). The issue at stake in verses 38-42 is basic in human relations: How should we respond to injury and insult—and to those who make unjust demands upon us? The law governing all of this in ancient Israel is a rule known as the *lex talionis* (law of retaliation; it goes back at least as far as the Code of Hammurabi, which had class distinctions lacking in the OT). Jesus cites this law in verse 38, quoting the graphic words *an eye for an eye and a tooth for a tooth* (cf. Exod. 21:23-25; Lev. 24:19-20; Deut. 19:21).

The law of talion actually served a twofold purpose. On the one hand, it upheld the right of injured parties to compensation or retribution. On the other hand, it limited the extent of retaliation to punishment appropriate for the crime committed. Later the law was sometimes applied less severely, so that fines could take the place of exact retribution. The right to redress for wrongs committed remained intact, however, and individuals (then as now) generally exercised that right.

Over and against this way of responding to wrongs, Jesus urges his hearers: *Do not resist an evildoer.* The word translated *resist* (Greek: *anthistēmi*) means to *set oneself against* something or someone (cf. James 4:7; Gal. 2:11; Acts 6:10). Here the more precise meaning is supplied by the context: Do not retaliate against those who injure or harm you. Do not act as the adversary who must settle the score. Do not insist on your rights as an offended party.

There follows then a set of illustrative statements, each dealing with a situation in which the issue might arise: (1) A slap on the right cheek, thus most likely a slap with the *back* of the hand, an extremely insulting action according to Jewish law. (2) A lawsuit in which a creditor seeks to take one's shirt (*coat* in the NRSV is misleading), the garment worn next to the skin. (3) Being commandeered to carry baggage or serve as a guide for the authorities (here likely Roman troops), a practice that originated with the Persians. (4) Requests from beggars or would-be borrowers, who have not actually wronged us, but who make what often seems to be unreasonable demands.

For each of these cases Jesus proposes a course of action that takes the hearer by surprise: Turn the other cheek! Let your creditor take *all* your clothes! Perform double the duty required! Give freely to all who ask! In each instance the respondent does the opposite of what is expected, acting on a basis other than the *lex talionis*. The intent of these proposals is not to legislate behavior in the four cases cited. Their purpose is, rather, to refocus our approach to every such case—and to force us to look for new ways to respond (cf. Tannehill: 67-77; Yoder, 1982:100-101, 130-133).

Instead of succumbing to an escalating cycle of hostile acts, eager to secure or defend our rights, we are to act in such a way that the cycle is broken. This might mean letting go of wounded pride, in order to deescalate a conflict situation. It might mean yielding ground in a legal or other dispute, in order to pacify one or more irate parties. Or it might mean pursuing a new level of reciprocity, in which we seek to meet evil with good stronger than evil (cf. Prov. 24:29; Rom. 12:17-21; 1 Thess. 5:15; 1 Pet. 2:23). In these and other ways, we act as the peacemakers Jesus commends in 5:9.

5:43-48 Love That Includes All

The sayings in verses 43-48 conclude the six sets of antitheses on the law. Here the *old word* goes back to the book of Leviticus, which commands the people to love their fellow Israelites (19:17-18) and also the sojourners who live in their land (19:33-34). Nowhere in the Torah is there a command to *hate your enemy.* Love of *neighbor*, however, could imply that love is limited to those within the community, and that opponents and outsiders fall in a different class. The Psalmist thus can boast of hating God's enemies (Ps. 139:19-22). Similar in tone is the language used in some of the writings from Qumran (cf. 1QS 1:3-4, 9-10). There the faithful are described as those who "love all the sons of light, each according to his lot in God's design, and hate all the sons of darkness, each according to his guilt in God's vengeance."

Jesus challenges this perspective in his *new word* concerning love in verse 44: Instead of limiting love to the neighbor, Jesus says, love even the outsider who seeks to destroy you (cf. Rom. 12:14, 20-21; 1 Pet. 3:9; Luke 23:34; Acts 7:60). Already in the OT we find texts that call for compassion toward the enemy (Exod. 23:4-5; Prov. 25:21-22), and rabbinic writings sometimes speak of a love for all humankind (cf. Aboth 1:12). Jesus' appeal for love that includes the enemy, however, has a direct and forceful quality unparalleled elsewhere.

Verses 45-47 go on to make a case for this inclusive love. To love only when it pays off, or to greet only our own kind, is to love as the world loves. But to love without limit, offering peace even to those who threaten and oppose us, is to love as *God* loves. We thus prove ourselves to be *children of God* when our love makes no distinction between the neighbor and the enemy.

In verse 48 we find a short summary statement: *Be perfect, therefore, as your heavenly Father is perfect* (cf. Lev. 19:2; Deut. 18:13). The Lukan version of the saying (Luke 6:36) speaks of being "merciful," as God is merciful. There the summary deals only with sayings on love of enemy and nonretaliation. For Matthew, however, the summary gathers up the whole series of Jesus' pronouncements in verses 21-47.

So it is that Jesus speaks of the need to be *perfect* (Greek: *teleios*), which means complete, fully developed, or all that God intends. At no point is this completeness better defined than in the words about love that we have just considered. *To be perfect as God is perfect is to love as God loves, openhearted to all, full of mercy and blessing, faithful in every way* (cf. Driver: 97-99; Meier, 1980:54-55; Snyder/Shaffer: 9-10). When this kind of love is operative in our lives, our righteousness *will* greatly exceed earlier models, and the law and the prophets will truly be fulfilled (cf. 5:17-20).

THE TEXT IN BIBLICAL CONTEXT

The theme of law as discussed in 5:17-48 is a theme with deep roots in the story of Israel. *[Torah, p. 428.]* From Sinai on, Israel lived in a covenant with God, and law was an integral part of that covenant. One of the questions that was bound to arise in the early church was how life in the new covenant relates to all this. Has Israel's Torah now been superseded? Or does the Christian community, in one way or another, still live out of the covenant and law of Sinai? Matthew 5 reflects the struggle over questions such as these and offers its own perspective for dealing with the issues.

Part of Matthew's answer is that the law remains valid as a revelation of God's will. It is more than a relic of Jewish culture and history. On the other hand, the church does not simply take over the law as given to *those of ancient times.* The radical part of Matthew's stance is that the law remains valid *as redefined by Jesus*. He unfolds the will of God to which the law points, and he unfolds it in a full and definitive fashion. Everything in the Torah is still a basis for teaching, but everything is now refracted through Jesus and his word.

A counterpart to Matthew 5:17-48 is the commentary on the law in the letters of Paul. Like Matthew, Paul believes that the law reveals God's will. In itself it is "holy and just and good" (Rom. 7:12). Paul is convinced, however, that our experience under the law is anything but positive. Because of who we are as sinners, the law means curse and captivity (Gal. 3:10ff.). It reveals the extent to which we fall short of God's will and makes us accountable for all our actions (Rom. 3:19ff.). It thus holds us in bondage, like children in the care of a custodian or governess (Gal. 3:23ff.), against which we are constantly prone to rebel (cf. Rom. 7).

Even those bent on keeping the law miss the mark, falling prey to the trap of self-justification (Rom. 10:1-3; Phil. 3:4ff.). In short, the law is unable to bring us into the right relationship with God that the law itself demands. The one who does that, for Paul, is Jesus Christ (Gal. 3:25ff.). And while in Matthew, Jesus Christ *redefines* the law, in Paul's message Jesus Christ *takes the place of* the law. He alone is the basis and center of our life. Knowing and doing God's will is thus no longer a matter of simply observing a written code. It is a process of heeding the Spirit at work in the body of Christ (Gal. 5:16-25; Rom. 8:1-17).

Although their views on the place of the law clearly differ, Matthew and Paul have more in common than is usually recognized. On the one hand, Paul can speak in a Matthean way about *fulfillment* of the law (Rom. 8:4; 13:8). When he at one point refers to Christ as "the end of the law" (Rom. 10:4), he means not only that Christ ends the era of life under law, but that the goal or aim of the law is fulfilled in Christ (cf. Matt. 5:17).

On the other hand, Matthew shares Paul's view that the *basis* of life in the Christian community is not the law, but Christ. The *yoke* that Jesus' followers are invited to assume is not the traditional yoke of the law but a relationship with Christ himself (11:28-30). And when the church meets to consider or decide ethical issues, it acts in and through Christ's presence in its midst (18:18-20; cf. 28:20).

The most striking convergence of Matthew and Paul concerns the lifestyle that corresponds to God's will for human life. Whatever role or place is assigned to the law, the bottom line is that "*love is the fulfilling of the law*" (Rom. 13:8-10, emphasis added; Gal. 5:13-15; Matt. 5:43-48; 7:12; 22:39-40). For Matthew and Paul alike, faithfulness to God's will means living a life of love that builds up the church and seeks peace with all.

THE TEXT IN THE LIFE OF THE CHURCH

The discussion about the law that begins in the NT has occupied the church throughout its history. At two major junctures, debate over Matthew 5:17ff. played a critical role (cf. Luz: 261-264; 272-273). The first of these episodes was the controversy with Marcion in the second century. Believing that the Christian gospel and Jewish law have nothing in common, Marcion rejected the idea that Jesus came to *fulfill* the law. Opposing Marcion were leaders such as Irenaeus and Tertullian, who taught that Christ came to complete the law and/or expand its scope.

Later, in debates between mainline Reformers and Anabaptists, the issue at stake was how *new* Jesus' teaching really is. For the Reformers, the assertion that Jesus came to fulfill the law pointed first and foremost to the continuity of the two testaments. Accordingly, Jesus' statements in the Sermon on the Mount were viewed as a true exposition of the law, not as new commands which revoked earlier ones.

For the Anabaptists, however, Jesus' fulfillment of the law meant something more radical. They perceived that Jesus' commands supersede the law at certain points and insisted that Jesus' followers must obey those commands. One such point was the taking of oaths, about which Menno Simons has this to say:

> Christ Jesus does not in the New Testament point His disciples to the Law in regard to the matter of swearing—the dispensation of imperfectness which allowed swearing, but He points us now from the Law to yea and nay, as to the dispensation of perfectness. . . . To swear truly was allowed to the Jews under the Law; but the Gospel forbids this to Christians. (Menno Simons: 518-519; cf. Klaassen: 282-289)

Another point at which the Anabaptists saw Jesus superseding the law was his teaching on nonresistance and love for the enemy (cf. Klaassen: 265-281). Where the Reformers limited the applicability of Jesus' words to the private sphere, the Anabaptists held that Jesus' word should govern the conduct of believers in societal relationships as well. For example, after citing Jesus' sayings in Matthew 5:43-48, Menno Simons (555) puts the question: "Tell me, how can a Christian defend Scripturally retaliation, rebellion, war, striking, slaying, torturing, stealing, robbing and plundering and burning cities, and conquering countries?"

Menno goes on, in the same treatise (556), to describe Jesus' true followers as a people of peace:

> They are the children of peace; their hearts overflow with peace; their mouths speak peace; and they walk in the way of peace; they are full of peace. They seek, desire, and know nothing but peace; and are prepared to forsake country, goods, life, and all for the sake of peace. For they are the kingdom, people, congregation, city, property, and body of peace.

"We Are People of God's Peace" is a contemporary hymn based on this text from Menno.

All of this is as pertinent to life today as it was for those who lived in the sixteenth century. Now as then, the usual norm by which society conducts its life is the *lex talionis*. One thinks of the epidemic of litigation in the courts, of the cycle of terrorism and counterterrorism, of popular support for capital punishment, of arsenals of weapons with which to threaten national enemies. To be a people of peace who take Jesus' word seriously is to challenge this "law" and to model a different way. Where conventional wisdom says there must be winners and losers, a peacemaking church looks for negotiated settlements that guard the dignity of each party. Where conventional wisdom focuses on punishing and humiliating wrongdoers, a peacemaking church seeks for ways to restore broken relationships between offenders and victims. Where conventional wisdom dictates that violent revolution is the only way to break the bonds of oppression, a peacemaking church engages in symbolic demonstrations to create an opening for nonviolent change. (For further reflection on the call to peacemaking, see Yoder, 1983; Hauerwas, 1983.)

True Piety and False

Matthew 6:1-18

PREVIEW

In Matthew 6:1-18 Jesus continues to talk about a righteousness which exceeds that of the scribes and Pharisees. Up to this point the focus has been on acting rightly in our relationships with fellow humans. Now the focus shifts to right actions in our relationship with God, to pious deeds or practices. The specific practices Jesus mentions include almsgiving (vv. 2-4), prayer (vv. 5-15), and fasting (vv. 16-18). All three were customary expressions of piety in Judaism (cf. Tob. 12:8; Sir. 7:10; Acts 10:2). At issue is the *right way* to engage in these practices or disciplines, which Matthew assumes will still be observed by Jesus' followers.

Once again Jesus contrasts an old way and a new way, using a set pattern to frame his comments on each practice:

When you ______________,
Do not do it, as some do, to be seen in public.
Truly, they get what they seek.
But when you ______________,
Do it privately (for God alone to see).
And God who sees in secret will give you your reward.

Only in Matthew's Gospel do we find this systematic discussion of almsgiving, prayer, and fasting (though cf. G. Thom. 6, 14, in which the same series of topics comes up). Perhaps a collection of sayings such as those in verses 2-4, 5-6, and 16-18 was already being used in Matthew's church before the writing of his Gospel. To this collection Matthew may have added the introductory statement in verse 1 and the additional material on prayer in verses 7-15.

Of primary importance here is the Lord's Prayer in verses 9-13, for which we find a parallel in Luke 11:2-4. Whatever its form in the underlying source, it is likely that the Matthean church used the prayer in teaching and worship long before it found its present setting in Matthew 6. In any case, Matthew's inclusion of the Lord's Prayer guaranteed its future role in teaching and worship in churches using his Gospel (cf. Did. 8:1-3). With the several additional sayings on prayer, the topic of prayer receives special emphasis in the unit.

OUTLINE

Public or Private Piety, 6:1

The Practice of Giving Alms, 6:2-4

The Practice of Prayer, 6:5-15

6:5-6	The Manner of Prayer
6:7-13	The Language of Prayer
6:14-15	Forgiveness and Prayer

The Practice of Fasting, 6:16-18

EXPLANATORY NOTES

Public or Private Piety 6:1

To introduce the admonitions on almsgiving, prayer, and fasting, Matthew warns his readers about the wrong way to practice piety. The opening word, *beware,* occurs six times in Matthew and stresses the need to pay attention and be on guard (cf. 7:15; 16:6). The danger Matthew wants to avert is using the forms of religious piety to gain human admiration (cf. 6:1-2, 5, 16; 23:5). Although this public show of piety leads to a *reward* of sorts, it does nothing to enhance one's relationship with God.

By contrast, true acts of piety are intended for God's eyes only and seek a blessing that God alone can give. It is important to note that the word translated *piety* in 6:1 is the same word translated *righteousness* in 5:20 and elsewhere. This is a clue that Jesus is ready to develop further the proposition of the Sermon announced in 5:17-20. The sayings in 6:1-18 will give us yet another picture of a righteousness that fulfills and exceeds.

The Practice of Giving Alms 6:2-4

The first practice Jesus addresses is that of almsgiving. The phrase *give alms* translates a Greek expression which reads literally *do kindly deeds,* but which is used here with the more specific meaning of contributing to the poor and needy. Among the settings in which alms were given were public gatherings such as festivals and synagogue services. Sometimes this was done in a quiet, unpretentious way (as the rabbis encouraged). At other times those eager to impress others with their generosity might make a public announcement of their gift.

With colorful hyperbole, Jesus describes such persons as *those who sound a trumpet* before them and labels them *hypocrites.* The latter term, which Matthew frequently uses for the scribes and Pharisees (cf. 15:7; 22:18; 23:13ff.), refers literally to actors in a play. It thus suggests persons who are doing something for show, performing for an audience, and whose deeds may be little more than playacting. Those who practice piety in this way, Jesus says, *have already been paid in full* (GNB). Their reward is the public acclaim they seek. Beyond that, they receive nothing.

Jesus goes on then in verses 3-4 to depict the right way to give alms. With yet another hyperbole, he states that one should not let the left hand know what the right hand is doing! The point of the expression is that we should practice charity as quietly and unobtrusively as possible. As verse 4 puts it, we are to give alms *in secret.*

This does not imply that we are to go out of our way to hide what we are doing. It simply underscores the fact that charitable deeds should be done for God alone to see and recognize, not to enhance our public image. When we give alms in the right way, as a genuine act of piety, then the one who sees our innermost thoughts and motives will acknowledge our deeds. This too Jesus calls a *reward,* although it is really more of a gift than a payment. It is a gift that comes from one we know as our *Father,* who seeks and values a close relationship with us.

The Practice of Prayer 6:5-15

6:5-6 The Manner of Prayer

As noted above, Matthew devotes special attention to the practice of prayer. The extended section on this topic begins with a commentary on the manner of prayer, parallel in form and content to the sayings on almsgiving and fasting (cf. Preview). Prayer played a significant role in Jewish life, both in the worship of the community in the synagogue and temple and in the practice of devout individuals. Some prayers were committed to memory and used at fixed times during the day. The Eighteen Benedictions, for example, were to be prayed three times a day, in the morning, afternoon, and evening.

Whether at fixed times of prayer or more generally, some persons chose to call attention to themselves by praying in public places, such as an intersection of major streets (*street corners*). Again, Jesus rejects the attempt to parade one's piety before others. *Whenever* you *pray,* Jesus says, *go into your room and shut the door* (cf. Isa. 26:20, LXX). The Greek word for *room* refers to a small interior room without windows, used for storage (cf. KJV, *closet*). The point of this vivid metaphor is not that we should confine our praying to dark, private places, but that we should pray with the sole intent of communion *with God*, whose presence is hardly a *public* phenomenon. Only then can we receive the true *reward* of prayer.

6:7-13 The Language of Prayer

Having dealt with the *manner* of prayer, Matthew turns to another issue, the *language* of prayer. Once again the discussion gets underway with a negative example (vv. 7-8). Here, however, it is the prayer habits of *the Gentiles* that we are to avoid, in particular the tendency to *heap up empty phrases.* The words quoted refer to the practice of babbling on and on in prayer, using endless divine names and special prayer formulas to ensure that one's petition is heard (cf. 1 Kings 18:26-29). With fitting sarcasm, the philosopher Seneca describes such a practice as "fatiguing the gods" (*Epistulae Morales* 31.5).

Jesus' critique of such prayers is based on his view of God. Unlike the Gentiles, Jesus says, you have no need to be anxious about whether God will hear you. God is aware of your needs even before you list them (cf. 6:32). Thus, it is unnecessary to bombard heaven with words to get God's attention.

To illustrate the *right* way to speak when we pray, Jesus offers us a sample prayer (vv. 9-13), which we know as the Lord's Prayer. It is likely intended both as a prayer for us to pray and as a model for other prayers. As noted above, the prayer also appears in Luke's Gospel, in a briefer and perhaps earlier version (cf. Luke 11:2-4). There too, the context is one of instruction on how to pray (11:1-13). In Matthew's version of the Lord's Prayer, the prayer consists of an address (*Our Father*. . .), three petitions which ask God to act on *his* agenda (vv. 9c-10), and three petitions which ask God to care for *our* needs (vv. 11-13).

Older translations sometimes conclude the prayer with a doxology: *For thine is the kingdom and the power and the glory, forever. Amen.* Since it does not appear in our best Greek manuscripts, the doxology was probably a later addition to Matthew's text. It is, nonetheless, a fitting way to end the prayer. Doxologies were common in Jewish prayers, and this doxology may be based on one we find in the OT (cf. 1 Chron. 29:10-13).

In Luke's version of the prayer, Jesus addresses God simply as *Father,* which was an unusually intimate way of speaking to God. The corresponding Aramaic word *Abba* was the term a Jewish child would use in addressing his or her father. It apparently was customary for Jesus to pray to God in this way (cf. Mark 14:36; Matt. 11:25), which in turn influenced the prayer language of the early church (cf. Gal. 4:6; Rom. 8:15-16).

In the text before us, Jesus addresses God with a somewhat fuller formula, more common in the Jewish world: *Our Father in heaven.* On Jesus' lips, however, the words *Our Father* are more than a traditional Jewish formula. Jesus has a special relationship with God as Father and enables his followers to enter into that familial relationship (cf. Matt. 11:27; 12:50). This for Matthew is why Jesus can invite us to pray, *Our* Father. The additional words, *in heaven,* serve to distinguish this Father from other fathers and to identify him as *God*. The phrase also points to God's sovereignty. It does not, however, imply that God is distant from us.

The first three requests directed to God in the Lord's Prayer are often labeled *you-petitions*:

Let *your* name be hallowed.
Let *your* kingdom come.
Let *your* will be done.

In each petition we are saying to God: "Do what is important to you. Make yourself central in our world." The agenda for God set forth in these petitions appears in a number of Jewish prayers. A particularly striking parallel occurs in a doxology known as the Kaddish, the earliest form of which may well go back to the time of Jesus:

"Magnified and sanctified be his great name in the world, which he created according to his will; and may he establish his kingdom in your lifetime and in your days and in the lifetime of all the house of Israel, quickly and soon."

In both the Kaddish and the Lord's Prayer, the petitions to God have an eschatological flavor. They ask God to usher in the endtime era of salvation in which all of life will reflect God's purposes. For Jesus' followers, such petitions for the future are closely linked to what is already happening. They beseech God to *complete* the work of salvation inaugurated in Jesus' ministry (cf. Harner: 80).

As a closer look at the you-petitions reveals, the topics of the three requests are much interrelated. The first petition speaks of God's *name*, which represents God's person or being. God's name is *hallowed* when people acknowledge God's holiness and live accordingly (cf. Isa. 29:23), or when God himself acts to vindicate his holy nature (cf. Ezek. 36:22-23). In the petition before us, we likely are praying for both things to happen: "Act in such a way, O God, that the world sees your greatness and praises you for who you are!"

The divine act that will accomplish this is spelled out in the second petition: "Let your *kingdom* come. Manifest your reign in its fullness. Take control of life and history in every way." When God's rule is fully established, then the request of the third petition will also be granted: The *will* of God will *be done on earth as it is in heaven*. God's will can refer either to God's purpose for history (cf. Isa. 46:10,13; 1 Macc. 3:60; Matt. 26:42) or to God's will for our lives in an ethical sense (cf. Ps. 40:8; Matt. 12:50). Here again it is likely that both meanings are intended: "So rule in our midst, O God, that your redemptive purpose is accomplished, and that our lives exhibit the righteousness you desire."

Having prayed first for *God's* agenda, we may then offer petitions to God concerning our own needs. These are the focus of the three "we-petitions" in verses 11-13:

Give *us our* daily bread.
Forgive *us our* debts.
Do not bring *us* to the time of trial, but rescue *us*.

A major question for interpreters is how these petitions are related to the first three. Do these petitions, like the preceding ones, deal with things yet to come (messianic banquet, final judgment, endtime testing)? Or do they deal with day-to-day issues that Jesus' followers face at all times? The second view is probably more nearly correct. Jesus most likely is enumerating needs that relate as much to the present as they do to the future. At the same time, the eschatological hope expressed in the you-petitions forms the backdrop for the we-petitions. We turn to God with our immediate needs as those who *strive first for the kingdom of God and his righteousness* (6:33), and who know that everything we receive from God here and now is a foretaste of what is yet to come.

The first we-petition is for *bread,* which refers primarily to food or nourishment, but may suggest other basic provisions for life as well. Modifying the word *bread* is a rare term (*epiousios*) found only in the Lord's Prayer and in one or two other obscure, ancient texts. It could mean *necessary, for today, for the future,* or *for the morrow* (cf. NRSV footnotes), the latter meaning being the most probable. Eduard Schweizer picks up that meaning in his paraphrase of the bread-petition: "Grant that we may lie down to sleep, not with a sense of abundance or surety against hard times, but simply without despair, knowing the coming day has been provided for" (154).

No less important than bread for our bodies is forgiveness for our sins, the subject of the next petition. The metaphor Jesus uses for sins is that of *debts,* which suggests unmet obligations in our relationship with God. Here as elsewhere (cf. Matt. 5:7; 18:21-35; Sir. 28:2), God's forgiveness is linked to forgiveness at the human level. When we ask God to forgive *our* indebtedness, we are to do so as those who have already forgiven the unmet obligations of others.

The final petition is a double request, one which seeks God's help in facing evil yet before us: *Do not bring us to the time of trial, but rescue us from the evil one* (or *from evil*). Here (as in similar petitions in Jewish evening and morning prayers found in the Talmud) *trial* and *evil* are equivalent terms and refer to everything that could endanger our relationship with God. In praying the final petition, we ask God to protect this relationship: *Do not bring us into situations that might overwhelm our faith, but rather deliver us from every peril that awaits us* (cf. 2 Tim. 4:18; 2 Pet. 2:9; Sir. 33:1).

6:14-15 Forgiveness and Prayer

The saying that concludes the section on prayer returns to the theme of the fifth petition of the Lord's Prayer. Using a form sometimes labelled a sentence of holy law, Jesus correlates God's forgiveness and human forgiveness in precise terms:

If you forgive, God will forgive.
If you do not forgive, God will not forgive.

A partial parallel occurs at Mark 11:25, which may or may not be the basis for the saying here. As noted earlier in our discussion of the beatitude on mercy, the point made is not that we have to earn or prove ourselves worthy of God's forgiveness. Matthew agrees with the view expressed elsewhere in the NT (Col. 3:13; Eph. 4:32) that God's forgiveness precedes and underlies our forgiveness of one another (Matt. 26:28; 18:23-35). The point of Jesus' saying is that there has to be a reciprocity between the way we respond to the misdeeds (*trespasses*) of others and the way God responds to our own. If we refuse to practice forgiveness in our relationships with others, then we void God's forgiveness in our own lives as well.

The Practice of Fasting 6:16-18

The final saying in 6:1-18 deals with the practice of fasting. Like prayer, fasting played an important part in Jewish life—and was sometimes viewed as an auxiliary to prayer. In addition to major fasts in which the whole nation took part, such as the Day of Atonement, fasting was observed as an individual discipline by various persons and groups. The Pharisees fasted twice a week, on Mondays and Thursdays (cf. Luke 18:12; Did. 8:1).

Fasting could be an expression of grief or mourning, a mark of remorse and penitence, or simply a sign of humility before God. Because of these associations, persons fasting would often simulate mourners in their appearance. They would wear sackcloth, sprinkle ashes over their heads, go unbathed without anointing the head or body, and look generally sad. Needless to say, this provided yet another opportunity to call attention to one's piety in public. And once again Jesus is sharply critical of those who do so. With a play on words, Jesus remarks that such persons make their faces unrecognizable (*aphanizousin*), in order that they might be recognized (*phanōsin*)!

Although fasting apparently was not part of the lifestyle of Jesus and his disciples (cf. Mark 2:18ff.; Matt. 11:18-19), Jesus does not reject the practice as such. The saying before us assumes that there will be appropriate times for Jesus' followers to fast, and that fasting has value as a spiritual discipline. Jesus insists, however, that we engage in fasting in the same unpretentious way in which we are to give alms and pray. Instead of looking like dismal mourners, Jesus says, look like normal persons: Anoint your head and wash your face, as anyone else would (cf. the actions of David when he breaks a fast of mourning in 2 Sam. 12:20). Jesus' counsel here concludes on the same note that it does in verses 2-4 and 5-6: Let your fasting be something that takes place between you and God. Then God can receive and acknowledge it as a righteous deed, a genuine act of piety.

THE TEXT IN BIBLICAL CONTEXT

In its critique of the public piety of *hypocrites,* Matthew 6:1-18 works at an issue that other biblical writers address as well: What kind of piety and worship is appropriate for God's people? Not surprisingly, the issue often surfaces in the context of a problem with faulty practice. Isaiah 58 condemns those who make a big production out of national days of fasting, but who are unwilling to alter their lifestyles to feed the hungry, give workers a decent wage, or provide shelter for the homeless.

In the New Testament, Luke 18:9-14 relates the story of a religious leader who prays privately enough, but who engages in prayer as an exercise in self-congratulation rather than approaching God with a humble spirit. Acts 5:1-11 reports the judgment that befalls a couple who seek to impress the community with the magnitude of their charitable gift, all the while stashing away a part of that gift for their private use. And 1 Corinthians 14 speaks of persons who are so eager to parade their spiritual gifts before others in worship that the celebration turns into sheer chaos.

Common to all of these problem situations is a preoccupation with self or self-image, which inevitably distorts the practice of piety. By contrast, true acts of piety take us outside ourselves. They focus our attention on God, expand our vision of righteousness, and seek the good of the larger community.

Within the discussion of piety in 6:1-18, a particular name for God is used no less than ten times. That name is *Father,* a familial metaphor of which Matthew is especially fond. References to *my Father* and *your Father* occur repeatedly throughout the Gospel (cf. 7:21; 18:19; 25:34; 6:26; 10:20; 23:9 and numerous other passages). Here Matthew reflects a linguistic phenomenon that is widespread in early Christian literature (see especially the writings of John and Paul).

This use of *Father* as a name for God is rooted in earlier biblical language but goes beyond it in two respects: First, the image of *Father* is only one of many ways of referring to God in the OT, and a relatively infrequent one at that. In Matthew and most of the NT, however, *Father* has clearly become a *primary* name for God.

Second, there is a shift in the meaning of knowing God as *Father*. The Hebrew Scriptures generally use the image to express God's covenantal relationship with Israel as a people (cf. Isa. 64:8-9; Jer. 31:9; Hos. 11:1-2; Jub. 1:24-25). For the Christian community, however, *Father* suggests not only One to whom we belong as a people, but One whom we know in an intimate, familial way through Jesus Christ. Paul states it succinctly in Romans: "When we cry 'Abba! Father!' it is that very Spirit bearing witness with our spirit that we are children of God" (8:15-16; cf. 8:9-17; Gal. 3:25—4:7).

THE TEXT IN THE LIFE OF THE CHURCH

Matthew 6:1ff. has influenced the practice of Christian piety in a number of ways (cf. Luz: 360-61, 366, 372-74, 387-88). As one would expect, it has encouraged a highly personal and private approach to religious piety, which has both its strengths and its weaknesses. Thus the Pietists found support for worshiping in small house groups in Jesus' counsel to withdraw into an inner room for prayer. Another point at which the text has played a role is in the critique it offers of heaping up empty phrases in prayer. More than one group has seized on this saying as a basis for criticizing Christian prayers that run on and on with this formula or that.

Most important of all, however, is the influence of the Lord's Prayer in 6:9-13, which is certainly the most-used prayer in the Christian world. A writing from the beginning of the second century urges believers to pray this prayer three times a day (Did. 8:3), and it became a regular part of the Christian liturgy at an early period. Beyond its use in worship, it has served as a significant resource for spiritual nurture. Many Christians would concur with Martin Luther when he writes: "To this day I suckle at the Lord's Prayer like a child, and as an old man eat and drink from it, and can never get my fill" (cited by Luz: 374).

As we wrestle with the meaning and practice of prayer in our own lives, the text raises at least three issues for us:

(1) What is the true purpose of prayer? The correct answer to that question, on the basis of Matthew 6, is communion with God. Prayer that has another agenda, whether it be showing off our skill with language or trying to preach to our fellow worshipers, fails to qualify as real prayer.

(2) What is the right way to address God in prayer? Jesus invited his hearers to pray to God as *Father*, because that name conveyed

loving and open access to God. For many Christians today, it still does. For others, however, an exclusively male image of God as *Father* actually gets in the way of feeling near to God in prayer. How might we overcome that stumbling-block as we name God in corporate prayer?

(3) What is the appropriate focus for prayer? All too often, the prayers we pray bear a striking resemblance to birthday want-lists and thank-you notes. In the Lord's Prayer, however, we pray for God's agenda before our own, and we speak of *our* needs rather than *my* needs. At both points this model prayer has much to teach us.

A Focused Life

Matthew 6:19—7:12

PREVIEW

The issue of righteousness addressed in 5:17-48 and 6:1-18 receives yet further attention in 6:19—7:12. The sayings we find in this unit differ from those in the preceding units in at least two respects: (1) They are much more loosely connected to each other and to the larger context than either the antitheses of 5:17-48 or the sayings on piety in 6:1-18. (2) They belong largely to a different literary genre than the preceding sayings, the genre of wisdom sayings such as we find in Proverbs and Sirach.

Rather than giving us norms for the right way to act in specific situations, these sayings offer counsel of a broader sort on the right way to orient our lives as a whole. Running throughout the unit are a number of *do not* statements, which point out wrong ways to orient our lives. Jesus supports these prohibitions with a variety of other material, including parables, proverbs, and rhetorical questions. Illustrations from nature and everyday life abound here, as they do elsewhere in Jesus' teaching (cf. Mark 4:30-32; Matt. 20:1-16; Luke 13:6-9) and in earlier wisdom material (cf. Prov. 6:6-8; 30:24-28; Job 12:7-10). At the end of the unit (7:12), we find a saying that serves as a summary for the entire central section of the Sermon. There Matthew picks up the topic of *the law and the prophets* with which he began in 5:17.

For nearly all of the sayings in 6:19-7:12, we find parallels in the Gospel of Luke. Some of these parallel sayings occur in Luke's Sermon on the Plain (Luke 6:31, 37-42). In other instances, however, the parallel sayings appear in different contexts (cf. Luke 11:33-36; 12:22-34; 16:10-13) and may have had a different setting in the underlying tradition as well. Once again, then, we observe Matthew at work as a compiler, taking sayings of Jesus from a variety of contexts and arranging them in a particular way to highlight certain themes. It is also worth noting the number of parallel sayings found in the second-century apocryphal work known as the Gospel of Thomas (G. Thom. 2, 24, 26, 36, 47, 76, 92-94). This confirms that the sayings before us were highly valued and widely circulated in the early church.

We have noted already that 6:19—7:12 has a somewhat loose pattern of organization. On the surface, it seems as though Matthew has used this unit as a catchall section for sayings on a variety of topics. Closer examination, however, reveals at least two thematic connections that link the sayings with one another and with the rest of the Sermon.

First, all the sayings relate in one way or another to issues dealt with in Jesus' instruction on prayer in 6:5-15, or more particularly to topics of the Lord's Prayer. For example, the sayings in 6:25-34 on anxiety about food and clothing relate to the petition for daily bread, and the words on judging others in 7:1-6 tie in with the admonitions on forgiveness in 6:14-15.

Second, all the sayings in the unit before us deal with the *focus* of our life as disciples. Refusing to be distracted by the quest for possessions, anxiety about our needs, or finding fault with others, we are to focus our lives on God and seek God's reign and righteousness (6:33).

OUTLINE

Let God Be Your Focus, 6:19-24

Trust in God's Goodness, 6:25-34

Don't Focus on Others' Faults, 7:1-6

Pray with Trust in God's Goodness, 7:7-11

God's Will in a Nutshell, 7:12

EXPLANATORY NOTES

Let God Be Your Focus 6:19-24

In verses 19-24 we find a cluster of three sayings, which Matthew uses to develop the theme of a life with *one* focus. The cluster begins with a saying on *treasures* in verses 19-21 (cf. Luke 12:33-34), which builds on the *reward* motif in 6:1-18. As he does throughout the sermon, Jesus makes his point by contrasting one thing with another. One kind of treasure is a chest full of earthly goods, such as clothing and precious metals. The problem with this kind of treasure is that it is all too perishable (cf. Isa. 51:8; James 5:2-3; Job 24:15-16, REB). Beautiful clothing is often eaten by moths or worms (the word translated *rust* most likely refers to an insect in the larva stage; cf. Mal. 3:11 LXX). And precious metals can be easily stolen when thieves break into (literally: *dig through* the wall of) the storeroom where one's treasure chest is kept.

By contrast, *treasures in heaven* are imperishable. In Jewish writings, treasure in heaven is frequently associated with keeping the law or charitable deeds (cf. Sir. 29:11-12; Tob. 4:7-11; 1 Tim. 6:17-19), and Matthew could have this association in mind (cf. 6:1-18). The point of the whole saying, however (see v. 21), is not that we should try to accumulate merit points in heaven, but that the thing we treasure most should be God rather than possessions. As Robert Guelich puts it: "To have one's *treasure in heaven* means to submit oneself totally to that which is *in heaven—God's sovereign rule*" (Guelich: 328).

The saying that follows in verses 22-23 talks about eyes and light and darkness (cf. Luke 11:33-36; Mark 4:21-23). According to one interpretation, the saying warns us not to view life from a selfish, possessive perspective. The eye that is *unhealthy* would refer to a mean, stingy, or greedy eye (cf. Deut. 15:9; Sir. 24:8-10), while a *healthy* eye would be one that looks on others with a liberal or generous attitude.

A more likely interpretation, however, is that Jesus is dealing with need for a clear vision of God's will and telling a parable to make his point. When we have good (*healthy*) eyes, our world is one of light, and we see and walk clearly. But when our eyesight is poor (*unhealthy*), life is a dark and blurry affair. So it is, Jesus suggests, with the spiritual realm. If we have only a shadowy awareness of God's will, how dark life will be! If on the other hand our vision is focused on God and illumined by God (cf. T. Iss. 4:1-6), our lives will be full of light.

In the third saying, found in verse 24 (cf. Luke 16:13), Jesus uses yet another illustration to make the case for a life focused on God. This time the parable comes from the world of slaves and hired servants—and their relationships with owners or employers. To divide one's basic loyalties between two masters, Jesus says, simply doesn't work. We will inevitably come to prefer one over the other (this is the meaning of the verbs *love* and *hate* here), or feel attached to one while actually despising the other.

The application of all this to the world of faith occurs in the final phrase: *You cannot serve God and wealth* (KJV: *mammon*). The word translated as *wealth* (*mamōna*) refers to material possessions of every sort, including property, money, and belongings. Here we return to the theme of treasures introduced in verse 19, and again Jesus confronts us with clear alternatives for our priorities in life: Will we be devoted to our possessions? Or will we be devoted to God?

Trust in God's Goodness 6:25-34

Unlike the shorter pronouncements in verses 19-24, the saying in verses 25-34 is developed at great length (cf. the parallel in Luke 12:22-31). Jesus begins with a *do not* statement (v. 25), offers a series of arguments to support the prohibition (vv. 26-30), restates the prohibition and offers a positive alternative (vv. 31-33), and concludes with a postscript to the whole discussion (v. 34).

The prohibition *do not worry* translates a Greek verb which can mean either *worry about* or *strive after.* In the saying before us, both ideas are likely present: Don't let anxiety about life lead to preoccupation with getting enough to eat and wear. Jesus, however, says this in a much more poetic manner:

Do not worry about your life, what you will eat,
Or about your body, what you will wear.
Is not life more than food,
And the body more than clothing?

The rhetorical questions here invite the answer *yes,* at the same time making us wonder: *How* is life *more than* food and clothing? Not until we get to verse 33 do we find an answer in the text.

In the arguments he sets forth to counter an anxious approach to life, Jesus deals first with *food* and urges us to *look at the birds.* (The verbs *look at* in verse 26 and *consider* in verse 28 suggest close observation.) While Luke 12:24 identifies the birds as ravens (unclean birds!), the saying in Matthew speaks more generally of *birds of heav-*

en or *birds of the air,* a common biblical expression (cf. Gen. 1:26; Job 12:7; Matt. 8:20). In any case, Jesus invites his listeners to learn from the way God cares for the birds (cf. Job 38:41; Matt. 10:29-31; Ps. Sol. 5:8-10): If God supplies the birds, who do nothing deliberate to raise their own food, will God not also supply you who are worth much more than birds?

Verse 27 reads like an afterthought, reinforcing the first argument with yet another rhetorical question. One could translate the text to read *add a cubit to one's stature* (about eighteen inches). It is more likely, however, that Jesus is using cubit in a figurative way to refer to a short span of time. We could then paraphrase Jesus' question: What good is it to worry about provisions, when doing so will not *add even an hour to one's life?*

In the second main argument (vv. 28-30), Jesus talks about *clothing* and directs our attention to *the lilies of the field.* The words quoted could refer to a specific flower (perhaps anemones) or simply to wild flowers in general (cf. Ps. 103:15). Whichever is the case, we are dealing here with colorful weeds rather than flowers planted in a garden. The transient nature of such flowers is underscored in verse 30 (cf. Ps. 90:5-6; Isa. 40:6-8), where they are described as field grass destined for use as fuel. Nevertheless, Jesus says, their splendor exceeds that of Solomon (cf. 1 Kings 9:26—10:29), and through no effort of their own! It is God who clothes them and gives them their beauty.

As in verse 26, Jesus makes his case by arguing from the lesser to the greater: If God clothes wild flowers which have no lasting value, will God not also *clothe you—you of little faith?* The final phrase is a favorite Matthean expression (cf. 8:26; 17:20), denoting a weak or fragile faith. Here it refers to those whose anxiety gets in the way of trusting in God's providence.

When he restates the command *do not worry* in verses 31-33, Jesus lists some of the anxious questions that accompany worry. He then proceeds to contrast a life controlled by such questions and a life in which these questions find their answer in a different way. If we are always preoccupied with material necessities, Jesus says, we are acting like Gentiles (like those outside the community). We are forgetting that God is already aware of our needs (cf. 6:7-8). If on the other hand our striving is a striving for God's kingdom, we know that *all* our needs will be cared for because of who God is (cf. Phil. 4:6; 1 Pet. 5:7). Here at last we learn how life is *more than* food and clothing (cf. v. 25). The quest that should govern all our activity is the quest for

God's rule in the world and God's will in our lives.

As noted above, verse 34 provides a postscript to the discussion on anxiety. Missing in the parallel passage in Luke, this pronouncement offers a pragmatic clincher to the preceding arguments. Some scholars propose a soft or optimistic interpretation of the verse: Tomorrow's concerns will take care of themselves; today is all you need to deal with. Other interpreters, however, find a cynical or pessimistic tone in Jesus' words: It is bad enough dealing with today's problems; don't add on tomorrow's before they get here! One way or another, the text advises us to live one day at a time, and not to succumb to anxiety about the future.

Don't Focus on Others' Faults 7:1-6

Of all the material in 6:19—7:12, the sayings in 7:1-6 are more unlike the rest than any of the other groups of sayings. The admonitions on not judging (cf. Luke 6:37-42; Mark 4:24-25) seem to deal with a different agenda than those urging us to make God the center of our lives. No less than the preceding sayings, however, the words of Jesus in 7:1-6 criticize a pattern of life that can divert us from a focus on God's kingdom. Here the threat to singleminded trust and commitment is finding fault with others rather than attending to our own discipleship.

The saying begins with yet another *do not* statement, coupled with the warning that God will judge us as harshly at the last day as we judge others now. Similar sayings can be found in a number of Jewish and Christian writings. One such is Sota 1:7 in the Mishnah: "With what measure a man metes it shall be measured to him again." More familiar to Christian readers is the statement of Paul in Romans 2:1: "Therefore, you have no excuse, whoever you are, when you judge others; for in passing judgment on another you condemn yourself, because you, the judge, are doing the very same things" (cf. James 4:11-12; 5:9).

In verses 3-5 Jesus points up the hypocrisy of faultfinders, giving us another sample of his penchant for hyperbole. Those who judge others are described as moral zealots who make it their mission to remove specks of sawdust from their neighbors' eyes, all the while having two-by-fours in their own eyes! The imagery in these verses recalls the prior comments on eyes and seeing in 6:22-23, and Matthew may well be saying: Here is another case of unhealthy or distorted vision.

The summary admonition in verse 5 can be understood in two ways. If we read *first* and *then* in a fairly straightforward manner, then Jesus is telling us that it is permissible to deal with the faults of others after we correct our own. It may be, however, that Jesus is speaking ironically, saying in effect: Your primary concern should be your own shortcomings, not those of others. In all of this, it is important to note that the behavior Jesus rejects is relating to others with a judgmental spirit, a readiness to condemn. Caring accountability to one another in the community of faith is another matter (cf. Matt. 18).

The pronouncement in verse 6 is one of the most enigmatic sayings in the Gospels. Occurring only here, it may or may not have been attached to the preceding words on judgment in Matthew's source. The only feature of the saying that seems relatively clear is its chiastic structure (*a b b' a'*):

a. Do not give what is holy to dogs,
  b. And do not throw your pearls before swine,
  b'. Or they [swine] will trample them under foot,
a'. And [dogs] turn and maul you.

Somewhat more tentatively, we can identify possible meanings of key words in the saying. Dogs and swine were both regarded as unclean animals (cf. 2 Pet. 2:22) and so were common metaphors for Gentiles in the Jewish world (cf. Matt. 15:26). Along the same lines, *what is holy* may reflect language in Leviticus describing sacred food, which outsiders were not allowed to eat (cf. Lev. 22:10). And *pearls* in some way signifies that which is valuable (cf. Matt. 13:45-46).

The difficult task is determining what all this means. At some point, the saying could have served as a prohibition against a mission to the Gentiles. In the present context, however, that can hardly be its function. Most interpreters conclude that either (1) we frankly don't know what the saying meant to Matthew and his community, or (2) the saying serves to balance off the preceding saying on not judging. In the latter case, Jesus would be arguing that judgment is necessary in the way we relate to unbelievers or apostate members, even though it is out of place in the community.

A more plausible interpretation is that the saying continues the main thrust of Jesus' counsel not to judge, and that *what is holy* and *pearls* refer to our relationships with one another in the church. We might then paraphrase the saying: Do not condemn one another in the midst of a hostile world, lest the world turn on you and take advantage of your weakness. (Cf. the analogous appeal in 1 Corinthians 6:1-8, where Paul admonishes Christians not to bring judgments against each other in Gentile courts.)

Pray With Trust in God's Goodness 7:7-11

In contrast to the sayings we have already examined, the material in 7:7-11 does not revolve around a prohibition. Instead, Jesus invites his listeners to take positive action, encouraging them to turn to God with all of their needs (cf. Luke 11:9-13). The focused life is thus defined as a life of prayer, a subject addressed earlier in 6:5-15. The saying begins in verses 7-8 with two series of short statements, arranged in a symmetric pattern (abc, a'b'c'). Sounding a note heard elsewhere in Scripture (cf. Prov. 8:17; Jer. 29:12-13; Mark 11:24), Jesus assures us that God responds to those who ask, search, or knock.

To support this promise, he introduces the rhetorical questions found in verses 9-10. Here it is helpful to note that a loaf of bread in Jesus' time often had the same round, flat shape that a stone had, and that there was an edible eel-like fish that resembled a snake. The obvious answer to the two questions is thus: No, no parent would mock the request of a needy child by giving the child a worthless gift that merely looks like the real thing. In verse 11, then, Jesus argues (as he has done previously) from the lesser to the greater: If you are capable of giving good gifts to children in spite of your sinful tendencies, how much more will the One who is righteous in every way give good things to *his* children!

God's Will in a Nutshell 7:12

The saying found in 7:12 is the familiar Golden Rule. In the parallel passage in Luke, it is sandwiched in the middle of the sayings on love of enemy (cf. Luke 6:31). Matthew, however, uses the saying to sum up the entire central section of the Sermon, 5:17—7:12. In fact, 7:12 forms a literary inclusion with 5:17. Having told us at the outset that he came to fulfill the law and the prophets, Jesus tells us in 7:12 that their intent *will* be fulfilled when we live by this rule.

Parallels to this saying abound in the ancient world, in both Jewish and other sources. One of the best known formulations is the response allegedly given by Jesus' contemporary, Hillel, when asked to summarize the Torah while standing on one foot: "Whatever is displeasing to you, do not do to your neighbor; that is the entire Law, and everything else is interpretation" (bShab. 31a; cf. Tob. 4:15; Did. 1:2b). A parallel stated positively rather than negatively appears in Sirach 31:15: "Judge your neighbor's feelings by your own, and in every matter be thoughtful" (cf. 2 Enoch 61:2).

In itself, the Golden Rule could be construed as an appeal for an ethic based on self-interest or common sense. In its present context, however, it is much more than that. Matthew clearly views the saying as a summation of everything Jesus has taught in the Sermon. To do to others as we would have them do to us, therefore, is to practice the way of love that Jesus commends to his followers.

THE TEXT IN BIBLICAL CONTEXT

The sayings in 6:19—7:12 touch on several key issues in the biblical story, one of which is the topic of wealth and possessions. In the OT and related Jewish writings, we find widely differing assessments of riches. Many passages speak favorably of wealth, making it clear that wealth is preferable to poverty (Prov. 10:15; 15:6; Exod. R. 31:12). Wealth is commonly viewed as a sign of God's blessing, a confirmation that persons are living in a right relationship with God (Deut. 28:1-14; Pss. 1:1-3; 112:1-3). Other texts, however, look on riches quite critically. They point out how the quest for wealth can so consume persons that it destroys faith and life (Sir. 31:5-8; Prov. 30:8-9). And wealth acquired by exploitation, or withheld from those in need, is roundly condemned (Amos 5:11-12; 8:4-6; Sir. 13:3-4; 14:3-10; 1 Enoch 94:6-9).

When the NT writers enter into this discussion, they come down hard on the side of wealth as a problem. To be sure, there is no categorical rejection of wealth, and those who use their abundance for the good of the church are upheld as models (Acts 4:32-37; Rom. 16:1-2; 2 Cor. 8—9). Most of the relevant texts, however, echo the same twofold critique of riches that we find in the OT. Wealth is associated with oppression and insensitivity (James 2:6-7; 5:1-6; Luke 6:24; 16:19-31; Rev. 18). And the threat that wealth can pose for faith and discipleship is underscored again and again (Mark 10:17-25; Luke 12:16-21; 1 Tim. 6:9-10; Rev. 3:17). The latter issue is the one Matthew addresses in 6:19ff. There Jesus makes it clear that we must choose between a life that serves mammon and a life that serves God.

In Jesus' call to live a life with a single focus, we observe yet another link between this text and other texts. At the outset of Israel's story, we find the ancient commandment to have no other gods before Yahweh (the Lord; Exod. 20:2) and the related summons to love God with one's total being (Deut. 6:4-5). One of the themes that runs through the OT is the need to choose between loyalty to God and competing loyalties (Deut. 11; Josh. 24; 1 Kings 18:20-40; Jer. 2).

Nowhere is the language more striking than in Elijah's challenge to the people on Mt. Carmel: "How long will you go limping with two different opinions? If the Lord is God, follow him; but if Baal, then follow him" (1 Kings 18:21). The choice that faced Israel faces Jesus himself in his testing in the wilderness, an episode in which Jesus models the singleminded commitment he seeks in his followers (Matt. 4:1-11/Luke 4:1-12). All of that is in the background as Jesus instructs his listeners to seek first God's reign (Matt. 6:33).

THE TEXT IN THE LIFE OF THE CHURCH

With its poetic language, Matthew 6:19-34 is a quotable text. Numerous phrases and images have found their way into our literature. Dealing with the issues raised in the text, however, has been a difficult task for the church. In addressing the question of wealth (cf. Hengel, 1974), individuals and groups have tended to take one of three approaches:

(1) Wealth can be either a help or a hindrance, depending on how it is used. If used generously to assist the less fortunate, great wealth can be a positive good. This is essentially the classic Jewish position as well.

(2) Wealth is incompatible with the lifestyle Jesus envisions for disciples—and for all who would be *perfect.* This approach has led persons to take vows of poverty, sometimes as a part of the discipline of a monastic community.

(3) Neither wealth nor poverty is God's intent for human life, but rather a modest lifestyle in which basic needs are met and excess is avoided. In advocating this approach, some groups have spoken of "simplicity" or "the simple life." Appeals for a less-affluent lifestyle are increasing in our own day, reflecting both the ecological urgency of reducing our level of consumption and the desire to stand in solidarity with the poor in their struggle for justice.

As our earlier analysis disclosed, the larger issue behind Jesus' critique of seeking wealth is the question of what is *first* in our lives. No one has addressed this dimension of the text more powerfully than the Danish philosopher, Søren Kierkegaard. One of his better-known parables depicts the issue as follows:

> When the prosperous man on a dark but star-lit night drives comfortably in his carriage and has the lanterns lighted, aye, then he is safe, he fears no difficulty, he carries his light with him, and it is not dark close around him; but precisely because he has the lanterns lighted, and has a strong light close to him, precisely for this reason he cannot see the stars, for his lights obscure the stars, which the poor peasant driving without lights can see gloriously in the dark but starry night. So those deceived ones live in the temporal existence: either, occupied with the necessities of life, they are too busy to avail themselves of the view, or in their prosperity and good days they have, as it were, lanterns lighted, and close about them everything is so satisfactory, so pleasant, so comfortable—but the view is lacking, the prospect, the view of the stars. (1948:123)

The "view of the stars" is, of course, a vision of God's kingdom, that which Jesus calls us to seek first and foremost. In a series of essays based on our text, Kierkegaard probes what it means to seek first the kingdom. As a starting point, he suggests that we need to learn from the silence before God that the birds and the lilies exemplify so well:

> That thou in silence mightest forget thyself, what thy name is, thine own name, the renowned name, the pitiful name, the insignificant name, for the sake of praying in silence to God, "Hallowed be *Thy* name!" That thou in silence mightest forget thyself, thy plans, the great, the all-comprehensive plans, or the petty plans regarding thy life and its future, for the sake of praying in silence to God, "*Thy* kingdom come!" That thou in silence mightest forget thy will, thy self-will, for the sake of praying in silence to God, "*Thy* will be done!" (1961:330)

If we develop our life priorities in this kind of waiting before God, questions of wealth and possessions will care for themselves (cf. also TLC for 19:16—20:16).

A Critical Choice

Matthew 7:13-29

PREVIEW

The final group of sayings in Matthew 7 constitutes the section of the Sermon identified earlier as an epilogue. It is customary in an epilogue for the speaker to sum up the major issue(s) of a speech and to challenge the hearers to take appropriate action. That is clearly what Jesus is doing in 7:13-29, and doing it in a typical manner.

Throughout the Sermon we have observed a pattern of stating issues in terms of sharp alternatives. The material here exhibits that same pattern. Using one image after another, Jesus contrasts broad and narrow roads, sound and bad trees, good and evil fruit, talkers and doers, and wise and foolish builders. When we look later at the larger biblical context of this passage, we will comment further on the motif that governs these images, the theme of the *two ways*. For now it is sufficient to note its function in the text, which is to confront the reader with the need to make a choice.

Literarily, the sayings in the epilogue are somewhat of a mixture, blending wise counsel and prophetic admonition. For most of these sayings, we find parallels in Luke's account. Some are found in the Sermon on the Plain (Luke 6:43-45, 46-49), while others appear in a different setting (Luke 13:22-30). Following the parable that concludes Jesus' sayings, we find a narrative postscript to the Sermon as a whole (verses 28-29, cf. Luke 7:1; Mark 1:22). The purpose of this concluding narrative is to make explicit what is already evident throughout the Sermon, that Jesus teaches with authority.

OUTLINE

The Two Ways, 7:13-14

Known by Their Fruits, 7:15-20

I Never Knew You, 7:21-23

Tale of Two Houses, 7:24-27

As One with Authority, 7:28-29

EXPLANATORY NOTES

The Two Ways 7:13-14

In the saying that begins the epilogue, Jesus uses the twin metaphors of *gate* and *road*. (Note the parallel in Luke 13:24, which speaks of entering a "door.") The word for *gate* suggests a public entry point, such as the gateway to a walled city (cf. Rev. 22:14) or one of the gates to the temple (cf. Ps. 24:7-10). *Road* refers to a street or highway, on which persons are traveling to some destination. How Matthew conceives of the relation between the gate and the road is somewhat less clear. Does the gate open onto a road? Does the road lead up to the gate? Or are *gate* and *road* actually used synonymously? In any case, Jesus distinguishes between two different gates and roads. There are a *narrow* gate and a *constricted* road that lead to *life.* And there are a *wide* gate and a *spacious* highway that lead to *destruction* (cf. REB and NIV).

The meaning of all these images is not hard to decipher (cf. the similar use of language in 2 Esd. 7:3-16; T. Abr.[B] 8). As the verses to follow indicate, *life* is another word for the kingdom, while *destruction* alludes to the final judgment. Correspondingly, the narrow road or gate that leads to life in the kingdom is the way of righteousness set forth in Jesus' teaching. This is the road that Jesus invites his hearers to *enter* now, so that they may *enter the kingdom* at the end of their journey (cf. 5:20; 7:21).

According to the text, only a *few* will *find* and follow this road, while most will travel the broad road to destruction. (In some manuscripts, the statement about the *few* reads as an exclamation: How narrow is the way that leads to life, and how few those who find it! Cf. NAB). The purpose of such a statement is not to propound a dogma on how many will be saved, but to invite the hearers of the Sermon to act on what they have heard. They have in fact *found* the way that eludes so many, and it is critical that they decide to follow it.

Known by Their Fruits 7:15-20

In both Matthew and Luke, Jesus' sermon contains sayings on good and bad fruit (cf. Luke 6:43-45). Matthew, however, applies these sayings to a particular problem facing the church, the problem of false prophets (cf. 7:15, 22; 2 Pet. 2:1; 1 John 4:1; Did. 11). Later in the Gospel, false prophets are associated with the tribulation of the endtime (24:11-12, 24), and Matthew may well view their activity in his community in that light. It is likely that these prophets were teachers who wandered from city to city (cf. the words *come to you,* v. 15), in much the same way that Jesus instructed his disciples to go forth (cf. 10:5-15).

Less certain is whether these prophets were linked to a particular "party" in the early church. They have been variously identified as antinomians who saw no place for law, as Jewish-Christian rigorists with a pharisaic spirit, or as charismatic enthusiasts more concerned with miracles than faithfulness. Whatever their bent, false prophets pose a threat to hearing and doing Jesus' word. And that leads Matthew to say again: *Beware!* (cf. 6:1).

The sayings describing the false prophets use a mixture of metaphors. In verse 15, a saying peculiar to Matthew, we are told that these teachers appear to be like any other members of God's flock. Like wolves, however, they are really out to devour the community to satisfy their own needs (cf. Acts 20:28-29; Ezek. 22:27; Did. 16:3).

As deceptive as false prophets are, the church can identify them *by their fruits* (7:16, 20). The tree and fruit imagery in verses 16-20 occurs elsewhere in Scripture (cf. Matt. 12:33-37; James 3:12; Sir. 27:6; Gal. 5:22-23) and stresses the correspondence of character and conduct: What we do reveals who we are. In the case of false prophets, *bad fruit* gives them away and will eventually lead to their judgment (cf. 7:19 and 3:10). It is noteworthy that the criterion given here for knowing who the wolves are is not a particular false doctrine or teaching. Instead, it is the pattern of their lives.

I Never Knew You 7:21-23

Having warned his audience about false prophets, Jesus goes on in verses 21-23 to talk about their destiny. These verses incorporate sayings which are widely separated in Luke's Gospel (cf. Luke 6:46; 13:26-27) and portray a scene at the last judgment. *On that day,* the text tells us, the false prophets will acclaim Jesus as all believers do (*Lord, Lord*) and list their credentials as Jesus' witnesses (cf. 7:22; 10:1; 24:24; Mark 9:38-39).

To their surprise, however, Jesus will disavow any relationship with them (*I never knew you*) and send them away from his presence (cf. 25:12, 41; and Ps. 6:8a). The basis for this harsh judgment is evident from verse 21. In spite of their Christian confession, the false prophets fail to practice the will of God as expounded by Jesus. That is why they are labeled doers of *evil* (Greek: *anomia*, the same word used of the scribes and Pharisees in 23:28). And that is why they cannot *enter the kingdom* (cf. 5:19-20, to which 7:21-23 may well allude).

Tale of Two Houses 7:24-27

Jesus concludes the Sermon on the Mount by telling a parable, a not uncommon practice among Jewish teachers. It is a story about two builders—and the fate of the houses they construct. In Luke's version of the parable (Luke 6:47-49), both houses apparently are built on a river plain, and rising floodwaters destroy the house which lacks a deep foundation. Matthew, on the other hand, envisions houses in two different locations, one on the rocky terrain of a mountainside, the other on sand in a valley. Here the destruction of the second house results from a combination of wind, torrential rain, and swollen streams rushing down the mountainside into the valley.

In both versions, the picture of destruction by water is a metaphor for God's judgment (cf. Ezek. 13:10-16; Isa. 28:17-18; Matt. 24:37-39). And Jesus' teaching is the solid rock on which the parable encourages us to build our lives to avoid judgment. (A similar theme appears in a parable attributed to Rabbi Elisha ben Abuya, where good works and knowledge of the Torah provide a foundation against the flood; cf. Luz: 452). To build thus is to be numbered among the wise rather than the foolish, a motif that comes up again in the parable of the ten bridesmaids, in 25:1-13.

As One with Authority 7:28-29

The brief narrative postscript to the Sermon in 7:28-29 forms a sequel to the narrative introduction in 5:1-2. Here Matthew reminds us of the presence of the crowds and describes their reaction to the Sermon. The postscript begins with the formula: *When Jesus had finished saying these things. . . .* Similar statements occur at the end of the other four discourses of Jesus in Matthew (cf. 11:1; 13:53; 19:1; 26:1). In the parallel passages, the formula serves as a transition to a new story or subject. In 7:28, however, it is part of the narrative framework of the Sermon itself, leading into the comment that *the crowds were astounded at his teaching.* The word for *astounded* could also be translated *overwhelmed* or *shocked.*

The reason for this reaction is the *authority* with which Jesus teaches. Unlike the scribes, who appealed to texts or tradition when they taught, Jesus declares God's will in a direct and authoritative fashion. He speaks for God, redefines the law, and makes his word the final word. In the presence of such a teacher, astonishment is quite in order—for both the hearer and the reader.

THE TEXT IN BIBLICAL CONTEXT

A popular assumption in some circles is that the roads of life will eventually all come together and lead to the same goal. A quite different assumption governs the world of biblical faith, an assumption which finds a classic formulation in the opening words of the

Didache: "There are two ways, one of life and one of death; and between the two ways there is a great difference" (Did. 1:1; cf. Barn. 18:1).

Rooted in traditions at least as old as the time of the prophets, the concept of *two ways* is reflected in a wide spectrum of Jewish texts. (Cf. Deut. 11:26; 30:15-20; Ps. 1:6; Jer. 21:8; 1QS 3:20-21; 2 Enoch 30:15; T. Asher 1:3-9; and the entire book of Proverbs.) As is obvious from our analysis of the text, the epilogue of Jesus' Sermon bears the imprint of this tradition. For Matthew, there are two different roads to travel, two different ways to build, here and now. And they will lead in the end to contrasting outcomes (cf. the parables of the end in chap. 25). Choosing the *right* way is thus a matter of greatest importance.

A second point at which the epilogue brings us into a wider biblical conversation is its emphasis on *doing* what Jesus teaches. Like the authors of Deuteronomy and James, Matthew insists that it is the doers of the word who will saved (cf. Matt. 7:21, 24; Deut. 32:45-47; James 1:22; 2:24). On the surface, it might seem that Matthew supports the view of salvation by works which Paul rejects so vehemently in his letters (Rom. 3:20; Gal. 2:16).

In reality, however, Matthew operates out of a theology of grace no less than Paul does. For Matthew, Jesus' ethical demands are not a means by which we weasel our way into God's favor. Rather, they offer a way to life that God makes known to us as a gift, just as the covenant at Sinai was a gift. Correspondingly, our obedience to Jesus' demands is a faithful response to God's gift, not unlike the response Paul calls for in Romans 12:1-2. That is what doing the word is all about.

Yet a third point at which 7:13-29 invites further comment is the issue of Jesus' authority. By what authority is Jesus able to speak for God and redefine the law? Is there a special role or capacity in which Jesus is acting as he teaches? Some scholars believe that Matthew portrays Jesus as a new Moses, bringing a new law to the people of Israel. While the setting of a mountain does evoke memories of the revelation at Sinai, the authority Jesus manifests on the mountain really exceeds that of a Moses. A more probable view is that Matthew perceives Jesus as the personal presence of the divine Wisdom.

Late in the OT period, Jewish writers began to personify wisdom as a figure present with God at creation and active in Israel's history (cf. Prov. 8:1-31; Sir. 24; Wisd. of Sol. 7:22-30; John 1:1-5, 9-13). In some passages, Wisdom is associated with the law and invites persons to come and learn from its bounty (Sir. 24:19-29; 51:23-30).

Rather strikingly, Jesus himself speaks in the language of Wisdom found in Sirach in Matthew 11:28-30 (cf. again Sir. 51:23-27). Other passages also confirm that Matthew identifies Jesus with Wisdom (cf. 11:2, 19; 23:34/Luke 11:49). In short, as the divine Wisdom behind the law, Jesus has full authority to redefine the law and bring it to fulfillment. And he exhibits this authority in the Sermon.

THE TEXT IN THE LIFE OF THE CHURCH

In discussing the biblical context of 7:13-29, we have already surfaced some key issues for the church in its engagement with the text. A case in point would be the relationship of obedience to salvation, a much-debated subject throughout the church's history. It would be interesting to delve further into this and other issues. Since the epilogue brings the Sermon to its conclusion, however, we do well to turn our attention to a larger question, that of the church's approach to the Sermon as a whole. How has the church across the centuries heard and applied Jesus' ethic in the Sermon on the Mount?

As the history of interpretation reveals (cf. Guelich: 14-22, Schweizer: 193-209, and the surveys by Kissinger and Bauman), Jesus' ethic has been understood in a variety of ways. One approach distinguishes between teachings binding on all Christians and more difficult teachings for the few who would be perfect. According to others, the more radical parts of Jesus' ethic are meant to guide all believers in face-to-face relationships, but are not applicable to the various roles we must play in the social order. Another position is that Jesus' ethic is one for believers to practice in every area of their lives, and that believers should separate themselves from societal structures and roles that might compromise that ethic.

More utopian in outlook are those who treat the Sermon as a social blueprint for all humanity, viewing it as directly applicable to both individual conduct and corporate policy. Still others question whether Jesus' intent was to offer an ethical blueprint for anyone or any group: Some would argue that the Sermon focuses on attitudes and dispositions, while others contend that Jesus' demands are so beyond our reach that they compel us to abandon hope in our own perfection and to look to God for mercy. Finally, there are those who view Jesus' teaching as an endtime ethic in a restricted sense, whether as an "interim ethic" for disciples who saw themselves living in the last days, or as a way of life for the dispensation (time) of Jesus' millennial reign.

What an array of views! As we ourselves enter into this history of interpretation, the wisest course is to try to take our clues from the Sermon itself. How does *Matthew* want us to hear and understand Jesus' ethic? The following seven theses attempt an answer to that question:

(1) Jesus' ethic is an ethic of the kingdom. From beginning to end, Jesus' message in Matthew is a message of God's reign. Jesus calls us to reorder our lives in light of the rule of God that will encompass history at the end, and that is already drawing near to us in Jesus' ministry.

(2) Jesus' ethic is an ethic for the community. As Jesus teaches on the mountain, he envisions a community of followers who will embody his word and be a light to the world. To put it another way: Jesus' teaching is an ethic for those who welcome God's rule and who seek to live by its vision.

(3) Jesus' ethic is more than a community code. Because the kingdom is wider than the church, the ethic of the kingdom relates to life outside the church. It both defines the way believers are called to live in society and reveals the will of God for all life throughout the world.

(4) Jesus' ethic holds act and attitude together. As the antitheses indicate, Jesus calls for righteousness in our total being, not merely correct performance. At the same time, Jesus calls us to *do* what he teaches, and he indicates some of the points at which our righteousness must be concrete.

(5) Jesus' ethic is an ethic of provocation. When Jesus redefines the law, he does not go the route of prescribing detailed legislation. Instead, he sets a new direction—and then uses stories and language that *provoke* us to discover new and appropriate ways to act.

(6) Jesus' ethic is an ethic of love. Although the word *love* does not occur until 5:43-48, Jesus is teaching what love requires throughout the six antitheses. He calls for love that makes peace, love that honors boundaries, love that keeps commitments, love that speaks the truth, love that endures evil, and love that includes all.

(7) Jesus' ethic is rooted in spirituality. As we discovered at several points, obedience to Jesus' word does not occur in a vacuum. Rather, it grows out of a life of trust and prayer. To put it another way: It is those who seek God who will seek first God's kingdom, and who will find the strength and courage to live for its coming.

Matthew 8:1—9:34

Jesus Acts with Authority

PREVIEW

In Matthew 11:20-24, Jesus names some of the Galilean cities where his ministry occurred and speaks of the *mighty works* (RSV) done in their midst. We get a picture of these mighty works in the collection of stories in 8:1—9:34. Here Jesus cleanses a leper, heals many who are sick or disabled, calms a storm at sea, casts out demons, forgives sin, and raises up a child who was dead. Through this panorama of miracles, we see that the authority which Jesus manifested in his teaching extends to his actions as well. He displays the power of God to deliver those in need and to make life whole. For Matthew, the meaning of these mighty works is not at all ambiguous. The deeds Jesus performs are the deeds of *the Messiah* (11:2, cf. 11:2-5).

The plan or design of 8:1—9:34 is a matter on which scholars disagree. An older hypothesis is that Matthew gives us an exhibit of ten miracles, ten positive wonders that form an antitype to the ten plagues described in Exodus 7—12. Some have questioned, however, whether the incidents Matthew reports really add up to ten. More important, this proposal fails to account for the material on Jesus' disciples which breaks the progression of the miracle stories (cf. 8:18-22; 9:9-17). A more recent proposal is that 8:1—9:34 is organized on a topical basis. According to one view, Matthew works at the issue of Christology in 8:1-17, at discipleship in 8:18—9:17, and at faith in 9:18-34. The problem here is that issues of Christology and faith are not confined to the sections indicated but rather permeate the whole of 8:1—9:34.

The most adequate proposal on Matthew's design in this section is that he has organized the collection in terms of alternating sections on miracles and discipleship (cf. Meier, 1980:79-80; Gundry, 1982:138). What we have then are three groups of miracle stories, each containing three narratives (8:1-17; 8:23—9:8; 9:18-34), and two sections of material on discipleship which serve as interludes (8:18-22; 9:9-17). Through this arrangement of material, Matthew portrays the disciples as apprentices in mission, who will soon be called to perform mighty works in Jesus' name (9:35—10:42).

As in most narrative sections, Matthew's primary source for the stories in 8:1—9:34 is Mark's Gospel. Seven of the nine accounts of Jesus' miracles are drawn from Mark, as is one of the sections of material on Jesus' disciples. Several shorter collections of miracle stories in the Second Gospel (cf. Mark 1:21-45; 4:35—5:43) may have suggested the idea of assembling materials of this sort. The remaining stories and sayings have parallels in Luke and apparently come from the common source Matthew and Luke used in addition to Mark.

In compiling this material, Matthew has left his imprint in several ways. First, he has constructed a new geographical framework for the stories, in which Capernaum serves as the hub for Jesus' movements. Second, he has rearranged the order of several Markan accounts, so that they fit better in the new framework. Third, he has greatly compressed most of the narratives, focusing on essentials. More specifically, Matthew (cf. Bornkamm, Barth, Held: 225):

(1) Uses compact, stock phrases to tell his stories.
(2) Gives little attention to secondary characters or actions.
(3) Repeats certain catchwords to link and unify his material.
(4) Lets Jesus' dialogue with supplicants stand out as central.
(5) Gives special prominence to the theme of faith.

Because of the particular design of 8:1—9:34, we approach this section in a different manner. First we analyze each of the five units in 8:1—9:34. Then The Text in Biblical Context (TBC) and The Text in the Life of the Church (TLC) will discuss the section as a whole. Comments there will explore the background and significance of miracle stories and reflect on ways these stories have been used.

Mighty Works, Cycle 1

Matthew 8:1-17

PREVIEW

The first three narratives on Jesus' mighty works are set in the framework of Jesus' return to Capernaum following the Sermon: In the first story, a leper approaches Jesus as he is coming down from the mountain. Then a centurion comes out to meet Jesus as he is entering Capernaum. Finally, Jesus proceeds to Peter's house in that city, and there the events of the third account unfold. More significant than the geographical detail are the persons we encounter in these stories. As John Meier writes, these narratives "group three types of people who were excluded from or enjoyed diminished rights within the Israelite community: a leper, a Gentile soldier, and a woman" (Meier, 1980:82; cf. Minear: 62). From the outset, therefore, Matthew wants us to appreciate the inclusive character of Jesus' mission. His mighty works break through social barriers of every sort.

All three of the accounts in 8:1-17 can be described as healing stories. In a typical Matthean healing narrative, a person comes to Jesus with a request for help. Jesus then responds, sometimes granting the petition at once, sometimes engaging the person in further conversation. Once the request is granted, the story concludes with a statement confirming that the healing has occurred. The first two accounts in 8:1-17 follow this pattern.

In the third account, however, several things are different. Here we have a composite story, reporting the healing of both one and the many. Another unique feature is that Jesus takes the initiative in this story, not waiting for a request for help. Especially noteworthy is the fulfillment quotation at the end of the account. With these words from Isaiah 53, Matthew makes the point that a ministry of healing is part of the calling of God's servant.

OUTLINE

From Unclean to Whole, 8:1-4

Healing for the Gentiles, 8:5-13

He Takes Away Our Infirmities, 8:14-17

EXPLANATORY NOTES

From Unclean to Whole 8:1-4

As Jesus comes down from the mountain, the *great crowds* who had listened to the Sermon continue to accompany him. They thus become witnesses to Jesus' mighty deeds as well as his teaching (cf. 8:18; 9:8; 9:33). The first miracle they behold is the healing of a leper (cf. Mark 1:40-45/Luke 5:12-16 and a related story in Luke 17:11-19). In the Bible, the term leprosy can refer to various skin diseases, which may or may not have included the disease we know as leprosy (Hansen's disease). What is clear is that lepers were viewed as unclean (cf. Lev. 13—14), and had to live apart from the community until healed and ritually cleansed.

Such a person approaches Jesus in verse 2 and models a believing response to Jesus: He addresses Jesus as *Lord* and kneels before him, worshiping him (the Greek word for *kneel, proskuneō*, is the same word used earlier for the adoration of the magi). Disregarding the taboo against contact with lepers, Jesus responds to the leper's request for healing by reaching out and *touching* him. And he is healed at once.

The description of the incident is a good example of Matthew's narrative style. Note the compact language and the reiteration of certain key words:

If you choose, you can make me clean.
I do choose; be made clean.
Immediately his leprosy was cleansed.

The story concludes with follow-up instructions for the leper. First, Jesus commands him not to publicize the event (cf. 9:30). The secrecy theme comes from Mark, who features it in a number of miracle stories; its meaning there is still a disputed matter. For Matthew, the command to secrecy relates to Jesus' servant role as described in 12:15-21: Jesus does not wish to "make a lot of noise," but prefers to carry out his calling as unpretentiously as possible.

Jesus' second command to the leper is to appear before the priest for certification of healing and to offer the sacrifice mentioned in Leviticus 14. In the Greek text, the words translated *to the people* read simply *to them,* which could refer either to the public or to the priests. *Testimony to them,* therefore, can mean either evidence for the community that a cure has taken place or proof to the religious authorities that Jesus honors the law of Moses (cf. 5:17).

Healing for the Gentiles 8:5-13

The second mighty work that the crowds behold occurs as Jesus is entering Capernaum. For this story we have parallel accounts in both Luke and John (cf. Luke 7:1-10; John 4:46-54). Here the petitioner who comes to Jesus (in Luke's version he sends delegations to Jesus to make his request) is identified as a *centurion*. The title is that of a Roman officer who commanded a hundred men in a Roman legion. Since Roman legions did not occupy Galilee in Jesus' day, the title may be used somewhat loosely here. The centurion in our story is likely a Syrian Gentile in the service of Herod Antipas, stationed at Capernaum with a small garrison of troops because of its location as a border city and customs post.

In any event, the centurion approaches Jesus on behalf of his *servant,* who is *sick in bed . . . unable to move, and suffering terribly* (GNB). The word translated as *servant* (Greek: *pais*) is somewhat akin to our English word *boy*. It can mean both *son* or *child* (as in John 4:51, cf. 4:46, 50) and *slave* or *servant* (as in Luke 7:7, cf. 7:2-3). In Matthew 8 the text allows us to accept either meaning.

Jesus' response to the centurion in verse 7 can be taken in different ways. In the translation given in the NRSV, Jesus offers to go to the centurion's home. The structure of the Greek text, however, suggests that Jesus could be asking a question: *Am I to come and cure him?* Or to paraphrase the question: Am *I* to go with *you*, a Gentile, to your home? If this is the case, then Jesus' response to the centurion is analogous to his response to the Canaanite woman in 15:21-28.

Whatever the centurion hears in Jesus' words, he replies that a visit is not appropriate (*I am not worthy*), nor is it necessary. A mere *word* will suffice. "As a military officer," he goes on, "I know what it is to receive and give orders, and how orders lead to action." By analogy, a simple command from someone with the authority Jesus has can surely heal the sick. This expression of trust leads Jesus to commend the centurion's faith in a manner none too flattering for the crowds: *I have not found anyone in Israel with such great faith* (NIV). For Matthew, the faith of this Gentile officer is both a judgment against unbelief in Israel and a preview of Gentile acceptance of the gospel.

Matthew continues to reflect on the issue of Gentile faith and Jewish unfaith in verses 11-12. Here he incorporates a saying of Jesus that does not appear in Luke 7:1-10, but which is found in a different setting in Luke 13:28-29. The scene depicted in this saying is the messianic banquet at the end (cf. Isa. 25:6; Luke 14:15-24; Rev.

19:9), hosted by the patriarchs of Israel (cf. 4 Macc. 13:17; Pesah. 119b; Exod. R. 25:8). What is surprising is who is included and who is excluded. The statement about persons coming *from east and west* uses OT language that referred to the gathering of Jewish exiles (cf. Isa. 43:5-6; 49:12; Ps. 107:3). Now, however, this language is applied to Gentiles streaming into the kingdom.

By contrast, the people of God to whom the kingdom was originally promised (the *heirs* of the kingdom) find themselves on the outside looking in (cf. 21:43). Their lot is described as one of darkness, weeping, and gnashing of teeth, traditional images of judgment (cf. Ps. 112:10; 1 Enoch 108:3-7; Matt. 13:42; 22:13; 24:51; 25:30). For Matthew's community, the saying in verses 11-12 is a sobering reminder that the kingdom is open to all but guaranteed to none. Only those who believe as the centurion believed will sit at table with Jesus and Abraham.

As for the centurion, his request is finally granted in verse 13. Jesus speaks the word that sets his power in motion—and healing results from his command. Similar commands can be found at the end of other stories yet to come (cf. 9:29; 15:28). In each instance, Matthew stresses the role of faith in giving us access to Jesus' power.

He Takes Away Our Infirmities 8:14-17

Once Jesus is in Capernaum, he goes to the home of Peter, who has a family, we now discover (cf. 1 Cor. 9:5). There the third story of healing unfolds (cf. Mark 1:29-34/Luke 4:38-41), and it begins with Peter's mother-in-law. Her ailment is defined as a *fever,* which in the ancient world refers not merely to a symptom but to some illness characterized by fever. As noted above, Jesus does not wait for a plea for help in this episode, but initiates the action. When the fever departs, Peter's mother-in-law rises and *serves* (*diakoneō*) Jesus. The literal meaning is that she offers Jesus hospitality. For Matthew, however, her action may have an extended symbolic meaning as well: She typifies the way all those restored by Jesus should *serve* him.

The story continues in verses 16-17 with the healing of a number of people brought to Jesus, either residents of Capernaum or persons from *the crowds.* In the parallel account in Mark, "all" the sick and possessed are brought to Jesus, and "many" are cured. Matthew writes, however, that *many* are brought to Jesus and *all* those brought are healed, underscoring even more the effective power of Jesus' *word* (cf. 8:16b; 8:8-9).

The quotation from Isaiah 53:4 concludes the narrative and attests Matthew's creative use of the OT. In the Hebrew text of Isaiah, sickness or infirmity is a metaphor for suffering related to sin, which the Servant takes upon himself and bears vicariously (cf. Isa. 53:4-6; 1 Pet. 2:24). As cited by Matthew, however, Isaiah's words describe physical diseases or infirmities, which Jesus removes through his ministry of healing. This too is a part of Jesus' fulfillment of the biblical promise.

Following Jesus, Interlude 1

Matthew 8:18-22

PREVIEW

As noted earlier, Matthew separates the three cycles of miracle stories in 8:1—9:34 with *interludes* on discipleship. The brief unit we find in 8:18-22 is the first of these interludes. For this material Matthew has drawn on a group of sayings in which Jesus addresses prospective disciples (cf. Luke 9:57-62). Each of these sayings uses forceful and picturesque language, on which we will comment shortly. The unit as a whole serves at least three purposes in Matthew's narrative: (1) It reintroduces disciples into the story line, preparing the way for a literal adventure in *following* Jesus in 8:23-27. (2) It makes the reader aware that Jesus is adding disciples as the story moves along (cf. 9:9), so that we are ready for the appearance of *twelve disciples* in 9:35—10:42. (3) It highlights the radical character of discipleship, an important theme both for the story and for Matthew's community.

OUTLINE

No Place to Call Home, 8:18-20

Forsaking All Else, 8:21-22

EXPLANATORY NOTES

No Place to Call Home 8:18-20

Periodically in the Gospels, the story moves away from the crowds and focuses on the smaller circle of Jesus and his disciples. The narrative statement in verse 18 marks one such transition and (anticipating the story to follow in verses 23-27) comes from Mark 4:35-36a. No reason is given for Jesus' decision to get away from the crowds at this particular time. According to some, Jesus' intent is to distance himself from the kind of popular acclaim his miracles are creating. In any event, the decision to leave Capernaum provides a setting for separating disciples from the crowd, and the command to go across the lake becomes in effect a call to discipleship. In the sayings that follow in verses 19-20 and 21-22, two would-be disciples respond to that call.

The first respondent is identified as *a scribe,* which may account for why he addresses Jesus as *Teacher.* In some Matthean texts, scribes are linked with Pharisees as opponents of Jesus (cf. 15:1; 23:13). Scribes can also become disciples, however (cf. 13:52; 23:34), and the scribe in 8:19 is intended to illustrate readiness to follow Jesus to any destination. Jesus' reply to the scribe, which urges him to count the cost, compares the relatively secure lot of foxes and birds with the homeless state of the *Son of Man.*

Behind the phrase *Son of Man* lies the Aramaic expression *bar naša*, which means simply *man* or *human one* (cf. the related Hebrew phrase in Ps. 8:4; Ezek. 2:1). In the NT, *Son of Man* occurs almost exclusively in sayings attributed to Jesus, twenty-nine times in Matthew. One of the most disputed questions is whether Jesus used the phrase as a messianic title or simply as an indirect way of referring to himself as a human figure (cf. Lindars). For Matthew, the expression seems to function as both a self-designation for Jesus and a title, such that *Son of Man* and *I* or *me* are interchangeable. As used in 8:20, *Son of Man* carries the sense of *this man* or *a person like me.* It clearly refers to "Jesus himself in his earthly wanderings, devoid of all middle-class security" (Schweizer: 219). To follow Jesus, then, is "to join the Son of Man in his insecurity and share his fate" (Schweizer: 220; cf. 1 Cor. 4:11).

Forsaking All Else 8:21-22

The second respondent is described as *another of his disciples,* a proleptic way of speaking of what the two men are about to become. (It is possible to translate the text *another man, one of the disciples,* which would contrast *disciple* with *scribe,* but this is somewhat forced.) Here the respondent seeks permission to care for another matter *first* before he follows Jesus. And it is no little matter. Burial of parents was a religious obligation incumbent on all devout Jews (cf. Tob. 4:3-4).

For Jesus, however, the "call into the new world of discipleship admits of no half measures or hesitations" (Meier, 1980:87). The admonition to *let the dead bury their own dead* is another instance of Jesus' use of shocking hyperbole. It can mean either "let the old order care for itself" or "discipleship takes precedence over other priorities." In any case, Jesus issues a clear command to *follow me,* recalling an earlier such command in 4:19.

Mighty Works, Cycle 2

Matthew 8:23—9:8

PREVIEW

For Matthew's second group of miracle stories, the backdrop is a trip across the lake and back. The first episode occurs on the outbound voyage and features Jesus calming a storm that nearly swamps the boat. Sometimes labeled a nature miracle, this event really belongs to the category of an epiphany, a mysterious revelation of who Jesus truly is. The second story unfolds in the Decapolis, a federation of Greek cities east of Galilee and Samaria. In this foreign setting, Jesus casts out the evil spirits afflicting two demoniacs and causes havoc when he sends them into an unsuspecting herd of pigs. For the third miracle, Jesus returns by boat *to his own town,* Capernaum. There he manifests another aspect of his power to restore life, the power to forgive the sin that cripples a paralytic.

Unlike the narratives in 8:1-17, none of the three stories in 8:23—9:8 is primarily a story of healing. Even in the account of the paralytic who walks again, the topic of healing is subordinate to another topic, that of forgiveness. What the three stories in this unit *do* have in common is their focus on the dramatic scope of Jesus' power or authority. In one instance Jesus demonstrates authority over the elements. In another it is authority to destroy demonic powers. And in the third account Jesus confronts us with his authority to forgive sin. The question that all three stories raise for the reader is the question found in 8:27: What sort of person is this, who commands such authority?

OUTLINE

Authority over the Elements, 8:23-27

Authority over the Demonic, 8:28-34

Authority to Forgive Sin, 9:1-8

EXPLANATORY NOTES

Authority over the Elements 8:23-27

Tales of storms at sea grip the reader in a special way, and the story from Mark related here is certainly no exception (cf. Mark 4:35-41/Luke 8:22-25). Adding to the power of the story is the way its language evokes memories of an earlier drama at sea, that of Jonah's voyage to Nineveh (cf. Jon. 1:4-6). Sudden storms were not uncommon on the Sea of Galilee, caused by winds sweeping down onto the lake from deep ravines in the hills surrounding it. It is such a windstorm, stirring things up unexpectedly, that threatens the boat carrying Jesus and his disciples across the lake.

Especially noteworthy is the term Matthew uses for the storm, the Greek word *seismos (shaking)*, which usually refers to an earthquake. Because of the association of earthquakes with the endtime (cf. Matt. 24:7; 27:51-54; 28:2; Rev. 6:12), a storm described as a *seismos* poses a terror all its own. Jesus, however, is more than equal to the wind and the waves. Arising from his sleep, he *rebukes* the elements (as he *rebukes* an evil spirit in 17:18). And with this command, he does what the psalmist attests can only be done by the power of God: "He made the storm be still, and the waves of the sea were hushed" (Ps. 107:29; cf. Pss. 65:5-8; 107:23-32).

In relating this episode, Matthew goes to great lengths to draw the church into the story. At the beginning of the narrative, we read that Jesus' disciples *followed him* into the boat, a clear allusion to the command *follow me* in the preceding verse. The journey about to transpire, therefore, is presented as a venture in discipleship. A second striking feature is the disciples' plea for help when the storm comes up. The words *Lord, save us! We are perishing* have a liturgical ring, conveying the cry of the community at worship.

Jesus' response to this plea is also noteworthy. Before he attends to the raging storm (which is the first thing he does in Mark's account), he deals with a "religious" issue: He addresses the faltering faith of his followers (cf. 6:30; 14:31; 16:8). Finally, there is the reference to people who marvel at Jesus' authority at the end of the story. While the immediate object of *they* is the group of disciples, the reference is sufficiently broad to incorporate later hearers of the story as well. To put it another way, it is the larger community of faith that ultimately responds in awe: *Who is this that commands even the winds and the sea?*

Authority over the Demonic 8:28-34

The story of Jesus' encounter with the demoniacs among the tombs comes from Mark 5:1-20 (cf. Luke 8:26-39). In retelling the story, Matthew omits a number of features of the colorful Markan narrative, writes of *two* demoniacs instead of one, and modifies the geography of the story. According to Mark, the incident takes place near Gerasa, a city thirty miles southeast of the Sea of Galilee. Matthew, however, places the event in the country around *Gadara*, which was only six miles from the lake. Gadara fits better with the scene of swine plunging into the sea at the end of the narrative, and this may account for the relocation of the incident. Whether Gerasa or Gadara, we should note that the episode unfolds in Gentile territory (indicated by the presence of pigs), although we must be careful not to draw false inferences from this. It is too soon for a mission of Jesus and his disciples to the Gentiles (cf. 10:5), and the story here makes a different point. As noted earlier, it highlights Jesus' power to destroy demonic powers. And what better place to confront demons than the unholy ground of a foreign land!

Demons appear regularly in texts from the biblical world and refer to "evil spirits, opposed to God and God's people" (Achtemeier: 217). As the demoniacs in the story illustrate, it was believed that demons could enter and possess persons, causing illness and unusual behavior. However we may view the subject, the Gospels link demon possession with the reign of evil in the world, and see the casting out of demons as a sign of God's reign overpowering evil (cf. Matt. 12:22-28 and the comments on that passage). The story before us reinforces that view.

The demons in 8:28-34 know that judgment awaits them in the endtime (cf. T. Levi 18:12; 1 Enoch 15—16; Jub. 10:8-9) and ask why Jesus is harassing them *before the time* (v. 29). Jesus, however, reveals that the time has already come. Although he grants the request of the demons to find a new home in a herd of swine, the pigs respond by carrying the demons to their destruction in the sea! For the residents of Gadara, the power Jesus exhibits is far too threatening to have around (vv. 33-34). Who knows what that power is likely to do next?

Authority to Forgive Sin 9:1-8

Upon returning to Capernaum, Jesus is met by several persons carrying a paralytic *lying on a bed.* The common bed in Jesus' day was a mattresslike pad, which could easily be used as a stretcher. The story of the paralytic comes from Mark 2:1-12 (cf. Luke 5:17-26; John 5:1-18), where the setting for the action is Peter's house. According to some scholars, Mark's account weaves together a story of healing and a story of a dispute about forgiveness. Be that as it may, Matthew 9:1-8 reads as a unified narrative and concentrates on the issue of Jesus' authority to forgive sin. To appreciate the story, one must keep in mind two tenets of Jewish faith that govern the discussion. One is the belief that sin and sickness are connected in some way (cf. John 9:2; 5:14). The other is the belief that only God can forgive sin (cf. Mark 2:7).

It is the first of these two tenets that leads Jesus to offer *forgiveness* to the paralytic as the gift he needs most. Jesus' initial word, *take heart*, is reminiscent of the phrase "do not fear" in the OT (cf. Isa. 43:1). Then his declaration *your sins are forgiven* leads Jewish scribes present to accuse Jesus of uttering *blasphemy* (the same charge the high priest brings against Jesus in 26:65, implying in both instances that Jesus claims divine attributes for himself). The response that Jesus makes to the scribes in verses 4-6 assumes that as sin and sickness are related, so are forgiveness and healing. If Jesus can free the limbs of the paralytic, it will be a sign that he also has authority to free the man from his sin. And so he speaks to the paralytic a second time and says, *Stand up,* which the paralytic does to the amazement of all.

In responding to the scribes, Jesus again refers to himself with the phrase *Son of Man* (cf. comments above on 8:20). According to some interpreters, the thrust of verse 6 is that the one who will judge and acquit others at the end has authority to forgive sin on earth as well. Others argue, however, that the issue at stake is whether a *human* can forgive sin on God's behalf, and that Jesus is proposing to demonstrate that God has in fact granted such authority to one who is human. This is clearly the sense in which the *crowds* of verse 8 hear Jesus' words, and the crowds likely speak for the author as well. For

Matthew himself, the reference to God giving *authority to human beings* to forgive sin likely carries a further meaning. The plural form hints at a community with which Jesus will share his authority to remit sin, the community we know as the church (cf. Matt. 16:19; 18:18; John 20:22-23).

Following Jesus, Interlude 2

Matthew 9:9-17

PREVIEW

The stories on following Jesus in 9:9-17 come from Mark 2:13-22. In Mark's narrative, this material is part of a collection of *controversy stories* (Mark 2:1—3:6). Each of these accounts lifts up some facet of Jesus' activity that upsets the Jewish community and leads to questions or a dispute. In Matthew 9, the element of controversy is still prominent. The primary purpose of the stories, however, has shifted. Matthew is interested in the episodes included here because of their focus on Jesus' disciples. They continue to develop the story line of Jesus' call: *Follow me.* And they depict a community of salvation that gathers around the disciples and Jesus.

The narrative framework for the unit is, once again, carefully crafted. Jesus apparently is still in the process of entering Capernaum as the unit begins. Somewhere along the way he passes a tax office, where the episode in verse 9 takes place. From there the action moves quickly to a meal hosted by Jesus in someone's house. Exactly whose house it is, the text leaves open; it could be Peter's, Matthew's, or Jesus' own home (but see 8:20). In any case, the setting for the meal is rather open, allowing visitors to drop by and question what is going on. Verses 10-13 deal with the objections of a group of Pharisees, while verses 14-17 relate an inquiry from disciples of John the Baptist.

OUTLINE

An Office Call, 9:9

Grace at Table, 9:10-13

New Calls for New, 9:14-17

EXPLANATORY NOTES

An Office Call 9:9

In the brief call story in Matthew 9:9, the unlikely candidate for discipleship is a tax collector (cf. Mark 2:13-14/Luke 5:27). Taxes of various sorts were assessed in the Roman empire, including a poll tax, income tax, tribute, and duties on transported goods. While some taxes were gathered directly by Roman officials, the collection of other taxes was contracted out to so-called publicans or tax farmers. These in turn hired subordinates from the local populace, and the tax collectors mentioned in the Gospels likely fall in this category. The tax office in which Matthew worked was probably a customs post on the edge of the city, where duties were demanded for goods passing into Galilee from the territory of Philip (cf. Luke 3:1). Ultimately, then, Matthew was in the service of Herod Antipas, to whom Rome had granted authority to levy taxes in his domain.

Interestingly, only the First Gospel identifies the tax collector in the story as *Matthew.* Mark refers to him as "Levi," and Luke follows Mark. How shall we account for this divergence? One proposal is that the tax collector was known by two different names. While this is not impossible, a more probable explanation is that the author of our text has substituted Matthew for Levi as the tax collector in his story. His reasons for doing so were likely twofold:

(1) It was his view that the body of disciples during Jesus' ministry was limited to the twelve (cf. TBC on 4:17-25). A tax collector who became a disciple, therefore, must have been one of the persons named in 10:1-4.

(2) The disciple Matthew may have been active in the church for which the First Gospel was written. By altering the story of Levi's call into that of Matthew's call, the author is able to say to his community: Here is where our own discipleship to Jesus Christ has its beginning! However Matthew makes his way into the story, he responds like Peter and others when Jesus says: *Follow me* (cf. 4:18-22).

Grace at Table 9:10-13

One characteristic feature of Jesus' ministry was his table fellowship with *tax collectors and sinners* (cf. 11:19; Luke 7:36-50; 15:1-2; 19:1-10). To his contemporaries, Jesus' choice of table companions was astonishing. Tax collectors were frequently shunned because of their collaboration with the government, their link with Gentile money and commerce, and their reputation for dishonesty. *Sinners,* which the GNB aptly paraphrases *other outcasts*, refers to persons careless in observing the strict requirements of the law, whom the Pharisees likewise tried to avoid as much as possible.

Such is the crowd that joins Jesus and his disciples for the dinner occasion described in 9:10-13 (cf. Mark 2:15-17/Luke 5:28-32). For Matthew, the table fellowship depicted here is significant in at least three ways: (1) It manifests Jesus' power to make God's acceptance and forgiveness available to all who come to him (cf. 9:6; 1:21). (2) It anticipates the messianic banquet at which an even wider circle will sit at table with Jesus (cf. 8:11; 22:1-14). (3) It offers a foreglimpse of the eucharistic fellowship of the church that will grow up around Jesus and the disciples.

Not surprisingly, the Pharisees who drop in on Jesus and his companions take offense at what they behold. The question they raise in verse 11 suggests that Jesus should not risk contamination by associating with the unclean and irreligious. In his reply, Jesus first cites a Greek proverb on who really needs help, then goes on to quote some words from Hosea 6:6 (which Matthew will insert again in another dispute in 12:7). *Go and learn* is a rabbinic formula, urging the hearer to appropriate the meaning of a Scripture lesson.

What the Pharisees need to learn from Hosea is that showing mercy to tax collectors and sinners is more important than maintaining ritual purity. Jesus concludes his reply by applying both the proverb and Scripture to his mission (cf. Luke 19:10; 1 Tim. 1:15). Here *the righteous* may describe those who already enjoy fellowship with God, or it may refer sarcastically to those who think Jesus and John have nothing to offer them (cf. 21:28-32). In any event, Jesus has come to extend God's mercy to all who need it, and his open table at Capernaum embodies that mercy.

New Calls for New 9:14-17

Still at dinner, Jesus and his friends are approached by a second group of inquirers (cf. Mark 2:18-22/Luke 5:33-37). As noted earlier, this group consists of disciples of John the Baptist (who will pay another visit to Jesus in 11:2-6). The question they raise is not who eats with Jesus, but the more fundamental question of why Jesus and his companions are more inclined to feast than to fast! In this respect, Jesus' practice differed both from that of the Pharisees (who fasted twice a week) and from the ascetic lifestyle of John and his followers (cf. 11:16-19).

Jesus responds to his questioners by conceding that a time will come when mourning and fasting will have their place (v. 15b). For the time being, however, Jesus' presence with his disciples is like a wedding party in which the bridegroom is mingling with the wedding guests (v. 15a). Who can fast at a time like this? The wedding imagery used here recalls passages describing God's covenant with Israel in terms of a marriage relationship (cf. Isa. 54:4-6; 61:10; 62:4-5; Hos. 2:16-20). In addition, it confirms the fact that Jesus' meals with his followers anticipate the messianic banquet of the endtime (cf. 22:2; Rev. 19:9).

The sayings that follow in verses 16-17 move beyond the specific issue of fasting and deal more broadly with the new situation that Jesus' ministry creates for his followers. At one time, the garment/patch and wine/wineskins sayings may have circulated apart from their present context. Already in Mark, however, they have become a commentary on the worship patterns of Jesus' followers, which diverge in various ways from the practice of the synagogue.

The point that both metaphors make is that the new thing God is doing through Jesus cannot simply be tacked onto or poured into ex isting structures. On the contrary, the reign of God present in Jesus' ministry calls for a radical transformation of life and worship. For the reader, the sayings in verses 16-17 raise a critical question about the direction the story is going: Can Israel itself be sufficiently transformed to receive what God is doing through Jesus? Or do *fresh wineskins* hint at the formation of a new community of God's people? *Matthew's* answer to that question will come in chapter 16.

Mighty Works, Cycle 3

Matthew 9:18-34

PREVIEW

In 9:18-34 Matthew concludes the collection of stories that began at 8:1. Like the first trilogy of stories (in 8:1-17), the three narratives included here focus on Jesus' power to *heal*: A chronic disease is finally cured. A dead child is raised up. The blind receive the gift of sight. A deaf mute begins to speak.

For the author, the deeds reported in these stories are significant at two levels. First, they anticipate the catalogue of miracles ascribed to Jesus in 11:1-5, illustrating some of the deeds for which we have not yet had examples. Second, they provide further evidence that the coming age of salvation is drawing near in Jesus' work. Together with the healing of the paralytic reported earlier, these deeds fulfill the promise of Isaiah 35:5-6: "Then the eyes of the blind shall be opened, and the ears of the deaf unstopped; then the lame shall leap like a deer, and the tongue of the speechless sing for joy."

From a literary perspective, several features of the stories in this unit should be noted:

(1) The *house* in Capernaum where Jesus and his disciples shared a meal remains the pivot of Jesus' activity in 9:18-34. Again there is some vagueness as to whose house it is.

(2) Two of the narratives in this section are brief doublets of stories that will be told later on (cf. 9:27-31/20:29-34; 9:32-34/12:22-30). As suggested above, they are used here to complete the exhibit of Jesus' deeds.

(3) Two of the narratives conclude with a notice of Jesus' spreading fame (cf. vv. 26, 31). Along with the summary to follow in 9:35ff., these notices recall the words of 4:23-25 and prepare the way for later stories on the response to Jesus' deeds.

(4) Themes Matthew has introduced in previous miracle stories resurface here with special emphasis. Among these are the themes of *touch* (cf. 8:3; 8:15; 9:21; 9:29) and of *faith* as the crucial link to Jesus' power to heal (cf. 8:10; 9:2; 9:22; 9:28-29).

OUTLINE

Double Deliverance, 9:18-26

Faith and Sight, 9:27-31

Like Nothing Else, 9:32-34

EXPLANATORY NOTES

Double Deliverance 9:18-26

The story of healing that begins at 9:18 consists of two stories in one (cf. Mark 5:21-43/Luke 8:40-56). While the meal described in 9:10-17 is still going on, a ruler (or *leader of the synagogue*) bursts in with an urgent plea for his daughter. Jesus and his disciples go with the ruler, but are accosted along the way by a second petitioner, a woman who has *been suffering . . . twelve years* of menstrual bleeding. Only after Jesus cares for the woman and her need can the story of the ruler's daughter move on to its conclusion.

Once again Matthew has adapted the story he found in Mark, calling attention to certain features while abbreviating the whole. One detail worth noting is the way Matthew describes the ruler and his request. Like the leper in 8:2, he kneels before Jesus in a gesture of faith and worship. What he requests, moreover, is not merely the healing of a child who is mortally ill (as in Mark 5:23), but the restoration of a child who has already *died.* We thus know from the beginning that this will be a Lazarus story.

Verses 20-22 contain the story within the story. From the reference to the *hemorrhage* that has lasted twelve years, we learn at least two things. First, the woman has a condition that is apparently incurable. Second, the woman has a condition that Jewish law viewed as unclean (cf. Lev. 15:25-30). This does not deter her, however. In a bold and presumptuous act, she comes up behind Jesus and touches *the fringe of his cloak.* (*Fringe* may refer to the tassels prescribed in Numbers 15:37-41, which faithful Jews wore as a reminder to keep the law.)

In an equally striking act, Jesus accepts the woman's touch as a gesture of faith and declares that this faith *has made you well* (whereupon healing follows). The word translated *made well* in verses 21 and 22 is the Greek verb *sōzō*, which elsewhere is used to speak of being "saved" (cf. Acts 2:21; 1 Cor. 1:18; Eph. 2:8). For Christian readers, therefore, Jesus' words to the woman embody the good news that we are saved by faith!

When story one resumes in verse 23, we get immediate confirmation that the ruler's daughter is dead. The crowd at the *leader's house* is wailing loudly (*making a commotion*), and the musicians hired to assist with the mourning (*the flute players*) are already busy. To be sure, Jesus declares that *the girl is not dead but sleeping.* What he means, however, is not that the girl is perhaps only comatose, but that God's power can awaken us from death as readily as we awaken from sleep. Death is not the end.

In the description that follows, Jesus sends the crowd outside and restores the child to life while he alone is with her. The language used recalls stories of Elijah and Elisha, who each revived a child in a somewhat similar manner (1 Kings 17:17-24; 2 Kings 4:32-37). Together, the stories of the woman and the girl establish that (1) Jesus' power to restore life is total, and (2) faith that reaches out to Jesus lets us receive that power.

Faith and Sight 9:27-31

The next supplicants who turn to Jesus are afflicted with blindness, a condition more common in the biblical world than in our own. Their story appears to be based on the story of Bartimaeus (cf. Mark 10:46-52/Luke 18:35-43), which Matthew will use again in 20:29-34. Perhaps to compensate for his omission of another Markan story on blindness (Mark 8:22-26), Matthew doubles the characters here and speaks of *two* blind men. (Cf. the same phenomenon in the account of the two demoniacs in 8:28-34, likely for the same reason.)

The episode begins as Jesus is heading home after reviving the ruler's daughter. Following Jesus and his entourage, the blind men cry out for Jesus to *have mercy.* The plea they make is not for pity, but for Jesus to *show* mercy by restoring their sight. In addressing Jesus, the blind men use the messianic title *Son of David,* which denotes a ruler descended from David (cf. 1:1). It is a title that normally carries a political meaning. For Matthew, however, the Messiah not only rules God's people but fulfills all of God's promises. So it is that *Son of David* is linked to Jesus' power to heal, not only in this passage but in other texts as well (cf. 12:23; 15:22).

Jesus' response to the blind men does not occur on the road but is delayed until he arrives at *the house* where he is staying. Apparently the two men pursue Jesus into the house, and there he engages them in a dialogue about faith:

Do you *believe* that I can do what you seek?

Yes, Lord.

Then according to your *faith* let it be done for you.

This conversation is clearly the central feature in the story, and its contours allow the reader to become one of the participants. As the narrative continues, faith leads to sight, and Jesus commands the two men to keep the healing a secret (cf. Mark 5:43, and see comments on 8:4). What happens, however, is that the word spreads far and wide (cf. 9:26; Mark 1:45), setting the stage for public reaction to Jesus and his work.

Like Nothing Else 9:32-34

The final candidate for healing in Matthew 8—9 appears at Jesus' doorstep as the men who were blind are just leaving. According to the text, he is *a demoniac who was mute,* the same demoniac mentioned in the story in 12:22-30 (cf. Luke 11:14-23). The word translated *mute* is the Greek word *kōphos*, which can mean either *deaf, speechless*, or both. While the healing that occurs in verse 33 emphasizes restored *speech*, Matthew likely views the man as both deaf and mute—and views his healing as an act that completes the series of deeds attested in 11:5.

The story concludes by noting two differing reactions to Jesus' mighty works. On one side are the crowds, who marvel that Jesus' deeds exceed anything previously witnessed (but who stop short of faith). On the other side are the Pharisees, who attribute Jesus' power to Satan rather than God, and who thus typify a rejection of Jesus that later becomes total. For the reader, this divided response is a clue to what is coming in the chapters still ahead.

THE TEXT IN BIBLICAL CONTEXT

The miracle stories we find in Matthew 8—9 did not develop in a vacuum. As a matter of fact, reports of healings and exorcisms abound in the NT era. Some of these accounts are linked with healing shrines dedicated to pagan deities, especially Isis and Asclepius. Such sanctuaries were found in a number of cities in the Mediterranean world. Other reports are associated with individual miracle workers, such as Apollonius of Tyana (a philosopher from Asia Minor) and Chanina ben Dosa (a first-century Jewish rabbi). The NT refers to the itinerant activity of various persons of this sort, including Jewish exorcists (cf. Acts 19:13; Matt. 12:27) and Christian miracle workers (cf. Matt. 7:22; 2 Cor. 12:12; Acts 8:4-8; 28:1-10). At one level, therefore, the miracle stories of the Gospels are part of a larger picture of which we need to be aware.

What is unique in the Gospel accounts is not so much the deeds they report as the way these deeds are understood. For Matthew and the other evangelists, Jesus' miracles find their meaning in the acts and promises of God in the story of Israel. There God is revealed as one who intervenes to deliver those in need. One strand of this story is Israel's witness to the exodus, where God works signs and wonders through Moses and Aaron (cf. Deut. 26:8; 34:10-12; Ps. 105:26-27).

Another facet of the story, to which we have already referred, is the promise of salvation linked to Israel's return from exile (cf. Isa. 35:5-6; 65:17-19). Both the earth and its people will one day be restored to the wholeness God intends. All of this is in the background as Jesus travels through Galilee and performs his mighty works. To those who behold these deeds with eyes of faith, he demonstrates the rule of God which frees creation from sin and suffering (cf. Matt.

12:28) and makes the healing of the age to come a reality here and now (cf. 11:2-6; 8:17).

A striking feature of miracle stories is the way they address the theme of *boundaries* (cf. Theissen, 1983:75-80; 129-152). In accounts of healing, the fundamental boundary is sickness or suffering. It is a barrier that stands between wholeness and the one who is ill. As a typical story unfolds, other obstacles emerge (boundary-stressing motifs) which further compound the problem. Thus in the stories of Matthew 8—9, we find obstacles such as ritual uncleanness, being a Gentile, sin, skepticism, unholy ground, religious objections, demon possession, and even death. To overcome such boundaries seems difficult if not impossible. But that is precisely what happens in the *boundary-crossing* actions described in the stories.

On the part of those in need, these actions include touch, worship, cries for help, and, above all, faith. On Jesus' part, there are words of assurance, reasoned argument, a healing touch, and decisive commands. In each case these actions lead to healing, a crossing of the boundary of suffering in which the power of God prevails.

In the context of Matthew's narrative, miracle stories play a double role. Their function within the story line of the Gospel is to highlight Jesus' messianic authority. It is not that Jesus' miracles correspond to a traditional view of what the Messiah would do. What they do, however (together with Jesus' preaching), is fulfill the promise of God to transform life in the age to come. For this reason, Jesus' deeds may be called the deeds of *the Messiah* (11:2; cf. 12:23), even though the power displayed is therapeutic rather than military.

The second function of the miracle stories relates to their hearing in Matthew's community. In addition to reminding the church of what Jesus did in Israel, the stories serve as paradigms or parables of salvation (cf. Kingsbury, 1978:568-573). They invite members of the church to approach Jesus with petitions for help in the face of their own crises. And they assure those who do so that Jesus' power can deliver all who reach out in faith (cf. 14:28-33!). For a community facing boundary situations of its own, whether distress within the church or persecution from the outside, the miracle stories offer a resource for strengthening faith and hope.

THE TEXT IN THE LIFE OF THE CHURCH

Jesus' miracles and the stories about them have influenced the church in a number of ways. Among these is the use of the language of the miracle stories in music and worship. For example, a statement of the Gentile centurion appears in the Roman liturgy for the celebration of Eucharist: "Lord, I am not worthy that you should enter beneath my roof, but say only the word, and my soul will be healed."

Poems and hymns in the modern era provide further examples. One thinks of the poem "The Touch of the Master's Hand," by Myra Brooks Welch; of the nineteenth century gospel song "Master, the Tempest is Raging"; and of the lyrics by Edward H. Plumptre in "Thine Arm, O Lord, in Days of Old" (usually sung to a tune by the name of St. Matthew!). Perhaps the best known hymn using the language of the miracle stories comes from the pen of Charles Wesley. In the lyrics of "O For a Thousand Tongues to Sing," we sing of some of those whom Jesus healed and set free:

> Hear him, ye deaf; his praise, ye dumb,
> Your loosened tongues employ.
> Ye blind, behold your Savior come,
> And leap, ye lame, for joy.

A second level at which miracles are closely tied to the life of the church is that of witness or mission (cf. Theissen, 1983:259-264; MacMullen: 17-42; Senior, 1985a). There are several aspects to this linkage:

(1) The miracle stories (as noted above) attested the power of God to break through barriers. Both directly and indirectly they thus supported the Gentile mission and encouraged the sharing of the gospel across all cultural boundaries.

(2) The miracle stories sometimes served as evangelistic media for inviting others to faith in Christ. Such was likely the case with the collection of stories on Jesus' signs on which the Fourth Gospel draws (cf. John 2:11; 20:30-31).

(3) The miracle stories paved the way for mighty deeds by Christians in the communities in which they lived. From all we can tell, such deeds played a major role in evangelizing the Roman empire. And stories of *Jesus'* deeds helped to create anticipation for Christian miracles in Jesus' name.

A final way in which miracles have figured in the Christian story is as a point of controversy (cf. Theissen, 1983:287-302; Fuller: 8-17, 110-114). Within the gospel accounts themselves, we hear the first round of this debate: Jesus' opponents accuse him of being in league with the devil and discredit his mighty works as acts of sorcery. In our own era the controversy occurs at a different point; the miracle stories are either dismissed as fantasies of wish fulfillment or explained in "natural" ways that satisfy the modern mind.

In reacting to those who depreciate the miracle stories, the church has sometimes engaged in questionable apologetics. At times this has taken the form of attempting to *prove* the gospel miracles, so that faith becomes dependent on rational proof or argument. Such an approach clearly violates the biblical witness to Jesus' deeds. A proper "defense" of the miracle stories consists of manifesting the power of God to which the deeds of Jesus point. When the world can look at God's people and see healing and transformation at work, the miracle stories will be received and valued for what they are.

Matthew 9:35—10:42

Jesus Commissions His Disciples

PREVIEW

Throughout the major section that begins at 4:17, Jesus is preparing for others to share in his mission. The direction is set in the call stories, in which Jesus invites persons to follow him as disciples (4:18-22; 8:18-22; 9:9). As followers, these persons receive instruction from Jesus (5:1-2), behold Jesus' power and authority (8:23-27), and learn the meaning of Jesus' mission as they sit at Jesus' table (9:10-17).

The vocation of the disciples to which all of this is leading is spelled out in 9:35—10:42. Here Jesus commissions *his twelve disciples* in a formal way and gives them a discourse on mission as he sends them out. What is impressive in this presentation is the extent to which Jesus' mission and that of the disciples are one and the same. As Jesus' emissaries, the twelve will go forth with his authority, adopt his itinerant style, preach the message he preaches, perform the deeds that he performs, and share the fate that awaits him too.

Earlier accounts of the disciples' mission provide the basis for Matthew's account. These include the commissioning story in Mark 6:7-13 (cf. Luke 9:1-6) and a parallel story found in Luke 10:1-16. While Luke relates the two accounts to separate incidents (the second involving a larger group of seventy persons), Matthew has a single commissioning that draws on material from both sources. In addition, Matthew has incorporated other material that fits the topic and occasion. Especially noteworthy are the list of disciples taken from Mark 3:13-19, sayings on the cost of discipleship, predictions of suffering from apocalyptic passages, and words about the link between sender and sent. The final product is thus an expanded commentary on mission, put together in a manner characteristic of Matthew's work.

Matthew's purpose in this composition is basically twofold. At one level he is writing as the narrator of a story of God's faithfulness to Israel. Jesus' mission is first and foremost a mission to Israel (cf. Rom. 1:16), and that task must be completed before the mission can be broadened. So it is that *twelve* disciples are chosen and sent out, symbolizing the twelve tribes of Israel in earlier days. Thus also, until a greater commission is given later (cf. 28:19), these twelve will restrict their work *to the lost sheep of the house of Israel.*

At another level Matthew is writing as the member of a community that is itself called to mission. Although the words limiting mission to Israel no longer apply, the church inherits the commission Jesus gives to the twelve. It represents Jesus in the world, faces rejection and persecution, and needs encouragement for its task. Accordingly, Matthew 10 includes sayings on Christian witness before Gentile rulers. And everything that Jesus says to warn and strengthen the twelve warns and strengthens their successors.

Laborers for the Harvest

Matthew 9:35—10:4

PREVIEW

The material in 9:35—10:4 forms a transitional unit, linking the Sermon and miracle stories with the mission discourse in chapter 10. Among the smaller pieces Matthew uses to create the unit are a summary of Jesus' work in *all the cities and villages,* statements on the crowds and disciples extracted from Markan stories, a mission-saying on the need for harvest laborers, and a list of the names of the so-called *twelve apostles.* The various pieces are joined to produce a story with two panels, in which the commissioning of the twelve in 10:1-4 responds to the need described in 9:35-38.

OUTLINE

Help Wanted, 9:35-38

Position Filled, 10:1-4

EXPLANATORY NOTES

Help Wanted 9:35-38

The summary of Jesus' work in verse 35 reiterates the summary given in 4:23. It thus forms an inclusion with 4:23, while at the same time providing a basis for the observation that follows in verse 36 (which comes from Mark 6:34): Seeing the crowds to whom his ministry is directed, Jesus realizes their desperate situation.

The expression *sheep without a shepherd* reflects OT language (cf. Num. 27:16-17; 1 Kings 22:17; Ezek. 34:5; Zech. 10:2) and depicts Israel as a flock in need of new leadership. In Numbers 27, the subject is the need for someone to step into Moses' role, which parallels the issue in Matthew. The phrase *harassed and helpless* relates to the sheep metaphor and suggests a flock that is lying on the ground, exhausted. On such a people, the text tells us, Jesus has *compassion* (cf. 14:14; 15:32; 20:34). More than a human emotion, *compassion* here recalls the pity God has on Israel, which is sometimes linked with the last days (cf. T. Zeb. 8:2; Luke 1:78).

In verses 37-38, the metaphor changes from sheep and shepherd to harvest and harvest laborers (cf. Luke 10:2; John 4:35). The saying containing this imagery underlines the urgency of a mission to God's people. A common metaphor for God's endtime action (cf. Isa. 27:12; Hos. 6:11; Joel 3:13; Matt. 3:12; Rev. 14:14-20), *harvest* can refer both to the ingathering of God's people and to the destruction of the wicked. Here the imagery suggests a redemptive harvest, in which the dawning kingdom fulfills God's promises of salvation, and harvest laborers invite persons to enter into this joyous event.

At least two things are noteworthy in this picture. First, an event usually linked with the final judgment is beginning to happen in the present hour. Second, God is entrusting to human laborers the task of harvesting traditionally reserved for himself or assigned to angels (cf. 3:12; 13:30, 41-43)! The mission for which Jesus invites the disciples to prayer, therefore, is indeed an awesome one.

Position Filled 10:1-4

As if in answer to the prayer request in 9:38, Jesus convenes his group of disciples and prepares to send them out. In Mark's Gospel, Jesus appoints the twelve to share his authority in 3:13-19, but does not send them out until 6:7-13. Matthew, however, in his use of Mark, reports the commissioning and sending out as part of a single event.

Although only five disciples have been identified by name up to this point (Peter, Andrew, James, John, and Matthew), Matthew has made us aware of an ongoing call-process in the preceding narratives. This prepares us for the reference to Jesus' *twelve disciples* (whose special role as *the twelve* was common knowledge in the early church; cf. 1 Cor. 15:5). To these twelve Jesus gives *authority* to act in his name and to restore life as he does (cf. the parallel wording in 9:35 and 10:1). To put it another way: Jesus commissions the twelve to be his partners in mission.

The list of names that follows in 10:2-4 is arranged in sets or parallels and is one of several such lists in the NT (cf. Mark 3:16-19; Luke 6:14-16; Acts 1:12-14; G. Eb. 1). Some of the names call for further comment. Although Peter is always the first to be named, the text here explicitly refers to him as *first,* implying that Peter enjoys a special prominence or priority (cf. 16:18-19). In the case of Matthew, the First Gospel adds the phrase *the tax collector,* reminding us that this is the disciple mentioned in the story in 9:9.

As for Simon the Cananaean, the adjective translated *Cananaean* probably reflects an Aramaic word meaning *zealot* (cf. Luke 6:15). He may have received this name because of his zealous nature, or because of his prior affiliation with the revolutionary Zealot party (cf. NIV and GNB, though many scholars now question whether the Zealot party existed as early as the time of Jesus). The last person to be named is Judas Iscariot, who is identified here as elsewhere as Jesus' betrayer. *Iscariot* is a word of uncertain origin and could mean *man of Kerioth* (a town in Judea), *man of Issachar* (one of the twelve tribes), or *the assassin* (from the Greek word *sikarios*).

THE TEXT IN BIBLICAL CONTEXT

One of the problems for interpreters of ancient and modern texts is that writers may use the same words but use them in different ways. Such is the case with three terms in 9:35—10:4, the nouns *disciple* and *apostle* and the adjective *twelve* (which is sometimes used as a substantive, *the twelve*). Up to a certain point, we can assign definitions to these terms which fit their usage throughout the NT: A *disciple* is one who follows Jesus as an adherent to his movement. An *apostle* is one who is sent out as a representative of Jesus. And *the twelve* refers to the group of followers named in 10:2-4, who played a symbolic role in Jesus' ministry to Israel, and who (with the substitution of Matthias for Judas; Acts 1:12-26) contributed to the life of the early church in Jerusalem. Where the NT writers differ is the scope of the group(s) to whom the terms disciple and apostle apply.

In the letters of Paul, the term *disciple* does not appear at all. There are ample references, however, to apostles, who are persons who have seen the risen Christ and are sent forth as his witnesses (cf. 1 Cor. 9:1; Rom. 16:7). For Paul, the twelve represent a smaller circle within the total circle of apostles, which includes Paul himself (cf. 1 Cor. 15:3-11; 1 Thess. 2:5-7).

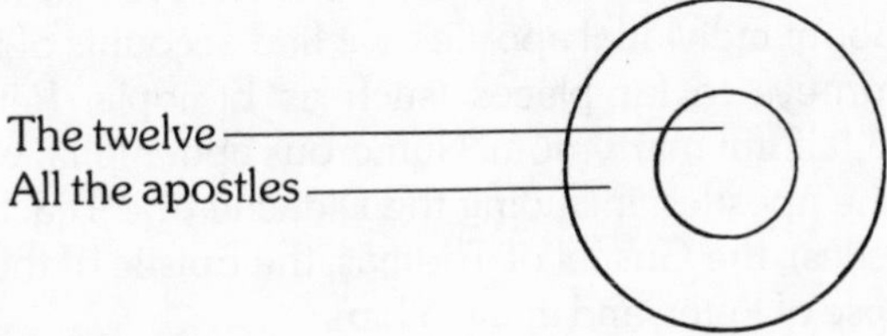

A different pattern is found in the writings of Luke (the Gospel of Luke and Acts). Here many persons become Jesus' disciples (= believers), both in the course of his ministry to Israel and in the subsequent life of his growing community. Except for one story, however (Acts 14:14), Luke limits the title of *apostle* to the twelve, whose witness underlies the witness of Paul and others.

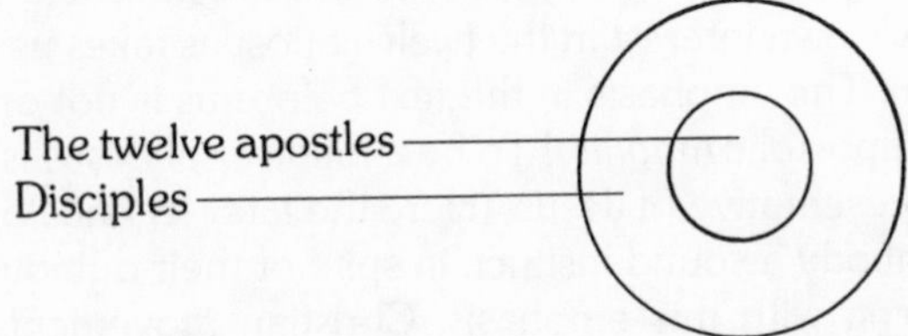

The most restricted use of the three terms occurs in the First Gospel. For Matthew, the twelve = the disciples = the apostles. To be sure, Matthew 28:18-20 envisions a broader community of disciples as the great commission is carried out (hence the open circle in the diagram). But in the context of Jesus' ministry to Israel, there are only twelve disciples, who are also the twelve apostles.

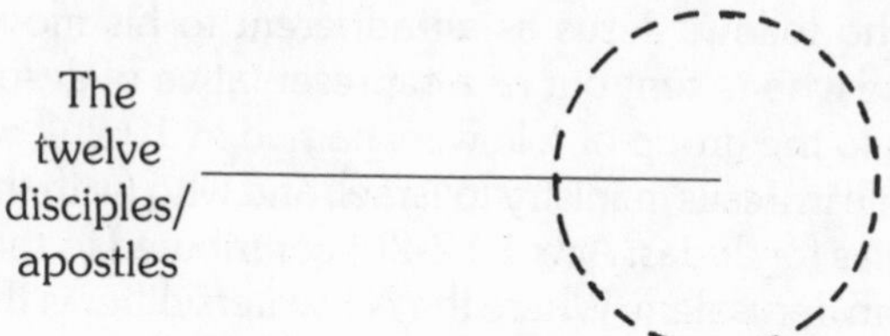

THE TEXT IN THE LIFE OF THE CHURCH

From the earliest days on, the twelve apostles have been popular figures in Christian piety and literature. The NT itself provides relatively little information on the life and work of these persons. Where historical tradition leaves off, however, legend takes over. In the colorful stories told about individual apostles, we find accounts of impressive miracles, journeys to far places (such as Ethiopia, Persia, India, Scythia), and faithful martyrdom. Numerous apocryphal writings are credited to the apostles, including the Didache (the Teaching of the Twelve Apostles), the Gospel of Thomas, the Epistle of the Apostles, the Apocalypse of Peter, and many others.

Literature such as this attests a growing veneration of the apostolic witness as the basis of Christian faith. Already in Ephesians we have a reference to "apostles and prophets" as the foundation on which the church is built (Eph. 2:20, cf. 3:5; Rev. 21:14). Apostolicity thus became a criterion for valid tradition in the church and one of the tests for determining which Christian writings were canonical. The same concern is evident in the Nicene-Constantinopolitan creed, which affirms faith in "one holy catholic and *apostolic* church."

Matthew's own interest in the twelve apostles takes us in a different direction. The emphasis in the text before us is not on apostolic stability but apostolic *mobility*! To be a follower of Jesus is to be *sent out* as a representative of Jesus. (Here the later legends of apostolic journeys embody a sound instinct, in spite of their dubious historicity.) In keeping with this emphasis, Christian movements stressing faithful discipleship have frequently assigned high priority to mission and evangelism. Such was the case with a number of groups in the left wing of the Reformation, including the early Anabaptists, Quakers, and Pietists (cf. Durnbaugh, 1968:226-241). For us, the commissioning of the twelve is a reminder that our own calling as disciples cannot be a closet affair. Whatever form our sending may take, we are called to be part of a centrifugal community, moving outward as Christ's witnesses and demonstrating his power in the world.

The Mission of the Twelve

Matthew 10:5-15

PREVIEW

The instruction of the disciples that begins in 10:5 and continues through 10:42 makes up the second of the five discourses of Jesus in Matthew. Linked as it is to the sending out of the twelve, it is frequently called the mission discourse. The first part of this discourse contains Jesus' charge to the twelve and describes their mission (10:5-15). In the sayings that follow (10:16-42), Jesus offers counsel on the opposition his messengers will encounter, underscoring the cost (and reward) of discipleship.

The charge to the twelve in the unit before us draws on similar collections of sayings found in Matthew's sources (cf. Mark 6:8-11; Luke 10:3-12). In the early church, these brief treatises on mission may have been used to instruct various groups of itinerant prophets and miracle workers. Although there are no sharp breaks in the unit, the charge does address a series of three topics: Verses 5-6 set the boundaries for the mission (limiting it to Israel). Verses 7-10 give a number of detailed commands on what to do and how to travel. And verses 11-15 deal with the reception of Jesus' messengers in the towns they visit.

OUTLINE

Restricted to Israel, 10:5-6

Rules for the Road, 10:7-10

Reception and Rejection, 10:11-15

EXPLANATORY NOTES

Restricted to Israel 10:5-6

As Jesus sends out the twelve, he limits the boundaries of their mission to the boundaries of his own activity. "Do not travel to foreign areas," Jesus says, "neither to Gentile lands [cf. NEB], nor to Samaritan communities." The Samaritans were an ethno-religious group based in Samaria who shared a common heritage and ancestry with Jews, but who over a period of centuries had developed a life separate from and in tension with the Jewish community. In the NT period, Jews regarded Samaritans as unclean and virtually equivalent to Gentiles (cf. John 4; Luke 17:18).

The people to whom Jesus and his disciples *are* sent are *the lost sheep of the house of Israel* (cf. 15:24). These lost sheep include not only certain despised persons within Israel, but the entire Jewish community as a *harassed and helpless* people (9:36; cf. Ezek. 34; Jer. 50:6). Since the words restricting mission to Israel are found only in Matthew, their origin is disputed. Whatever earlier use they might have had, their purpose in Matthew is to underscore the *priority* of Israel in Jesus' mission (cf. comments in TBC). At the end of the Gospel, the restriction to Israel will be lifted, and the disciples will be sent out to *all* the nations (28:19).

Rules for the Road 10:7-10

The rapid-fire orders Jesus gives in verses 7-10 deal with the substance and style of the disciples' mission. Following in Jesus' footsteps, the twelve are to engage in a ministry of *word* and *deed*, of proclamation and healing. Not surprisingly, they are to announce the coming of the *kingdom* proclaimed by John the Baptist and Jesus (v. 7, cf. 3:2; 4:17), and the mighty works they perform (v. 8a) will exhibit the power of the kingdom evident in Jesus' own miracles.

The twelve are also to take their cues from Jesus in the way they conduct themselves as itinerant messengers (cf. 8:20). Like Jesus, they are to use their authority as a gift to bless others, not as a means to fill their pockets (v. 8b; cf. 1 Cor. 9; Acts 20:33), and they are to move from town to town in the leanest possible manner (vv. 9-10). Jesus not only forbids taking along basic provisions (money, food bag, change of clothes), but also rules out normal means of protection against the harsh terrain, snakes, and wild animals (sandals, walking stick). Through these prohibitions (which are more severe than those in Mark 6:8-9), Matthew depicts Jesus' messengers as both defenseless and unencumbered. They go forth trusting God to protect them in the face of danger and to supply their needs through the hospitality of their hearers (cf. 6:25-34; 1 Cor. 9:4-7, 13-14; 1 Tim. 5:18; Did. 13:1).

Reception and Rejection 10:11-15

Building on the final phrase in verse 10, verses 11-15 focus on the issue of hospitality. Hospitality to visitors was an important part of Semitic culture, all the more so when visitors came as messengers from God (cf. Gen. 18:1-15; Heb. 13:2). The *worthy* home that Jesus' messenger is urged to seek out, then, is a *receptive* home, one ready to hear the word of the kingdom and offer hospitality.

Finding such a home, the messenger is to *greet it,* to proclaim God's blessing of peace upon it (cf. Luke 10:5). The greeting reflects the Hebrew *shalom*, which here signifies the peace of the kingdom, the wholeness of life that comes with God's reign. So closely is God identified with this word of peace that blessing occurs as blessing is pronounced (cf. Isa. 55:11), though only where it is welcomed.

If rejected, the blessing returns to Jesus' messenger, who must then communicate a message of judgment. The graphic act by which this is done is shaking the dust from one's feet as one leaves (cf. Acts 13:51), a gesture saying in effect that God is abandoning this house or town. Such a town, Jesus says, is in a worse position than Sodom or Gomorrah, cities that epitomized evil and judgment (cf. Isa. 1:9-10; Jer. 23:14; 2 Pet. 2:6; Jude 7). Behind this unfavorable comparison lies the inhospitable behavior of Sodom toward the messengers who visited Lot in Genesis 19:1-11. As John Meier puts it: "Sodom and Gomorrah showed disrespect to the angels, the Old Testament messengers of Yahweh; worse still is the disrespect shown to the apostles, the New Testament messengers of Christ" (1980:108).

THE TEXT IN BIBLICAL CONTEXT

The sending out of the twelve described in Matthew 10 is much more than an isolated incident. As the NT data confirms (cf. Theissen, 1978:8-23), itinerant prophets or teachers were a common feature in the landscape of early Christianity. (Theissen calls these first missionaries "wandering charismatics.") While Matthew 10 and its parallels relate primarily to activity in Israel, the phenomenon is larger than that. Paul and his co-workers traveled extensively in carrying out the mission to Gentile communities, and references in his letters indicate that many other apostles were on the road as well, for better or worse (cf. 1 Cor. 4:9-13; 9; 16:5-18; 2 Cor. 11-12).

Looking back on all of this, the author of Luke-Acts makes the idea of *journey* a central motif in his writing, closely paralleling the mission travels of Jesus, his earliest witnesses, and Paul. From other writings it is evident that itinerant ministry was still going on at the end of the first century, and that one of the problems facing Christian communities was how to discern "false" messengers while remaining hospitable to those who were worthy (cf. Matt. 7:15-23; 1 John 4:1-6; 2 and 3 John; Did. 11-13).

A second point at which Matthew's picture of mission is part of a larger exhibit is his emphasis on the priority of Israel in the drama of the Gospel. As Luke describes the growth of the early church in Acts, he establishes the fact that Israel is *first* in two ways: (1) He builds the entire narrative around the order of mission projected in Acts 1:8, "in Jerusalem, in all Judea and Samaria, and to the ends of the earth." (2) He portrays Paul as a missionary who always begins his work in the synagogue before going to the Gentiles (cf. Acts 13:5, 14-15, 44-48; 14:1; 17:1-2, 10-11).

While Paul himself has little to say about going to synagogues, he clearly affirms the priority of Israel in theological terms. Writing to the Romans, he notes that the gospel is "the power of God for salvation to everyone who has faith, *to the Jew first* and also to the Greek" (Rom. 1:16, emphasis added; cf. Rom. 9—11). There is a fundamental consensus in the NT, therefore, that the promise of salvation must first be fulfilled in the community to whom it was given, before it can be fulfilled for the rest of humankind.

THE TEXT IN THE LIFE OF THE CHURCH

At various times in the story of the church, individuals or groups have tried to model the pattern of itinerant ministry to which Jesus called the twelve. One thinks here of the mendicant friars of the late Middle Ages (for example, the followers of Francis), the Waldensians of the thirteenth century (and later), and to a certain extent the missionary movement of the modern era. Still another way in which the text has functioned in some groups is to undergird the idea of an unsalaried or free ministry (whether at home or on the road).

Undoubtedly there are dangers in trying to copy a pattern that is rooted in the circumstances of an earlier time and place, and that may or may not be pertinent to our own situation. Nevertheless, the text raises some intriguing questions: What does the picture of the vulnerable apostle who travels light say to contemporary evangelists with empires of wealth and technological glitter? Or to sharpen the issue, how should the substance of Christian witness affect the style of Christian witness?

For those of us on the receiving end, the text may ask a somewhat different question: How hospitably do we open ourselves and our communities to those who come as God's messengers—not only those who preach a familiar word, but those who bring a vision of the kingdom that pulls us in a new direction? Today, as in Matthew's day, God's *peace* comes only to those who welcome it.

The Cost of Discipleship

Matthew 10:16-42

PREVIEW

The mission discourse begun in 10:5 continues in 10:16-42, but with sayings that look beyond the sending out of the twelve. Here Jesus offers more general counsel on witness in a hostile world, words appropriate for Christian messengers in any era. In composing this unit, Matthew has assembled various kinds of sayings. Some are words of warning and encouragement, marked by terms such as *beware, have no fear,* and *do not worry* (cf. 16-23, 26-33). Anticipating persecution and martyrdom, these sayings promise endtime blessing to witnesses who remain faithful.

In other sayings the mood is not one of assurance, but rather one of sober reflection. Here the emphasis falls on the costliness of discipleship, and Jesus urges his listeners to consider the consequences (cf. 34-39). Finally, there are sayings that underscore the solidarity of Jesus and his witnesses. He is present with and received through his messengers (vv. 40-42), who in turn can expect the same reception he gets (vv. 24-25). From these various sayings Matthew has constructed a powerful statement on faithful witness.

OUTLINE

Faith on Trial, 10:16-23

A Common Fate, 10:24-25

Fearless Witness, 10:26-33

A Price to Pay, 10:34-39

Channels of Grace, 10:40-42

EXPLANATORY NOTES

Faith on Trial 10:16-23

The relatively hopeful tone of verses 5-15 gives way to a more somber note in verses 16-23, which are based largely on Mark 13:9-13. As Jesus' witnesses go forth, they are warned that they will be placed on trial for their faith. They will appear before Jewish religious authorities and Gentile civil authorities (vv. 17-18), facing charges brought by their opponents, including members of their own families (vv. 21-22; cf. 34-37; Mic. 7:6).

Knowing this will happen, Jesus' witnesses should be shrewd enough to avoid their persecutors where possible (*wise as serpents*; cf. v. 23a). At the same time, they should live in such a way that their conduct testifies in their favor if they are apprehended (*innocent as doves*; cf. Romans 16:19; 1 Peter 3:14-16). As noted earlier, warning is coupled with encouragement in the sayings we find here. Jesus' messengers are assured that judicial hearings provide an opportunity to bear witness (v. 18), that the Holy Spirit will guide them in their testimony (vv. 19-20), and that those who endure suffering now will enjoy salvation at the end (v. 22).

The statement in 10:23b returns to the original topic of the mission of the twelve to Israel and promises that the Son of Man will come before that mission is completed. Unique to Matthew (though cf. Mark 9:1), this saying appears on the surface to be an unfulfilled promise. It is possible, however, that Matthew wants us to view the saying not as a reference to the *parousia* (Jesus' coming at the end), but as a promise of Jesus' coming to the eleven following his resurrection (28:16-20). In this case, the promise concerning mission to Israel in 10:23 has been fulfilled—and at the same time superseded by a new promise in 28:20 concerning the larger mission to every nation: *Remember, I am with you always, to the end of the age.*

A Common Fate 10:24-25

Proverbial sayings on the need for disciples to be like their teacher (or slaves their master) can be found in a number of Christian and rabbinic texts (cf. Matt. 10:24; Luke 6:40; John 13:16; 15:20; bBer. 58b). Here the correspondence stressed is a likeness in rejection and suffering, which picks up the theme of persecution in the preceding verses. Since Jesus encounters hostility and abuse, his disciples can expect more of the same.

As an example, Jesus refers to a controversy yet to be reported

(12:22-30), in which his opponents accuse him of sorcery and attribute his powers to *Beelzebul*. Beelzebul was originally the name of a Philistine god (cf. 2 Kings 1:2, Beelzebub) and was one of many names given to Satan in the intertestamental period. Since the name itself means "head of the house" or "lord of the dwelling," Jesus is actually making a pun in 10:25b: If persons call the head of (God's) house the head of (Satan's) house, how much more will they discredit the rest of the household?

Fearless Witness 10:26-33

Like the earlier sayings in verses 16-23, the sayings in 26-33 offer encouragement in the face of persecution and martyrdom (cf. Luke 12:2-9). The opening words on what is *covered up* and what is *known* may originally have dealt with the revelation of good and evil in the endtime. For Matthew, however, they serve as an appeal to fearless witness: What Jesus has revealed to his disciples in private instruction, they are now to proclaim openly for all to hear.

In spite of the fact that this will arouse opposition, Jesus tells his witnesses not to be intimidated. No less than three times he urges them to *have no fear* (vv. 26, 28a, 31), supporting this appeal with two arguments: (1) The power of persecutors to destroy life is after all a *limited* power. (2) The One who wields ultimate power over life and death does not view our life cheaply (cf. 6:25-34). The only prospect that should evoke fear in the disciple is being unfaithful, which cuts one off from the giver of life.

All of this comes to a conclusion in verses 32-33, in which we again find the imagery of trials and courts. According to Jesus, the conduct of his witnesses before earthly tribunals will determine what happens at the tribunal of the final judgment. At that time, Jesus will claim or *acknowledge* those who have publicly affirmed their solidarity with him, but will disavow any relationship with those who have disowned him. In its earliest form, the pronouncement here may have been a Son of Man saying (cf. Luke 12:8-9; Mark 8:38). In Matthew's version, however, the pronoun *I* takes the place of the phrase *Son of Man,* making it all the clearer that judgment rests with *Jesus*. To be a faithful advocate of Jesus before humanity, therefore, is to know that Jesus will be our advocate at the end.

A Price to Pay 10:34-39

As noted above in the preview of the unit, verses 34-39 stress the high cost of following Jesus. Matthew has combined several shorter sayings here (cf. Luke 12:49-53; 14:25-33; 17:33). In the first saying (vv. 34-36), Jesus speaks of the conflict (*sword*) that his mission evokes and contrasts this with the peace expected in the messianic era (cf. Isa. 9:2-6). The source of this conflict is the need to decide for or against Jesus, which divides households right down the middle. As a result, family members may turn against each other, a situation described with language from Micah 7:6 (cf. v. 21).

The second saying (vv. 37-38) continues to address the topic of family opposition, making it clear that discipleship must take precedence over all other relationships (cf. the even stronger language in Luke 14:26). In this saying we find the first of two references in Matthew to taking up one's *cross* (cf. 16:24). Here the metaphor denotes a readiness to endure family hostility—and the violent end to which that ultimately might lead. The final saying, on finding and losing one's life (v. 39), is found in one form or another in all four of the gospels (cf. Mark 8:35; Luke 17:33; John 12:25). According to Jesus, faithful witnesses who endure martyrdom will find life anew in the kingdom. Those who deny Jesus to preserve their lives, however, will lose the life that matters most.

Channels of Grace 10:40-42

In the sayings that conclude the mission discourse, Matthew returns to the theme of the reception of Jesus' messengers (cf. vv. 10-15). The commissioning story in one of Matthew's sources apparently ended on a similar note (cf. Luke 10:16), and Matthew has augmented the saying there with related pronouncements on receiving Jesus (cf. Mark 9:37, 41; John 13:20; 12:44-45). With these various sayings Matthew underscores the significance of the disciples' mission: Jesus is active in and through his messengers, and the response to his representatives is a response to Jesus himself (cf. 25:31-46!), and ultimately a response to God.

The idea expressed here reflects the traditional Jewish view that "a man's emissary is like the man himself" (Ber. 5:5). For Matthew, the messengers to whom this applies include not only the apostles, but *prophets* (later missionaries), the *righteous* (most likely elders or teachers in a congregation), and the *little ones* (the least of Jesus' followers). To respond to these envoys with hospitality (even with *a cup of cold water*) is to ensure one's own *reward,* that is, a place in the life of the kingdom yet to come.

THE TEXT IN BIBLICAL CONTEXT

The sayings in Matthew 10 about the persecuted messenger belong to a tradition that spans the OT and NT. Its roots lie with the prophets of ancient Israel, who were well acquainted with rejection and hostility. "Jerusalem, Jerusalem, the city that kills the prophets and stones those who are sent to it!" (Luke 13:34; cf. Jer. 26:20-23; 2 Chron. 24:20-22; Luke 11:47-51; Acts 7:52; Heb. 11:32-38). Since the prophets met with persecution, both Jesus and his messengers can expect a similar fate (cf. Matt. 5:12; 21:33-41; 22:1-6; 23:29-36; John 15:18-20; 1 Thess. 2:14-15). The story of the spreading Christian witness in Acts is thus sprinkled generously with accounts of arrest, trial, imprisonment, and martyrdom (cf. 5:17-42; 6:8—8:1; and 21:27—26:32). And a letter written to believers in Asia Minor near the end of the first century notes that they "have had to suffer various trials" (1 Pet. 1:6; cf. 4:12—5:11), perhaps the same trials that beset the churches addressed in Revelation.

Wherever the theme of the persecuted witness appears in the NT, we find several important subthemes: (1) The coming of God's kingdom evokes strong opposition and conflict in the world. (2) Faithfulness to God in the midst of this conflict can be a costly matter. (3) Suffering links believers with Jesus, whose faithfulness in suffering provides a model for his followers. (4) God is aware of the trials of the faithful, and is in fact present with them in their ordeal. (5) Those who endure suffering and whose witness remains steadfast will be rewarded for their faithfulness. Each of these subthemes is evident in the theology of mission in Matthew 10, a theology in which discipleship, sending, and suffering are closely linked.

THE TEXT IN THE LIFE OF THE CHURCH

Persecution of Christians in the NT era tended to be local and sporadic. Later, however, there are periods in which persecution became more thoroughgoing and widespread. One thinks of the suffering of the church under the emperor Diocletian in the early fourth century, of the violence of Christians against each other in the sixteenth and seventeenth centuries, and of the harassment of Christians in our own time where the church has opposed tyranny and injustice.

In these and other circumstances, Matthew 10 has proven to be a powerful resource for strengthening those facing persecution. So, for example, we find numerous references to this chapter in classic Anabaptist works such as the *Martyrs Mirror* and Menno Simons' "Cross of the Saints." For all of us, the text serves as a reminder that the message of the kingdom is not always received with joy and openness. Instead, it arouses enmity and opposition, even in societies supposedly friendly to the church. When that happens, Jesus calls for witness that remains faithful, whatever the cost.

Part 3

Israel Responds to Jesus

Matthew 11:1—16:20

PREVIEW

The focus of attention in the first ten chapters of Matthew is Jesus' calling as God's Son (1:1—4:16) and the way Jesus' messianic mission begins to take shape in Galilee (4:17—10:42). In the new section that begins at 11:1, we learn how various persons and groups in Israel *respond* to Jesus' mission. The unhappy theme which dominates this section is the rejection of Jesus by the greater part of Israel. Because of their hardness of heart (13:15), the people fail to comprehend Jesus' teaching (13:13-14), are unresponsive to his mighty works (11:20-24), and take offense at him (13:53-58). The reaction of the leaders is even more antagonistic. Their attitude is consistently critical (12:1-14; 15:1-20), they refuse to acknowledge Jesus' divine authority (12:22-45; 16:1-4), and they begin to plot his destruction (12:14).

Fortunately, there is a group of persons who respond to Jesus in a quite different manner, the small band of Jesus' disciples. Unlike the others, they know who Jesus really is (11:25-27; 14:28-33; 16:13-17), understand Jesus' message and mission (13:11, 16-17), and are ready to do what God commands (12:46-50). They thus become the foundation of a new community (16:18), to whom Jesus gives the keys of the kingdom (16:19).

Throughout this portrayal of faith and unfaith, the issue of Jesus' messianic identity is constantly before us. John the Baptist raises the question at the outset when he asks: *Are you the one who is to come, or are we to wait for another?* (11:3). And at the end of the section we find twin questions: *Who do people say that the Son of Man is? . . . Who do you say that I am?* (16:13, 15).

Lest there be any doubt, the correct answer to the question of identity is supplied at several points. It is found in the messianic witness of Jesus' deeds (11:4-6), in Jesus' self-identification with divine Wisdom (11:28-30), in Jesus' fulfillment of the servant role described in Isaiah (12:15-21), in the implications of the miracles of feeding (14:13-21; 15:32-39), and in the preliminary confession of the disciples at sea (14:28-33). Not until the episode at Caesarea Philippi, however, do we find the definitive statement. It is there that Simon Peter, responding to Jesus' question, utters the classic confession of faith: *You are the Messiah, the Son of the living God* (16:16).

In terms of literary composition, we can delineate three larger blocks of material within 11:1—16:20. The first of these, 11:1—12:50, consists of stories and sayings illustrating Jesus' authority and Israel's refusal to accept that authority. Equally topical in character is the collection of parables in 13:1-52, all of which deal with *the kingdom of heaven,* and which only the disciples are able to comprehend. In the third subsection, 13:53—16:20, Matthew begins to follow the Markan narrative rather closely (cf. Mark 6:1—8:30), a narrative in which we continue to find both believing and unbelieving responses to Jesus' ministry.

OUTLINE

Faith and Unfaith, Part 1, 11:1—12:50

11:1-19	John the Baptist and Jesus
11:20-30	Who Receives Wisdom?
12:1-21	Jesus and the Sabbath
12:22-37	By What Power?
12:38-50	Show Us a Sign

Many Things in Parables, 13:1-52

13:1-35	Secrets of the Kingdom
13:36-52	Disciples and the Kingdom

Faith and Unfaith, Part 2, 13:53—16:20

13:53-14:12	Unwelcome Prophets
14:13-36	Mercy and Majesty
15:1-20	Who Really Is Defiled?
15:21-39	Compassion with No Boundaries
16:1-20	The True Israel

Matthew 11:1—12:50

Faith and Unfaith, Part 1

PREVIEW

When we read the account of Jesus' ministry in 4:17—10:42, it is easy to identify with the reaction of the crowds. Like them, we marvel at the authority with which Jesus teaches and heals (cf. 7:28-29; 9:8) and sense that something unparalleled is happening in Israel (9:33). Such a mission has every right to succeed. This, however, is not to be.

In the same chapters that tell of popular acclaim, we find hints of rejection. The residents of Gadara beg Jesus to leave their country (8:34). Jewish leaders accuse Jesus of blasphemy, sorcery, and keeping bad company (9:2-3, 11, 34). And Jesus himself laments the lack of faith in Israel (8:10-12). The same note is sounded in Jesus' teaching to his messengers in chapter 10. While some homes and towns will be receptive to the good news (10:12-13, 40-42), a hostile response is just as likely (10:14-15, 24-25).

The stories and sayings in chapters 11—12 build on these earlier hints of rejection and portray the scope of Israel's unfaith (cf. comments above on the larger section, 11:1—16:20). Early in the first unit of material (11:1-19), Jesus encourages those assessing his ministry not to reject him (v. 6). The units that follow, however, attest that rejection is precisely what takes place. Unmoved by either Jesus or John the Baptist, the cities of Galilee refuse to repent (11:16-30), while the scribes and the Pharisees fault Jesus and his disciples for violating the Sabbath (12:1-21), attribute Jesus' miracles to demonic power (12:22-37), and insist that Jesus validate his mission with a sign (12:38-50).

As noted above, it is only among the disciples that we find a different response. Through God's revelation, these *infants* perceive what *the wise* fail to perceive (11:25-27), and say yes to God's will (12:46-50). In a story that is predominantly a story of unfaith, therefore, they signal the continuing possibility of faith.

John the Baptist and Jesus

Matthew 11:1-19

PREVIEW

In our comments on Matthew 3:1-12, we noted the interest of the early church in John the Baptist and his relationship to Jesus. That interest is attested in the unit before us, an expanded edition of a collection of material used by both Matthew and Luke (cf. Luke 7:18-35; 16:16). The three vignettes included in this collection deal in turn with Jesus as the coming one proclaimed by John (11:1-6), John as the forerunner of Jesus who sets things in motion (11:7-15), and the reception of John and Jesus by their contemporaries (11:16-19).

Stylistically, there are several features that serve to link the three vignettes, which originally were likely separate pieces of tradition: (1) Each of the episodes uses *who* or *what* questions to pose the issue under discussion (cf. verses 3, 7-9, 16). (2) There are references to the *coming* of John and/or Jesus in each of the accounts (cf. verses 3, 14, 18-19). (3) The unit begins and ends with statements about Jesus' deeds, the two statements forming an inclusion (cf. verses 2, 19).

For Matthew, this material was well-suited to introduce the section before us. First of all, the question that John raises in verse 3 is the question that all of Israel must answer. It thus sets the stage for the responses to Jesus and his mission in the narratives to follow. Second, the picture of *this generation* in verses 16-19 makes it clear that Israel's response to Jesus is one of rejection. This is the theme that Matthew wants to highlight in the stories ahead, and the parable of the children in the marketplace allows him to set the tone at the outset.

OUTLINE

Who Is Jesus? 11:1-6

Who Is John? 11:7-15

How Were They Received? 11:16-19

EXPLANATORY NOTES

Who Is Jesus? 11:1-6

Verse 1 is transitional; a typical Matthean formula links the preceding discourse of Jesus with the story to follow (cf. 7:28-29; 13:53; 19:1; 26:1). To our surprise, Matthew does not tell us how the twelve fared on their mission to the towns of Israel (cf. 10:5ff.). We hear instead of the resumption of Jesus' own activity, news of which has reached John the Baptist in prison (v. 2, cf. 4:12; 14:3-12; Luke 7:18-23).

Most translations paraphrase the underlying Greek text of 11:2, which states that John hears of *the deeds of the Messiah,* the deeds depicted in the preceding chapters. Unlike the narrator who formulates these words, John himself has yet to perceive the messianic significance of Jesus' deeds. Jesus' activity does not quite measure up to the fiery program that John assigned to *the coming one* (cf. 3:11-12). The cataclysmic final judgment has not occurred. So it is that John sends followers to ask whether faith in Jesus is misplaced faith: Are you God's Messiah, or shall we keep on looking (v. 3)?

Jesus' answer to John in verses 4-5 is indirect and suggestive. Rather than give John any new data, Jesus invites John to look at what he already knows about Jesus' work in the light of Scripture. From the book of Isaiah, Jesus describes his deeds with language promising the salvation of God's people (cf. Isa. 35:5-6; 29:18-19; 26:19; 61:1-2). The list of deeds climaxes with a reference to Jesus' preaching, his proclamation of hope to those who need it most, *the poor* (cf. 5:3; Luke 4:18-19; Isa. 61:1).

If John views Jesus' work in this light, he will find the answer to his question. He will discover that Jesus is fulfilling God's promise for the future, even if the shape of fulfillment differs from John's expectations. Jesus' reply to John concludes in verse 6 with a beatitude, a type of saying found elsewhere (cf. 5:3-12; 24:46; Luke 11:27-28). Speaking to all potential followers and not merely to John, Jesus urges persons not to stumble over the fact that he doesn't fit their preconceptions of messiahship: *Blessed* are those who do not *wait for another,* but who in faith accept what God is doing through Jesus.

Who Is John? 11:7-15

Having established that Jesus is indeed *the coming one,* the text shifts our attention to the one who precedes Jesus: Who is John the Baptist? Jesus invites the crowds to reflect on John's role through the rhetorical questions he poses in verses 7-9, each set of which begins: *What did you go out to see?* Or: *Why did you go out? To see. . . ?* However we translate the questions, the issue is what drew the people to the wilderness of Judea (cf. 3:1). Was the attraction only a natural phenomenon—perhaps the tall cane grass of the Jordan valley blowing in the wind? Hardly. Or did the people expect to find a fancy dresser, decked out in royal linen and silk? Here the crowd must certainly have laughed, knowing that John's attire consisted of a hairy mantle and leather girdle (3:4)!

Finally, in verse 9, Jesus identifies the real attraction. The crowds flocked to the wilderness to see *a prophet,* a messenger of God. In fact, Jesus adds, John was *more than a prophet,* one who not only *spoke* of things to come, but who also played a part in their coming. This is confirmed by John's location in the wilderness, which itself had messianic significance (cf. 24:26; 3:1; 4:1; Isa. 35; 40:3-11; 1QS 8:12-14).

In the sayings that follow, Jesus comments further on John's role and stature. Two of these sayings, verses 10 and 11, were already part of the vignette on John in the tradition Matthew received (cf. Luke 7:24-28). The proof text in verse 10 comes from Malachi 3:1 (cf. Mal. 4:5), but is modified with language from Exodus 23:20. In this adapted form of the text, the messenger promised by God is no longer God's own forerunner ("before *me*") but the forerunner of the Messiah (before *you*). And John the Baptist *is the one about whom it is written.*

According to verse 11, John's stature exceeded that of all his forebears (*born of women* is a poetic way of referring to humanity; cf. Job 14:1; Gal. 4:4). Even that greatness will be eclipsed by the grandeur of life in the kingdom, which the *least* of Jesus' followers will enjoy. But that in no way diminishes John's importance in the drama of God's activity in history.

Building on all of this, Matthew appends a related saying about John and the kingdom in verses 12-13 (cf. Luke 16:16), then supplies a postscript on John's role in verses 14-15. The saying in 11:12-

13 speaks of violence that attends the coming of the kingdom. In an earlier form of this saying, violence may have been a metaphor for the forceful coming of the kingdom, which Matthew and Luke interpreted in different ways. Luke 16:16 relates the saying to the *preaching* of the kingdom—and to the forceful enthusiasm of those who seek to enter the kingdom. While some scholars find a similar positive thrust in Matthew 11:12 (cf. NIV), Jesus' words here likely convey a darker meaning: God's reign is fiercely assailed by those who oppose its coming, opponents like Herod (who executed John) and the Pharisees (who seek to destroy Jesus).

In any case, the advent of the kingdom begins with John, who sets in motion the events that fulfill the hope of *all the prophets and the law.* More specifically, John fulfills Israel's hope in the return of Elijah (vv. 14-15, cf. 17:10-13; Mal. 4:5-6; Sir. 48:10). Elijah's role was to call the people back to covenant relationship with God. To accept John as Elijah requires an act of faith (just as faith plays a part in receiving Jesus as the Christ). And Jesus calls for such faith when he appeals to the crowd to *hear* what he has revealed (cf. 13:9; 19:12d).

How Were They Received? 11:16-19

Jesus continues to speak to the crowd in the sayings we find in verses 16-19 (cf. Luke 7:31-35). Here the subject addressed is the crowd itself, whom Jesus refers to as *this people* or *this generation.* In a short but poignant parable, Jesus compares his contemporaries to children sitting in the marketplace. A few of the children have been trying to get a game started, either a wedding game or a funeral game. (Like the games of children throughout the world, the games of Jewish children mimic adult life.) No matter what is proposed, however, some persons object: "We don't want to play *that*!" And the result is no game. Rather than play, the children sit and complain.

This is the way it has gone, Jesus says, as John and I labored among you. When John sang his mournful tune and abstained from the normal pleasures of life, you wrote him off as strange and possessed. When I, however, played a joyous song of salvation, inviting all to eat and drink at a table of grace, you found fault with that too and called me a reveler (cf. 11:19; Deut. 21:20). Like the children in the parable, the generation of John and Jesus refused to play along. They rejected God's appeal, no matter how it was presented.

Nevertheless, Jesus tells us in 19c, the wisdom Israel rejects will be *vindicated.* Wisdom here refers to divine Wisdom, which is linked elsewhere with the sending of prophets, and which Matthew identifies with Jesus himself (cf. Luke 11:49/Matt. 23:34). In the parallel passage in Luke 7:35, Wisdom is vindicated "by her *children*," by those who recognize God's voice and so receive God's messengers (cf. Prov. 8:32; Sir. 4:11; John 1:9-13). According to Matthew, however, Wisdom is vindicated by her *deeds*, the deeds of the Messiah mentioned above in verse 3. These deeds speak for themselves and glorify the One who does them. (In some manuscripts Matthew 11:19 has the Lukan wording *by her children,* and is so rendered in the KJV, but the best manuscripts support the reading *by her deeds.*) Whether by deeds done or disciples made, Wisdom leaves a witness that vindicates God in spite of Israel's unbelief.

THE TEXT IN BIBLICAL CONTEXT

As already observed in our notes on the text, OT language of hope and promise abounds in Matthew 11:1-19. There are images of salvation drawn from the book of Isaiah (v. 5). There is the promise from Malachi of a messenger who prepares the way for another (v. 10). And there is a reference to the return of Elijah prophesied by both Malachi and Sirach (v. 14). One of the ways the text relates to the larger biblical tradition, therefore, is in terms of promise and fulfillment. It links the work of John and Jesus to certain expectations of Israel for the age to come.

In its portrayal of the relationship *between* John and Jesus, Matthew 11 invites comparison with passages in the other Gospels. All four Gospels (and Acts as well) cast John the Baptist in the role of Jesus' forerunner (cf. TBC for 3:1-12). Each of the Gospels, however, develops this theme in its own way, with a view to issues important in the author's community. Walter Wink offers a good summary of the different nuances in the Gospel accounts (Wink, 1968:110-111; cf. Mark 9:9-13; Luke 1:5-80; John 1:6-8, 19-34):

> *Mark* portrays John as Elijah incognito whose sufferings prepare the way of the Lord and serve as an example to persecuted Christians at Rome. *Matthew* uses John as an ally of Jesus against the hostile front of opposition he was encountering in the Judaism of his day. . . . *Luke* accepts the traditional picture of John as the forerunner with minor changes and adapts it to his panoramic conception of [salvation history]. And finally, *the Fourth Evangelist* holds up before the church the representation of John as a "type" of the ideal Christian evangelist, whose function it is to witness that Jesus is the Christ. (italics mine)

THE TEXT IN THE LIFE OF THE CHURCH

As a text of the *church*, the unit before us could be approached in a variety of ways. We might survey the attention John the Baptist has received across the centuries, from the veneration of John by remnants of his followers (and later still by the Mandaean sect) to the depiction of John in classic Christian art and drama. Again, we might explore the way the contrasting lifestyles of John and Jesus are picked up in Christian piety—and ask whether we ourselves are more indebted to John or to Jesus.

The reflection that may be most pertinent, however, is on the way the text poses the issue of faith. According to Matthew 11, faith sees the same events in history that everyone else sees, but sees them in a quite different light. Where some see only a deluded desert fanatic, others see Elijah. Where some see only a wonder-worker chased by crowds, others see the dawning of the kingdom. Where some see only a man who likes to party, others see the Messiah offering fellowship with God. For every generation, the question is the same: As we behold the story of Jesus, and as we interpret our own story, *what do we see*?

Who Receives Wisdom?

Matthew 11:20-30

PREVIEW

Matthew 11:20-30 is a two-panel unit, contrasting the judgment coming on those who reject Jesus with the *rest* promised to those who receive Jesus. In the first panel (vv. 20-24), we find a *woe-saying* directed to the towns of Galilee, rebuking the people for their failure to repent (cf. the longer series of woe-sayings in chap. 23). As the GNB paraphrase suggests, the words *Woe to you* convey the sense of *How terrible it will be for you!* This type of saying has its roots in funeral dirges and songs taunting fallen enemies (cf. Num. 21:27-30). Later, as a part of prophetic speech, woe-sayings are used to announce judgment and destruction yet to come (cf. Isa. 5:8-23; 30:1-5). There are numerous examples in the OT of woe-sayings against cities or lands such as we find in 11:21-24 (cf. Isa. 28:1-4; Jer. 13:27; Ezek. 24:9; Amos 6:1-3; 2 Esd. 15:46-47; Sib. Ora. 3:303).

In the second panel of the unit (vv. 25-30), we find sayings with a wisdom flavor about Jesus and those who *come to* him. Here the emphasis falls on knowledge of God and God's mysterious purposes—and on Jesus' role as the mediator of such knowledge. The language used in these sayings reflects both the broader wisdom tradition of Proverbs, Sirach, and the Wisdom of Solomon, and the concern for wisdom about the endtime in Jewish apocalyptic literature (cf. Dan. 2:19-23; 2 Esd. 4:21ff.; 1 Enoch 60:10). Similar language is found in the writings of the Qumran community, especially in the texts of the Hymn Scroll.

OUTLINE

A Pronouncement of Woe, 11:20-24

A Promise of Blessing, 11:25-30

EXPLANATORY NOTES

A Pronouncement of Woe 11:20-24

The subject of Jesus' messianic deeds introduced in 11:2 (cf. v. 19) remains the topic of discussion in 11:20-24. Here Matthew refers more specifically to Jesus' mighty works or *deeds of power* (cf. Mark 6:2; Acts 2:22). Behind the phrase *deeds of power* lies the Greek word for *power, dunamis*, which in this context suggests the power of God at work in Jesus' miracles. In spite of this display of divine power, we are told that the people *did not repent* (cf. John 12:37). It is this that moves Jesus to utter the saying in verses 21-24 (cf. Luke 10:12-15), which in Matthew consists of two parallel pronouncements (21-22, 23-24). Each pronouncement contains:

(1) A *woe* statement or its equivalent (21a, 23a).
(2) An *if . . . then* statement (21b, 23b).
(3) An *I tell you* statement drawing the consequences (22, 24).

Of the two towns named in verse 21, little is known of Chorazin except its probable location two miles NNW of Capernaum. Bethsaida is mentioned several times in the Gospels (Mark 8:22-26; Luke 9:10-17; John 1:44; 12:21) and was a fishing village on the NE corner of the Sea of Galilee, east of the Jordan. The Phoenician cities of Tyre and Sidon, with which Chorazin and Bethsaida are unfavorably compared in verses 21b-22, were famous for their wealth and power, but condemned by the prophets for their pride (cf. Isa. 23; Ezek. 27—28).

In the second pronouncement, in verses 23-24, Jesus takes language from a dirge mocking a fallen ruler's delusions of grandeur (Isa. 14:13-15) and applies it to Capernaum, the city that served as the base for his ministry. Here the city of comparison is Sodom, which together with Gomorrah appears as a paradigm of evil and God's judgment on evil in the OT (cf. Gen. 18:16-21; 19:24-28; Isa. 1:9-10; Ezek. 16:48-50; Amos 4:11). To appreciate the force of these unfavorable comparisons, we must remember that Tyre, Sidon, and Sodom were all *foreign* cities. What Jesus is saying, then, is that *Gentiles* repent more readily than Israel (cf. 12:41-42), and that accordingly they will fare better than God's own people at the judgment.

A Promise of Blessing 11:25-30

In the wisdom sayings of verses 25-30, Matthew gives an expanded version of a saying also found in Luke 10:21-22. Hymnlike in character, this material exhibits a three-part structure:

(1) A prayer of thanksgiving for God's revelation (25-26).
(2) A statement about Jesus' role as revealer (27).
(3) An invitation by Jesus to receive his instruction (28-30).

The formula of thanksgiving in verses 25-26 is reminiscent of Sirach 51:1 (cf. 1QH 11:28-30). The idea of the simple discerning what the wise fail to perceive is likewise a familiar biblical theme (cf. Isa. 29:14; Ps. 119:130; Wisd. of Sol. 10:21; 1 Cor. 1:18-31). Here the knowledge to be disclosed is the meaning of Jesus' messianic deeds; the *infants* to whom God reveals *these things* are the disciples; and *the wise and the intelligent* from whom this knowledge is hidden are the scribes and the Pharisees. All of this, Jesus says, is a matter of God's own choosing.

According to verse 27, Jesus plays a pivotal role in the process of revelation. Note the formula of authorization in 11:27a, which appears again at the end of the Gospel (28:18a). There Jesus announces that he has been given *dominion over all*. Here the claim is that Jesus has been granted *knowledge of all*, which he in turn shares with others: God alone knows the divine purpose at work in Jesus' mission; and Jesus alone has access to this divine understanding.

The Father/Son language in which the saying is couched occurs rarely in the synoptic Gospels, but permeates the Fourth Gospel (cf. John 3:34-35; 7:29). Partial parallels for this vocabulary of sonship can be found in texts dealing with the king as God's son (2 Sam. 7:14) and with the righteous individual as God's son (Wisd. of Sol. 2:13-18; Sir. 4:10). At the most profound level, however, the basis for this language is Jesus' intimate relationship with God as *Abba*.

Jesus' invitation to come and learn in verses 28-30 (cf. G. Thom. 90) echoes a number of passages in which Wisdom appeals to persons to receive instruction (cf. Prov. 1:20-23; 8:32—9:6; Sir. 24:19-22). Nowhere is the parallel more striking, however, than in Sirach 51:23-27 (cf. also Jer. 6:16). In Sirach, Wisdom is identified with the Torah (cf. Sir. 24:23-29), and the "yoke" of Wisdom is the yoke of the law of which the rabbis spoke (cf. Aboth 3:5; Acts 15:10).

In Matthew 11, Wisdom is incarnate in Jesus himself, and the *yoke* of Wisdom is a relationship with Jesus in which Torah takes on a new quality. Unlike the teachers of the law who lay heavy burdens on others (23:2-4), Jesus offers Torah (teaching) that lightens our load and leads to peace and satisfaction. With him we find the *rest* of completion or fulfillment, a Sabbath rest like God enjoyed on the seventh day of creation (Gen. 2:1-3), and a foretaste of endtime peace and wholeness (cf. 2 Bar. 73:1; Heb. 4:1-11).

THE TEXT IN BIBLICAL CONTEXT

In our comments above, we have already identified some of the strands of the OT taken up in our text, especially that of the wisdom tradition. Other linkages to be noted include the focus on divine revelation elsewhere in Matthew (cf. 10:26-27; 13:10-17; 16:17; 18:20; 28:20) and a similar emphasis in other NT writings. The earliest witness to an emerging theology of revelation indebted to the wisdom tradition is 1 Corinthians 1:18—2:16, where Paul is addressing a community divided by competing claims of true spiritual understanding. While agreeing with the Corinthians that the Spirit bestows revelation and understanding, Paul stresses that this wisdom is linked to Christ and the cross, and so hardly a matter for human boasting.

Later writings in which a Christian theology of revelation is developed more fully include Ephesians and John. In the rich prose of Ephesians we hear of the mysterious purposes of God fulfilled in Christ, revealed to apostles and prophets, and now made known to the church in "a spirit of wisdom and revelation" (1:17ff.; cf. 1:9-14; 3:1-21). In John we find a hymn based on wisdom motifs praising the Word or *logos* (1:1-18), long discourses in which Jesus speaks as the divine revealer (cf. 5:19-47), and sayings about the Spirit who carries on Jesus' revealing activity in the church (cf. 14:25-26; 16:12-15). The view of the church as a community of revelation, therefore, is a view which is central to NT faith.

THE TEXT IN THE LIFE OF THE CHURCH

Together with related texts, the *revelation* sayings in Matthew 11:20-30 helped to shape the Christology of the church. In some instances, the end result was less than desirable. One of the dangers in focusing on Christ as the revealer of truth is that we can construe salvation solely in terms of spiritual understanding, and lose sight of God's concern for history and the world. This is exactly what happened in the early heresy known as *Gnosticism*, in which Christ was seen as bringing self-knowledge that liberates us from the earthly realm and reunites us with the divine.

Among the church fathers who opposed Gnosticism, texts like Matthew 11:25-30 exerted a different kind of influence. For them too, the language of wisdom and sonship witnessed to Jesus' unique relationship with God, but without implying that Jesus is only a divine visitor in our midst. In the creedal statements of the early councils, therefore, we find an attempt to uphold Jesus' deity *and* humanity, and to underscore the fact that redemption occurs *in history*. Today as then, Jesus' appeal to come and learn from him is not a summons to leave the world, but an invitation to discover the will of God that transforms the world.

Jesus and the Sabbath

Matthew 12:1-21

PREVIEW

The word that best describes the narratives Matthew has assembled in chapter 12 is that of conflict or controversy. One of the points of controversy is observance of the Sabbath, which is the topic of the two stories in 12:1-14. Taken from an earlier collection of conflict stories in Mark 2:1—3:6 (cf. 2:23-28; 3:1-6), these accounts read like rabbinic disputes about the law. In each of the episodes, the Pharisees question Jesus on what is *lawful* on the Sabbath, to which Jesus replies with arguments of various kinds. The third vignette in the unit (12:15-21) does not deal with a particular point of contention, but rather reflects on how Jesus moves away from conflict and attends to his mission. Here the material presented consists of a brief narrative summary, followed by a lengthy fulfillment quotation.

From an editorial standpoint, it is not hard to see why Matthew chose to introduce conflict stories at this juncture in the narrative.

The stories illustrate the gathering storm of opposition to Jesus, and so contribute to the overall theme of Israel's rejection of Jesus. Nor is it surprising that the first two conflict stories deal with Jesus' attitude toward the *Sabbath*. As others have observed, the topic of Sabbath picks up Jesus' promise of *rest* in 11:28-30. And in the approach Jesus takes to the Sabbath, he demonstrates how the yoke he asks his followers to assume is in fact an *easy* yoke. Rather than impose burdensome regulations, he frees persons to enjoy the Sabbath rest the law intended.

OUTLINE

Hunger on the Sabbath, 12:1-8

Healing on the Sabbath, 12:9-14

A Low-Profile Messiah, 12:15-21

EXPLANATORY NOTES

Hunger on the Sabbath 12:1-8

Keeping the Sabbath has always been an important part of Jewish practice, one rooted in the Decalogue (cf. Exod. 20:8-11; Deut. 5:12-15), and defined with great care in rabbinic teaching. According to the Mishnah, thirty-nine kinds of work are forbidden on the Sabbath, including reaping and winnowing (cf. Shab. 7:2). When the Pharisees, therefore, observe Jesus' disciples plucking grain (likely wheat or barley) on the Sabbath (12:1-2), they accuse the disciples of breaking the Sabbath. (On any other day, plucking wheat in a neighbor's grainfield would have been permitted; cf. Deut. 23:25.) In the Markan account which is Matthew's source here (cf. Mark 2:23-28/Luke 6:1-15), Jesus' reply defending the disciples consists of one basic argument. In Matthew 12:1-8, that argument is supplemented with two others, and all three appeal to Scripture.

The first argument (vv. 3-4) is haggadic in character, based on an anecdote or story (haggadah). Found in 1 Samuel 21:1-6, the story cited by Jesus relates how David and his soldiers satisfied their hunger by eating holy bread in the tabernacle, bread which only priests were supposed to eat (cf. Lev. 24:5-9). Here we find a precedent for a servant of God permitting his followers to set aside a ritual law because of hunger.

The second argument (vv. 5-6) is based on a law or rule (halakah), and so can be labeled halakic. With Numbers 28:9-10 and similar texts in mind, Jesus notes that priests are authorized to perform duties in the temple on the Sabbath without incurring guilt. If then, Jesus argues, there is an exemption from Sabbath law in the lesser case of priests serving in the temple, how much more so in the case of Jesus and his co-workers, who are serving in a cause that is *greater than the temple.*

In the third and final argument (v. 7), Jesus invites his opponents to consider the true intent of Sabbath law. Citing Hosea 6:6 (a passage quoted earlier in 9:13), Jesus argues that mercy and human well-being are what Sabbath is all about, not ritual correctness. Therefore, it is acceptable to pluck grain to relieve hunger on the Sabbath.

Having argued his case, Jesus goes on in verse 8 to state the authority with which he addresses the Sabbath issue. As the one who has come to fulfill the law and the prophets, he is *lord of the Sabbath* and the rules that govern it. He thus can redefine the way that those who follow him should keep the Sabbath.

Healing on the Sabbath 12:9-14

In the second conflict story, the issue is *healing* on the Sabbath (cf. Mark 3:1-6/Luke 6:6-11). We can assume from the number of such stories in the Gospels that healing on the Sabbath was a major point of contention between Jesus and his opponents (cf. Luke 13:10-17; 14:1-6; John 5:1-18; 9). According to rabbinic law, it was permissible to administer relief on the Sabbath to someone whose life was in danger (cf. Yoma 8:6; Mek. Exod. 22:2; 23:13), but not to one afflicted with a less serious illness. Jesus, however, was not confined by such distinctions, as the healing of a man with a withered hand clearly illustrates.

The setting for the story is a synagogue, which Jesus visits on the same Sabbath mentioned in 12:1-8. (Note how Matthew puts distance between church and synagogue by referring to *their* synagogue; cf. 4:23; 10:17; 13:54.) Once again the story is cast in the form of a dispute, in which Jesus responds to a hostile question from his opponents (v. 10). The argument Jesus develops in verses 11-12 resembles the case he makes in another Sabbath controversy (Luke 14:3-5) and may well be taken from that episode. In any event, Jesus argues here in typical fashion from the lesser to the greater: If it is right to help a *sheep* on the Sabbath, how much more so a human being?

Interestingly, not all Jewish teachers would have accepted Jesus' basic premise. Opinion was sharply divided on how much help one could offer on the Sabbath to an injured or endangered animal (cf. bShab. 128b; CD 11:13-14). Jesus, however, does not base his case on a rabbinic position, but addresses his hearers more pragmatically: What if *your* animal, your one and only animal, fell in a pit on the Sabbath? What would you do?

Having established that it is right *to do good on the Sabbath* (v. 12b), to sheep and humans alike, Jesus proceeds to heal the man whose hand was diseased (v. 13). It is a deed of mercy (cf. v. 7), restoring wholeness to life. In the response of Jesus' opponents, however, a different kind of deed begins to take shape (v. 14). Here, for the first time, we learn of a plot to destroy Jesus, a plot that eventually leads to his arrest and crucifixion.

A Low-Profile Messiah 12:15-21

The brief narrative summary in 12:15-16 is an abbreviated version of Mark 3:7-12. Matthew highlights three things in this summary, including Jesus' withdrawal from conflict with the Pharisees, his healing of all those who followed him, and his command not to publicize his deeds of mercy. In the fulfillment quotation that follows in verses 17-21, each of these three elements is picked up in some way: Thus we are told that God's servant will not wrangle with others (v. 19a). He comes to restore those broken in body and spirit (*bruised reeds* and *smoldering wicks*) rather than crush them in pursuing his own ends (v. 20). And he will not seek publicity for himself as he carries out his mission (v. 19b). For Matthew, every detail of Jesus' ministry is anticipated in Scripture.

The quotation we have been discussing comes from Isaiah 42:1-4, although the form of the text found here does not agree either with the Hebrew text or the LXX. What we have is more like a Christian targum, a paraphrase that interprets the text of Isaiah in the process of quoting it. Along with the phrases mentioned above, there are two elements of the quotation that call for comment: (1) The description of Jesus as God's beloved servant or child (Greek: *pais*) recalls the story of Jesus' baptism in 3:16-17. (2) The references to the servant's mission to the nations or Gentiles indicate that Pharisaic opposition to Jesus will not defeat God's purposes. Whether accepted or rejected by the leaders of Israel, Jesus will *proclaim justice* to the nations beyond Israel: He will reveal God's righteous and saving will, so that all may find and walk in the way of righteousness.

THE TEXT IN BIBLICAL CONTEXT

The debate about the Sabbath in Matthew 12:1-21 is a debate growing out of a long and rich biblical tradition. While the origin of the Sabbath is somewhat uncertain, its importance for Israel's life is attested in many ways. One strand of tradition relates the Sabbath to the story of creation, in which God himself rests on the seventh day, making that day a holy or special day (cf. Gen. 2:1-3; Exod. 20:8-11). In Deuteronomy the Sabbath is linked to God's deliverance of Israel from slavery, the memory of which should lead the people to provide Sabbath rest for every creature in Israel (cf. Deut. 5:12-15; 15:12-18).

Yet a third strand of material speaks of the Sabbath as a sign of the special relationship between God and Israel, a practice that sets Israel apart from other peoples (cf. Exod. 31:12-17; Ezek. 20:12-13). The latter emphasis grew in importance in postexilic Judaism, in which observance of the Sabbath became a badge of Jewish identity in a world controlled by Gentiles.

In the debate between Jesus and his opponents in the Gospels, there is agreement that this Sabbath tradition is important. The issue is not whether persons should *keep* the Sabbath—but *how* to keep the Sabbath. Does one observe the Sabbath by observing rules designed to protect it? Or does one observe the Sabbath by letting it be what God intended? According to Matthew, the Sabbath is a day for the renewal of human life. It is a day for doing good, for practicing God's mercy. The way to *keep* the Sabbath is to let it serve these ends.

THE TEXT IN THE LIFE OF THE CHURCH

The discussion of the Sabbath in the Gospel accounts is a discussion that might have ended in the NT period. With Jesus himself modeling freedom in relation to Sabbath issues, the early church did not feel bound by Jewish practice and soon adopted a new day as its primary day of worship (cf. Acts 20:7; 1 Cor. 16:2; Rev. 1:10). Later, however, Sabbatarian restrictions begin to turn up in conjunction with the Christian Sunday. The first signs of this development appear in the fourth century, when both the emperor and the church forbade or discouraged work on Sunday.

In the churches of the Reformation, Sabbatarian tendencies can be dated from the publication in 1595 of Nicholas Bound's *True Doctrine of the Sabbath*, which equated the Christian Sunday with the Jewish Sabbath. Such a position easily led (though it need not so lead) to Sunday closing laws, to restrictions on Sunday sport and recreation, and to a view of the Lord's day remarkably similar to that of the Pharisees. A different type of Sabbatarian faith is found in those Christian groups who believe that Jesus did not abrogate the traditional Jewish Sabbath, and that the church should still observe the seventh day as its holy day. In the Anabaptist tradition, an early proponent of this position was Andreas Fischer (cf. Liechty, 1988).

For most churches today, austere traditions of Sabbath observance are more a memory than a present reality. In this regard, our situation differs from that in Jesus' day. In another way, however, our situation is much like that of the Jewish community in the first century. We too live in the midst of a Gentile culture that knows little about Sabbath, whether on the seventh day or first day. We are part of a world that never shuts down, in which people are consumed by relentless busyness. In that kind of culture we have to ask afresh the question posed earlier: How do we keep the Sabbath? For us, as for Matthew's church, Jesus provides important clues.

By What Power?

Matthew 12:22-37

PREVIEW

Like the stories in the preceding unit, 12:22-37 presents a conflict or controversy. This time the debate between Jesus and his opponents concerns his work of casting out demons: By what power does Jesus cast out demons from the possessed? In reporting this controversy, Matthew appears to have drawn both on Mark's account of the episode (cf. Mark 3:20-30) and on another version of the same story found in Luke (Luke 11:14-23). In addition, Matthew has incorporated sayings from another context that expand Jesus' reply to his critics (cf. 12:33-37; 7:15-20; Luke 6:43-45). The end product is a narrative with three parts: First, we hear of the deed that leads to the dispute and how it evokes both wonder and criticism (vv. 22-24). Next, we find Jesus' defense and interpretation of his ministry of curing persons so bound (vv. 25-30). Finally, Jesus goes on the offensive, admonishing his critics (vv. 31-37).

OUTLINE

A Controversial Act, 12:22-24

Kingdom Against Kingdom, 12:25-30

The Unforgivable Critic, 12:31-37

EXPLANATORY NOTES

A Controversial Act 12:22-24

The episode that triggers the dispute over Jesus casting out demons is reported with notable brevity (cf. the doublet of the story in 9:32-34). We are provided just enough narrative detail to set the stage for the sayings that follow. What we learn in verses 22-24 is that Jesus is able to heal a demoniac who is both blind and mute (a severe case), and that this raises afresh the question of Jesus' power.

When the text says that the crowds *were amazed,* the verb used suggests that the people were beside themselves with astonishment. They even toy with the possibility that Jesus might be the Messiah. Much different in tone is the assessment of the Pharisees, who continue to appear in the forefront of the opposition. They argue that Jesus' power over demons is that of a sorcerer (note the similar accusation in John 7:20; 8:48; 10:20-21). In their view, Jesus acts as an agent of the devil (cf. the comments on Beelzebul in 10:25).

Kingdom Against Kingdom 12:25-30

Jesus responds to his critics with a variety of arguments. First of all, Jesus replies, it is absurd to think that the one who rules the forces of evil would invite someone to attack those forces (vv. 25-26). Such a course would lead to the collapse of Satan's kingdom. In his second argument (v. 27), Jesus suggests that the position of his critics leaves them vulnerable: If *my* power over demons comes from the devil, Jesus says, what does this say about the exorcists among your own ranks (Greek: *sons*)? (Cf. the account of Jewish exorcists in Acts 19:13-19.)

Finally, Jesus counters the position of the Pharisees with his own interpretation of the power he exhibits (v. 28). According to Matthew, Jesus casts out demons *by the Spirit of God,* by *God's power* (cf. Luke 11:20, "by the finger of God"). If that is so, then *God's reign* is taking shape in and through Jesus' deeds, overcoming the forces of evil. And Jesus' critics are in the position of opposing God's rule!

The sayings in verses 29-30 comment further on the theme of kingdom versus kingdom. Using a brief but vivid parable, Jesus speaks in verse 29 of the binding of a *strong man* and the plundering of his house. The meaning is that Jesus' healing ministry binds or limits Satan's power, liberating those caught in the grip of evil (cf. Isa. 49:24-25). Here is a significant claim: The binding of Satan associated with the last days (cf. Ass. Mos. 10:1; T. Levi 18:1; Rev. 20:2) is already taking place. The saying that follows stresses that there is no neutral ground in the conflict between Jesus and Satan. God's rule is now challenging the reign of evil in the world, and we either support or stand in the way of what God is trying to do.

The Unforgivable Critic 12:31-37

Having defined the *power* by which he acts, Jesus goes on to address the danger of speaking *against* that power. In verses 31-32, Jesus accuses his critics of *blasphemy* (cf. Mark 3:28-30; Luke 12:10; G. Thom. 44). The term *blasphemy* covers a variety of offenses, including slander, cursing God, claiming divine authority for oneself, and other actions disrespectful to God. Here it refers to the words of the Pharisees in verse 24, ascribing Jesus' deeds to the power of Satan rather than God.

In the saying, Jesus distinguishes between two kinds of blasphemy—that which can be forgiven and that which cannot. To be specific, one can speak against *the Son of Man* and be forgiven, but speaking against the Holy Spirit *will not be forgiven, either in this age or in the age to come.* Interpreters differ on the meaning of this distinction. According to some, the saying distinguishes between rejection of Jesus during his ministry to Israel and rejection of Jesus' work as risen Lord through the Holy Spirit. It is more likely, however, that the saying distinguishes between rejection of Jesus as God's messenger and rejection of the One who empowers Jesus. To criticize the *messenger* is a forgivable offense, but to discredit the power of *God* by which the messenger frees and heals is an offense without pardon.

Verses 33-37 continue to address the issue of evil speech, using sayings found earlier in the Sermon on the Mount (cf. 7:16-20; Luke 6:43-45). There Matthew applies the tree and fruit metaphors to the problem of false prophets. Here the diseased trees are the Pharisees who revile Jesus, and bad fruit refers to the words used to revile or criticize. The emphasis in verses 33-35 is on the way the tongue betrays our basic character: People who are evil, who oppose God's purposes in their hearts, will reflect that in evil or malicious language.

In the final two verses, Jesus warns of the consequences for those who utter *careless words,* words that fail to serve a worthy end. Because the words we speak reveal who we are (cf. 15:18-19), God will acquit or condemn us on the basis of our words. For Matthew, this warning applies not only to Jesus' contemporaries, but to later generations as well. It rebukes rabbinic critics of Jesus' community in Matthew's day. And it admonishes the community itself, especially those called to teach (cf. 5:19; James 3:1-12).

THE TEXT IN BIBLICAL CONTEXT

The problem of evil as addressed in the OT is basically a problem between God and humankind. Although we find occasional references to evil or hostile spirits (cf. Lev. 16:6-10; Ps. 91:5-6; Isa. 34:14; 1 Sam. 18:10), there is little evidence of the fascination with the spirit world that characterizes other ancient cultures. Satan appears in a few texts (Job 1—2; 1 Chron. 21:1; Zech. 3:1-2), but as a member of the divine council (cf. Pss. 82:1; 89:7), not as the commander of an evil empire.

The picture begins to change, however, in the postexilic era. Partly because of Israel's diminished power and sense of captivity in a hostile world, and partly due to exposure to the dualism of good and evil spirits in other cultures (especially Persian), increasing attention is paid to the demonic aspect of life. This is reflected in Jewish apocalyptic, where Satan and similar figures are depicted as fallen angels, leading hosts of evil spirits which threaten humankind (cf. 1 Enoch 6—10; Jub. 10:1-14; 11:5; L. Adam 12—17). In this view of the world, God and evil are locked in cosmic conflict until the endtime, when God finally prevails (cf. 1 Enoch 54:5-6; T. Levi 18:12; T. Jud. 25:3).

As a text like Matthew 12:22-37 illustrates, the NT assumes and builds on this approach to the problem of evil. References to demons and evil spirits abound (cf. Matt. 8:28-34; Mark 1:21-28; Luke 10:17-20), and Satan or the devil appears as the evil archenemy of God and the faithful (cf. Luke 22:3; John 8:44; 2 Thess. 2:9; 1 Pet. 5:8). Related concepts occur in several letters ascribed to Paul, where we hear of *principalities and powers* with which God must contend (cf. Rom. 8:38; Eph. 6:12; Col. 2:15).

The most dramatic portrayal of the conflict between God and evil is set forth in the visions of Revelation, the early Christian book that most resembles Jewish apocalyptic. Central to NT faith is the conviction that God challenges and defeats the forces of evil through Jesus Christ. This occurs both through Jesus and his community casting out demons and through Jesus' death and resurrection. It is the latter event that clearly establishes God's lordship over all, freeing God's world from bondage to alien powers.

A second point at which 12:22-37 belongs to a wider family of texts is its discussion of the unforgivable or unpardonable sin. The roots of such a concept can be found in the book of Numbers. There, in the midst of legislation dealing with sin and atonement, the writer refers to those who "highhandedly" defy God and God's command (Num. 15:30-31). Such persons, we are told, "shall be utterly cut off." Building on this tradition, the rabbis argue that those who deny the covenant and repudiate the way of the Torah have no share in the life of the age to come (cf. Aboth 3:12; Yoma Bar. 85b).

In the NT, we find several passages that parallel Jesus' comments on unpardonable blasphemy. First John speaks of "sin that is mortal" (1 John 5:16-17), sin so grave that it leads to death and destruction. And the author of Hebrews writes of the impossibility of restoring those who receive the Holy Spirit and then commit apostasy (Heb. 6:4-8). When we compare the various statements in this family of texts, we see that all are dealing with extreme circumstances, situations in which our faith itself is in question. The sin that is ultimately unforgivable is breaking faith with the God who offers forgiveness, turning away from God and opting to go our own way.

THE TEXT IN THE LIFE OF THE CHURCH

Demonic evil and human evil have both received their share of attention in the church's faith and life. From early times, the church developed and practiced certain rites of deliverance from demonic powers. Some were associated with the baptism of newly instructed converts (cf. the vestiges of such rites in baptismal promises to renounce the devil). Other rituals dealt with persons actually "possessed" by evil spirits.

In our own time, the church has tended to move to one of two extremes on the subject of demonology. Some persons dismiss belief in the devil and demons as a prescientific view of evil, while others display an almost occult fascination with the topic. James Efird offers a more balanced perspective when he writes: "The idea that there are evil forces in the world that manifest themselves in various ways is still valid. How one articulates this idea may change from one culture to another" (Achtemeier: 218). In whatever ways we ourselves choose to talk about evil forces, it is clear that persons and groups can be held captive by such forces. And the text reminds us that God's intention is to liberate the possessed.

While fear of demons has troubled some in the church in every era, many more have worried about "the unforgivable sin." Matthew 12:31-32 has at times led to morbid self-examination, especially on the part of persons with overly sensitive consciences. As commentators usually seek to clarify, however, Jesus' words are not intended to frighten the faithful, but to warn those on the brink of rejecting God in unfaith.

Augustine relates the text to those who separate themselves from the one true church (the fellowship of the Spirit in which sin is forgiven), while the Reformers point to those who reject and malign God's revelation. Calvin is typical when he writes: "They sin against the Holy Spirit who, with evil intention, resist God's truth, although by its brightness they are so touched that they cannot claim ignorance" (1960:3.3.22). Similar comments can be found in Anabaptist texts (cf. Balthasar Hubmaier in Williams: 122; Menno Simons: 1004). In one way or another, the motif that keeps surfacing in discussion of the text is hardness of heart, willful and persistent opposition to God's appeal. It is this that leads to *blasphemy against the Spirit* and that keeps God's forgiveness beyond reach.

Show Us a Sign

Matthew 12:38-50

PREVIEW

The dispute over Jesus' power in 12:22-37 finds its sequel in the controversy in 12:38-50. In fact, the two units share a common narrative setting. It is the same Pharisees who accuse Jesus of being in league with Satan in 12:24 who, along with the scribes, insist that Jesus show them *a sign* in 12:38. Unfazed by Jesus' words condemning blasphemy against the Spirit, they challenge him to prove his claim that he acts with divine authority. Does God really stand behind Jesus' work, or is Jesus only an imposter (cf. 21:23)?

In constructing this unit, Matthew draws on several pieces of material from his sources. One of the pieces presents the debate over a sign, including Jesus' sayings about *this generation* (vv. 38-42). For this core material, Matthew is indebted both to Mark 8:11-13 and to a saying also found in Luke 11:29-32 (cf. 11:16). The second component is a saying about the return of the unclean spirit (vv. 43-45). In the Lukan parallel (Luke 11:24-26), the saying is included in the dispute over Jesus casting out demons. Matthew uses it, however, to expand Jesus' critique of *this generation.*

To complete the unit, Matthew turns to a Markan story linked to the dispute over casting out demons (vv. 46-50, cf. Mark 3:31-35). In this story Jesus' relatives come looking for him, and Jesus uses the occasion to identify his "true" family. What we have then in the unit is a "gallery of contrasting attitudes" (Senior, 1977:130), much like the two panels in 11:20-30. The larger canvas depicts *an evil and adulterous generation,* faithless Israel as represented by the leaders who reject Jesus. But alongside this dismal picture is a portrait of the disciples, who accept Jesus' claims and do the will of God.

OUTLINE

An Evil Generation, 12:38-45

Jesus' True Family, 12:46-50

EXPLANATORY NOTES

An Evil Generation 12:38-45

The *sign* sought by Jesus' opponents is not just another miracle, but rather a sign from heaven that would validate Jesus' credentials (cf. 3:16-17; 4:5-6; Luke 11:16; John 2:18). Signs from God frequently play a positive role in the story of Israel (see TBC below). Here, however, the demand for a sign masks a desire to discredit Jesus. It is similar in tone to the mocking appeal for God to act as Jesus hangs on the cross (cf. 27:39-43).

Perceiving that this is the case, Jesus refuses to give his opponents what they want, but instead rebukes them for the unfaith that leads to their demand: *An* evil *and* adulterous *generation asks for a sign* (emphasis added). The harsh language Jesus uses is from the OT. In Deuteronomy, the people of Israel are described as "a perverse and crooked generation" (Deut. 32:5). And the prophets repeatedly use the metaphor of adultery for Israel's unfaithfulness (cf. Hos. 2; 3:1; Jer. 3:1-10; Ezek. 16).

To such a generation, Jesus says, the only sign that will be given is *the sign of the prophet Jonah* (v. 39). But what is this sign? According to Luke 11:30, the sign consists of someone coming to preach a message of repentance. Jonah served as such a sign to the people of Nineveh, and Jesus plays the role of Jonah in his ministry to Israel.

Matthew, however, relates the sign to a different feature in the Jonah story. According to verse 40, the sign consists of a miraculous deliverance from death. Just as Jonah was delivered from the belly of a great fish (Jon. 1:17; 2:10), so Jesus will be delivered from entombment in the earth. This will be God's way of validating Jesus' work (although it too will be disputed; cf. 28:11-15). Whatever meaning is assigned to *the sign of the prophet Jonah,* it is a sign that judges those who refuse to repent.

The sayings that follow in verses 41-42 underscore the gravity of this refusal. Jesus is not only *like* Jonah, but in fact *greater than Jonah* and *greater than Solomon.* More than a prophet, he *fulfills* the prophetic hope. More than a sage, he is Wisdom in person. The failure of *this generation* to repent (cf. 11:16; 12:45; 17:17) is thus all the more inexcusable. Consequently, Jesus says, the *Gentiles* of old who listened to Jonah and Solomon (cf. Jon. 3:1-5; 1 Kings 10:1-13) will testify *against Israel* at the final judgment (cf. 11:20-24).

As noted earlier, Jesus continues his critique of Israel's unfaith in verses 43-45. (Note how *evil generation* in verse 45 forms an inclusion with *evil and adulterous generation* in verse 39.) Here a parable stressing that it is not enough simply to purge the evil from one's life is given a social application. According to Matthew, Jesus has broken the grip of Satan in Israel's life through casting out demons (cf. 12:28-29). But unless Israel aligns itself with God's redemptive purpose, its final state will be more pathetic than was the case before Jesus appeared.

Jesus' True Family 12:46-50

From the narrative comments in verse 46 and 13:1, we learn that the whole of 12:22-50 transpires in a *house* (cf. 9:10). Now, in the final scene of this narrative, members of Jesus' family appear outside the house, asking to speak to him (cf. Mark 3:31-35/Luke 8:19-21; G. Thom. 99). Verse 47, in which a bystander conveys their request to Jesus, is missing in some manuscripts. The most likely explanation for the omission is that a copyist's eye accidentally skipped from the Greek word at the end of verse 46 (*lalēsai, to speak*) to the same word at the end of verse 47.

In any case, Jesus responds to the request of his relatives by raising a theological question: Who *really* are my kin? Who belongs to my true family, *God's* family? Jesus answers his own question in verses 49-50: The true family of Jesus consists of his *disciples*, who have left their former families to follow him (cf. 8:21-22; 19:29). By doing *the will* of God, they verify that they are kin of the one who calls God, *my Father.*

THE TEXT IN BIBLICAL CONTEXT

Writing to the church at Corinth, Paul notes that "Jews demand signs and Greeks desire wisdom" (1 Cor. 1:22). The prominence of *signs* in the biblical story is hard to overlook. In some accounts, signs are given to confirm God's promise and faithfulness (cf. Gen. 9:13; Judg. 6:17-18; Isa. 7:10-14; Luke 2:12). In other texts, signs are portents of coming events, especially endtime events of judgment and salvation (cf. Joel 2:30-31; Mark 13:4ff.). Still other passages speak of signs as occurrences that reveal God's power and glory (cf. Jer. 32:21; Acts 4:30; and especially John 2:11, referring to the glory manifested in *Jesus*' signs). In one form or another, then, signs are intrinsic to the way God relates to history and to people.

The problem with the demand for a sign in Matthew 12 is not that signs have no place in what Jesus is doing (on the contrary, cf. 11:2-6). The problem is, rather, that this particular demand is the product of unfaith. To put it another way: Signs are for those who seek to discover, not dispute.

A second point at which the text intersects other texts is the way it addresses the subject of *family*. As in most societies, both ancient and modern, the family was the basic unit of societal life in Israel. Family life supplies the story line for much of the biblical narrative (cf. the stories of Jacob, David, and others). Family concerns also loom large in the laws accompanying the story (cf. Exod. 20:12; Lev. 25; Deut. 21:15-21; 1 Kings 21:1-24). So closely are family and faith linked together, that kinship with Abraham and membership in Israel are virtually one and the same.

In the Gospels, however, we find several sayings that challenge this linkage of family and faith. Thus John the Baptist warns some of his visitors at the Jordan not to boast of their patriarchal descent, for *God is able from these stones to raise up children to Abraham* (Matt. 3:9). Elsewhere Jesus argues that following him may lead to conflict with the family, in which case one must choose between family and faith (cf. 10:34-39; 8:21-22). A third example is the saying in the text before us. According to Matthew, ties of kinship count for little in the relationship with God which Jesus offers to his people. What counts is choosing to hear and do the will of God.

THE TEXT IN THE LIFE OF THE CHURCH

The issue of *who* belongs to Jesus, and *how* we belong to Jesus, is one the church has wrestled with throughout its history. In the early Christian communities attested in the NT, it is clear that belonging was based on faith and repentance—in spite of the fact that these communities were frequently organized as house churches. Later, however, as church and state became partners in the social establishment, the nature of belonging began to shift. As was true in ancient Israel, family and geography were the factors that determined who belonged to the community.

Proponents of a believers church contested this development, arguing that "the church consists of the voluntary membership of those confessing Jesus Christ as Lord" (Durnbaugh, 1968:32). Alexander Mack is typical when he writes in his "Basic Questions" (Durnbaugh, 1958:339): "The true brotherhood of Christians has always been founded upon true faith and obedience to Jesus Christ and His gospel. . . . He, Christ himself, considers only those His brethren who do the will of God (Matthew 12:50)." Even in the believers' church tradition, however, family boundaries all too often determine the boundaries of the faith community. Where congregations are little more than extended families at worship, or where common ancestry is more important to who we are than a common calling, we have departed from Jesus' vision of who belongs to *his* family.

Matthew 13:1-52

Many Things in Parables

PREVIEW

Jesus' teaching in the Gospels abounds in figurative language. He castigates his opponents as *a brood of vipers* (12:34) and likens them elsewhere to *whitewashed tombs* (23:27). He speaks of his ministry as an effort to gather Israel *as a hen gathers her brood under her wings* (23:38). He describes his disciples as *the salt of the earth* and *the light of the world* (5:13-14) and sends them out *as sheep into the midst of wolves* (10:16).

In addition to using simple metaphors and similes such as these, Jesus frequently tells *stories* which use language in a figurative way, stories that we call the *parables* of Jesus. There are 30 to 40 such stories in the Gospels, depending on how broadly we apply the term *parable*. The term itself comes from the Greek *parabolē*, which means *a comparison,* and which the LXX uses to translate the Hebrew *mašal*. In the OT, *mašal* or *parabolē* can refer, not only to parables in the strict sense, but to other kinds of figurative material as well, including riddles, proverbs, and allegories.

A parable can be defined as a comparison "drawn from nature or common life, arresting the hearer by its vividness or strangeness, and leaving the mind in sufficient doubt about its precise application to tease it into active thought" (Dodd: 5). Because of its open-ended character, a parable tends to draw us into the plot, forcing us to examine our own lives in the light of that plot.

As retold in the early church, Jesus' parables were adapted in various ways. New features or interpretations were sometimes added to the stories, and the telling of the stories served a catechetical end. The parables were used to illustrate Jesus' message, to illumine the church's own story and calling, and to exhort believers to act in certain ways. In this process of adaptation, there was often a tendency to look for meaning in each of the narrative elements of a parable. To put it another way, parables were sometimes interpreted as allegories, a phenomenon we can observe in the text before us.

Matthew 13 is a collection of eight typical parables, supplemented by sections of commentary or explanation. Shaped in part along the lines of a shorter collection in Mark 4, this material makes up the third of the five discourses of Jesus in Matthew. The topic of the discourse is *the kingdom of heaven* (for example, v. 24), and the parables serve as a vehicle for revelation concerning the kingdom. According to Matthew, Jesus adopts this means of communication in response to Israel's unbelief. Since Israel has rejected Jesus' open proclamation of the kingdom, "Jesus withdraws from Israel into parabolic speech" (Meier, 1980:141), which only the disciples will be able to understand (cf. 13:10-17). The telling of parables *to* the crowds is thus a judgment *on* the crowds, who are cast in the same faithless role as their leaders.

In the layout of chapter 13, a major break occurs after verse 35, when Jesus leaves the public rostrum of a boat and retreats to a house for a private session with his disciples. We thus have two units of material to explore, verses 1-35 and verses 36-52. As a way of proceeding, it seems advisable to do the detailed analysis of the text for both units, and then to treat The Text in Biblical Context and The Text in the Life of the Church for the collection as a whole.

Secrets of the Kingdom

Matthew 13:1-35

PREVIEW

The material in 13:1-35 consists of four parables, an interpretation of one of these parables, and sayings on why Jesus is speaking in parables. It is this portion of the discourse that Matthew has patterned after Mark's account (cf. Mark 4:1-34), and as noted above, it is this portion that Jesus addresses to the crowds (cf. the inclusion formed by vv. 2-3 and 34). When we examine the four parables in the unit, we discern at least three common features: (1) Each of the four is formally introduced *as a parable*, which for Matthew carries the connotation of something puzzling, an enigma (cf. vv. 3, 24, 31, 34). (2) Each of the four talks about grain or seed (or the flour that comes from grain), drawing on some aspect of the cycle of food production. (3) Each of the four deals with the destiny of God's kingdom, affirming the ultimate triumph of the kingdom in spite of its almost imperceptible advent and many forces working against it.

OUTLINE

Seed and Soil, 13:1-9

Hearing and Understanding, 13:10-17

Four Kinds of Hearers, 13:18-23

How the Kingdom Comes, 13:24-33

Hidden Wisdom Made Known, 13:34-35

EXPLANATORY NOTES

Seed and Soil 13:1-9

The setting for 13:1-35 is the edge of the Sea of Galilee, near *the house* in Capernaum where Jesus frequently shows up. Pressed by the crowds, Jesus gets into a boat and sits as a teacher customarily would (cf. 5:1). Jesus does not, however, *teach* the crowds, but rather *speaks to* the crowds in parables which conceal his teaching. The first such parable (cf. Mark 4:2-9; Luke 8:5-8; G. Thom. 9) is one that we and Matthew alike call the parable of the sower (cf. v. 18). It was customary in Palestine to sow seed before plowing the ground, and that is what the sower is doing here, scattering or broadcasting the seed by hand.

According to the text, some of the seed ends up on the path and is never plowed under. Some falls on rocky terrain, where the soil is too thin to sustain life. Some lands in good soil and sprouts, but is choked out by other plants. And some finds the right soil and conditions for growth, yielding up to a hundredfold return at the harvest (note the hyperbole in the amount of the yield!). Later Matthew will supply us with an interpretation for this parable (vv. 18-23). Already, however, we may suspect that the story relates to Jesus' mission, his proclamation of the kingdom, and the results it is yielding.

Hearing and Understanding 13:10-17

Jesus' telling of a parable leads the disciples to ask why he is choosing this means of communication (cf. Mark 4:10-12, 25). It is important to note that the explanation given is related to the developing plot in Matthew's narrative. Elsewhere in the Gospels, we sense that the parables Jesus tells are used to *enhance* understanding, to engage listeners more fully in his message. Here, however, in the context of Israel's rejection of Jesus in the preceding chapters, Jesus uses parables to *withhold* understanding. "Jesus speaks to the people in parables because they have refused to see and hear his clear message, which he has been offering since chapter 4" (Meier, 1980:145).

From this point, the little understanding that the people have will become less and less (cf. v. 12), and Jesus' ministry of teaching will focus on the disciples. As he often does, Matthew cites a biblical basis for Jesus' action (vv. 14-15), quoting words from Isaiah 6:9-10. (Interestingly, this is the only instance in Matthew where a fulfillment quotation comes from Jesus' own lips.) For Isaiah himself, the words quoted were part of a bitter call to close the eyes and ears of the people through his preaching. For Matthew, the words describe a blindness and deafness that the people bring on themselves, which Jesus then confirms as he begins to speak in parables.

Not everyone, however, is blind or deaf. The message hidden in parables will not remain hidden for Jesus' disciples. By the grace of God which has already opened their eyes and ears, they will be given understanding that is withheld from others (vv. 11-12). Thus we find Jesus interpreting the parables to the disciples as a part of his discourse (vv. 18-23, 36-43).

To underscore the seeing and hearing of the disciples, Matthew appends a beatitude that Luke uses in a different context (vv. 16-17; cf. Luke 10:23-24). The beatitude congratulates the disciples for the happy situation in which they find themselves. They have witnessed deeds fulfilling the promises of God to their predecessors (cf. 11:4-6). And they have been given faith to perceive what these deeds in fact mean. Unlike the crowds, who *listen but never understand* and *look but never perceive,* the disciples have eyes that really see and ears that really hear.

Four Kinds of Hearers 13:18-23

Jesus continues to speak to the disciples in verses 18-23, interpreting the parable in verses 3-9 (cf. Mark 4:13-20; Luke 8:11-15). In the parable itself, the primary concern seems to be the fate of the seed. Here, however, the emphasis falls on the various kinds of *soil*, which are related to different types of hearers who receive Jesus' word: Some listeners never make it from hearing to faith. Some respond with a short-lived faith that vanishes when hard times set in. Some accept the word but allow worldly concerns to suffocate their faith. And some hear, believe, and actually do what God desires.

Through this interpretation, Matthew and his predecessors seem to be posing the question: Where do we find ourselves in the parable of the sower? As one might expect, Matthew adds his own touch to the interpretation as he passes it on to us: (1) He identifies the word sown as *the word of the kingdom* (v. 18), which is the subject of each of the parables in the collection. (2) He contrasts the first and last types of hearers in terms of who does and doesn't *understand* (vv. 19, 23), picking up the theme of the previous section. (3) He underscores the fact that hearing should lead to *doing*, adding a verb which here is translated *yields* (v. 23), but which is the same verb used elsewhere for one who *does* God's will (cf. 5:19; 7:21; 12:50).

How the Kingdom Comes 13:24-33

Having interpreted one parable, Jesus proceeds to tell three more. Each is introduced as *another parable,* and each begins with a certain formula of comparison: *The kingdom of heaven may be compared to* . . . (v. 24) or *The kingdom of heaven is like* . . . (vv. 31, 33). These formulas introduce other parables in Matthew (cf. 13:44; 18:23; 20:1; 22:2; 25:1), and a similar formula is sometimes found in rabbinic parables: "To what is the matter like?" In each case, the formula suggests a likeness between two situations. In verse 24, therefore, the point is not that the kingdom resembles a sower, but that the advent of the kingdom resembles the plot in the story ahead.

The first of the three parables (vv. 24-30) appears only in Matthew in the NT, although it turns up elsewhere in the Gospel of Thomas (G. Thom. 57). Like the parable of the sower in 13:1-9, the story deals with planting and growing. This time, however, the contrast is not between fruitful and unfruitful seed (or soils) but between wheat and weeds growing in the same field. (Cf. verse 36, where Matthew labels the story as *the parable of the weeds of the field.*) The weed in question is probably darnel, a poisonous plant that looks like wheat when the plants are young.

The novel element in the story is that the weeds do not simply spring up naturally, but are planted by a malicious neighbor to interfere with the crop. When the deed is finally evident, the householder must decide whether to uproot the weeds—or let the wheat and weeds contend with each other. For a detailed explanation, we must wait till verses 36-43. What the parable itself clearly tells us, however, is that the kingdom must contend with evil all around it, and that God permits evil and good to coexist until the end.

The two shorter parables in verses 31-32 and verse 33 form a matched pair in Luke as well (cf. Luke 13:18-21), which suggests that they were transmitted together in the underlying tradition. Note that one story is about a *man*, the other story about a *woman* (cf. a similar phenomenon in 24:40-41). In both parables, there is a striking contrast between a small or obscure beginning and an amazing end result. Thus a tiny mustard seed grows into a towering shrub, to which *the birds of the air come and make nests in its branches* (cf. Mark 4:30-32; G. Thom. 20). The imagery of a tree that provides shade and shelter comes from Daniel 4:10-22 (cf. Ezek. 31:5-6; 1QH 8:4-9), where it refers to a mighty nation or kingdom. Here it describes the kingdom of God, to which people will come from every nation on earth (cf. 8:11; 28:19).

In like manner, a bit of yeast leavens *three measures of flour* (about a bushel; cf. Gen. 18:6), and its effect is evident throughout the mass of dough (cf. G. Thom. 96). Leaven as a symbol most often implies corruption or contamination (cf. 16:6; 1 Cor. 5:6-8; Gal. 5:9). Here, however, the meaning is positive: Although the presence and power of the kingdom is hidden for the moment, it will shape the future of all human history.

Hidden Wisdom Made Known 13:34-35

Verses 34-35 consist of a summary statement based on Mark 4:33-34, to which Matthew has added a fulfillment quotation. For Matthew, the observation that Jesus says nothing to the crowds apart from parables reiterates the point made in 13:10-15: A people unwilling to hear God's word is now deprived of the ability to understand that word.

However, the parables reveal as well as conceal, a point underscored in the following quotation. The words cited come from Psalm

78:2, a psalm ascribed to the musician Asaph. (Note that Asaph is called a "seer" in 2 Chronicles 29:30, which may explain why Matthew credits the citation to *the prophet.*) As the author of the psalm recites God's glorious deeds in his *dark sayings from of old,* so Jesus describes God's rule and activity through his parables. Or as John Meier puts it: "Jesus is the perfect wisdom-teacher who speaks forth mysteries hidden from creation, i.e., the apocalyptic revelation of God's coming as king" (Meier, 1980:149).

Disciples and the Kingdom

Matthew 13:36-52

PREVIEW

At the conclusion of Jesus' parable discourse in Mark, we are told that *privately to his own disciples he explained everything* (Mark 4:34). Matthew presents the sayings in 13:36-52 as the subject matter of this private session, which as noted earlier takes place in a *house.* (The setting of disciples gathered in a home for instruction anticipates the later assembling of believers in Christian house churches!) Included in these sayings are an interpretation of the parable of the weeds, three additional parables of the kingdom, and a special parable about those who interpret God's word for others. None of this material appears elsewhere in the NT, although we find several parallel sayings in the Gospel of Thomas (sayings 8, 76, 109).

OUTLINE

Explanation for Insiders, 13:36-43

Caught Up in God's Reign, 13:44-50

Scribes for the Kingdom, 13:51-52

EXPLANATORY NOTES

Explanation for Insiders 13:36-43

Responding to a request from the disciples, Jesus interprets the parable of the weeds among the wheat (cf. 13:24-30). This commentary on the parable consists of two parts. Verses 37-39 offer an allegorical explanation of seven elements in the parable (sower, field, seed, weeds, enemy, harvest, reapers). Then verses 40-43 depict a traditional apocalyptic view of the endtime which builds on this explanation: At the last judgment, evildoers will finally be purged from God's kingdom. The righteous, by contrast, will exhibit God's glory as they inhabit God's kingdom (cf. Dan. 12:2-3). The phrase *end of the age* (vv. 39,40) is a construction Matthew uses several times in the Gospel (cf. 13:49; 24:3; 28:20). It conveys the twofold idea of an *end* to the present age and of a time when God's purposes for history will be *consummated*.

As a part of Matthew's theology of the kingdom, this commentary or explanation makes several important points. Note that the *field* to which the drama of the parable relates is defined as the *world*, not just the church. And Jesus' reign as the Son of Man encompasses the world. What we have then is not a story of how believers should deal with evil in the church (which is the subject of Matthew 18), but a story of how God will deal with evil in the world, including the church.

Through the combined text of the parable and its explanation, Matthew assures us that God will judge evil and evildoers at the right time. Simultaneously, the text warns us that crusades on our part to eliminate the wicked are both misguided and dangerous. (Cf. the critique of those who would use violence to uproot the wicked by Menno Simons: 48, 605; and by Dietrich Philips in Williams: 252-253).

Caught Up in God's Reign 13:44-50

Like the three parables in verses 24-33, the three parables here begin with a similar introductory phrase: "*(Again) the kingdom of heaven is like. . . .*" This time the common theme is that of people becoming disciples, responding to the advent and attraction of God's reign. Rather significantly, none of the three stories is actually labeled a parable. Because Jesus is teaching disciples, who have the gift of understanding (cf. vv. 11, 51), these stories are not impenetrable mysteries but rather transparent revelation.

The first two parables highlight the priceless value of the kingdom, the joy or excitement in discovering it, and the total investment a true disciple makes in laying claim to this discovery. Both stories use treasure as a metaphor for the kingdom, in much the same way that Jewish tradition compares wisdom to precious metals and jewels (cf. Prov. 2:4; 3:13-15; 8:10-11,19; Job 28:12-19).

In the first story (v. 44), Jesus tells of a day laborer who stumbles accidentally onto buried wealth. It was common in the ancient world to bury treasure in a field, to keep it out of the hands of marauding troops or bandits. Finding such a stash (left behind by some previous owner), the worker sells all he has to buy the field—and thus have a rightful claim to the treasure.

In the second story (vv. 45-46), the main character is a jewel merchant who specializes in pearls (which some in the ancient world valued more highly than gold). Finding a priceless pearl on one of his ex peditions, the merchant sells his whole collection of jewels in order to obtain it (cf. Luke 14:33; Phil. 3:7-8; Acts of Thomas 108–113).

The parable of the dragnet (vv. 47-50) is a story about fishing in the Sea of Galilee. One of the methods used to catch a quantity of fish was to suspend a large, weighted net in the lake and pull it toward the shore (either by boats or hand-drawn ropes). Since the lake contained over twenty kinds of fish, the catch found in the dragnet was usually a mixed lot. A sorting process was necessary to eliminate those varieties that were either inedible or unclean according to Jewish law (cf. Lev. 11:9-12).

This then is a parable with two themes, attraction and separation. In the present hour, God is drawing or gathering persons of every sort to take part in the kingdom. In the future, however, there will be a sorting-out process, a time for separating *the evil from the righteous* (v. 49; cf. vv. 41-42). We find the same two themes later in the Gospel in the parable of the marriage feast: There guests of every stripe are invited or called, but only those rightly attired are allowed to stay and enjoy the celebration (cf. 22:9-14).

Scribes for the Kingdom 13:51-52

Jesus concludes his parable discourse by raising again the issue of *understanding* (v. 51) and by telling a parable about the task of those who understand (v. 52). Like the parable of the sower, this parable talks about communication—and in fact forms an inclusion with 13:3-9. The specific topic here is the role of the *scribe*, one who interprets God's word for others (cf. the portrait of a scribe in Sirach 39:1-11, a portrait with which Matthew appears to be familiar). According to Matthew, there are scribes *trained for the kingdom of heaven* (the word for *trained* is related to the word for disciple), just as there were scribes in the Jewish community.

But who exactly does Matthew have in mind? In the broadest

sense, every believer who studies and interprets the word is a scribe. In a narrower sense, *scribe* may refer to teachers who function like rabbis in Jesus' community (cf. 23:34). In this latter sense, Matthew may be alluding to himself as well, giving us a glimpse of the way he viewed his role as the writer of a Gospel.

Whether broadly or narrowly defined, a Christian scribe is *like the master of a household who brings out of his treasure what is new and what is old.* The word for *treasure* is better translated *storeroom* (cf. GNB, JB, NIV) and refers to a room where provisions were kept to supply a household. Some provisions would naturally be old or preserved goods, while others would be new or fresh. As applied to those who are scribes for the kingdom, old and new likely refer to old and new revelation. Those who communicate the gospel of the kingdom draw on the rich biblical heritage of ancient Israel (*what is old*). But they interpret this old word in the light of God's final self-disclosure through Jesus' message and ministry (*what is new*). Through such an endeavor, others are led to understanding, and the needs of the household of faith are fully supplied.

THE TEXT IN BIBLICAL CONTEXT

Like the fables of Aesop in Greek literature, parables turn up fairly early in the traditions of Israel. Some well-known examples include Jotham's fable of the trees (Judg. 9:7-15), Nathan's parable of the ewe lamb (2 Sam. 12:1-15), and Isaiah's song of the vineyard (Isa. 5:1-7). Later, we find the rabbis using parables as one of many ways of commenting on the Torah.

It is with Jesus, however, that parables become a distinctive or characteristic mode of communication. The synoptic Gospels are replete with his stories, and Matthew gives us a generous sampling. In addition to the material in Matthew 13, we find two shorter collections of parables (21:28—22:14; 25), as well as individual stories scattered here and there (cf. 18:10-14; 18:23-35; 20:1-16). The parable discourse of Matthew 13 thus belongs to a wider discourse in parables that shapes the language of faith in significant ways.

Another level at which Matthew 13 puts us in touch with a broader tradition is the picture it paints of God's rule over history. The theme of God's lordship is one that surfaces at numerous points in the biblical story. So, for example, the psalmist celebrates God's exalted reign over all the nations (cf. Pss. 93—100), and the author of Isaiah 40—55 attests the way God incorporates world politics into the divine plan of salvation.

The closest antecedents to the vision of God's reign in Matthew 13, however, are found in apocalyptic works like the book of Daniel. In this stream of literature, we find an emphasis on the painful conflict between good and evil in the present hour, coupled with the assurance that history is still in God's hands and that God's reign will triumph in the end. When that occurs, evil will be destroyed and the righteous will be vindicated. Such is the message we hear in the stories of Matthew 13.

THE TEXT IN THE LIFE OF THE CHURCH

The parables of Jesus have been treated in various ways across the centuries of Christian usage (cf. Kissinger, 1979). As noted earlier, one of the first approaches to the parables was to look for allegorical meaning in every detail. The allegorical approach, exemplified in Augustine's classic exposition of the story of the good Samaritan (Quaestiones Evangeliorum 2.19, cited in Dodd: 1-2), dominated parable study until the late nineteenth century.

With the advent of historical criticism, there is a shift away from allegorizing to an attempt to treat parables as simple stories with a single or primary point. Some scholars defined this point in terms of general moral and religious principles, while others (more appropriately) interpreted the message of the parables in relation to Jesus' proclamation of the kingdom. More recent parable study presupposes the research of the last hundred years, but raises certain questions that point in new directions: (1) Do parables simply illustrate truths that we can extract and state in other ways—or do parables require us to enter into the story they tell in much the same way that we enter into a play or movie? (2) Is it possible to pin down a single meaning for a parable—or are parables open to multiple levels of meaning as they are retold in new situations?

Of the parables found in Matthew 13, one in particular calls for comment here, because of the way it has fueled the long-standing debate about the nature of the church. This is the parable of the weeds of the field (13:24-30, 36-43). As understood by proponents of a territorial church, the parable portrays the *church* as a mixed community, where true believers and others are found together like wheat and tares. Calvin writes, for example: "So long as the church is in pilgrimage in this world, the good and sincere will be mixed in it with the bad and the hypocrites" (1972, 2:74-75).

The Anabaptists, however, disputed this interpretation. Calling attention to the way the text itself defines the field of action (cf. v. 38), Menno Simons and others insisted that the mingling of wheat and weeds describes the *world*, not the church (cf. Menno Simons: 750; Augsburger: 176-177). Jesus' will for the church, they argued, is defined in Matthew 18, which clearly envisions a disciplined community of the faithful. As a review of commentaries on the text reveals, the debate described above is still going on.

In addition to providing texts for study and debate, Jesus' stories have encouraged others to speak and write in parables. One such person was the Danish philosopher, Søren Kierkegaard, who used parables to critique the religious world of the nineteenth century (cf. the collection in Oden, 1978). Among his oft-retold stories are those about a royal coachman who knows how to train horses; wild geese who unwisely settle in a barnyard; a clown who tries to warn the crowd of a fire; and the carriage lights that obscure the stars (cf. TLC for 6:19—7:12). A modern-day equivalent of parables is found in cartoon strips such as Peanuts, which use pictures as well as words to tell stories in which readers recognize their own lives. Wherever and however we speak the truth in parables, we are acknowledging our indebtedness to the stories Jesus told to his hearers in Galilee.

Matthew 13:53—16:20

Faith and Unfaith, Part 2

PREVIEW

The new section that begins at 13:53 is primarily a *narrative* section, for which Matthew is doubly indebted to the Gospel of Mark. First, the stories told come from Mark's account. Among the stories included are those of Jesus' rejection in Nazareth, the feeding of the 5000, the healing of a Gentile woman's daughter, and Jesus' conversation with the disciples at Caesarea Philippi. Second, Matthew follows the *order* of the Markan narrative as he presents these stories (and will continue to do so from here on to the end of the Gospel). As a result, 13:53—16:20 is not as tightly structured as some of the topical collections that Matthew himself assembles.

Still, the theme of faith and unfaith which governs the larger section beginning at 11:1 pervades the stories here as well. As the plot unfolds in the episodes reported, the breach between unbelieving Israel on the one hand and Jesus and his disciples on the other becomes irreparable. Jesus rejects rabbinical tradition in the dispute over clean and unclean (15:1-20). He instructs his disciples to leave the blind leaders of Judaism alone and to beware of their teaching (15:13-14; 16:5-12). And he speaks explicitly of a community that *he* will build on a new foundation, with a teaching authority of its own (16:18-19). In all of this, we sense that Matthew is addressing his own community as it defines its identity over and against the synagogue.

The promise of the church in 16:18-19 comes in response to Peter's confession of faith in 16:16: *You are the Messiah, the Son of the living God.* With that confession, made on behalf of all the disciples, the portrayal of faith and unfaith in 11:1—16:20 reaches its climax.

Unwelcome Prophets

Matthew 13:53—14:12

PREVIEW

The two stories that comprise 13:53—14:12 come from Mark 6:1-6 and Mark 6:14-29. (Matthew has already used the intervening material in Mark 6:7-13 in the mission discourse.) What we have in these accounts is a two-panel unit on the fate of prophets. Panel 1 features Jesus' rejection in Nazareth, and panel 2 reports the beheading of John the Baptist in Herod's court. Linking the two stories and the two figures is the fact that both Jesus and John are identified as prophets (13:57; 14:5); the note that Jesus' powers evoke memories of John (14:1-2); and the reader's awareness that Jesus' rejection will lead to a fate similar to John's (cf. 17:9-13).

OUTLINE

Jesus in His Hometown, 13:53-58

John in Herod's Court, 14:1-12

EXPLANATORY NOTES

Jesus in His Hometown 13:53-58

When Jesus finishes his parable discourse (note the usual formula for the end of a discourse and beginning of a new section in v. 53; cf. 7:28-29; 11:1), he goes to *his hometown.* Nazareth is implied (cf. 2:23; 4:12-13), but the vagueness of the language in the Greek text (literally *his native place*) lets the story that follows typify Israel as a whole (cf. v. 57).

Among the things that we learn from this account are the names of Jesus' brothers and the family trade of Jesus' father. (According to Mark 6:3, it was Jesus' own trade as well.) The Greek word for *carpenter* has a broader range of meanings than our English translations would suggest. It can refer to anyone who works with wood, stone, or metal, whether as a craftsman who fashions objects or as a builder engaged in construction. What exactly Joseph did for a living, then, remains uncertain.

In any case, the purpose of the story is not to reconstruct Jesus' family background, but to tell how Jesus fares among the hometown folk who know that background. The outcome is predictable, and it is presented effectively in the series of questions the people raise in verses 54-56. Note that the series begins and ends with the provocative inquiry: *Where did* he *get this wisdom and these deeds of power?* For the reader, the question points to Jesus' special relationship with God. For the residents of Nazareth, however, the question implies a skeptical reaction to Jesus. "We know his relatives," the people say, "and they're as common as the rest of us" (cf. John 6:41-42). They are *astounded* by what they see and hear, but their astonishment stays at the level of disbelief rather than moving them toward faith. As the text puts it, recalling words from 11:6, the people *took offense* at Jesus.

Jesus sums up the episode in verse 57b with a saying about the experience of prophets everywhere. At home, Jesus says, one gets no respect. This saying may have circulated as a popular proverb in Jesus' day, and it turns up in each of the Gospels (cf. Mark 6:4; Luke 4:24; John 4:44; G. Thom. 31). In any event, the unbelief that denies honor to Jesus denies something to Nazareth as well (v. 58). It leads Jesus to *restrict* his ministry there, so that the people get only a smattering of all that Jesus has to give.

John in Herod's Court 14:1-12

Matthew 14:1-12 consists of a story within a story, much abbreviated from the parallel account in Mark 6:14-29. When Herod hears reports of Jesus' unusual powers, he speculates that Jesus is none other than John the Baptist returned to life (vv. 1-2; cf. 16:13-14). The reader, however, has not yet been informed of John's *death*, and so Matthew (following Mark) provides a flashback to explain how and why John died as Herod's prisoner (vv. 3-12; cf. 4:12; 11:2). Josephus also reports that John was executed by Herod (*Antiquities* 18.116-119), although the details in his account differ from those in the Gospels.

Here it is John's rebuke of Herod's marriage to his niece and sister-in-law Herodias (cf. Lev. 18:16; 20:21) that gets him into trouble. (Herodias had been married previously to another Herod about whom we know little. Verse 3 refers to him as Philip, perhaps confusing him with Philip the tetrarch, who married Herodias' daughter.)

According to the text, a gala birthday party for Herod provides the royal family with an opportunity to eliminate their critic. The colorful tale of this event contains all the ingredients of a TV miniseries, including seduction (vv. 6-7), intrigue (vv. 8-9), and finally violence (vv. 10-11). At least three features of the story call for further comment:

(1) The dance by Herodias' daughter, likely at her mother's bidding, is unprecedented. Entertainment of this sort would normally be provided by harlots, not by a member of the royal family.

(2) The story is told in such a way as to recall earlier biblical events. In her scheming to destroy John, Herodias is cast as Jezebel (cf. 1 Kings 19:3). And Herod's promise to give her daughter anything she wants echoes language from the story of Esther (cf. Esth. 5:2-3; Mark 6:22-23).

(3) Herod appears as one who *himself* wants to destroy John (v. 5a; cf. the somewhat different picture in Mark 6:20), and Herodias' request for John's head merely forces the king's hand. Herod's only regret (*the king was grieved,* v. 9) is that executing John will upset the people who revere him (v. 5b; cf. 21:46 and 26:4-5, where fear of the people restrains *Jesus*' enemies.)

As suggested earlier, John's gruesome end at the hands of Herod points ahead to Jesus' tragic end at the hands of Pilate. This is where rejection and unbelief will finally lead. And when John's disciples report the prophet's death to Jesus (v. 12), they are in effect announcing Jesus' own impending fate.

THE TEXT IN BIBLICAL CONTEXT

In a passage yet to come in Matthew's Gospel, Jesus castigates his opponents as *descendants of those who murdered the prophets* (23:31), who follow in the steps of their hostile ancestors (cf. 23:29-39). The theme of the unwelcome and persecuted prophet (discussed earlier in TBC for 10:16-42) plays an important role in the biblical tradition. And the two stories in 13:53—14:12 clearly illustrate that theme.

In each instance, there is a striking OT episode that parallels the story at hand. We have already noted the way John's demise recalls the peril Elijah faced in Ahab's court because of Jezebel. And when Jesus is rejected in Nazareth, we are reminded of the hometown reaction of the people of Anathoth to Jeremiah's preaching: "You shall not prophesy in the name of the Lord, or you will die by our hand" (Jer. 11:21; cf. 1:1). The parallel with Jeremiah is even closer in Luke's version of the episode at Nazareth, which reports an attempt to take Jesus' life (Luke 4:29; cf. 4:16-30). With or without violence, the Nazareth story makes the point that Jesus "came to what was his own, and his own people did not accept him" (John 1:11).

THE TEXT IN THE LIFE OF THE CHURCH

In appropriating the stories of 13:53—14:12, the church has frequently focused on secondary issues. A favorite topic of commentators is the debauchery of Herod's birthday party. Thus, in a sermon on the story by the church father John Chrysostom, we find a warning about the dangers of dancing, drunkenness, and wanton women (296-303).

Another such side issue is the status of the brothers and sisters of Jesus mentioned in 13:55-56 (cf. 12:46-50). Did Jesus have brothers and sisters born to Mary and Joseph in the usual manner? Or does the text refer to children of Joseph by a previous marriage? Or is Matthew thinking of extended family members such as cousins? The latter two views are often linked with the tradition of Mary's perpetual virginity. Today, however, most interpreters are wary of reading the text through the lenses of that tradition.

More germane to the concerns Matthew himself is addressing is the use of the text as a paradigm for the fate of God's servants in the world. The Jewish proverb Jesus cited in 13:57 has become a stock saying in the Christian world as well. And the story of John has provided a resource for both Christian martyrology and church-state issues. In "The Cross of the Saints," Menno Simons includes John in a series of biblical saints who suffered and alludes to John's fate with the words: "O Lord, so lamentably and grievously have the righteous been destroyed on account of their piety by this abominable, bloody, murderous world" (592).

No less graphic are the comments of Martin Luther, which focus on the picture of Herod in the text. According to Luther, the mighty rulers of the world "are all Herods," crafty foxes who want to appear pious and respectable, but all the while bent on pursuing evil (491-492). Luther's words are rather harsh, and many rulers doubtless deserve a kinder verdict. What is true and has been true in every age, however, is that prophets and kings often find themselves in conflict, and that prophets all too often pay a price for their witness.

Mercy and Majesty

Matthew 14:13-36

PREVIEW

Earlier in the narrative (cf. chaps. 8—9), Matthew presented a collection of stories of Jesus' miracles or mighty works. Two more such stories are featured in 14:13-36, which is based on Mark 6:30-56 (cf. Luke 9:10-17; John 6:1-21). In the first story, Jesus performs a *gift miracle* (cf. Theissen, 1983:103-106), feeding a hungry crowd in a remote or secluded setting (vv. 15-21). Among the characteristics of this type of miracle story (cf. John 2:1-11 for another example) is the unobtrusiveness of the miracle, which becomes apparent only gradually and then only to a few.

The second story can be described as both a *rescue miracle* and an *epiphany*, an event in which God or divine attributes are revealed (cf. Theissen, 1983:94-99). In this particular epiphany, Jesus walks on water and enables Peter to do likewise (vv. 22-33). Like the miracle stories already discussed, the accounts here play a twofold role: (1) They disclose the messianic authority with which Jesus acts in Israel. (2) They depict how Jesus acts in or relates to the church.

Bracketing the stories of food in the wilderness and walking on water are brief summary statements at the beginning and end of the unit (vv. 13-14 and 34-36). Both of these statements refer to crowds of people who seek Jesus and pursue him. And both speak of Jesus' healing of the sick. The statements form an literary inclusion, holding together a body of material that highlights the *compassion* of Jesus (v. 14).

OUTLINE

A Great Throng in Need, 14:13-14

Food for the Hungry, 14:15-21

Salvation at Sea, 14:22-33

All Were Made Well, 14:34-36

EXPLANATORY NOTES

A Great Throng in Need 14:13-14

Adapted from Mark 6:30-34, the narration in verses 13-14 provides a transition from the preceding episode to the feeding of the crowds. A key word in these verses is the word *withdrew*. Earlier, when Herod imprisoned John the Baptist, Jesus *withdrew* into Galilee to begin his ministry (4:12). Now, when Jesus hears that Herod views him as a re-embodiment of the murdered prophet (14:1-2), he *withdraws* again, this time from public view (14:13). Both references are part of a larger strand of material in which Jesus moves from one place to another to avoid danger or hostility (cf. 2:22; 12:15; 15:21). In each instance, God's purpose is carried forward in spite of threatening circumstances.

The *deserted place* to which Jesus withdraws is not identified. Nor does it remain lonely or secluded for long. A huge crowd of townspeople is present to greet Jesus when he goes ashore. The reference in verse 14 to Jesus' *compassion* on the people recalls similar language in 9:36. As noted in the comments there, this compassion is more than human emotion. It denotes the divine compassion for Israel that Jesus manifests in his messianic ministry. In the Markan parallel, this compassion leads Jesus to *teach* the crowds (Mark 6:34). In the Matthean narrative, however, where the crowds have already forfeited the opportunity to understand Jesus' message (cf. 13:10-15), compassion results instead in the healing of the sick (cf. also Mark 10:1 and Matt. 19:1-2).

Food for the Hungry 14:15-21

The feeding of the multitude is the most broadly attested miracle in the Gospels. It is recounted by each of the four Evangelists (cf. Mark 6:35-44; Luke 9:12-17; John 6:1-14). In addition, Mark and Matthew both report a second feeding incident (cf. Mark 8:1-10; Matt. 15:32-39), which likely grew out of the same tradition. The account before us closely follows the Markan account, but with some abbreviation and with greater solemnity. Here there is less fumbling around to determine what to do with the crowds in the conversation the disciples have with Jesus. The miracle itself, however, takes shape in the same way in both accounts.

Rather than send the crowds away hungry, Jesus has them sit for supper and somehow feeds them all with the meager resources of five loaves and two fish. How this occurs is not spelled out, and there is no evidence that the crowds themselves are aware that something extraordinary has happened. For the reader, the scope of the miracle becomes apparent only at the end of the story (vv. 20-21). There we learn that (1) over 5000 persons took part in the meal, (2) everyone ate till they were full, and (3) there were even twelve containers of leftovers!

To grasp the power of this story for Matthew and the early church, we need to recognize its many allusions to the OT and Jewish tradition: First, the gift of bread to crowds in *a deserted place* (Greek: *erēmos topos*, vv. 13, 15) recalls the gift of manna to crowds in the *wilderness* (*erēmos*) in Exodus 16. Second, the loaves, leftovers, and basic theme of the narrative remind us of a story in 2 Kings 4:42-44, where Elisha feeds a hundred men with twenty loaves. Third, the *twelve* baskets of leftover food, like the twelve disciples themselves, probably symbolize the twelve tribes of Israel, suggesting provisions for all of Israel. Finally, when Jesus praises God in a prayer of blessing and then breaks and distributes the bread (v. 19), he is acting as the head of a Jewish family would in presiding over a meal (cf. Acts 27:33-36).

Taken together, these allusions inform the reader that *Jesus is a gracious host who supplies the needs of God's people as Yahweh (the Lord) did in days of old*. He spreads "a table in the wilderness," giving the people "food in abundance," so that "they ate and were well filled" (Ps. 78:19-29).

Salvation at Sea 14:22-33

The story of Jesus' epiphany at sea in verses 22-33 is based on Mark 6:45-52 (cf. also John 6:15-21), but expanded with the episode involving Peter in verses 28-31. This is the first of several stories in which Matthew appears to be drawing on a special tradition concerning Peter (cf. 16:17-19; 17:24-27; 18:21-22). Setting the stage for the action to come, the text first tells us how Jesus and the disciples get separated (vv. 22-23), and how the disciples are imperiled as they make their way across the lake by night (v. 24). We learn that the disciples are struggling with an opposing wind and the waves it is whipping up. Furthermore, the boat carrying the disciples is *far from the land* (Greek: *many furlongs from the land*).

Such is the scene when Jesus appears *walking toward them on the sea* (v. 25), sometime between 3 a.m. and 6 a.m. (Greek: *the fourth watch of the night,* cf. NIV). As is typical in an epiphany (cf.

17:6-7; Isa. 6:5; Luke 24:36-37), the first reaction of the disciples is one of fear or terror (v. 26). They assume that they are seeing an apparition. With Jesus' words of assurance, however (v. 27), and with the quieting of the sea when Jesus enters the boat (v. 32), fear gives way to worship (v. 33; cf. 8:27).

Once again we have a story full of allusions to OT texts and themes. Like the psalmist and others, the author depicts the sea and its turbulent waters as a place of chaos and destruction (cf. Gen. 1:2; Pss. 69:2; 74:13-14). There is a power greater than that of the sea, however, and Jesus clearly exhibits that power. When he appears walking on the sea, the picture is reminiscent of Yahweh walking on or through the sea at creation (Job 9:8; 38:16; Ps. 77:19) and making a route through the sea for Israel (Isa. 43:16).

Divine authority is equally evident in the assurance Jesus offers in verse 27: His words to the awestruck disciples echo the affirmation "I am" in Exodus 3:14 and the consoling words "Do not fear" in Isaiah 43:1-2. Finally, Jesus' action in reaching out to rescue Peter recalls the testimony to God's deliverance in Psalm 18:16: "He reached down from on high, he took me; he drew me out of mighty waters" (cf. Pss. 69:1-2; 144:7). All of this leads to the ringing acclamation of the disciples in verse 33: *Truly you are the Son of God.*

As in the sea story of 8:23-27, this account can be viewed as a parable of salvation; the boat beset by wind and waves serves as a metaphor for the church. Such a function of the story becomes clear in several features of the episode involving Peter. Note, for example, how Peter's initial words and action model true discipleship: He asks Jesus to command him and then obeys that command (vv. 28-29).

Peter continues to typify the church, albeit less gloriously, when fear and doubt take over and he begins to sink (v. 30). Here Peter's behavior represents the wavering faith of the church in hard times. (*Little faith* and *doubt* in verse 31 do not mean *un*belief, but a faith too easily swamped when the going gets rough; cf. 6:30; 8:26; 16:8.) Finally, in the midst of his dilemma, Peter voices the cry of the community in distress in every age: *Lord, save me* (v. 30; cf. 8:25). Hearing that cry, Jesus proves that he is able to deliver his community, both from raging waters and from faltering faith.

All Were Made Well 14:34-36

The summary statement with which the unit concludes (based on Mark 6:53-56) brings Jesus and the disciples back to land and back to the crowds. For the first time in the unit, a specific geographical location is mentioned. *Gennesaret* can refer either to a town by that name, to the fertile plain where the town is located on the northwestern shore of the sea of Galilee, or to the sea of Galilee itself (cf. 1 Macc. 11:67; Luke 5:1). Here the town is implied, a Roman town built on or near the site of the OT city of Chinnereth. (Like Gennesaret, Chinnereth could refer to the surrounding area or to the lake as well as the town; cf. 1 Kings 15:20; Deut. 3:17.)

As noted earlier, the summary here forms an inclusion with the summary at the beginning of the unit in verses 13-14. And the content is typical of summary statements found at a number of places in the narrative (cf. 4:23-25; 8:16-17): All the sick *throughout the region* are brought to Jesus, and all who are brought are *healed.* The unit ends then, as it began, by attesting the divine compassion of Jesus for those in need of wholeness.

THE TEXT IN BIBLICAL CONTEXT

From our observations thus far, it is already apparent that the miracle of the loaves is part of a wider biblical tradition about the feeding of God's people. We have identified some of the ways the story is linked to the heritage of Israel that precedes it, most notably to the tradition of bread in the wilderness. There are other connections, however, which are no less significant.

One of these links is with the family of texts that focus on *eating with Jesus*, including stories of Jesus' controversial meals with a wide circle of hosts and guests (cf. 9:10-13; Luke 14:1-14), the account of the Last Supper with the disciples (26:20-29), and references to the eucharistic fellowship of the early church (cf. Acts 2:46; 1 Cor. 11:17-34). The story in 14:15-21 is told in such a way as to suggest a eucharistic celebration.

To be specific: (1) The story begins with the same phrase that introduces the last supper in 26:20 (identical in Greek: *When evening came/When it was evening*). (2) Jesus' actions in blessing God, breaking the loaves, and giving bread to the disciples anticipate the scene described in 26:26. (3) The prominent role of the disciples in distributing the food invites us to think of deacons or others administering a love feast. As Paul Minear writes, "Matthew intended his readers to see the analogy between this Galilean meal and their own suppers" (89).

If the feeding of the 5000 anticipates meals in the church, it also anticipates the messianic banquet of God's people in the kingdom. Another connection of the story, therefore, is with the strand of tradition that depicts the salvation of the age to come in terms of a meal or feast. Among the many texts attesting the tradition (cf. Isa. 25:6-9; Matt. 22:1-14; Luke 22:15-16; Rev. 19:9) is the exclamation by a table companion of Jesus in the Third Gospel: "Blessed is the one who will eat bread in the kingdom of God" (Luke 14:15). Occasionally such texts reflect hope in a literal reenactment of the food miracle of the wilderness period (cf. 2 Bar. 29:8).

In the story at hand, the miraculous feeding does not itself constitute an endtime meal, whether of manna or more sumptuous fare. What it does provide, however, is a foretaste of Jesus satisfying the hunger of those who seek him. In so doing, it confirms the promise of the fourth beatitude (5:6) and links the nourishment of the endtime to Jesus' own power and mercy.

The episode of salvation at sea also invites comparison with other texts. In our earlier analysis of the story, we looked at some of these texts and noted how Jesus' power over the sea parallels that of Yahweh in the OT. Another body of texts to which the passage relates is that of the epiphany stories found throughout the Bible. Among the epiphanies in Matthew's own narrative would be Jesus' baptism (3:16-17), the previous storm at sea (8:23-27), Jesus' transfiguration (17:1-8), and the events accompanying Jesus' death (27:51-54).

It is in the appearances of Jesus after his resurrection, however, that the fullest manifestation of Jesus' transcendent power occurs (28:9-10, 16-20). According to some scholars, the story of Jesus' walking on water may have originated as a report of a postresurrection appearance (cf. John 21:1-14), later combined with an account of a storm at sea during Jesus' ministry. Be that as it may, the epiphany in the text before us clearly anticipates the revelation of Jesus' glory in the resurrection.

THE TEXT IN THE LIFE OF THE CHURCH

For the most part, the church's interpretation of the feeding of the 5000 has been governed by allegorical or moralistic approaches to the story. Thus the five loaves have often been identified with the five books of Moses, and the miracle construed as the transformation of law into gospel. Or attention is drawn to Christ's act of blessing, which is treated as an example for Christians on receiving God's gifts with gratitude and thanksgiving.

Not until modern times does the eucharistic interpretation of the text proposed above become prominent. Nevertheless, the story has left its imprint on Christian meals (and vice versa). Already in the Fourth Gospel, we find a eucharistic commentary on the story (John 6:51-58). Later, loaves and fish appear as symbols in Christian art, whether in conjunction with eucharist or other celebrative meals. And later still, Jesus' gesture of lifting his eyes to heaven (14:19) became part of the prayer of consecration for the host in the Roman Mass.

Another dimension of the church's discussion of the feeding story is the lively debate over "what really happened." Among the theories proposed, one of the least likely explains the incident in terms of contagious generosity: When Jesus and his disciples shared the little bit of food they had brought, others reached into their picnic baskets and did likewise! Others argue that the story is based on a symbolic meal in the wilderness with messianic connotations (an "eschatological sacrament," in the view of Albert Schweitzer). According to this theory, the miraculous elements in the story are a later accretion.

There are also interpreters, however, who prefer to take the form of the story as we now have it at face value, and who contend that a miracle of some sort is the best way to account for the tradition. Whatever may or may not lie behind the narrative is hidden from our inspection. What *is* accessible is the message that Jesus supplies the needs of his people, just as Yahweh supplied their needs in former times. That message is unmistakable, whether we treat the story in a more literal or more symbolic fashion.

In the case of Jesus' epiphany at sea, the parabolic significance of the story highlighted earlier has not gone unnoticed. The phrase *walking on the water* has come to epitomize unusual powers or unusual faith. And the boat has been widely used as a symbol for the church (as in the logo of the World Council of Churches). One of the earliest statements on the boat as a metaphor comes from the church father Augustine: "The ship which carries the disciples, i.e., the Church, is tossed and shaken by the tempests of temptation; and the contrary wind, i.e., the devil her adversary, rests not, and strives to hinder her from arriving at rest. But greater is 'He who maketh intercession for us' " (337; cf. 337-339).

It is in Peter's adventure that the depiction of the church in the story reaches its climax. And Christian teachers in every era have sought to define the lessons on faith that Peter illustrates. At one level the story of Peter is a story of failure, with a stern rebuke for insufficient faith. It is precisely in failure, however, that Peter learns (as we must learn) "the kind of faith that rivets its attention solely on the word of Jesus" (Schweizer: 323). Such is the faith that Matthew commends to his readers.

Who Really Is Defiled?

Matthew 15:1-20

PREVIEW

As we move into chapter 15, we find Jesus embroiled in another conflict or controversy (cf. the conflict stories in chapter 12). The immediate issue in the conflict is whether the disciples *defile* themselves when they fail to observe the rabbinic tradition of washing hands before eating. (According to Luke 11:38, Jesus himself failed to observe the practice.) In responding to those who pose the question, Jesus raises a more fundamental question about the rabbinic tradition itself: Does this tradition help us understand and obey the will of God expressed in the Torah? Or does it distort and sometimes circumvent the Torah and thereby mislead God's people?

Verses 1-9 present the formal dispute within which this attack and counterattack take shape. This is followed in verses 10-20 by a parabolic saying of Jesus and the subsequent discussion it evokes. Here Jesus returns to the subject of defilement and offers his own judgment on what really defiles a person.

Matthew's source for this material is Mark 7:1-23. If we compare the two texts, we see that Matthew has adapted the Markan account in several ways: (1) He has omitted the description in Mark 7:3-4 of ceremonial acts of washing in Judaism, customs with which Matthew's community was already familiar. (2) He has sharpened the language and rearranged some of the material in the dispute, so that the format of a dispute and the issues at stake emerge all the clearer. (3) He has added the sayings found in verses 12-14, where Jesus pronounces a harsh verdict on the Pharisees and rejects their teaching authority. (4) He highlights the role of *the mouth* in the definition of defilement in verses 10-20, so that the accusing words of Jesus' opponents become a prime example of the things that defile.

OUTLINE

Scripture and Tradition, 15:1-9

The Things That Defile, 15:10-20

EXPLANATORY NOTES

Scripture and Tradition 15:1-9

In the brief statement introducing the dispute in verse 1, an ominous note is sounded. Matthew informs us that the scribes and Pharisees questioning Jesus are a delegation *from Jerusalem.* This gives the dispute the character of an official inquisition, anticipating the conflicts that will shortly occur *in* Jerusalem (cf. 21:23—23:39). In the verses that follow, the dispute unfolds in a sequence of four moves:

(1) The scribes and Pharisees ask a leading question (v. 2): Why do your disciples transgress our religious tradition?

(2) Jesus asks a counterquestion (v. 3): Why do *you* transgress the law itself through your tradition? (Note the parallel structure and vocabulary of the two questions.)

(3) Jesus illustrates his counterquestion by showing the conflict between the Ten Commandments and a practice sanctioned by the tradition (vv. 4-6).

(4) Jesus draws on a quote from the prophets to describe his critics and clinch the argument (vv. 7-9).

The *tradition of the elders* was a body of material from rabbinic teachers interpreting or applying the law, later codified in the Mishnah and Talmud. According to the famous rabbi Akiba (a contemporary of Matthew), this tradition served as a fence around the law, to prevent persons from transgressing the law itself (Aboth 3:14).

The particular tradition of washing hands before eating may have been based on a biblical text commanding *priests* to bathe before eating sacred food (Lev. 22:1-9). That text is part of a longer catalogue of ritual laws urging the people of God to distinguish "between the holy and the common, and between the unclean and the clean" (Lev. 10:10), to avoid defilement from touching or partaking what is unclean (cf. Lev. 11), and to wash away defilement when it occurs (cf. Lev. 14:1-9; 15:1-33; Exod. 30:17-21).

In the NT period, the struggle of the Jewish community to maintain a distinct identity in a Gentile world gave added significance to the injunctions in Leviticus. Thus ritual ablutions played a major role in groups such as the Pharisees and Essenes (cf. CD 10:11-13; 1QS

5:13-14). And discussions of the issue of clean and unclean eventually yielded enough material to fill twelve tractates in the Mishnah.

As already noted, Jesus does not comment directly on the issue of defilement in his response to the Pharisees and scribes. Instead, he challenges the credibility of his critics, pointing out how they allow tradition to take precedence over Scripture. (Note the inclusion verse 6 forms with verse 3.) To illustrate his point, Jesus cites the practice of dedicating property to the temple with a binding oath (cf. Num. 30:2), thereby preempting any claims others might make on it. (One did not thereby give up use of the property, but simply changed its legal status from secular to sacred.) According to the text, this stratagem could even be used to deny support to aging parents.

Later, Jewish teachers disputed whether an oath taken for such a purpose was in fact irrevocable. In Jesus' day, however, the practice apparently had rabbinic support, and Jesus condemns it in no uncertain terms. It is a flagrant violation of the fifth commandment, Jesus argues, allowing persons to *not honor* their father and mother (cf. Exod. 20:12; Deut. 5:16; Exod. 21:17; Lev. 20:9). For Jesus, the societal obligation to care for parents that God commands in the Decalogue has priority over the seemingly sacred act of vowing to give one's resources to a religious institution.

The biblical text with which Jesus concludes his reply in verses 7-9 comes from Isaiah 29:13 (cited here in the form we find it in the LXX). As the quoted words suggest, the *hypocrisy* of Jesus' opponents lies in the way their tradition nullifies the very word of God they claim to uphold. The practices they advocate have the appearance of promoting devotion to God. In reality, however, they mask a profound insensitivity to the will of God revealed in the Torah.

The Things That Defile 15:10-20

When the topic of defilement surfaces again in verses 10-11, the dispute with the delegation from Jerusalem is over, and Jesus is speaking to the crowds. The miniparable he tells in verse 11 is sufficiently opaque that even the disciples will shortly request an explanation. To Jesus' opponents, however, the parabolic saying is clear enough to offend, and the disciples report this to Jesus in verse 12. This in turn provides an opportunity to introduce the sayings in verses 13-14, through which Jesus continues his blistering critique of the Pharisees.

The first of the two sayings (cf. G. Thom. 40) revolves around the image of a plant. It is an image used elsewhere as a metaphor for Israel as God's planting (cf. Isa. 5:1-7; 60:21; 61:3; Jer. 45:4) and as a self-designation of groups who considered themselves to be the true Israel (cf. Ps. Sol. 14:3-4; 1QS 8:5; 11:8). Doubtless the Pharisees thought of themselves in this way. According to Jesus, however, "Israel and its ruling class of Pharisees is not the vineyard planted by God but a wild thicket!" (Schweizer: 327).

The second saying (cf. Luke 6:39; G. Thom. 34) is equally unflattering. Jewish leaders instructed in the law viewed themselves as "a guide to the blind, a light to those who are in darkness" (Rom. 2:19; cf. Isa. 42:6-7). Jesus labels them as a case of the blind leading the blind (cf. 23:16-26). The guidance they offer is not dependable, but leads to destruction. Consequently, Jesus tells his followers to *let them alone* (v. 14). Instead of looking to the rabbinic tradition which the Pharisees represent, Jesus' community is to look to his own teaching as the final word on what God wills.

With that point established, Jesus goes on in verses 15-20 to explain the saying in verse 11 for the sake of the disciples. The language used is quite blunt. What is taken into the mouth cannot defile, Jesus says, because it does not remain in a person. It passes into the stomach and then *goes out into the sewer.* What does defile is the deep-seated evil within, which often expresses itself in *what comes out of the mouth,* namely lies, slander, and false teaching (cf. 15:8-9). Evil speech is part of the list of sins in verse 19, a list briefer in scope than the catalogue of vices in Mark 7:21-22, and so constructed that the list corresponds to the last half of the Ten Commandments (cf. Exod. 20:13-16).

In short, Jesus defines defilement in moral terms rather than ceremonial. It is not failure to observe a particular ritual of cleansing that defiles or profanes, but failure to act with wholeness in our relationships with God and fellow humans. Jesus underscores this point in his concluding pronouncement in verse 20, which recalls the issue raised at the outset of the story (v. 2) and proclaims the disciples innocent of any substantive offense.

THE TEXT IN BIBLICAL CONTEXT

Among the terms Jesus uses to flay his opponents in Matthew 15 is the epithet *you hypocrites.* Hypocritical religious practice is one of the sins for which the prophets roundly criticize ancient Israel. At times the burden of the criticism is on the way the people delight in elaborate religious celebrations, but permit social injustice to erode the very covenant with God that they are celebrating (cf. Isa. 1:10-17; Amos 5:21-24; Mic. 6:6-8).

At other times the focus of attention is on the way the leaders allow this sorry state of affairs to develop, causing others to stumble by the faulty instruction they give (cf. Jer. 23:9-32; Mic. 3:9-12; Mal. 2:7-9). Matthew draws on this tradition more than once in his Gospel (cf. 6:1-18; 9:13; 12:7), most dramatically in the *woes* Jesus pronounces when he confronts the scribes and Pharisees in the temple (chapter 23). The same tradition is clearly evident in 15:1-20.

The parallel account in Mark reveals yet another point at which the text relates to a wider conversation. According to Mark, Jesus "declared all foods clean" when he told his parable on what does and doesn't defile (Mark 7:19b). Clarity on this point was not achieved as easily as Mark's statement might suggest. We find evidence in a number of NT passages that the early church struggled long and hard with the issue of clean and unclean foods—and with the related issue of table fellowship between Jew and Gentile (cf. Acts 10:9-16; 15:19-20, 28-29; Gal. 2:11-14; Col. 2:20-23).

The most extended discussion of the issue occurs in Romans 14. There Paul, like Mark, affirms that in principle no foods are unclean for the Christian community. At the same time, Paul recognizes that old traditions of clean and unclean make certain foods problematic for some members. Where this is so, Paul argues, we should forego a menu that causes offense and so maintain a common table for all believers.

THE TEXT IN THE LIFE OF THE CHURCH

Matthew 15:1-20 has proven to be a fertile plot for Christian interpreters. Although in some ways *defilement* is a peculiarly Jewish topic, a clean life is in fact a Christian concern as well, and commentators sometimes work the text from this angle. A good example is the homily on the passage by Chrysostom, who writes these words: "Let us learn then what are the things that defile the man; let us learn, and let us flee them. For even in the church we see such a custom prevailing amongst the generality, and men giving diligence to come in clean garments, and to have their hands washed; but how to present a clean soul to God, they make no account" (319).

A second point at which the text has fascinated interpreters is its depiction of religious practice as an enemy of true faith. As noted above, even a sacred vow can become unholy if it conflicts with a fundamental moral obligation. Martin Luther devotes attention to this facet of the text and relates it to the issue of idolatry. According to Luther, idolatry begins at the point where we attempt to honor God in ways we ourselves define, rather than in the ways God commands (499-500). The text pushes us to consider, then, whether the piety we practice supports or hinders the call to justice that is central to God's covenant.

Finally, the text provides a framework for defining the relationship between Scripture and tradition—and judges those who permit tradition to have priority over Scripture. Needless to say, it has not been difficult for interpreters to point to situations where this has been the case. In the Reformation era, Jesus' critique of Jewish tradition was often applied to the practices and institutions of Roman Catholicism (cf. Luther: 497-498; Calvin, 1960:4.10.10 and 4.10.23; Calvin, 1972, 2:159-161; Menno Simons: 178, 362). The reign of tradition, however, is really a generic problem, not the failing of one particular branch of Christendom. Every church must ask itself: Does Scripture control our traditions, or do our traditions control Scripture?

Compassion with No Boundaries

Matthew 15:21-39

PREVIEW

Having challenged traditional ways of viewing clean and unclean (15:1-20), Jesus proceeds to take a journey to an *unclean* land. He heads for *the district of Tyre and Sidon* (15:21), the Gentile area of southern Phoenicia (modern-day Lebanon). After an episode with an inhabitant of this region, Jesus returns to the area around the northern edge of the Sea of Galilee (15:29). Here too, however, there are hints that the events described are taking place on the boundary of the Jewish world. Unlike the typical audiences up to now, the crowds here respond to Jesus' ministry with fervent praise. And the very name *Galilee*, as understood by Matthew, denotes a place of hope for other nations as well as Israel (cf. 4:15-16; 28:16-20).

What we have then in 15:21-39 are several episodes which look ahead to the salvation of the Gentiles, even though Jesus' mission is itself confined to Israel. Each of the episodes attests Jesus' miraculous power, so that formally the unit is a collection of miracle stories. In the first episode (vv. 21-28), a conversation on how far Jesus' mercy may extend leads at last to the healing of a woman's possessed child. The second story consists of a Matthean summary (vv. 29-31), describing the healing of numbers of people with a variety of diseases and disabilities. And in the third and final account (vv. 32-39), we find a gift miracle which reads like a reprise on the story in 14:15-21.

OUTLINE

Crumbs for a Canaanite, 15:21-28

Mercy on the Mountain, 15:29-31

Food in the Wilderness, 15:32-39

EXPLANATORY NOTES

Crumbs for a Canaanite 15:21-28

Using a word discussed earlier (cf. notes on 14:13-14), Matthew tells us that Jesus *went away* or *withdrew* to a foreign land. The text leaves open whether Jesus actually crosses into the district of Tyre and Sidon, or is only approaching the border when the woman mentioned in verse 22 comes out to meet him. Whichever the case, the woman in question is clearly a Gentile, a non-Jew.

In the parallel account from Mark on which Matthew is drawing (cf. Mark 7:24-30), the woman is identified as *a Gentile of Syrophoenician origin.* Matthew himself calls her a *Canaanite,* a pejorative term used for the pagan occupants of the Promised Land in the OT. This harsh tone governs the conversation that follows between Jesus and the woman. Thus the saying in verse 26 likens Jews to children in a household, but Gentiles to pet dogs who have no place at the table.

In spite of this, the woman's request for the healing of her daughter will eventually be granted. And the woman herself emerges as an impressive model of faith. This faith is evident in the first words she utters. Gentile though she is, she acclaims Jesus as the *Son of David,* thereby acknowledging his messianic authority.

Even more striking is the way the woman persists with her request when that request seems hopeless. Neither silent rebuff (v. 23) nor the argument that Jesus' mission is to Jews alone (v. 24, cf. 10:6) persuades the woman to give up. She keeps pressing her need (v. 25).

And when Jesus utters the saying about children and dogs (v. 26), the woman proceeds to debate Jesus on his own terms: She implores Jesus for some of the crumbs from the table that even dogs are privileged to enjoy (v. 27).

It is this persistence that finally leads Jesus to exclaim: *Woman, great is your faith!* (v. 28). Like the centurion at Capernaum in 8:5-13, the woman illustrates Gentile faith that puts Israel to shame (cf. 11:21). And like the centurion's servant or son, the woman's daughter is cured instantly when Jesus says: *Let it be done* (cf. 15:28; 8:13).

Mercy on the Mountain 15:29-31

In Mark's Gospel, the healing of the woman's daughter is followed by the healing of a deaf mute (cf. Mark 7:31-37). Matthew, however, absorbs this story into the summary we find in verses 29-31, a summary that enumerates various categories of people whom Jesus heals. If we compare this summary with the one in 4:23-25, we observe some striking parallels. There too we find a catalogue of various ailments; there too Jesus goes *up the mountain* (5:1); and likewise we have the sense of crowds coming from all directions rather than from any particular location. The summary here thus forms an inclusion with 4:23-25, inviting the reader to recall all the reports of healing since Jesus' ministry began.

If the form of 15:29-31 links it with other summaries, the content links it with two additional texts. One is the passage in 11:2-6, where Jesus responds to John the Baptist, reciting the mighty works that accompany his ministry. The other text is Isaiah 29:17-24, which speaks of a coming time of salvation when "the eyes of the blind shall see" and the redeemed "will sanctify the Holy One of Jacob, and will stand in awe of the God of Israel" (cf. 29:18, 23; Matt. 15:31b).

What makes the Isaiah text all the more significant is that Isaiah 29:13 was the source of Jesus' words criticizing the scribes and Pharisees in 15:7-9 (cf. Isa. 29:20-21). By using language from Isaiah 29, Matthew creates a picture of a "contrast people," who praise God for Jesus' deeds rather than take offense. As they do so, they represent the mixed church community that worships the God of Israel.

Food in the Wilderness 15:32-39

The story of food in the wilderness in verses 32-39 is based on Mark 8:1-10, and involves the same crowds portrayed in verses 29-31.

Like the earlier feeding episode in 14:15-21, the miracle here reflects Jesus' compassion (v. 32), begins with a quandary on the part of the disciples (v. 33), depicts Jesus as a gracious host in charge of the situation (vv. 34-36a), includes the disciples as key figures in distributing bread to others (v. 36b), and results in more than enough food (vv. 37-38). Only the numbers are different. This time there are *seven* loaves and *seven* baskets of food left over (note that an everyday Greek word is used for *baskets,* whereas the parallel word in 14:20 denotes baskets typically used by Jews). And *4000* men are fed, along with women and children.

While interpreters differ on the significance of these figures, the numbers most likely carry symbolic meaning. *Seven* is a number that connotes perfection or completeness (cf. Rev. 1:4 and the multiples of seven in Matthew's genealogy). And *4000* is a multiple of *four*, which is linked with the idea of universality (cf. the four corners of the earth in Isa. 11:12 and Rev. 20:8, and the four winds from the four quarters of heaven in Jer. 49:36). If viewed alongside other data in the unit, the numbers suggest that the feeding in 15:32-39 is not merely a repetition of 14:15-21. There the focus was on Jesus as the Messiah who provides for Israel. Here, however, the crowd that is fed represents not only Israel, but the worldwide community that looks to Jesus in the church.

As in 14:22, the story ends with the dismissal of the crowds and a departure by boat (v. 39). This time, however, the journey across the lake does not generate a new story. We are simply informed that Jesus *went to the region of Magadan* (cf. Mark 8:10), the location of which remains unknown.

THE TEXT IN BIBLICAL CONTEXT

For the food miracle in 15:32-39, the wider context in Scripture includes a series of texts featuring food and meals. We have already discussed some of the texts from this tradition in our comments on the earlier food miracle in 14:15-21. Rather than reiterate this material here, we will concentrate instead on the story of the Canaanite woman. For this episode, the wider context consists of everything in Scripture that bears on the Jew-Gentile issue (passages such as Acts 15 or Eph. 2:11—3:6), but especially certain stories in which Gentiles like the woman gain access to Israel's God.

One such story is set in Zarephath (near Sidon!), where the deceased son of a widow who feeds Elijah is revived by the prophet

(1 Kings 17:8-24). Another Gentile who receives divine help is the commander of the Syrian army, Naaman, who is cured of leprosy by the prophet Elisha (2 Kings 5:1-19). Army officers are also featured in two stories from the NT: One is the nameless centurion whose son or servant is healed by Jesus (Matt. 8:5-13; Luke 7:1-10). And the other is Cornelius, also a centurion, whose household receives the Spirit during a visit from Peter (Acts 10).

Like the persons in these and other related stories, the Canaanite woman shows that the power of God to save can cross ethnic boundaries. (Cf. the comments on boundary-crossing as a characteristic theme of miracle stories, in TBC for 8:1—9:34.) Such boundaries may prove to be formidable, certainly, as the woman herself discovers when she solicits Jesus' help. In the final analysis, however, salvation is God's gift "to everyone who has faith, to the Jew first and also to the Greek" (Rom. 1:16; cf. Bornkamm, Barth, Held: 197-200).

THE TEXT IN THE LIFE OF THE CHURCH

For many readers, the story of the Canaanite woman belongs to that handful of texts which we label "problem passages." We are offended by the way Jesus relates to the woman. He seems to reflect the ethnic biases of his contemporaries, and he gives the woman a rather hard time.

If we read the text on its own terms, however, Jesus' behavior appears in a different light. What the story seeks to portray is how faith enables Gentiles to receive God's mercy. And Jesus' resistance to the woman provides a foil which allows her Gentile faith to stand out. To put it another way, it is the crossing of the hurdles that Jesus places in her path (hurdles of some importance to Jews and Jewish Christians) that reveals just how *great* the woman's faith really is.

Not surprisingly, Menno Simons selects this woman as one of ten examples in a list of biblical persons who illustrate true faith (cf. 383-391), and other writers view her faith with equal admiration. In some texts the facet of faith lifted up is her humility (she accepts the label *dog* and only asks for crumbs of mercy). In other cases the emphasis falls on the quality of persistence, on faith that refuses to give up. Luther's comments on this point are especially perceptive: The woman demonstrates unshakable confidence in God's grace and goodness, even when it seems that God is turning aside and saying no. This, as Luther remarks, is the essence of true faith (cf. 507-511).

The True Israel

Matthew 16:1-20

PREVIEW

From 11:1 on, Matthew has been showing how various persons and groups in Israel *responded* to Jesus' ministry. The general response is one of rejection and unfaith. Only among the twelve does Jesus find a receptive following. That state of affairs forms the backdrop for the question Matthew pursues in 16:1-20: Where is the *true* Israel to be found? According to the text, the true Israel will not be found in the temple or synagogue. Instead, it will be found in the community that Jesus himself builds, to which he gives authority to develop a life of its own. There believers will discern the will of God and disciple one another, free from the constraints of Jewish leaders and their teaching.

The narrative in which this theme is developed consists of three episodes. A controversy over signs sets things in motion in verses 1-4 and pits Jesus against a coalition of two Jewish parties. Those same two parties are named in a conversation Jesus has with the disciples in verses 5-12, where a saying of Jesus is misunderstood and has to be clarified.

A subsequent conversation in verses 13-20 takes us from confusion to confession: In a twofold act of naming, Peter acclaims Jesus as God's Son, and Jesus acclaims Peter as a rock on which to build. Most of the material in these three vignettes is drawn from Mark 8 (vv. 11-21 and 27-30). For the sayings on Peter and the church, however, Matthew is indebted to a special tradition concerning Peter (cf. 14:28-31; 17:24-27; 18:21-22). This tradition could conceivably have reported a commissioning of Peter following Jesus' resurrection (cf. 1 Cor. 15:5a; Luke 24:34; John 21:15-19), which Matthew chose to incorporate here rather than at the end of the Gospel. In any case, Matthew offers us an expanded account of the episode at Caesarea Philippi.

OUTLINE

Yet Another Test, 16:1-4

Watch What You Consume, 16:5-12

The Messianic Community, 16:13-20

EXPLANATORY NOTES

Yet Another Test 16:1-4

The request for a *sign* in verses 1-4 is based on Mark 8:11-13 and poses the issue of Jesus' authority: What sign from heaven can Jesus produce to validate his message and ministry? For those who have followed Matthew's narrative up to this point, the episode here will recall two earlier incidents. One is the *test* Jesus undergoes in the wilderness before his ministry begins, when Satan himself urges Jesus to show a sign of his sonship (4:1-11). The other is the request for a sign in the round of controversies in chapter 12 (12:38-42), which may draw on the same underlying tradition as the account before us (cf. also Luke 11:16; John 2:18-19; 6:30; G. Thom. 91).

As reported by Matthew, the request in 16:1 comes from an unlikely coalition of *Pharisees and Sadducees,* parties with widely differing agenda. Frequently they found themselves in conflict (cf. Acts 23:6-10). Here, however, they represent a united front of Jewish leaders, seeking to discredit Jesus and his work.

In most translations, Jesus' reply to the Pharisees and Sadducees begins with the saying in verses 2-3: You are adept at reading signs that forecast the weather, Jesus says, but blind to what has been going on in my ministry (*the signs of the times*). This saying is missing, however, in the earliest Greek manuscripts (cf. the footnote in the NRSV and NIV) and may have been added to Matthew's text by a later copyist (cf. Luke 12:54-56).

In any case, Jesus refuses to grant what his opponents seek. The only sign they will get is his return from death (*the sign of Jonah,* v. 4; cf. 12:39-40). God will vindicate Jesus in his resurrection, but Jesus will not try to force God's hand to satisfy critics. The account ends with the brief note that Jesus *left* his opponents. More than a piece of information, the statement depicts Jesus walking away from Israel's leadership, ready to look elsewhere.

Watch What You Consume 16:5-12

After the episode in 16:1-4, the disciples rejoin Jesus, and an interesting dialogue follows. Based on Mark 8:14-21 (cf. Luke 12:1), the account is constructed in chiastic form (*a b b' a'*), which we might diagram as follows:

a. Jesus warns the disciples about the *yeast* of the Pharisees and Sadducees.

b. The disciples misunderstand Jesus' saying because they are preoccupied with their lack of food.

b'. Jesus deals with this misunderstanding and with the *little faith* reflected in concern about food. (After the two feedings, the disciples should know that Jesus can supply their needs at will.)

a'. The disciples finally understand Jesus' saying about the yeast of Jewish leaders.

Here and elsewhere in Scripture (and in rabbinic texts as well), yeast or leaven is a symbol for something that corrupts (cf. 1 Cor. 5:6-8; Gal. 5:7-9; Matt. 13:33 is an exception). In Mark's account, the leaven of Jewish leaders is not defined, and we (like the disciples) are left wondering what Jesus means. In Matthew, however, the disciples finally *understand* what Jesus is getting at (v. 12), and their discernment is shared with the reader of the story: The yeast to be avoided is the *teaching* of Israel's leaders, teaching that misleads the people who consume it (cf. 15:7-9 and 15:13-14). If this is so, then those who seek the will of God must go where true instruction is offered. And the place where this occurs is, for Matthew, the church.

The Messianic Community 16:13-20

The conversation of Jesus with his disciples in verses 13-20 occurs somewhere in the vicinity of Caesarea Philippi (= Philip's Caesarea), at the northernmost boundary of ancient Israel. Known earlier as Paneas or Panion, the city of Caesarea Philippi was located at the foot of Mt. Hermon and had been rebuilt and renamed by Philip the Tetrarch (cf. Luke 3:1). The new name both honored the emperor, Caesar Augustus, and distinguished this Caesarea from the coastal city with the same name (cf. Acts 10:1).

In the parallel account in Mark's Gospel (Mark 8:27-30), the conversation at Caesarea Philippi has one basic topic: Who is Jesus? In Matthew's account, however, a second topic emerges: Who are the disciples? The dual answer of the text is that Jesus is the Messiah, and that his disciples make up the messianic community. To put it another way, the text links the topics of Christ and the church, of Christology and ecclesiology. And the one who embodies this link in the narrative is Simon Peter. It is he who confesses faith in Jesus, on behalf of all the disciples. And it is he, therefore, who receives Jesus' promise of what the disciples will soon become.

The question of *Jesus*' identity is explored in verses 13-16 through two subquestions: (1) What is the general opinion of Jesus in

Israel? (2) How do the disciples themselves view Jesus?

When Jesus poses the first question, the disciples respond with a list of popular views. In each case, people are identifying Jesus with an earlier figure in Israel's history who has supposedly returned to life or whose role is fulfilled anew in him. He could be John the Baptist (the view Herod espouses in 14:2), or Elijah (whose return was promised in Mal. 4:5-6), or Jeremiah (who is depicted in 2 Macc. 15:13-16 as alive and active in heaven), or another such figure (cf. Deut. 18:15-22). Common to each of these popular views is the idea that Jesus is a *prophet*. While this is true in one sense, it is an insufficient view from the standpoint of the Gospels. It confines Jesus to the roles and possibilities of the old era.

So it is that Jesus continues to probe with his second question: What do *you* my followers see as you behold me at work? The answer Peter gives as the disciples' spokesperson has already been anticipated in 14:33. Here, however, as a direct response to Jesus' inquiry, the words take on added significance. More than a prophet, Jesus is *the Messiah*, one with authority to *fulfill* Israel's prophetic hope. Like the anointed kings who preceded him, therefore, he may be called *God's Son* (cf. 2 Sam. 7:14; Pss. 2:7; 89:26-27), but with a status far exceeding theirs. *His* sonship is not merely one of adoption, the result of an act of coronation, but a sonship that comes from a unique and intimate relationship with God (cf. 11:27). He is *the Son of the living God* par excellence, because the living and life-giving God has been present in his life from the very beginning (cf. 1:18-25). *[Christ/Christology, p. 418.]*

In verses 17-19, the focus of the conversation shifts to Peter and the community of believers he represents. Here we find three succinct pronouncements by Jesus, including a beatitude (v. 17), an act of naming and the related promise (v. 18), and a formula of investiture (v. 19). The beatitude addresses Peter by his old family name (*BarJona = son of Jonah*), setting the stage for the new name he will receive in the next verse. As in beatitudes elsewhere (cf. 5:3-12), the phrase *blessed are you* could be paraphrased: "How fortunate you are!" Nevertheless, this is a gift from God, not luck.

Peter is in a favorable situation because he is able to perceive Jesus in a way that goes beyond human understanding (*flesh and blood* denotes that which is human or earthly; cf. 1 Cor. 15:50; Gal. 1:16). Human perception sees in Jesus no more than a great prophet. By divine revelation, however, Peter and his fellow disciples behold Jesus as God's Son (cf. 11:25-27, and the way Paul describes his reception of the gospel in Gal. 1:11-12, 15-16).

The promise Jesus gives in verse 18 is to build a durable community which he calls *my church* (cf. 18:17; 1 Cor. 1:2; Acts 9:31). The Greek word for *church* is *ekklēsia*, the same word used for the assembly of Israel in the LXX (cf. Deut. 31:30; Judg. 20:2; 1 Kings 8:14). What Jesus promises, then, is to reconstruct the people of God, to fashion a messianic community of faith with its own foundation and destiny. And Peter is somehow related to this building project. As the NRSV and NIV footnotes indicate, verse 18 begins with a provocative play on words: *You are Peter (Petros)*, Jesus says, *and on this rock (petra) I will build my church. Petros* is a masculine noun meaning *stone* or *rock*, and so usable as a male name; *petra* is a feminine noun conveying the idea of a rock foundation (as in 7:24).

The key question here is whether the rock foundation of the church is Peter himself, or something to be distinguished from Peter. If the latter, Jesus could be speaking of Peter's *faith*, or of the *revelation* Peter received. It is more likely, however, that the rock on which Jesus promises to build the church is in fact *Peter himself*, *Peter the first disciple* (cf. 4:18; 10:2), who represents the whole group of disciples from which the church will be formed. At least four considerations support this view:

(1) When a person in the biblical story receives a new name, the name points to a new identity or role for that person (cf. Gen. 17:5-6, 15-16; 32:27-28). It is thus natural to relate the name Peter receives to a role he will have in the founding of the church.

(2) The Aramaic saying which likely lies behind the Greek text here would have used one and the same word for both *Peter* and *rock* (the word *kepha*), thus identifying the two. (It is from the Aramaic word that the name *Cephas* is derived, the name Paul uses for Peter in his letters; cf. 1 Cor. 1:12; Gal. 1:18.)

(3) The view that the church is built on the foundation of the apostles is found elsewhere in the NT (Eph. 2:20). Further, there is evidence that Peter was revered as one of the *pillars* of the church among believers in Judea (cf. Gal. 2:9).

(4) The OT speaks of Abraham as the rock from which Israel was hewn (Isa. 51:1-2), and it is fitting that the first disciple to respond to Jesus should be identified in the same manner. Like Abraham, Peter signifies the origin of a special people, a people through whom God will bless all the nations.

The second part of Jesus' promise is that *the gates of Hades will not prevail against* the church. According to some interpreters, the language depicts a church on the move, storming the bastions of hell and conquering evil. The problem with this view is that the basic image of the church in verse 18 is that of a building on a rock, not a moving army. A clue to a correct understanding of the promise is found in the imagery of *the gates of Hades.* Hades or Sheol, the underworld abode of the dead, was pictured by the biblical writers as a watery abyss (cf. 2 Sam. 22:5; Job 26:5-6; 38:16-17). Were not its gateways sealed, turbulent waters could break through and destroy the earth with floods.

As a metaphor, therefore, the gates of Hades represent the threat of destruction, in the face of which one seeks a secure place (cf. Isa. 28:14-22; 1QH 6:23-27; 1QS 8:7). According to Jesus, the community he builds is such a place, capable of withstanding destruction. However fierce the floodwaters that beat against the church, its foundation is secure, and it will not be overwhelmed.

As noted earlier, the third saying in verses 17-19 reads like an act of investiture: Jesus entrusts *the keys of the kingdom* to Peter (from whence comes the picture of Peter guarding the gates of heaven) and endows him with authority to *bind* and *loose.* At first glance, we might think that Jesus is granting Peter a prestigious office in the church. And some Christians have interpreted verse 19 in this way. Other passages, however, suggest that Matthew is not thinking along these lines. The authority granted to Peter in 16:19 is granted to *all* the disciples in 18:18. And Jesus' sayings in 23:8-12 forbid anyone to assume hierarchical authority over others in the church.

To understand the text correctly, we need to recall Peter's function throughout 16:13-20. He serves as the representative of the disciples as a group. When Peter, therefore, receives the keys and the power to bind and loose, he does so *on behalf of the church.* To put it another way, the saying in verse 19 does not grant Peter special authority in the church, but grants the church special authority within history.

Both of the two metaphors for this authority are rooted in Jewish tradition. The image of the keys likely comes from an oracle in Isaiah, which speaks of the installation of a new majordomo or steward in Hezekiah's palace. There we read: "I will place on his shoulder the key of the house of David; he shall open, and no one shall shut; he shall shut, and no one shall open" (Isa. 22:22). Matthew 16:19 envisions a similar role for the church. As the steward governed access to the royal household, so the church governs access to God's kingdom. Unlike the leaders reproached in 23:13, however, who were guilty of blocking the way to the kingdom (cf. Luke 11:52), the church is called to use the keys to make the kingdom more accessible.

The metaphor of binding and loosing sometimes refers to casting out demons, but here reflects a usage that comes out of the synagogue. In this context, *binding* and *loosing* could refer either to (1) the forbidding and permitting of certain actions, or (2) the imposing and lifting of a sentence of excommunication. In short, the authority to bind and loose is the authority of a community to establish and enforce norms for its life. According to Matthew, Jesus gives the church this kind of authority, authority ratified in heaven itself. As a result, the church can interpret Scripture and make community decisions without looking to the synagogue.

In verse 20, Matthew returns to the Markan narrative (cf. Mark 8:30) and to the theme of Jesus' messiahship. Although Jesus has accepted Peter's confession of faith (v. 16), he now forbids the disciples to proclaim that he is *the Messiah.* The reason for this prohibition is not stated, but may be inferred from the material that follows (cf. 16:21-28). Only after the cross will the true nature of Jesus' messiahship be understood. Until that time, the political connotations of the title *Messiah* could arouse false expectations and hinder Jesus from fulfilling his mission.

THE TEXT IN BIBLICAL CONTEXT

Who do you say that I am? The question Jesus asks his disciples in 16:15 was a question repeatedly asked in the early church. Implied in the question is the belief that Jesus himself is central to the Christian message. Correspondingly, we find a number of NT texts which either call for or illustrate a confession of faith like Peter's. Thus the author of 1 John writes to his community: "God abides in those who confess that Jesus is the Son of God, and they abide in God" (1 John 4:15; cf. 4:1-3; 5:1; Acts 16:30-31; Rom. 10:9-10). And explicit statements of faith can be found both in the gospel narratives (cf. Matt. 27:54; John 1:49) and in creedal summaries imbedded in letters from Paul and others (cf. Rom. 1:3-4; Phil. 2:5-11; 1 Tim. 3:16).

Another strand of the NT to which the text belongs consists of passages describing the church as a *building*. While most of these passages have a common building in mind, the temple, they develop the metaphor in a variety of ways. In Matthew 16:18, Jesus plays the role of the builder, and Peter is identified as the foundation of the building. The roles are reversed in 1 Corinthians 3:9-17, where Paul and Peter (and other leaders) are depicted as the builders, while Jesus Christ is named as the church's foundation.

Yet a third picture is that of Christ as the *cornerstone* of a building, with prophets and apostles forming the rest of the foundation (Eph. 2:19-22; cf. Matt. 21:42 and parallels), and with believers as "living stones" built into the new structure (1 Pet. 2:4-8). Together, these texts attest both the importance of the temple motif in the early church and the transformation of that motif to describe a living community.

Finally, Matthew 16 contributes to a wider pool of texts which highlight Peter's role as an apostolic leader (cf. Brown, 1973). Within the First Gospel itself, Peter is cast in a leading or representative position at several points (cf. 10:2; 14:28-33; 17:24-27). Elsewhere in the Gospels, Peter is assigned the task of strengthening his "brothers" (Luke 22:31-32), granted a special appearance by the risen Lord (Luke 24:34), and instructed to care for Jesus' sheep like a shepherd (John 21:15-17).

The same sense of Peter's significance is attested in other parts of the NT. Thus in the story of Acts, Peter appears as the chief spokesperson for the disciples in Judea and Samaria (cf. Acts 1:15; 2:14; 8:14-25; 10:1—11:18). And Paul refers to Peter in the letter to the Galatians as the one who headed the mission "to the circumcised" (Gal. 2:6-10). Given data such as this, it is not surprising that Peter is called a rock at the base of the church's life.

THE TEXT IN THE LIFE OF THE CHURCH

The rock on which the church is built has been a topic of lively discussion throughout the history of interpretation. Interestingly, one can find proponents of each of the various understandings of *this rock* among the church fathers. While some identify the rock with Peter (Tertullian), others relate it to Peter's faith (Chrysostom), to Christ (Augustine), or to every disciple who confesses Christ (Origen). Later, the view that Peter is the rock became the prevailing view, and the text was increasingly used to support the primacy of the Roman bishops who allegedly succeeded Peter.

Thus the text became a point of controversy between Protestants and Roman Catholics, with Protestant leaders disputing Roman claims to possess an office granted to Peter. Fortunately, centuries of polemics are now yielding to a more judicious interpretation of the text. On the one hand, there is a growing consensus that the rock on which Jesus promises to build the church is in fact the disciple Peter. On the other hand, it is widely agreed by leaders of various confessions that Jesus' words do not decide the issue of who should govern the church.

A broader concern for faith and life is the role the text ascribes not to Peter, but to the *church*. At the beginning of the twentieth century, French critic Alfred Loisy made the provocative statement that "Jesus proclaimed the kingdom of God, and what came was the church" (cited in Küng: 69). Loisy's remark raises the question of the relationship between the kingdom and the church. Did the church develop because the kingdom failed to come? Or is the church an integral part of the coming of God's reign?

The historical question of how and when Jesus' followers became "the church" remains a matter of debate. From the very beginning, however, Jesus' message of the kingdom assumes that there will be *a community of the kingdom*, and Matthew 16 describes the church in precisely this manner. The church receives and exercises *the keys of the kingdom.* While God's reign extends further than the boundaries of the church, the church is the sphere where God's reign is made known, and where persons lay claim to its promise and demands. The text assures us, therefore, that the church is by no means an accident or afterthought, but rather central to God's plan to redeem humankind.

Part 4

Jesus' Final Journey

Matthew 16:21—20:34

PREVIEW

The phrase *from that time on* in 16:21 signals a major shift in Matthew's narrative (cf. the same phrase in 4:17). Up to this point, Jesus' ministry to Israel has been centered on Galilee. From now on, however, everything will be oriented toward the city of Jerusalem—and toward the fate awaiting Jesus when he gets to Jerusalem. One of the ways Matthew makes this shift clear to the reader is through sayings in which Jesus predicts his passion or suffering (cf. 16:21; 17:22-23; 20:17-19). In addition, Matthew uses the motif of a *journey* to Jerusalem as a narrative framework for the section (cf. 19:1-2; 20:17; 20:29). Although the journey does not actually begin until 19:1, Jesus' decision to make the journey is clear from the outset, and there is a mood of anxious anticipation from that moment on.

While the story is taking shape along the lines just described, Jesus is busy preparing his followers for what lies ahead. At one level, the instruction Jesus gives is preparing the twelve for the particular circumstances they will face in Jerusalem and beyond. At another level, Jesus is instructing disciples of every age, future members of the church he has promised to build (cf. 16:18-19). To put it another way, the teaching in 16:21—20:34 is a resource for the formation of faith and community.

Numerous topics or issues thus come up for discussion. There are sayings calling believers to take up the cross and share Jesus' suffering (cf. 16:24-28; 20:20-23). There is teaching on how disciples will relate to the old order of family life and possessions (cf. chapter 19). And there is counsel on the values that should shape the corporate life of the community and its leaders (cf. 17:24—18; 20:24-28).

Literarily, the material in 16:21—20:34 is quite diverse. We will say more about the form and origin of this material when we examine the various pieces that make up the section. For now, it is sufficient to note that Matthew gives the reader an expanded version of Mark's narrative (cf. Mark 8:31—10:52).

OUTLINE

Suffering and Glory, 16:21—17:21

16:21-28	The Way of the Cross
17:1-13	A Glimpse of Glory
17:14-21	A Crisis of Faith

Life in Jesus' Community, 17:22—18:35

17:22-27	Freedom and Submission
18:1-14	A Community of Caring
18:15-35	Dealing with Brokenness

Demands of Discipleship, 19:1—20:34

19:1-15	Marriage and Children
19:16—20:16	Giving and Getting
20:17-34	Status or Servanthood

Matthew 16:21—17:21

Suffering and Glory

PREVIEW

At the conclusion of the episode at Caesarea Philippi, Jesus places an embargo on the topic of his messiahship (16:20). He forbids the disciples to issue a news release announcing, Here is the Christ! To the disciples themselves, however, Jesus has a great deal more to say about his calling. He must clarify the route by which he finally will save his people (cf. 1:21). This sets the agenda for the material that follows, material Matthew takes from the Gospel of Mark (cf. Mark 8:31—9:29).

In the first account (16:21-28), Jesus makes the unwelcome point that a cross precedes the crown. Only after Jesus suffers many things will he reign in glory and will that glory be apparent. The second account offers a preview of Jesus' glory (17:1-13), through an epiphany usually labeled the "transfiguration." Jesus shines like the sun, and his preeminence is confirmed. As the story ends, however, the conversation returns to the theme of suffering (cf. verses 9-13). And the final account in the section (17:14-21) seems to wrestle with the question of life in Jesus' absence. Will the disciples be powerless when Jesus isn't there, or will they find the strength needed to deal with difficult situations?

The Way of the Cross

Matthew 16:21-28

PREVIEW

The unit that begins in 16:21 consists of two shorter segments, already linked in the Markan narrative (cf. Mark 8:31—9:1). In the first segment (vv. 21-23), the topic is Jesus' suffering and subsequent vindication. The material here includes the first of the so-called "passion predictions" (cf. 16:21; 17:22-23; 20:17-19; 26:1-2), followed by harsh words between Peter and Jesus concerning this forecast. In the second segment (vv. 24-28), the focus shifts from Jesus' fate to the suffering and vindication of his disciples. Here we find a collection of five sayings that were originally independent of each other, but now are joined to address the theme of the cost and reward of following Jesus. By presenting the two segments of material back-to-back, Matthew and Mark make an important theological point: As Jesus goes, so also must his followers. His cross provides a paradigm for Christian discipleship.

OUTLINE

Destined to Suffer, 16:21-23

Losing and Finding Life, 16:24-28

EXPLANATORY NOTES

Destined to Suffer 16:21-23

The passion prediction in verse 21 is cast in the form of a narrator's summary of Jesus' announcement. Several features are noteworthy in the language Matthew uses:

(1) We find a sample of apocalyptic vocabulary for the revealing of coming events. Jesus *shows* his disciples what *must* come to pass to fulfill the divine purpose (cf. the same language in Rev. 1:1).

(2) Matthew calls attention to *Jerusalem* as the place of Jesus' demise. As the site where earlier prophets met their doom (cf. 23:37), the holy city will once again become an unholy city.

(3) We learn that Jesus will be rejected by the religious authorities of Israel, including the *elders* (influential Jewish laypersons), the *chief priests* (the temple hierarchy), and the *scribes* (teachers of the law).

All three groups were represented in the Sanhedrin in Jerusalem, the highest Jewish council and tribunal.

(4) The text uses a phrase from an early Christian confession to describe Jesus' vindication following his passion. He will not be held by death, but will be raised *on the third day* (cf. 1 Cor. 15:4; Hos. 6:2).

The language used is also significant in the private exchange that takes place between Peter and Jesus (vv. 22-23). When Peter rebukes Jesus, he uses a formula that reads literally, *Gracious to you,* which means, *May God in his grace prevent this from happening to you.* The translation *God forbid* is a shorthand way of expressing this idea.

In responding to Peter, Jesus issues a rebuke of his own, and it is full of irony. Earlier Peter was acclaimed as one who discerned God's revelation (16:17), but now he is criticized for *thinking not as God thinks but as human beings do* (NJB). Earlier Peter was called the rock foundation of the church (16:18), but now he is called an obstacle in Jesus' path, something to stumble over (cf. Isa. 8:14-15; 1 Pet. 2:7-8). In fact, by seeking to divert Jesus from fulfilling God's plan, Peter assumes the role of Satan in tempting or testing Jesus. So it is that Jesus says, recalling his words in 4:10: *Get behind me, Satan! Do not hinder me from my mission.*

Losing and Finding Life 16:24-28

With the five sayings in verses 24-28, Jesus resumes his conversation with the entire group of disciples. The first saying (v. 24; cf. 10:38; Luke 14:27; G. Thom. 55) invites would-be disciples to *take up* their cross. For those who first heard this saying, the language would evoke pictures of a condemned prisoner (or someone conscripted to assist him) carrying a cross to the site of the execution (cf. 27:32). The metaphor is thus a strong one and signifies more than simply bearing the burdens of life. It calls for enduring animosity and suffering, to the point of death if necessary. Instead of seeking their own safety and well-being, true followers will deny self and pay the price of discipleship.

In the saying that follows (v. 25; cf. John 12:25), we learn that taking up the cross is not as foolish as it might seem. From a worldly point of view, sacrificing one's life means a total and irretrievable loss. Accordingly, self-preservation becomes a high priority. For Jesus, however, life in the fullest sense is life in God's reign, and obtaining *that* life is the all-important issue. The paradox here, as Jesus' words make clear, is that the persons who *find* life in the kingdom are not those who cling tenaciously to their present existence, but those who risk themselves on behalf of the new order.

The rhetorical questions in the next saying (v. 26; cf. Luke 12:15) underscore the importance of not losing the life that matters. Cast in the form of a wisdom pronouncement, the saying draws on the language of Psalm 49:7-9: "Truly no ransom avails for one's life, there is no price one can give to God for it. . . ." There *life* is the life we enjoy here and now. In Matthew, however, the *life* which worldly wealth can neither buy nor replace is life eternal in God's reign. How could one compensate for the loss of *that* life?

The final two sayings consist of promises Jesus makes to those who follow him. Both sayings use the language of apocalyptic and speak of the *coming* of the Son of Man to rule and to judge (cf. 13:41-43; 24:44; 25:31; 26:64; Dan. 7:13-14). Here as elsewhere in the Gospel, *Son of Man* refers to Jesus, but now with a view to his endtime authority. According to verse 27, Jesus will *repay* or reward his disciples when he settles up accounts with humankind at the judgment (cf. Ps. 62:12; Matt. 6:1-6; 25:14-30; Rom. 2:6; Rev. 22:12).

Moreover, verse 28 says that some disciples will get a glimpse of Jesus' coming before death overtakes them. Originally this saying may have meant, quite literally, that the end would occur while the first generation of Christians was still alive (cf. 1 Thess. 4:15). In Matthew, however, the saying likely refers to Jesus' appearance to the eleven in chapter 28 (cf. the comments on 10:23). When the risen one proclaims that he now commands authority in heaven and on earth (28:18), "his disciples see him coming with his royal power" (Meier, 1980:188) and thus enjoy a foretaste of his coming at the end.

THE TEXT IN BIBLICAL CONTEXT

The portrayal of Jesus as one who *must undergo great suffering* is not limited to the handful of passion predictions. Other texts as well speak of Jesus' death as part of the divine plan (cf. Matt. 26:39; Luke 12:50; Acts 2:23) and as a fulfillment of Scripture (cf. Luke 24:26-27; Acts 3:18; 1 Cor. 15:3). While no writer in the OT foresees a suffering *Messiah*, several texts and traditions depict a mission of suffering for God's servants in a broader sense.

Thus 2 Chronicles 36:15-16 attests the tradition of the rejected and persecuted prophet (cf. Luke 13:31-34). The apocryphal Wisdom of Solomon speaks of the righteous man who calls himself a son of God, whose adversaries condemn him to shameful death (Wisd. of Sol. 2:12-20; cf. Ps. 22). And Isaiah of the exile writes of a servant figure who bears the sins of others in his suffering and death (Isa. 52:13—53:12). Texts like these point to the divine *must* of the cross in Jesus' work as God's deliverer.

In the call to disciples to take up *their* cross, Matthew again sounds a note heard elsewhere in his Gospel (cf. 5:10-12; 10:16-39; 24:9-14) and a note picked up by others in the early church. An example is the counsel we find in 1 Peter: "For to this you have been called, because Christ also suffered for you, leaving you an example, so that you should follow in his steps" (1 Pet. 2:21; cf. Heb. 12:1-2; 13:12-13).

Nowhere is this theme developed more fully than in the letters of Paul. To the Galatians Paul writes: "I have been crucified with Christ; and it is no longer I who live, but it is Christ who lives in me" (Gal. 2:19-20; cf. 6:14, 17). Equally forceful is Paul's language in 2 Corinthians, where he speaks of his afflictions and persecution as "always carrying in the body the death of Jesus, so that the life of Jesus may also be made visible in our bodies" (2 Cor. 4:10; cf. 1:3-7). The cross thus provides an image for the Christian life that pervades the NT.

THE TEXT IN THE LIFE OF THE CHURCH

The church's response to the cross and Jesus' words about the cross has taken various forms. The most obvious could be called the domestication of the cross as a symbol of the faith. Since the time of Constantine, the cross has become the primary token of Christian art and piety. We wear it as jewelry, display it on altars, imprint it on letterheads, place it atop steeples, and mount it on grave sites. So prevalent is its use, one can easily forget what the cross represents—a death sentence. Even so, it has the power inherent in symbols to evoke important memories.

For some Christians the cross as a symbol has certainly taken on special meaning. It has become an emblem of suffering known firsthand in the struggle to be faithful. Here the response to the text is one of finding the church's fate reflected *in* the text—and thereby finding purpose in the tribulation at hand. Such is the case in "The Cross of the Saints," a work by Menno Simons encouraging fellow Anabaptists. There we read, in a paraphrase of the text, that "it can never be otherwise, as you well know, than that all who wish to obey and follow Jesus Christ . . . must take upon themselves the heavy cross of all poverty, distress, disdain, sorrow, sadness, and must so follow the rejected, the outcast, the bleeding and crucified Christ" (583). That, Menno says, is the experience of God's people throughout history, and that is the mark of the faithful church.

Whether persecuted or not, the church has wrestled with the implications of the text for its life. *What does it mean to be a community of the cross?* According to Jürgen Moltmann (97-98), the church is linked to the cross in at least three ways:

(1) The church derives its very life from Jesus' death on the cross. That sacrificial act both creates the church and defines its character.

(2) The church is a community *under* the cross. It is called to participate in Christ's journey to Jerusalem, confronting the false powers that oppose God's rule and enduring the suffering those powers inflict.

(3) The church is called to solidarity with the wretched who live in the shadow of the cross. Only in fellowship with the despised and rejected do we truly have fellowship with the crucified Christ.

A Glimpse of Glory

Matthew 17:1-13

PREVIEW

The story that begins in 17:1 is a story of revelation. Part of the disclosure occurs in conjunction with Jesus' transfiguration (vv. 1-8), another part in the subsequent discussion about Elijah (vv. 9-13). For those on the receiving end (an inner circle of disciples, to which the reader is privy), the revelation given achieves three things: (1) It confirms the uniqueness of Jesus as God's Son. (2) It offers a glimpse of the glory of Jesus' reign. (3) It reiterates the fact that Jesus first must suffer, just as *Elijah* had to suffer before him. At each point, this disclosure recalls and builds upon issues raised in chapter 16 (cf. 16:15-16, 21, 27-28).

Matthew's source for the material in 17:1-13 is the parallel account in Mark 9:2-13. In both accounts the story reads as one continuous narrative, related to a mountain and the trip down the mountain. This narrative, however, contains two distinct episodes, based on two separate pieces of tradition. One of these is the story of the transfiguration, a story that exhibits the form of an epiphany. Like other epiphanies narrated in the Gospels (cf. 3:16-17; 14:22-33; Luke 24:28-32), the transfiguration reveals Jesus' divine majesty. The second piece of tradition, the discussion about Elijah, likely stems from a dispute about endtime expectations. Whatever its earlier scope and setting, the dispute is now linked to the question of resurrection: How can someone be resurrected or *raised* and inaugurate the kingdom, when the prophet of the endtime has not yet appeared?

OUTLINE

The Glory of the Son, 17:1-8

Jesus and Elijah, 17:9-13

EXPLANATORY NOTES

The Glory of the Son 17:1-8

At several points in the Gospel, mountains provide the setting for events that reveal Jesus' power or authority (cf. 4:8-10; 5:1-2; 15:29-31; 28:16-20). So likewise the story in 17:1-8 unfolds on *a high mountain,* the site of which is left to the reader's imagination. In the first of four scenes, Jesus is *transfigured* before three of his disciples (vv. 1-2). The Greek word for *transfigure* can suggest either an inward transformation (cf. 2 Cor. 3:18; Rom. 12:2) or a change in outward appearance. Here the latter is the case, as Jesus' face and garments glow with unusual brilliance.

A somewhat similar event is related in the story of Moses' experience at Sinai (cf. Exod. 24:9-18; 34:29-35). Like Jesus, Moses ascends a mountain, accompanied by three close associates. After six days, the divine voice speaks from the cloud of glory that covers the mountain. And when Moses later comes down from the mountain, his face is shining because of his intimate encounter with God. The parallels are striking.

Shining faces, however, are associated with the future as well as the past. Various texts attest the view that, at the resurrection, the faces of the righteous will shine like the sun (cf. Matt. 13:43; Dan. 12:3; 2 Esd. 7:97; 2 Bar. 51:3). And the risen Christ is portrayed in the book of Revelation as one whose "face was like the sun shining with full force" (Rev. 1:16).

For Matthew, the event of the transfiguration thus has two meanings: (1) It proclaims that the glory which once surrounded Moses now surrounds God's Son. (2) It gives a preview of the glory of Jesus' universal reign following his death and resurrection.

The story continues in verses 3 and 4, as Jesus is joined by Moses and Elijah. What their presence signifies is still unresolved. Is Moses the prototype of Jesus? And is Elijah the forerunner of Jesus? Are both figures portrayed as prophets of the endtime (cf. Rev. 11:3)? Or do the two represent the law and the prophets (cf. 5:17)? In any case, the two men signify the old era that points ahead to Jesus, and their presence provides a backdrop for the scene in verse 5.

Meanwhile, Peter offers hospitality to Jesus and his guests: *It is well that we are here,* Peter says politely, *to care for your needs* (summarized). Peter proposes to build three *shelters* (NIV), which the NRSV designates *dwellings* (cf. Neh. 8:14-18) and the GNB *tents* (cf. Exod. 33:7-11). Whatever the precise nuance, it is clear that Peter wants Jesus and his guests to stay on the mountain, to make this the time and place when heaven and earth dwell together (cf. Zech. 8:3; Rev. 21:3). To put it another way: Peter wants this moment to last forever, to have glory within reach without taking up the cross!

This wish, however, flies in the face of God's plan. And while Peter is still speaking, heaven manifests itself to redirect his thinking (v. 5): A bright cloud hovers over Jesus' party and their guests, and a voice from the cloud begins to address them. What we have, as it were, is one epiphany within another, revealing Jesus' preeminence and urging hearers to act accordingly.

The cloud calls to mind the cloud of glory that covered Sinai (Exod. 24:15-17), and which later overshadowed the tent of meeting or tabernacle (Exod. 40:34-38). According to tradition, this cloud would reappear at some point in the future (2 Macc. 2:8). When God speaks *from* the cloud, the same announcement is made that we heard at Jesus' baptism: Jesus is God's Son, chosen by God to fulfill the divine purpose (cf. 3:16-17). The acclamation leads into an admonition, *Listen to him.* Echoing words from Deuteronomy applied to Jesus in the early church (cf. Deut. 18:15-22; Acts 3:22-26), this phrase conveys a message that brings the story to its climax: The right way to serve Jesus is not to linger on the mountain, but to follow his *word* wherever it leads! Even to the cross (16:24)!

The conclusion to the story in verses 6-8 (note how Matthew has reshaped the ending in Mark's account) follows a pattern found elsewhere in texts describing visions (cf. Ezek. 1:28—2:1; Dan. 8:17-18; 10:7-14; Acts 26:13-18; Rev. 1:17). Confronted with God's presence, the three disciples are awestruck and fall prostrate on the ground (v. 6), whereupon Jesus offers divine reassurance. He reaches out to touch the three and invites them to *get up* (v. 7), reminiscent of earlier scenes where Jesus raises the sick and dead (cf. 8:15; 9:25).

Suddenly then, the vision ends. As the three *look up* (v. 8, literally *lift up their eyes*; cf. Gen. 18:2; 22:13), only Jesus is with them, and in his normal human form. So it will remain until the end of the Gospel, until atop another mountain the disciples will again behold Jesus in his glory.

Jesus and Elijah 17:9-13

As noted earlier, the topic of discussion in verses 9-13 is the coming of Elijah. His brief appearance in verses 3-4 may explain why this discussion is now part of the narrative. In any case, verse 9 provides a statement of transition that leads into the discussion. When Jesus gives the command, *Tell no one about the vision* (only here is the transfiguration called a vision), he orders silence till the moment he is raised from the dead. This word recalls the sayings in 16:21-28 and prompts the question about the endtime that we find in verse 10.

Underlying the question is a Jewish objection to Christian claims about Jesus: How can one assert that Jesus reigns as God's Messiah, when the prophet Elijah has not yet returned (cf. Mal. 4:5-6; Sir. 48:10)? As taken up in the text, the objection is directed to Jesus himself: How can you speak of your resurrection and imminent reign, when we have not yet seen Elijah, who is supposed to come first?

Jesus' reply is presented in verses 11-12, introduced by the authoritative formula, *But I tell you* (cf. 5:21ff.). More orderly and more explicit than the parallel in Mark (cf. Mark 9:12-13), this reply makes several points: (1) The expectation that Elijah will return to restore Israel is a valid expectation. (2) Elijah has come already in the person of John the Baptist to herald God's kingdom. (3) No one recognized Elijah, and he was spurned and put to death (cf. 14:1-12; 1 Kings 19:1-2). (4) The fate of Elijah will be Jesus' own fate in his role as the Messiah.

With this sequence of ideas, Jesus leads the disciples back to the topic of his suffering. According to verse 13, the disciples *understand* the clarification about Elijah. Understanding Jesus' *suffering* will take considerably longer.

THE TEXT IN BIBLICAL CONTEXT

In the account Matthew gives of the transfiguration, the word *glory* does not appear. Glory is clearly present on the mountain, however (cf. 2 Pet. 1:17-18), and glory is a central theme in texts throughout the biblical story. Glory can be defined as weightiness or importance, a mark of which is the splendor that accompanies one who has it. So it is that light and brightness are often associated with glory. While humans can possess a certain measure of glory, the God of Israel is "the king of glory," majestic in every way (cf. Pss. 24:7-10; 29). Already visible in mighty deeds in history (cf. Exod. 15:11; Deut. 5:24), God's glory will one day be revealed in its fullness (cf. Isa. 35:2; 60:1-2).

The NT links this hope to God's presence in Jesus Christ. In him we behold the glory of God in human form (cf. John 1:14; Heb. 1:3), glory which the world will behold at his coming (Matt. 16:27; 25:31). The gospel can thus be called the gospel of Christ's glory (2 Cor. 4:4), and those who receive it become partakers of his radiance (2 Cor. 3:18). All of that is in the picture in 17:1-8.

For many in Israel, the hope of glory was related to *Elijah*, the prophet whose name appears at two points in the text, and whose career made a powerful impact on Israel's memory (cf. Sir. 48:1-11; 1 Kings 17:1—2 Kings 2:12). The expectations that grew up around Elijah are not surprising. According to 2 Kings 2:11 (cf. Sir. 48:9), the mighty prophet never died, but instead was taken up into heaven by a whirlwind. It was natural, therefore, to view Elijah as one who could return at any time, whether to help those in need (cf. Matt. 27:47, 49), or to play a decisive role in the advent of the endtime (cf. Sir. 48:10; 2 Esd. 6:26-28; Shek. 2:5; Sota 9:15).

The NT builds on the particular view of that role which depicts Elijah as a *forerunner*, originally in the sense of one who prepares for *God's* coming (Mal. 3:1; 4:5-6; cf. Isa. 40:3), but later in the sense of one who precedes the Messiah. This is the tradition that lies behind the question in 17:10. And this tradition, according to the Gospels, is fulfilled by John the Baptist (cf. 3:1-6; 11:7-15; Luke 1:16-17, 76-79).

THE TEXT IN THE LIFE OF THE CHURCH

Christology looms large in 17:1-8, and Christology has been the focus of Christian reflection on the text. Two aspects of the story have generated special interest, one being its *visual* message, the other its *verbal* message. Visually, the point of interest is Christ's glory, and what we learn from the splendor manifested on the mountain. While some interpreters treat the story as a preview of *future* glory, others treat it from the standpoint of a doctrine of incarnation, as a disclosure of who Christ was all along. In the latter case, the story is being read through the lenses of the Fourth Gospel.

The *verbal* message often stressed in commentary on the story is the command, *Listen to him,* which underscores the authority of Christ as *teacher*. Calvin writes, for example: "When He commands them to *hear Him*, He sets Him in authority as the highest and unique Doctor of His Church" (1972, 2:201; cf. 201-202; Luther: 578-579). For Calvin this meant that Christ's word ranks above the OT and church tradition.

The Anabaptists concurred, but pressed the issue even further. If we would listen to Christ, argued Menno and others, we must strictly observe every one of his commandments, including nonresistance, refusing oaths, etc. (cf. Menno Simons: 283, 518, 713, 735; Dietrich Philips in Williams: 250-251). Whatever our heritage, the text calls us to a faith that moves from vision to obedience, allowing Christ's word to shape and guide the church's life.

A Crisis of Faith

Matthew 17:14-21

PREVIEW

In the narrative that began in 16:21, the faith of the disciples comes up short at several points. Peter objects to Jesus' prediction of impending suffering and death (16:21-22), preferring glory on the mountain to the harsh reality of Jerusalem (17:4). Later, when Jesus talks about his resurrection, his three companions are mystified and voice a question that comes from Jesus' opponents, the scribes (17:9-10). Meanwhile, the disciples who did not accompany Jesus up the mountain are having problems of their own (17:16). With Jesus gone (a foreglimpse of days ahead), they find themselves unable to heal a troubled child.

The story in which this dilemma is portrayed once again comes from Mark (cf. Mark 9:14-29). Matthew, in typical fashion, greatly abridges Mark's account. Among the items omitted are the vivid description and illustration of the child's condition, the reference to an argument between the scribes and the disciples, and a classic dialogue on faith between Jesus and the child's father. In the process of condensation, the story acquires a new form and focus. No longer is it primarily a miracle story, concentrating on the plight of the boy and his father. Instead, the emphasis falls on the plight of *the disciples* and their need for greater *faith*. And the text that results can be described as a piece of *instruction for disciples* (cf. the conversation in vv. 19-20).

OUTLINE

Jesus Challenges Unfaith, 17:14-18

Jesus Counsels His Disciples, 17:19-21

EXPLANATORY NOTES

Jesus Challenges Unfaith 17:14-18

When Jesus and the trio mentioned in 17:1 reach the bottom of the mountain, a crowd awaits them. The immediate need is healing for a boy described as *an epileptic.* (The word translated *epileptic* actually means *moonstruck,* reflecting the ancient view that epileptic seizures were linked to phases of the moon.) Because of his condition, the text goes on, the boy was prone to fall into life-threatening situations (the fire, the water). Therefore, the father solicits Jesus' help. Note that, like other supplicants in the Gospel, he calls Jesus *Lord* and requests divine mercy (cf. 8:5; 9:27; 15:22), both marks of a believer. The strength of his faith contrasts sharply with the weakness of Jesus' own disciples (cf. v. 16), who as noted above have not been able to act as Jesus' agents of healing (cf. 10:1).

News of the disciples' failure leads Jesus to issue the harsh rebuke in verse 17. Speaking as God would speak in a prophetic complaint (cf. Num. 14:27-35; Jer. 5:20-31), Jesus castigates his *generation* for their evil and unfaith (cf. Deut. 32:5, 20; Matt. 12:39) and then asks, rhetorically: *How long is it going to take?*

This rebuke is startling in that it links the *disciples* with unbelieving Israel. Unfaith is threatening the very followers of Jesus, those who know who he is and understand his word. Before dealing with the problem of the disciples, however, Jesus cares for the needs of the epileptic boy. He issues another *rebuke* (v. 18), this time to the demon that afflicts the troubled child. And as in previous acts of healing (cf. 8:13; 9:22; 15:28), the boy is cured *from that hour* (NRSV: *instantly*).

Jesus Counsels His Disciples 17:19-21

In the private scene that follows (cf. similar scenes in 13:36-43; 15:12-20; 19:10-12), the disciples inquire about the reason for their failure. According to verse 20a, the inability to heal is the result of *little faith,* a failure of confidence or trust. (A second reason is given in verse 21, based on the statement in Mark 9:29, but this verse is not found in the earliest manuscripts and is likely an addition to the text by a copyist.)

The remainder of verse 20 appears to draw on two sayings found elsewhere in the Gospels. One is a saying about faith like a mustard seed (cf. Luke 17:6), the other a Markan saying about faith to move mountains (cf. Mark 11:22-23; G. Thom. 48, 106; 1 Cor. 13:2). Through the new composite saying, Jesus tells his disciples that faith is the link to the power they lack. If they truly trust God, even though that trust be miniscule, they will be able to do all that Jesus calls them to do—whether or not he is present (cf. John 14:12).

THE TEXT IN BIBLICAL CONTEXT

Throughout the First Gospel, there is a lively interplay between unfaith and faith. Israel fails to perceive what God is doing through Jesus, and so refuses to believe (cf. 8:10; 11:20; 13:13, 58; 17:17; 21:32). The disciples on the other hand *do* perceive what is happening and so believe and follow Jesus (cf. 11:25; 13:16; 16:15-17). Even the disciples' faith can falter, however, and Matthew's term for this is the word *oligopistia*, usually translated *little faith.* As suggested above, the connotation of *oligopistia* is weak or wavering trust, a shortage of confidence. Thus disciples may worry about provisions for their needs (6:30; 16:8), or fear for their safety in the midst of a crisis (8:26; 14:31), or doubt their ability to carry out their ministry (17:19-20).

The problem is one addressed by other writers as well, who like Matthew were dealing with pastoral issues in the church (cf. James 1:5-6; Heb. 10:23, 35-39). The opposite of *oligopistia* is the faith Paul ascribes to the patriarch Abraham: "No distrust made him waver concerning the promise of God, but he grew strong in his faith as he gave glory to God, being fully convinced that God was able to do what he had promised" (Rom. 4:20-21). Such is the faith that is able to move mountains.

THE TEXT IN THE LIFE OF THE CHURCH

The story in 17:14-21 is often treated as a sequel to the transfiguration. In the Vatican, for example, we find a painting by Raphael which portrays the glorious Christ atop the mountain as the answer to the chaos of human need below. The same juxtaposition of themes from the two stories can be found in many sermons, contrasting special "mountaintop" experiences of faith with the tough reality of life at ground level.

With or without the backdrop of glory, the scene in the text depicts the world which faith must inhabit and challenge, a world where crowds clamor, where skepticism reigns, and where deliverance is needed. How do we fare in that kind of world? According to one writer, the text warns us that "the church is always in danger of reverting to the unbelieving mentality of a secular-minded generation" (Sand: 360). The text also contains a word of promise, however: If we dare to trust God in the midst of unbelief, we will find the power needed to act in Jesus' name.

Matthew 17:22—18:35

Life in Jesus' Community

PREVIEW

Before Jesus and the twelve begin their journey to Jerusalem, there will be one last round of teaching in Galilee. The bulk of this teaching is the discourse we find in 18:1-35, the fourth such collection of Jesus' sayings in the Gospel. Its theme can be described as "relations within the church, the conditions necessary for healthy interaction among disciples" (Meier, 1980:200).

Formally, the discourse consists of two sections, one dealing with care for *little ones* in the church (18:1-14), the second with restoration of members who sin (18:15-35). Each of the two sections concludes with a parable, and each parable refers to the will of *the Father*. Leading into the discourse, as a bridge narrative, is the account in 17:22-27. While the issue in the foreground of this text is paying taxes, a broader concern in the story is not giving offense. And that concern is central to the discourse that follows.

In each of the five discourses, Matthew takes a core of material from one of his sources and expands it in various ways. Here the core comes from Mark 9:30-50, which itself has the form of instruction for disciples. To amplify this instruction, Matthew draws on other Markan sayings (cf. Mark 10:13-16), on another written source also used by Luke (cf. Luke 15:3-7), and on tradition that likely comes from his own community.

Freedom and Submission

Matthew 17:22-27

PREVIEW

The narrative in 17:22-27 begins with a passion prediction (vv. 22-23), then proceeds to a discussion of the temple tax (vv. 24-27). For the passion prediction and for the geographical framework of the text, Matthew is indebted to Mark (cf. Mark 9:30-33). The episode concerning payment of the tax, however, is found only in the First Gospel and likely reflects oral tradition from Matthew's community. Whatever its antecedents, the story now combines features of a debate or dispute, instruction for disciples, and a miracle story. Its topic is the freedom of Jesus and his community. On the one hand, the text says, we are free from obligations to the old social order. On the other hand, we must be sensitive to the way our actions affect others.

OUTLINE

Submission to Death, 17:22-23

Submission to the Tax, 17:24-27

EXPLANATORY NOTES

Submission to Death 17:22-23

In verse 22 we read of a *gathering* that occurs in Galilee, apparently a gathering of Jesus and the twelve. While the idea could be simply that of a regrouping after the events in 17:1-20, there could also be a sense of gathering for the journey that will begin in 19:1. Senior comments appropriately: "Jesus gathers his disciples together like a commander rallying his troops before a battle" (1977:173).

The first word that the reassembled group hears is an announcement of Jesus' impending fate, the second of the formal predictions of his passion (cf. Mark 9:31/Luke 9:44). Note the wordplay in the saying in v. 22b: *The Son of Man is going to be betrayed into human hands* (meaning: into the power of human authorities). According to some scholars, a riddlelike saying such as this might underlie all the more developed predictions of Jesus' death.

The saying introduces a key term, *betrayed* (Greek: *paradidōmi*), a word that can also mean simply handed over (REB) or *delivered*

(RSV). Here the more general meaning may be intended, and the passive voice may suggest divine action as well as human. Ultimately, it is *God* who both delivers Jesus *to* death and raises Jesus *from* death (cf. Rom. 4:25). In spite of the promise of resurrection after death, the prediction as a whole leaves the twelve *greatly distressed* (v. 23), *filled with grief* (REB, NIV). They are beginning to come to grips with the end awaiting Jesus, and the realization is painful.

Submission to the Tax 17:24-27

Earlier in the Gospel, Jesus began his ministry to Galilee in Capernaum (4:13-16). Now, before leaving Galilee, he returns to Capernaum to conclude that ministry. It is there that tax collectors inquire whether Jesus pays the *temple tax*. The text actually speaks of a *double drachma* or *two drachmas* (cf. NIV), Greek coinage equivalent to the Jewish half-shekel. However labeled, the tax in question is probably the contribution required annually from every male Jew over 19 years of age for upkeep of the temple (cf. Exod. 30:13; Neh. 10:32; Josephus, *Antiquities* 3.8.1; 18.9.1).

When the collectors question Peter about Jesus' practice (note Peter's role as an official spokesman), the wording they use assumes a positive answer: *Your teacher pays the tax, doesn't he?* Peter in turn replies, *Yes,* almost without thinking.

However, in the scene that follows in the house (the same house mentioned in 9:10 and other texts), Jesus engages Peter in a dialogue that leads to a more nuanced reply. Inviting Peter to reflect on tax exemption in the world, Jesus challenges the assumption that he and his followers pay taxes automatically: If the families of *human* rulers are exempt from taxation (and such was the case in the realms of ancient kings), how much more so the Son of God and his brothers and sisters (cf. 12:49-50; 13:38)!

From this perspective, Jesus and his community are free from the claims of institutions like the temple. They are not obligated to pay the tax. Nevertheless, Jesus counsels that the tax should be paid, so as to *not give offense* (v. 27), and he uses his freedom to supply the payment needed by means of a miracle. The coin that Peter will find is a Greek *stater*, equal in value to a shekel or four drachmas, the exact amount needed to cover the tax for both Jesus and Peter. As elsewhere in the Gospel, Peter here represents the community of disciples—and his payment of the tax sets a direction for the church.

A further matter is how Matthew viewed the bearing of the story on church life in his day. By the time Matthew wrote, the temple in Jerusalem had been reduced to rubble, and the yearly poll tax now went to Rome. How then does Jesus' counsel apply to the reader?

There are several possibilities: (1) Matthew is urging his readers to be sensitive to Jewish practice in general and to contribute to the needs of the Jewish community. (2) Matthew is using the story to address the issue of taxes in general, advising readers to pay taxes so as not to create a hostile climate for the church. (3) Matthew offers the story as a paradigm for his readers on how to live in community, whether within the church or in the larger society.

To put it another way, he includes the account to teach a basic lesson about freedom in Christ. Whatever the specific applications of the story, its use as a prelude to chapter 18 would suggest that the latter issue was foremost in Matthew's mind.

THE TEXT IN BIBLICAL CONTEXT

The discussion of the temple tax feeds into two broader discussions in the NT. One involves the question of whether Christians should pay *taxes*. Here the key related texts are Matthew 22:15-22 (cf. Mark 12:13-17; Luke 20:19-26) and Romans 13:1-7. We will look at this question while studying Matthew 22. The other circle of discussion to which the story contributes involves the question of *freedom*.

Here again Matthew's partner in the broader conversation is first and foremost Paul. Like Matthew, Paul defines the life of sonship as a life of freedom: "For freedom Christ has set us free. Stand firm, therefore, and do not submit again to a yoke of slavery" (Gal. 5:1; cf. Rom. 8:14-15, 21; Gal. 3:23—4:7). At the same time, Paul and Matthew agree that freedom in Christ is not reckless freedom. "You were called to be free," Paul writes, "but use your freedom to serve one another in love" (Gal. 5:13, paraphrased; cf. 1 Cor. 8:9; 9:1, 19).

A similar note is sounded in the letter of 1 Peter, where the subject is the Christian's obligation in society: "As servants of God, live as free people, yet do not use your freedom as a pretext for evil" (1 Pet. 2:16). Freedom, then, is rightly used when it builds up the church, promotes peace and wholeness, and seeks the welfare of all.

THE TEXT IN THE LIFE OF THE CHURCH

Most studies of the text deal in one way or another with the idea of "free, but. . . ." In Luther's comments, the topic is linked to the theme of two kingdoms (582-584). The text, Luther says, portrays Christ and his disciples as royalty of another kingdom, who now, however, are guests in the realm of earthly rulers. While here, they will pay their guest fees, so as not to offend their worldly hosts and provoke accusations of causing unrest.

A more recent word on freedom that helps illumine the text comes from Eduard Schweizer (357). On the one hand, Schweizer notes, the text underscores the importance of acting out of a sense of freedom: "Only after the distinction between free and slave is established can one ask whether there may be reasons for doing of one's own free will what one is no longer required to do."

On the other hand, the text does not support those who have to show off their freedom. According to Schweizer, we can be as "bound" by the pursuit of freedom as some are bound by the law: "There is a negative legalism that is no better than positive legalism when it supposes that fundamental freedom must be demonstrated at all costs." In contrast to the bondage of both the slave and the rebel, the text counsels a freedom with purpose and direction, a freedom that is coupled with caring and accountability.

A Community of Caring

Matthew 18:1-14

PREVIEW

The discourse of Jesus in Matthew 18 has been labeled in various ways. Some refer to it as a treatise on church order, the "rules of the house" for Jesus' followers. Others argue that what we have is not a set of legal prescriptions, but rather advice of the sort often found in wisdom literature. In this case, chapter 18 might be called community counsel, advice on how to live with one another in the church. However labeled, the discourse depicts the church as a community like a *family*, using terms from family life to refer to church members.

In 18:1-14, two such terms lifted up are *child* and *little ones.* Disciples of Jesus must become like children, assuming the lowly stance of the small and powerless young (vv. 1-4). Disciples, moreover, must look out for one another as one looks out for little ones, not harming or misleading weak and vulnerable members (vv. 5-9). Instead of looking on such members with contempt or embarrassment, true dis ciples will reach out to little ones with loving care (vv. 10-14).

OUTLINE

The Disciple as Child, 18:1-4

Don't Make Others Stumble, 18:5-9

Care for the Little Ones, 18:10-14

EXPLANATORY NOTES

The Disciple as Child 18:1-4

As Peter and Jesus conclude their discussion of the temple tax (17:24-27), the other disciples join them and pose a new issue, the issue of *greatness*. Mark's account of the incident portrays the issue as an outgrowth of a squabble among the disciples: Which of *us* is the greatest (cf. Mark 9:33-37)? In Matthew, however, the disciples raise the issue as a theological question, an inquiry about rank in the kingdom yet to come: *Who is the greatest in the kingdom of heaven?* The question was one discussed by the rabbis as well, where greatness is often linked to the teaching of the Torah. Jesus responds, however, in his own distinctive way.

Part of Jesus' answer is the signlike action reported in verse 2: He places a little child in the midst of the disciples, a person with no status or rank in the ancient world. Even without comment, this gesture says a mouthful. Jesus nonetheless proceeds to interpret his action in verses 3 and 4, which speak of children as a model for disciples to emulate. The pronouncement in verse 3, which Matthew has adapted from Mark 10:15, appears to have been a widely circulated saying (cf. the versions found in John 3:3, 5, and in G. Thom. 22).

In the phrase *change and become like children,* the verb for *change* could carry the technical meaning of *be converted,* but here likely calls for a change in the way the disciple thinks and acts. This reversal is further described in the saying in verse 4, where becoming like children is equated with self-humbling, with assuming the stance of those who know that they are *little* (cf. 23:12; Luke 14:11; 18:14). To become like children is thus to perceive ourselves afresh from the dependent vantage point of a child, with no illusions of self-grandeur or self-sufficiency. To put it another way, to become like children is to see ourselves as *the poor in spirit* of the Beatitudes. Such a stance, Jesus says, is both a condition for *entering* the kingdom and a measure of greatness *in* the kingdom.

Don't Make Others Stumble 18:5-9

In verses 5 and 6 (cf. Mark 9:37, 42), *child* becomes a metaphor for one who follows Jesus. *One such child* means a childlike disciple (not a child in the literal sense) and is equivalent to *one of these little ones who believe in me* (cf. 10:42; 11:25). The concern in these verses is how we act toward disciples *who are as vulnerable as children*. If we *welcome* weak disciples, act caringly and hospitably toward them, we serve Jesus himself in and through them (cf. 10:40). If we cause them to *sin* or *stumble,* however, the most dire judgment awaits us. (The *great* millstone around one's neck is the massive upper stone of a large mill turned by a donkey!)

The verb for *cause to stumble* or *put a stumbling block before* is *skandalizō*, which can mean specifically *entice another to sin* or more broadly *offend* or *be the downfall of* someone. As Senior suggests, the meaning here may encompass "a whole spectrum of obstacles thrown in the way of the weak person" (1977:178). *Skandalizō* and the cognate noun *skandalon* (offense, temptation, hindrance) are used several times in verses 5-9 and turn up frequently throughout the Gospel (cf. 5:29-30; 13:21; 16:23; 17:27; 24:10; 26:31, 33).

Verses 7-9 elaborate on the judgment facing those who cause little ones to stumble. The woe-saying in verse 7 appears in Luke as well (cf. Luke 17:1) and speaks apocalyptically of impending "stumbling blocks." Because the world is bent on its own evil course, it is inevitable that stumbling will occur—but how terrible for those who cause that to happen! To avoid this, disciples must be ready to take drastic action, as verses 8 and 9 indicate: If a part of the body causes problems, Jesus says, it is better to remove it than let it lead to our destruction.

Here Matthew is drawing on Mark (cf. the three parallel sayings in Mark 9:43-47), using sayings cited earlier in the discussion of adultery in the Sermon on the Mount (5:29-30). In the context of chapter 18, the sayings can be interpreted in two different ways. According to some writers, *cutting off* and *tearing out* refer to excommunication: The church must remove those members whose behavior endangers the faith of others and the life of the community (cf. 1 Cor. 5:2, 13, and Dietrich Philips in Williams: 246). It is more likely, however, that the sayings call for self-examination on the part of each believer: If any part of our life causes us to stumble, and therefore makes us an obstacle to the faith of other Christians, we must do whatever it takes to correct the situation (cf. the comments on 5:29-30).

Care for the Little Ones 18:10-14

Concern for weak disciples remains the topic of discussion in verses 10-14. At the center of this section is the parable of the lost sheep in verses 12-13, a story from the tradition that Matthew and Luke have in common (cf. Luke 15:3-7; G. Thom. 107). In Luke's account, Jesus tells the parable to support his ministry to outcasts, persons on the fringe of the Jewish community. Matthew, however, relates the parable to the issue of church members who have strayed, and calls the church to assume the role of the shepherd in the story. From the language used, it is not clear whether the wayward sheep simply wanders off—or is led astray by someone. Whichever the case, the straying member of the flock represents those who stumble. And the story highlights both the extraordinary concern devoted to reclaiming such persons and the extravagant joy to which this reclamation leads.

Bracketing the parable, and thereby telling us how to interpret it, are the sayings supplied by Matthew in verses 10 and 14. (Verse 11 is a later scribal addition to the text, based on Luke 19:10.) Both sayings use the expression *little ones,* keeping this image before the reader, and both sayings relate *little ones* to heaven's own agenda. Verse 10 makes the point that weak members have access to God through *their angels,* so that God is fully apprised of their plight.

The belief in angels who look out for the welfare of God's people was widespread in Judaism and is rooted in the OT (cf. Ps. 91:11; 1QH 5:20-22). It was believed, however, that only a few of the highest angels were privileged to commune with God face to face (cf. 1 Enoch 40), and it is precisely these angels who, according to the text, intercede for the little ones. To put it more simply, little ones have friends in high places!

In verse 14, Jesus tells us that God not only *knows* about the little ones, but *wills* that none should perish or be lost. When weaker members stray, therefore, the community must not despise them for their weakness, but rather act with loving care to find and restore them.

THE TEXT IN BIBLICAL CONTEXT

Among the features that link the text to a wider tradition is its use of *child* in the sense of *believer.* Already in the OT, the people of God are often called the "children" of Israel (cf. Exod. 19:6, RSV; Deut. 31:23, RSV; Isa. 17:3). In the NT, *child* and *children* can have varying connotations. There are texts, first of all, in which the image of the young alludes to *childlike traits* in members of the community.

Sometimes, as in Matthew 18, the traits described are positive or neutral in character, while in other texts childlike means fickle or immature (cf. Matt. 11:16-17; 1 Cor. 13:11; 14:20; Eph. 4:14).

A second set of texts points to the *child-parent relationship* in which children of faith find themselves and accents the intimate nature of this relationship. In some cases, the parent in question is the founder or leader of a community, eager to see its members grow (a usage of Paul and John: 1 Cor. 4:14; Gal. 4:19; 1 Thess. 2:11; 1 John 2:1). In other cases, the parent who calls us children and tenderly cares for the family is none other than God (cf. 1 John 3:1; 5:1; John 1:12; Rom. 8:16-17; Phil. 2:15).

As already noted, one of the nuances of *child* or *little one* in Matthew 18 is that of a *weak* Christian. And this motif links the passage to the discussion of the weak and strong in the letters of Paul. There the weak are members whose conscience can not handle eating meat offered to idols (cf. 1 Cor. 8:7-13; 10:23—11:1), or who have other scruples related to acceptable and unacceptable foods (cf. Rom. 14:1-4). Like Matthew, Paul calls for special sensitivity to the needs of the weak. He begins by reminding his readers that all of us come to faith through the "weakness" of the cross, so that we have no reason to despise those weaker than ourselves (cf. 1 Cor. 1:18-31).

To the contrary, Paul argues, "We who are strong ought to put up with the failings of the weak" (Rom. 15:1) and take care lest our liberty "become a stumbling block to the weak" (1 Cor. 8:9; cf. Rom. 14:13; 2 Cor. 11:29). More specifically, "if food is a cause of their falling, I will never eat meat, so that I may not cause one of them to fall" (1 Cor. 8:13). In texts such as these, Paul exhibits a pastoral approach similar to Matthew's—and even uses some of the same terminology.

Yet a third point at which the text recalls passages elsewhere in Scripture is in the parable Jesus tells about sheep and shepherding. So, for example, Jeremiah and Ezekiel use the shepherd image to depict Israel's rulers, criticizing them for the way they have abused and neglected the flock: "You have not strengthened the weak, you have not healed the sick, you have not bound up the injured, you have not brought back the strayed, you have not sought the lost, but with force and harshness you have ruled them" (Ezek. 34:4, cf. 34:1-6; Jer. 23:1-4). In the face of this situation, God promises to assume the shepherd role himself, to seek out the lost sheep, to do what Israel's leaders failed to do (cf. Ezek. 34:11-31; Isa. 40:11).

The NT picks up this promise and develops it in several ways. Central to the Christian story is the conviction that Jesus is the divine shepherd who seeks and saves the people of God (cf. Matt. 9:36; John 10:1-18; Heb. 13:20; 1 Pet. 2:25; Rev. 7:17). Shepherding, however, becomes a community assignment as well. The task of caring for the flock is entrusted both to leaders in the church (cf. 1 Pet. 5:2-4; Acts 20:28; John 21:15-17) and to every church member (Matthew 18).

THE TEXT IN THE LIFE OF THE CHURCH

Discussion of 18:1-14 in the church has often focused on the phrase, *unless you change and become like children.* As noted earlier, it is possible to take the phrase as a description of conversion. In this case, Jesus is stressing the need for spiritual regeneration or rebirth. This is the way the Fourth Gospel interprets the saying (cf. John 3:3, 5), and it is an understanding well-attested in the Anabaptist tradition (cf. Menno Simons: 213, 411; Augsburger: 215).

An alternate view, one that more likely corresponds to Matthew's own understanding, is that Jesus is calling for a childlike disposition among members of his community. Where 18:3 is so interpreted, we find a number of ingenious proposals on what it means to be childlike. Thus children are defined as trusting, or open, or innocent, or willing to be disciplined. The most probable proposal is that children *know* that they are *little* (cf. notes on 18:3-4), and thus are largely free from the pretensions about greatness that often characterize adults. It is at this point that the child becomes a model for the disciple.

Commentators have also been attracted to Matthew's concern for *these little ones.* Calvin's comments on the passage are especially perceptive (1972, 2:215-219), noting the link between pride, contempt for the weak, and giving offense; stressing the fact that God prizes the little ones and embraces them with special love; and encouraging Christians to reach out to the weak "and help them lovingly on their way."

Throughout the history of interpretation, some have treated the instruction that Matthew gives as a word for church *leaders*. According to Paul Minear, the text addresses "dangers faced by leaders in their treatment of weak and insignificant members of their congregations," making the point that "the salvation of the leaders requires their care for the sheep" (100, 101; cf. Luther: 598-601). While the view that the text speaks *only* to leaders is too restrictive, the counsel it gives is surely *critical* for those in leadership roles. More specifically, the text calls for leadership that is sensitive and nurturing, as opposed to leadership preoccupied with itself and running roughshod over others.

Dealing with Brokenness

Matthew 18:15-35

PREVIEW

The discourse which began at 18:1, a discourse on life in Jesus' community, continues in 18:15-35. A shift occurs, however, in the focus of the material. Having acknowledged the possibility of stumbling or straying, Matthew goes on to treat the question: What do we do as a community of faith when a member *sins*? As in verses 1-14, family language sets the tone for addressing the issue, and here the family term is *brother* (NIV, which the NRSV paraphrases either as *member of the church* or *brother or sister*; cf. vv. 15, 21, 35). In confronting sin, we are not called to act as crusaders or prosecutors, but as sisters and brothers seeking whole relationships with every member of the family.

To develop the point, Matthew brings together three pieces of material on sin and forgiveness. Verses 15-20 describe a sequence of three steps for dealing with sin, supported by several sayings on authority in the church. There follows then, in verses 21-22, a brief dialogue around the question of whether forgiveness has any limits: How often can one sin and still be forgiven? This in turn leads to the parable in verses 23-35, a kingdom story about debts and the cancellation of debts.

OUTLINE

When Sin Occurs, 18:15-20

Seventy Times Seven, 18:21-22

Be Merciful to One Another, 18:23-35

EXPLANATORY NOTES

When Sin Occurs 18:15-20

As many have noted, the approach to sin set forth in verses 15-17 has a markedly Jewish flavor. Two of the three steps are based on sayings in the Torah, and the process as a whole is reminiscent of the procedure apparently followed at Qumran (cf. 1QS 5:25—6:1). We may conjecture, therefore, that the process took shape in a Jewish-Christian community. It was likely intended, moreover, to cover any and all kinds of inappropriate behavior, not merely wrongs committed against a brother or sister. (The words *against you* in verse 15 are missing in some key early manuscripts and probably were a later addition to the text, based on the language of verse 21 and Luke 17:4.)

The first step in the process involves one-to-one confrontation with the member who has sinned. As the Jerusalem Bible puts it: *Go and have it out with him alone, between your two selves.* Behind the phrase *tell him his fault* in the RSV lies the verb *elenchō*. The same verb is used in Leviticus 19:17 in the LXX, where one is urged to "reason" with a neighbor or brother against whom one has a complaint. In the text before us, the verb suggests showing or demonstrating that wrongdoing has occurred, so as to convince another to alter personal behavior. If that happens, Matthew tells us, the offender is restored to a whole relationship with the family.

If not, one proceeds to the second step described in verse 16. The instruction to bring one or two witnesses into the conversation is drawn from Deuteronomy 19:15, which specifies the need for two or three witnesses to confirm a person's guilt in a judicial setting. In Matthew, the purpose of the witnesses is not to secure a legal judgment, but to buttress the attempt at fraternal correction, to make an even stronger appeal to the member who has stumbled to acknowledge sin and be restored.

If that too fails, then the issue must be brought before *the church* (*ekklēsia*), which here refers to the congregation or local gathering of believers. This final step is also taken to restore, not to punish. If one refuses, however, to heed the counsel of the congregation, separation is the end result: *Let such a one be to you as a Gentile and a tax collector,* as one who stands outside the circle of faith. What is envisioned is not isolation from the sinner, but a radical redefinition of the relationship. From this point on, the community will no longer relate to the person as a fellow disciple, but as someone of the world who has yet to be discipled.

Having followed the text thus far, the reader might well ask: Does the church have authority to act in this way? Verses 18-20 supply an answer to that question. According to verse 18 (which begins with the solemn formula *Truly, I tell you*), the power to bind and loose granted to Peter in 16:19 is now bestowed by Jesus on the disciples as a group, and thus on every community of believers. In the context of the discussion about sin in the church, *bind* and *loose* convey the sense of *convict* and *acquit*, and may allude to the extreme case of excommunication. The church, then, has authority to pronounce judgment in God's name, and the church has authority to release persons from that judgment and restore them to fellowship.

Verses 19-20 further define this authority and the way it functions. As described in the text, the community which God affirms in its binding and loosing exhibits several characteristics:

(1) It assembles in Christ's name.
(2) It seeks the will of God in prayer.
(3) It acts in agreement or consensus.

In such a community, however small (even *two or three* members), Jesus is present with the members to guide their deliberations (cf. G. Thom. 30). A striking parallel to 18:20 is found in an early collection of sayings by Jewish rabbis: "If two sit together and the words of the Law [are spoken] between them, the Divine Presence rests between them" (Aboth 3:2). What is noteworthy in 18:20 is the way Jesus assumes the role of the Torah in the synagogue. He himself is the one around whom the church gathers, and he himself is the presence of God in the community. Linked to God in this manner, the community is assured that God will grant its requests on behalf of those who sin.

Seventy Times Seven 18:21-22

If read the wrong way, the hard line on sin advocated in the text could spell the end of compassion. Matthew acts to guard against such a misunderstanding through the dialogue he presents in verses 21-22 (cf. Luke 17:4; G. Naz. 15). Once again Peter appears as the spokesman for the twelve (cf. 15:15; 16:16, 22; 17:4; 19:27), raising a question about forgiveness: *How often must* I *forgive the one who sins against* me?

Sin is now a very personal matter, and Peter's offer to forgive an offense up to seven times is fairly generous by human standards. It assumes, however, that our readiness to forgive must have *some limit*. Jesus challenges this assumption in his reply to Peter. Whether *seventy times seven* or *seventy-seven times* (cf. NRSV footnote), Jesus proposes a new number which tells Peter to stop counting. The number itself turns up early in the biblical record, in Genesis 4:24. There Lamech vows to avenge his enemies "seventy-sevenfold." In Matthew 18:22, Jesus reverses this cry for unlimited revenge and calls the church to extend unlimited forgiveness.

Be Merciful to One Another 18:23-35

Having introduced the topic of forgiveness, Matthew goes on to tell a story about debts and forgiveness. It is a story set in the court of an ancient monarch, who wants *to settle accounts* with the highly placed *slaves* or *servants* (NIV) who administer his kingdom, and who owe the king money. The debts in question may have to do with taxes collected from subjects but not yet paid to the king, or with funds from the royal treasury loaned out to the officials.

Whatever the circumstances, the account of one official is in arrears to the tune of *ten thousand talents,* an astronomical sum. A talent was the largest unit of money at that time, and ten thousand was the highest number used in counting. In our context, we would say: He owed billions of dollars!

It is a debt which the official can never hope to repay, so his plea for more time in verse 26 is both desperate and absurd. Nevertheless, the king relents from his threat to sell the man and his family. Looking with pity on the official's plight, he goes beyond the request for an extended payment period. In an unheard-of act of royal generosity, the king cancels the debt outright. He forgives the total amount.

As the story continues, we hear of a second servant, who owes *a hundred denarii* to the just forgiven servant. It is a small sum by comparison, for a denarius was merely a day's wages for a laborer. This time, moreover, there is a realistic prospect for repayment of the debt. Surely, we think to ourselves, the plot will repeat itself and mercy will lead to mercy. But this is not what happens.

When the two men meet, the creditor is brutal in his demand for payment and rejects the plea for time to come up with the money (the very plea *he* had made only a short while earlier!). Unyielding and unforgiving, he has his fellow servant thrown in prison. The reaction of the king to the news of this transaction is one of righteous indignation. He calls the official *wicked* because of the heartless way he has treated a brother servant. He points to the inconsistency of accepting a gift of mercy and withholding mercy from another. And he consigns the official to torture in prison until he comes up with the money. It is the same action the official himself took in relation to his fellow servant (cf. v. 30). Only now, where the debt in question can never be repaid, the implication of the sentence is imprisonment forever.

The plot of this story, we are told at the outset, says something about the plot of life in God's kingdom (v. 23). God as a gracious sovereign forgives the debt of all our unmet obligations. Freed and shaped by that gift, we in turn will forgive the shortcomings of fellow servants in the church. If instead we act contrary to the mercy we have received, denying forgiveness to our brothers and sisters, we place ourselves outside the orbit of mercy as well. This is the point stressed in the application of the story in verse 35, and it recalls earlier words on the theme of reciprocity in the Sermon on the Mount (cf. 6:14-15; 7:1-2). It is an unpleasant note on which to end the story and the discourse as a whole. This harshness, however, has a pastoral intent. It is a way of calling the church to examine its life, to make sure that mercy permeates every action members take to disciple one another.

THE TEXT IN BIBLICAL CONTEXT

Throughout the biblical story, sin in the community is a serious matter, all the more so in the case of the early church. How can sin find a place among those who have tasted God's endtime salvation? And if believers do sin after receiving God's grace, what hope do they have of gaining eternal life (cf. Heb. 10:26-31)? Nowhere is the struggle with such questions more apparent than in the epistle of 1 John. "We know," the author writes, "that those who are born of God do not sin, but the one who was born of God protects them, and the evil one does not touch them" (5:18; cf. 3:4-10).

In principle, that is true. Life in Christ is not a life of evil. But the author also knows that the reality of Christian experience is somewhat more complex, and that sin does occur. Thus he writes, "If we say that we have no sin, we deceive ourselves" (1 John 1:8). He thus counsels his readers to confess their sins (1:9) and pray for others who have erred (5:14-17), knowing that there is forgiveness through Jesus Christ, our advocate (2:1-2). That is the route by which we move toward the wholeness of a life "born of God." So it was that the church developed strategies to confront sin and restore erring members (cf. 1 Cor. 5; 2 Cor. 2:5-11). And Matthew 18 provides a glimpse of how it worked in at least some circles.

Forgiveness of sin is clearly central to the understanding of restoration in the text. Here and elsewhere in the Gospel, the evangelist works with three basic assumptions about forgiveness:

(1) God offers us forgiveness through Jesus Christ, who came to free us from sin (cf. 1:21; 26:28).

(2) God channels that forgiveness through redemptive actions of the faith community (cf. 18:18; 9:2, 8).

(3) God's forgiveness is a model for, and closely linked with, our forgiveness of one another (cf. 6:12).

These assumptions are in no way peculiar to Matthew, but part of the common faith of the NT church. God's provision of mercy is attested in many ways, for example in language about Christ as one sent as an expiation for sin (cf. Rom. 3:23-25; 1 John 4:9-10). The church's role as a channel of mercy is lifted up in the Fourth Gospel, in a Johannine parallel to Matthew 18:18: "If you forgive the sins of any, they are forgiven them; if you retain the sins of any, they are retained" (John 20:23; cf. James 5:15-16). Finally, we have texts like Ephesians 4:32, which admonishes believers to "be kind to one another, tenderhearted, forgiving one another, as God in Christ has forgiven you" (cf. 1 John 4:7-12).

THE TEXT IN THE LIFE OF THE CHURCH

Early in his ministry, Martin Luther proposed an "evangelical order" for believers who wanted to meet in small groups and work more seriously at their Christian calling. "According to this order," Luther wrote, "those who do not lead Christian lives could be known, reproved, corrected, cast out, or excommunicated, according to the rule of Christ, Matthew 18" (cited in Durnbaugh, 1968:3). The concern for a more faithful community was taken up to some extent in the Reformed tradition, which made discipline one of the marks of the church.

The most thoroughgoing implementation of Luther's vision, however, occurred in the Anabaptist wing of the Reformation, and in later movements committed to a similar understanding of the church. In the writings from this tradition, we find repeated references to Matthew 18:15-20—and to the practice of "the ban" or excommunication based on this text (cf. Dietrich Philips in Williams: 246-248; Menno Simons: 407-418; 453-485; 959-998; Alexander Mack in Durnbaugh, 1958:336-338; 365-370; Snyder and Shaffer: 17-20).

Frequently the ban was accompanied by shunning or avoidance of the separated brother or sister, a practice based on references in the letters of Paul.

At its best, discipline according to Matthew 18 functioned as a caring and loving attempt of the community to hold members accountable to their calling as disciples. Menno writes at one place: "We do not want to expel any, but rather to receive; not to amputate, but rather to heal; not to discard, but rather to win back; not to grieve, but rather to comfort; not to condemn, but rather to save" (413). The emphasis here is clearly on restoration.

Unfortunately, this was not always the case. Stories abound of a harsh and legalistic use of the ban, all too often to enforce conformity to the cultural traditions of a community, rather than as a means to promote greater faithfulness to the gospel. In reaction, many churches have tended to abandon the concept of a disciplined community. Whatever the abuses of the text in our history, Matthew 18 poses a question the faithful church can hardly ignore: How *will* we act to hold each other accountable in the community of faith, and how *will* we act to restore those members who stumble and fall? (Cf. Gish: 133-171; Jeschke; Klassen: 175-200.)

Other points at which Matthew 18 speaks helpfully have emerged in recent discussion of the text. One such point is *conflict* in the church and how we handle it. Whether caused by sin or simply misunderstanding, conflict is a regular part of human experience. And the process described in 18:15-17 offers a way to deal with conflict and settle our differences (cf. Snyder and Shaffer: 19-20). Among other things, the text urges us to confront brokenness rather than deny or run from it, to make a face-to-face attempt to resolve differences with the other party, and to seek mediation when a conflict cannot be resolved simply and directly.

A further point at which the text has a great deal to say is the role of the church as *a forgiving community*. Most Christians are heavily influenced by a tradition that privatizes the gift of forgiveness. For some the gift is sought in personal prayer, for others in the absolution declared by a priest. In Matthew 18, however, forgiveness is viewed as a process involving the whole community of faith (cf. Klassen: 140-173, especially 144-149). As sisters and brothers relate to each other, sin is named and confessed and pardon offered in Christ's name. A critical mark of the true church is thus whether its life and worship encourage this process—and so enable its members to experience God's forgiveness.

Matthew 19:1—20:34

Demands of Discipleship

PREVIEW

The journey to Jerusalem announced in 16:21 is finally narrated in 19:1—20:34. Along the way, Jesus disputes, teaches, speaks in parables, and heals, the same things he did earlier in Galilee. Although various players appear in the episodes that unfold, Jesus' primary agenda consists of issues with which *disciples* must wrestle as they pursue their calling, issues related to the classic topics of sex, wealth, and power. Thus 19:1-15 deals with marriage and divorce, celibacy, and children. The subject of 19:16—20:16 is the cost of eternal life and the kingdom as gift and reward. With 20:17-34, the question is status versus servanthood. In each instance, Jesus spells out certain demands or expectations for his followers.

Throughout the section, Matthew is following Mark's outline and drawing heavily on Markan material. At the same time, Matthew leaves his imprint on each of the three units that make up the section.

Marriage and Children

Matthew 19:1-15

PREVIEW

As indicated above, 19:1-15 deals with issues of sex and family, issues central to human life. How do disciples relate to this arena of life in the world? Under this broad question, the text addresses three specific questions: (1) Do disciples always marry? (2) If married, do disciples ever divorce their spouses? (3) Do children have a place in Jesus' community?

The unit begins with a transitional statement, marking the end of the discourse in chapter 18 and the beginning of Jesus' ministry to Judea (vv. 1-2; cf. Mark 10:1). Following this brief statement, we find a dispute involving the Pharisees, who approach Jesus and ask where he stands on the matter of divorce (vv. 3-9; cf. Mark 10:2-12). This in turn leads to a discussion between Jesus and the disciples, culminating in a word about celibacy found only in Matthew (vv. 10-12). Finally, we come to the episode where children are brought to Jesus for his blessing, and Jesus again offers a word to guide his community (vv. 13-15; cf. Mark 10:13-16; G. Thom. 22).

OUTLINE

From Galilee to Judea, 19:1-2

When Two Become One, 19:3-9

Called to Singleness, 19:10-12

Let the Children Come, 19:13-15

EXPLANATORY NOTES

From Galilee to Judea 19:1-2

Matthew again uses a typical formula (*when Jesus had finished these sayings;* cf. 7:28-29; 11:1; 13:53; 26:1) to lead the reader from a discourse of Jesus into a new segment of the story. Here the new development is Jesus' departure from Galilee and entry into *the region of Judea beyond the Jordan.* Technically, the land east of the Jordan to which the text refers is Perea. But Matthew subsumes this area under the category of Judea, which is Jesus' final destination. Judea is the territory from which Jesus and his parents had to flee earlier (cf. 2:13-23), and from which Jesus *withdrew* after he was baptized by John the Baptist, tested by the devil, and John the Baptist was arrested (4:12-16). Now he is returning to this place of threat and danger. As usual, Jesus is accompanied by crowds, and he continues to show divine compassion toward the crowds by healing the sick.

When Two Become One 19:3-9

The Pharisees who approach Jesus in verse 3 pose a question to *test* Jesus (cf. 4:1; 16:1; 22:15, 35), to trap him in what he says. There are at least two ways to understand this question, depending on the force of the phrase *for any cause.* According to some scholars, the Pharisees are asking Jesus where he stands in the debate among the rabbis on possible grounds for divorce: *Is it lawful to divorce one's wife for any reason one wishes?*

According to others, however, the Pharisees are asking a more fundamental question: *Is there* any *ground on which it is lawful to divorce one's wife?* (cf. NEB footnote). In this case, the Pharisees are acting with knowledge of Jesus' opposition to divorce (cf. 5:31-32) and seeking an answer that might put Jesus in conflict with Scripture and thereby discredit him. Whatever the precise shape of the question, it leads to a lively discussion, the form of which resembles a rabbinic dispute. (Note how Matthew has rearranged the material in Mark 10:2-12, constructing a series of arguments and counterarguments.)

The first move Jesus makes in his reply to the Pharisees (vv. 4-6) is to define the nature of marriage as a part of God's plan. To do so, he cites two texts from the story of creation, Genesis 1:27 and 2:24 (cf. a similar use of Genesis 1:27 in CD 4:21). On the basis of these texts, Jesus argues that "God made human beings for the precise purpose of lasting union" (Meier, 1980:215). Far from being just a legal convention, then, which one can set aside at will, marriage is a covenant joining life to life with God's promise and blessing, a relationship to nurture and protect.

The Pharisees counter with Scripture of their own (v. 7), this time the legislation providing for divorce in Deuteronomy 24:1-4. *If Moses so commands,* they ask Jesus, *who are you to forbid us to divorce our wives?* (paraphrased). In his response (v. 8), Jesus has the last word, subordinating Mosaic law to God's ultimate intent as set forth in Genesis. Moses *allowed* divorce, Jesus tells his opponents, because resistance to God's will made such provisions necessary. The norm for marriage, however, remains the vision embodied at the outset of creation, not later concessions made to deal with human failure.

Jesus goes on in verse 9 to make a pronouncement on divorce, a pronouncement that appears in various forms in the NT (cf. Matt. 5:32; Mark 10:11-12; Luke 16:18; 1 Cor. 7:10). The verse before us is itself found in several renditions (cf. NRSV footnotes), attesting efforts by copyists to assimilate its wording to that of 5:32. In its earliest form, Jesus' saying on divorce most likely did not contain the clause *except for unchastity* (cf. 5:32, *except on the ground of unchastity*), but rather spoke against divorce in unconditional terms. The exception clause represents an attempt to apply that unconditional saying to the life and practice of the community.

As noted earlier in our comments on 5:31-32, the Greek word for *unchastity* can carry one of two meanings here, either *adultery* or *incest.* If the issue is incest, Matthew is saying: Divorce is permissible in the case of Gentile converts married to persons with whom they are too closely related (according to Jewish law). If adultery is the issue, Matthew is saying: Divorce is permissible when the union created by marriage is already torn apart by sexual infidelity. In this case, we are again dealing with a concession due to *hardness of heart.* Even *with* the exception clause, however, the saying on divorce assumes that marriage is intended to be indissoluble. Its purpose is not to offer loopholes through which to end marriage, but to urge believers to uphold marriage as a lifelong relationship.

Called to Singleness 19:10-12

Both Matthew and Mark report a private conversation of Jesus with his disciples following the dispute with the Pharisees (cf. Mark 10:10-12). In Matthew's account, the conversation turns to a new topic, prompted by the severity of Jesus' stance on divorce and remarriage. *If marriage is as binding as you say,* the disciples ponder, *it would be better not to marry in the first place!* Jesus disregards the cynical tone of the disciples' remark, but agrees that for some, singleness may indeed be a preferable state.

According to verse 12, persons may live a sexually celibate life for one of three reasons. In some cases, persons are born without the capability to have sexual relations. A second category consists of those who have been castrated, perhaps for service in a role restricted to eunuchs. Finally, there are those who become eunuchs in a symbolic sense, who voluntarily refrain from marrying for the sake of a special calling. Here the special calling relates to God's kingdom, and singleness is chosen either (1) to prefigure a new order which transcends marriage and family, or (2) to pursue a ministry unencumbered by family interests and obligations (cf. 1 Cor. 7:32-36).

Jesus' use of the term *eunuch* as a metaphor for the single disciple is rather striking. In ancient Israel, eunuchs were viewed as impaired or blemished, and so excluded from the congregation (cf.

Deut. 23:1; Lev. 21:17-23). Later, however, we find sayings promising a place in God's community for eunuchs who are faithful to God (cf. Isa. 56:3-5; Wisd. of Sol. 3:14). So likewise, Jesus seems to be saying, there is a place in the church for disciples who serve God in their singleness rather than in marriage. At the same time, the vocation of singleness is not for everyone. Jesus' saying on celibacy is both prefaced and followed with the comment that it is a word for those who can *accept* it (cf. vv. 11, 12d). To put it another way: "Each has a particular gift from God, one having one kind and another a different kind" (1 Cor. 7:7).

Let the Children Come 19:13-15

The scene described in verses 13-15 casts Jesus in a traditional Jewish role. For Matthew's readers, the episode would call to mind scenes of children seeking the blessing of their parents, or students the blessing of their rabbis. There may even be an allusion to the blessing of children by the elders in conjunction with the Day of Atonement. In any case, the text tells us that children are brought to Jesus (most likely by their parents). And the references to prayer and the laying on of hands indicate that the reason they are brought is to receive Jesus' *blessing*.

Exactly why the disciples object to this request is not spelled out. By their objection, however, the disciples present Jesus an opportunity to deliver an important saying about children (v. 14). According to this saying, children typify those to whom God offers life in the kingdom—the weak, the helpless, the needy, the lowly (cf. 5:3; 18:3). Children thus have a special place in the fellowship of the kingdom and should be welcomed accordingly. Jesus symbolizes this when he proceeds to bless the children, providing a model for the life of the church.

THE TEXT IN BIBLICAL CONTEXT

As is evident from the discussion thus far, Matthew 19:1-15 is part of a wider Jewish and Christian tradition concerning marriage. Ephesians 5:21-33 calls for cooperation, love, and respect in marriage, which is compared with the relationship between Christ and the church. One particular text that invites comparison with Matthew 19 is 1 Corinthians 7, in which Paul addresses a number of questions related to sex and family life. Among the topics Paul explores is that of *divorce*, and the approach he takes is similar to Matthew's in two respects. On one hand, Paul affirms the teaching of Jesus that marriage is for keeps and that spouses are to give each other conjugal rights in marriage. He argues that neither spouse should act to sever a marriage relationship (1 Cor. 7:10-14).

On the other hand, Paul writes as Matthew did to a community struggling with problematic cases and attempts to apply Jesus' teaching to such cases in a sensitive manner. Accordingly, Paul concedes the possibility of separation so long as one remains single and/or seeks reconciliation (7:11). And he advises a Christian married to a nonbeliever who wants out of the marriage to grant the partner a divorce (7:15-16). To put it another way: Both Matthew and Paul offer us "exception clauses" as they interpret Jesus' word on divorce for the church.

A second issue which surfaces in both Matthew and 1 Corinthians is that of *singleness* or *celibacy*. Paul notes in his letter that he himself is single, makes it clear that he prefers this state, and advises other unmarried persons "to remain unmarried as I am" (7:8; cf. vv. 6-7, 40). It is not a matter of celibacy for *leaders*, for Paul indicates elsewhere that apostles generally enjoy the company of a spouse (1 Cor. 9:5). Nor does Paul view sexual relations in marriage as somehow inappropriate for believers (7:3-4).

Rather, Paul opts for singleness because he believes that marriage (1) enmeshes one in an old order that is about to vanish, and (2) distracts one from undivided devotion to Christ and the new order (7:25-35). At the same time, Paul concurs with Matthew that celibacy is not for everyone. He quickly concedes that marriage is preferable to a lifestyle of uncontrolled sexual passion (7:1-2, 9, 36). More importantly, he acknowledges that God endows us in different ways, some for service in marriage and some for service in singleness (7:7, quoted earlier). The bottom line for Paul is not whether we marry or remain single, but whether our lives manifest the new creation in Christ.

THE TEXT IN THE LIFE OF THE CHURCH

The church's teaching that marriage is a lifelong relationship is anchored in texts such as Matthew 19. Throughout much of its history, the church's efforts to uphold the text concentrated on making it difficult or impossible for persons to get out of a marriage. Wide ranging civil and religious law was developed to restrict or forbid divorce. For those who did divorce and remarry, the church's judgment was often harsh and unrelenting.

In today's more permissive culture, in the church and in society, a different issue confronts us. Divorce is easy to obtain, freedom is highly prized, and marital breakup is commonplace. For many persons, the possibility of a lifelong relationship seems questionable. How do we honor Jesus' vision for marriage in such a situation? The answer does not lie in a return to tough divorce codes, but in finding ways to help *marriages* become what Jesus intends. One of the most important things a church can do is model a communal life in which relationships are coming together rather than breaking apart. In so doing, the church serves as a laboratory where skills are learned and support received for building oneness in marriage.

The question of *whether* to marry, addressed in 19:10-12, has been handled in various ways in the Christian community. The church has generally adopted a pro-marriage and pro-family stance, not unlike that found in Judaism. Alongside this view of marriage as the norm, however, we find a tradition that looks back to NT texts on celibacy, lifting up the single state as most desirable for at least some believers. The most obvious example is that of celibacy for priests and bishops, mandated in the Western church as early as the fourth century (and a live issue in Roman Catholic circles today). Celibacy is also linked with religious orders and communities, whether as an optional or required lifestyle. A case in point in the believers' church heritage was the Ephrata Community in colonial Pennsylvania, which had both celibate and married orders.

More recently, churches have begun to look critically at the cultural bias in favor of marrying and the way that has influenced the church's life. Should not singleness as well as marriage be upheld as a valid option for those who follow Jesus? And if so, should churches not be more attentive to the needs of both single and married persons in their midst?

A third issue in Matthew 19 with which interpreters have wrestled is the church's practice in relation to *children*. The text clearly validates the presence of children in the community and points out the significance of that presence. But does it perhaps say more? Some have argued that Jesus' command, *Let the children come to me, and do not hinder them,* supports the practice of infant baptism (cf. the use of the same verb for *hinder* or *prevent* in Acts 8:36). As read by the Anabaptists, however, Jesus' saying teaches that children have access to God's mercy independent of any ceremony, and so have no need to be baptized (cf. Menno Simons: 280-281; Alexander Mack in Durnbaugh, 1958:333-335; 351-352).

Most interpreters today agree that the passage does not address the topic of infant baptism one way or the other. The text, nevertheless, invites the church to ask: How *might* we symbolize what Jesus himself signified when he blessed the children? Some believers church bodies, in response to the text, conduct a service of dedication for infants and parents. Indeed, one Anabaptist, Pilgram Marpeck, provided instructions for infant dedication in the congregation (Klaassen: 124-125). In such a service, the community has an opportunity to *receive* children, to embody God's blessing, and to affirm its role in the faith development of the young. Similar blessings for children older than infants are sometimes celebrated at milestones of life and spiritual development. Equally important are the occasions the church provides for children to contribute their gifts to the community—and thereby know that their presence is valued.

Giving and Getting

Matthew 19:16—20:16

PREVIEW

In 19:1-15, the overarching topic was discipleship and family life. A new topic emerges in 19:16—20:16, that of discipleship and *wealth*. On the one hand, we hear of riches which a disciple may have to give up. On the other hand, we hear of new riches which disciples will receive.

The unit begins with the story of the rich young man in 19:16-22, a narrative we might label an unsuccessful call story (cf. 4:18-22; 8:18-22). Based on Mark 10:17-22 (cf. G. Naz. 16), the account probes the question of the cost of eternal life. A conversation between Jesus and the twelve follows in 19:23-30, in which Jesus talks about both the difficulty riches pose and the rewards of discipleship. Here Matthew is drawing on Mark 10:23-31, supplemented with a saying cited by Luke in a different context (cf. Luke 22:28-30). Finally, as a commentary on the puzzling word in 19:30, Matthew offers us the parable of the laborers in the vineyard in 20:1-16. Found only in the First Gospel, the story reminds us that the riches of the kingdom are God's to bestow—as God chooses.

OUTLINE

EXPLANATORY NOTES

Too High a Price? 19:16-22

As Matthew retells the story of the rich man who meets Jesus on the journey to Jerusalem, he adds his own touch at several points. Thus the introduction focuses on the *good* that God seeks rather than on the issue of whether *Jesus* is good (cf. Mark 10:17-18). Later, in the listing of commandments from the Decalogue that define what is good (vv. 18-19), Matthew adds the summary statement on love of neighbor (Lev. 19:18).

Yet another new feature is the way the rich man himself acknowledges that he still lacks something—and asks what it is (v. 20; cf. Mark 10:21). In turn, Jesus speaks of the man's quest for something more as a quest to *be perfect* (v. 21; cf. 5:48!) and offers the call to become a disciple as a way to fulfill this quest. Finally, only in Matthew's account is the rich man identified as a *young man* (vv. 20, 22), someone under the age of 40.

It is clear from the story that the final answer to the question of how to gain eternal life, to enter the kingdom, is: *Come, follow me.* It is in following Jesus that one discovers the scope of the goodness God seeks—and the means to achieve it. The problem for the rich man is that the call to come and follow is linked to the command to give away his wealth. Like others before us, we may find ourselves wondering: Why does Jesus ask the man to part with his riches?

At one level, the demand can be viewed as a special requirement for itinerant ministry, as a step the man must take to be free to accompany Jesus in his mission to Israel (cf. 10:9-10). To this extent, the call to break with wealth is historically conditioned. At another level, however, the demand is a symbolic test of loyalty, a test that confronts every would-be disciple in one form or another: Will we serve God and seek first his kingdom, or will we serve wealth and status in pursuit of *our* ambitions (cf. 6:19-34)? When the rich young man goes away sorrowful (v. 22), he mirrors the tragic plight of all who choose the second option.

Compensation Beyond Measure 19:23-30

The conversation in verses 23-30 builds on the preceding episode and explores two themes: the dilemma of the rich (vv. 23-26) and the destiny of disciples (vv. 27-30). On each topic Jesus makes several forceful pronouncements, introduced by the solemn formula *Truly, I tell you* (vv. 23, 28).

One of those forceful statements is the proverblike saying in verse 24 about a camel going through the eye of a needle (rabbinic parallels speak of an elephant instead of a camel). Here we have another example of Jesus' use of hyperbole, a bold figure of speech that says in effect: It is *impossible* for the rich to reorient their lives so as to enter God's kingdom! For the disciples, the implication of Jesus' saying is most disturbing. From their point of view, wealth was a sign of good standing with God. If the rich don't make it into the kingdom, therefore, where does that leave the rest of us (v. 25)?

Jesus' reply to the twelve concedes their concern, but then comes at the question of what is possible or not from a wholly new perspective (v. 26; cf. Gen. 18:14; Job 42:2). No one, Jesus says, achieves salvation on their own. Any number of stumbling blocks can get in the way. By the power of *God*, however, persons can and do say yes to the call of the kingdom—perhaps even the rich!

The twelve, of course, *have* responded to Jesus' call, and in verse 27 the conversation turns to the topic of what the future holds for them. Peter once again speaks for all the disciples: *What then will we have?* In reply Jesus promises two things. According to verse 28, the twelve themselves will share in Jesus' messianic reign in the *new world* or *new age* (GNB), when the present order is radically transformed (cf. Isa. 65:17; Jub. 1:29; 1 Enoch 45:4-5; Rev. 21:1, 5). The verb for *judge* in this saying can also mean *rule* (cf. GNB), so the role ascribed to the twelve may be either that of governing the endtime people of God (cf. Ps. Sol. 17:26-29; Rev. 3:21) or of assisting in the final judgment of Israel (cf. 13:41-42; 1 Cor. 6:2). Future blessing is not restricted to the twelve, however. For *all* those who endure the hardship and separation that discipleship may entail, Jesus promises there will be compensation *a hundredfold.* That return is the gift of eternal life (v. 29).

Just how verse 30 relates to all of this is a disputed matter. There are essentially two ways of interpreting Jesus' reference to the *first* who *will be last* and *the last* who *will be first* (cf. Luke 13:30; G. Thom. 4). The saying could be a kind of summary statement, describing an endtime reversal of present fortunes: The rich and powerful will barely make it into the kingdom, if at all, while humble, poor disciples will be the first to get in (cf. 21:31; 5:3). On the other hand, the saying may be a special postscript for disciples, a word of caution to those pondering future rewards: Don't assume that your tenure or status in the church will put you ahead of others in the age to come! In this case, the saying leads naturally into the story that follows—and forms an inclusion with 20:16.

The Goodness of God 20:1-16

The parable of the laborers in the vineyard reflects the life and culture of Jesus' day at a number of points. Then as now, one of the pressing social problems was unemployment, which is why the landowner finds persons standing around the marketplace, waiting for work. The *denarius* offered to the workers by the landowner was the customary daily wage for a laborer. Finally, payment is made at the end of the day, in accord with Jewish law (cf. Lev. 19:13; Deut. 24:15). The scene described is thus, in many respects, a typical or normal scene.

What goes beyond the normal is the fact that the landowner pays all the laborers the same wages, whether they worked twelve hours, nine hours, six hours, three hours, or only one hour. Who wouldn't raise a question about that? Something unusual is going on. (Cf. the similar plot in a rabbinic parable cited by Jeremias: 138-139, where the focus however is on human merit.)

As readers, we know in advance that the vineyard in the story is not ordinary. It is a field of activity that relates to the kingdom, and the landowner is a metaphor for the God of Israel. The problem the text poses, then, is not one of justice in terms of human labor law, but an even larger issue—the justice of God! To be more precise: Is it fair for God to grant all disciples the same reward, eternal life?

According to the text, God both promises to be just (v. 4) and *is* just. No one receives less than agreed at the outset (v. 13). At the same time, God is free to exceed what is just by legal standards and act out of sheer generosity (v. 15). To take offense at this, Jesus says, is to look at God's *goodness* with an *evil* or envious eye (cf. the NRSV footnote on v. 15b, and note how this verse picks up the comment on God as good in 19:17). In the end, therefore, the parable of the laborers forces us to think about salvation in a way that bursts the framework of work and wages. Eternal life is finally a *gift from* God, not a *claim on* God.

For Matthew, it was important to balance the discussion of rewards in 19:27-29 with a story such as this. Although disciples can be sure that God will reward their faithfulness, they cannot turn this promise into a rating system. The founding members of the community have no advantage over the second and later generations. The strong will not go through the portals of the kingdom ahead of the weak. It is in this sense that Matthew wants us to understand the sayings about the first and the last (19:30; 20:16). The purpose of these sayings is not to establish a new order of precedence, but rather to tell us to stop calculating. As noted earlier, the riches of the kingdom are *God's* to distribute—and God is full of surprises!

THE TEXT IN BIBLICAL CONTEXT

In discussing Matthew 6:19-34, we noted some of the ways Scripture addresses the subject of riches. One of the issues the Gospels confronts is the question behind the text: *Can the rich be saved*? Luke pursues the question at length through materials found in the Third Gospel and in Acts. In some instances, the stories convey a clearly negative answer to the question. Such is the case with the accounts of the rich man intent on building bigger barns (Luke 12:13-21), the rich man and Lazarus (Luke 16:19-31), and the rich ruler (Luke 18:18-30, the Lukan parallel to Matt. 19:16-22).

Other stories, however, indicate that it is *possible* for the rich to be converted. The case in point in the Gospel is the story of Zacchaeus (Luke 19:1-10), while Barnabas and Lydia represent wealthy believers who supported the early church (Acts 4:36; 16:11-15). Actually, Matthew himself illustrates the fact that *for God all things are possible* near the end of the First Gospel. As he relates the story of Joseph of Arimathea, who provided a tomb for Jesus' burial (27:57-61), he tells the reader that Joseph is both *a rich man* and *a disciple of Jesus!* On occasion, then, a camel does go through the eye of a needle.

The story of the laborers in the vineyard has its own surprise or reversal of expectations, a feature common to a number of biblical narratives. Thus one thinks of the story of Ruth, a foreigner who becomes the unlikely grandmother of King David (cf. Ruth 4:13-17), or of David himself, a youngest son chosen over his brothers to be the king (cf. 1 Sam. 16:1-13). In the Gospels, unexpected outcomes occur in several of Jesus' stories, including the parable of the closed door (Luke 13:22-30) and the parable of guests invited to a great banquet (Luke 14:15-24; Matt. 22:1-14).

The most striking counterpart to 20:1-16, though, is the parable of the prodigal son and his brother (Luke 15:11-32). Like the first group of workers in Matthew's story, the elder brother in this account has labored faithfully a long time. The prodigal, by contrast, hasn't even worked an hour to prove himself. Nevertheless, the father restores him to his place in the family, showing the same generosity exhibited by the vineyard owner. And this act of goodness again evokes a sharp protest, a complaint of unfairness. As the story ends, Luke depicts the elder brother on the outside looking in, which is another way of saying that *the first will be last and the last will be first.*

THE TEXT IN THE LIFE OF THE CHURCH

Jesus' word to the rich man to give away his wealth is clearly a hard saying—and interpreters have struggled to accommodate its message. One of the classic approaches to the text distinguishes between what is necessary to be saved and what is necessary to *be perfect* (19:21). Here the renunciation of riches is praised as the highest ideal, to which a few will aspire, but it is not regarded as a requirement of faith.

A different approach is found in authors like Clement of Alexandria, who wrote a well-known treatise on Mark's account of the rich man, *Quis Dives Salvetur? (Who Is the Rich Man That Will Be Saved?)* According to Clement, Jesus does not call the rich to abandon their wealth in a literal sense, but rather to free themselves from an inward attachment to riches and to use their wealth to benefit others:

> For he who holds possessions . . . as the gifts of God . . . and knows that he possesses them more for the sake of the brethren than his own; and is superior to the possession of them, not the slave of the things he possesses; and does not carry them about in his soul, nor bind and circumscribe his life with them, but is ever labouring at some good and divine work . . . is able with cheerful mind to bear their removal equally with their abundance. This is he who is blessed by the Lord, and called poor in spirit, a meet heir of the kingdom of heaven, not one who could not live rich. (16)

Neither of the two approaches cited above is fully satisfactory. The demand Jesus makes in the text is part of a basic call to discipleship, not an assignment for extra credit. Moreover, it is a demand for concrete action, not merely a new attitude toward wealth. The only question is whether this demand is universal. *Does Jesus demand of all would-be disciples what he demands of the rich young man in the text?*

At least two considerations are pertinent here. On one hand, the NT does not prescribe a uniform course of action for the rich. There apparently was a place in the early church for both well-to-do patrons of congregations and for missionaries who had given up everything. On the other hand, the NT leaves no doubt that the pursuit of prosperity can seriously jeopardize the pursuit of the kingdom. How one acts to overcome that conflict may vary from case to case. For all disciples, however, possessions are part of the totality of life which we surrender in baptism.

A different sort of riches is the subject of the story about the workers in the vineyard. In exploring this story, the church has shown considerable imagination in identifying the various groups of workers who are hired. According to one interpretation, the groups represent successive generations in the history of redemption, with Christians or Gentiles as the eleventh-hour workers. Another view is that the different groups signify various stages of life at which persons become believers. Yet a third proposal is that the workers portray the developing Christian mission, with old established churches as the early morning workers and younger groups of Christians as the later arrivals.

More important than the identity of the groups is the issue that emerges from the *plot* of the parable—and where we find ourselves in relation to that plot. To be specific: How will we respond to the strange employer who offers all the same wages? Will God's flagrant disregard of our rules for compensation leave us bitter and envious? Or will we open ourselves to life in a world where grace and freedom reign?

Status or Servanthood?

Matthew 20:17-34

PREVIEW

Jesus' journey to Jerusalem is in its final stages in 20:17-34. Before it ends, however, Jesus addresses yet another facet of the everyday life of disciples. He has already clarified his expectations in regard to family life (19:1-15) and wealth (19:16—20:16). Now he speaks to the issue of *power* and *honor*. What does it mean, in God's scheme of things, to be great among others? And how does Jesus' own life exemplify the pattern he commends to his followers?

Based on Mark 10:32-52, the unit begins with a prediction of suffering (vv. 17-19). This is the third such prediction in Matthew (cf. 16:21; 17:22-23) and the most specific of the three. In the episode that follows (vv. 20-28), Jesus again speaks of impending suffering as he responds to a mother's request to grant her sons special honors. The response itself ends at verse 23, but has been expanded with the sayings on servanthood in verses 24-28. To illustrate Jesus' role as servant (cf. 8:17; 12:15-21), the unit concludes with an account of his healing of two blind men (vv. 29-34; cf. the doublet of this narrative in 9:27-31).

OUTLINE

En Route to Suffering, 20:17-19

The Way of the Servant, 20:20-28

The Gift of Sight, 20:29-34

EXPLANATORY NOTES

En Route to Suffering 20:17-19

The wording of the text in verses 17-19. underscores the destination of Jesus and his party. Twice we find the phrase *going up to Jerusalem,* once in the narration and again in Jesus' announcement. Also noteworthy is the detail with which Jesus' imminent suffering is spelled out, amounting to "a short summary of the whole passion narrative" (Meier, 1980:226; cf. 26:14-16, 45-57, 66; 27:1-2; 24-31). Among the new elements in this prediction are the statements that Jesus will be *crucified* (cf. 26:2), and that this will occur at the hands of *Gentiles* (Romans). Yet a third feature that strikes the reader is the way *the twelve* are drawn into the developing drama. *We* are going up to Jerusalem, Jesus says to his disciples, suggesting that the plot of suffering and vindication will determine *their* story as well. This sets the stage for the account of the Zebedees in verses 20-28.

The Way of the Servant 20:20-28

Though not mentioned by name, *the sons of Zebedee* in verse 20 are the disciples James and John (cf. Mark 10:35; Matt. 10:2). In Mark's account, the two brothers themselves approach Jesus and request positions of highest honor in the age to come. In Matthew, however, the petition is brought by the *mother* of James and John, whose intervention on behalf of her sons resembles that of other mothers from the biblical era (cf. 1 Kings 1:15-31; Gen. 27:5-17; 2 Macc. 7).

Whoever brings the request, Jesus addresses James and John directly in verses 22-23 (the pronoun *you* is plural in the Greek text). Jesus' initial response makes the point that the two brothers are asking for more than they realize (*You do not know*), because the route to future glory leads through suffering. The metaphor for suffering that Jesus uses here is that of a cup one must drink, an image sometimes linked with bearing God's judgment (cf. Isa. 51:17; Jer. 25:15; Ezek. 23:32-34; Ps. 75:8).

When James and John indicate their readiness to partake of such a cup, Jesus offers a second response, clarifying what he can and cannot give them: *I can promise you suffering and martyrdom,* Jesus says (paraphrased; cf. Acts 12:1-2), *but God alone determines the nature of one's exaltation in the kingdom.*

The indignation of the other disciples noted in verse 24 provides an occasion for Jesus to deliver the sayings found in verses 25-28 (cf. 18:1-4; 23:11-12; Luke 22:24-27). According to Jesus, the sign of stature in his community (note the three occurrences of the phrase *among you* in vv. 26-27) differs radically from that recognized by the world. In the world, greatness is measured by the degree of domination, but in the church by the degree of one's service to fellow members. The twin statements that make this point (vv. 26b, 27) exhibit a paradox that builds in force from one line to the next:

To be *great*, become a *servant*.
To be *first*, become a *slave*!

Equally forceful is the language in the final saying (v. 28), which cites Jesus' own ministry as a model of servanthood. Instead of lording it over persons, he chose to serve their needs and seek their well-being at considerable expense. The word for *ransom* (Greek: *lutron*) denotes a price paid to free captives such as slaves, those in debt, and prisoners of war. Here the bondage in question is the grip of evil, and Jesus' role as a deliverer is the role of the servant in Isaiah 53: He sacrifices *himself* to bring forgiveness to *many* (Isa. 53:10, 12), to *all* whose lives are linked with his life (cf. Matt. 26:27-28).

The Gift of Sight 20:29-34

The episode that concludes the journey narrative of 19:1—20:34 is located at Jericho, a city in the Jordan Valley northeast of Jerusalem. As Jesus is leaving the city, he is accosted by a pair of blind men who hope to regain their sight. (Note that Matthew speaks of *two blind men* instead of the sole "blind beggar" mentioned in Mark 10:46; a possible reason is given in the comments on 9:27-31.)

Twice the supplicants call on Jesus with the phrase later taken up in the church's liturgy: *Lord, have mercy* (vv. 30, 31). This form of address, together with the messianic title Son of David, casts the two men in the role of believers. The dialogue and narrative that follow lift up Jesus' power to act as God's servant, who gives sight to the blind (v. 33; cf. Isa. 42:7; 35:5). Manifesting the same divine pity or compassion mentioned in other stories in the Gospel (cf. 9:36; 14:14; 15:32), Jesus touches the eyes of the supplicants (cf. Mark 8:22-26) and so restores their sight.

The sequel to the miracle Jesus performs is found in the final two words of the text. With open eyes, the two men *followed him.* The ending to the story is noteworthy in two respects. At one level, it signifies a new development in the plot. Up to this point, the circle of Jesus' disciples has extended no further than the twelve. Now, Matthew tells us, anticipating the great commission at the end of the Gospel, the circle of followers is ready to expand! At another level, the narrative makes a theological point that is pertinent to each reader or listener: The appropriate response to the mercy of God that makes us whole is to follow Jesus as grateful disciples.

THE TEXT IN BIBLICAL CONTEXT

Jesus' sayings on servanthood are taken up in different ways by the writers of the Gospels. While Matthew follows Mark in his placement of this material, Luke makes it part of the conversation at the Last Supper (Luke 22:24-27). A dispute about greatness breaks out as Jesus and the twelve are seated at table, and Jesus uses this occasion to remind the disciples that he is with them *as one who serves.* The Fourth Gospel likewise links the discussion of servanthood to Jesus' final meal (John 13:1-20), but goes a step further. Here Jesus not only *speaks* of himself as one who serves, but performs an act of service as a model or example: Girding himself with a towel and pouring water into a basin, he, the Lord and Master, washes the feet of his disciples.

As noted earlier, the picture of Jesus as a servant is shaped in part by the servant songs in Isaiah 40—55 (cf. Isa. 42:1-4; 49:1-6; 50:4-11; 52:13—53:12). Matthew 20 is one of several NT passages that draw on the servant songs in one way or another.

Thus Matthew himself cites verses from Isaiah 42 and 53 elsewhere in his Gospel to describe Jesus' ministry of healing (8:17; 12:17-21). The witness of Philip to the Ethiopian eunuch identifies Jesus as the suffering servant mentioned in the scroll the eunuch is reading (Acts 8:26-35). And 1 Peter 2:21-24 reads like an early Christian paraphrase of Isaiah 53. A related text, though the influence of Isaiah on its language is disputed, is a hymnlike passage in Philippians 2. There Paul speaks of Christ as one who "emptied himself, taking the form of a slave," and who "humbled himself and became obedient to the point of death" (Phil. 2:7, 8). Together, these texts attest a Servant Christology, a Christology that Matthew emphasizes in his Gospel.

THE TEXT IN THE LIFE OF THE CHURCH

A popular twentieth-century hymn based on the text begins with the lines:

"Are ye able," said the Master,
"To be crucified with me?"
"Yea," the sturdy dreamers answered,
"To the death we follow Thee."

The mood here is one of heroism, a self-assured gutsy readiness to act nobly for a noble cause. In the text itself, however, what we find is a penetrating critique of the aspirations of heroes like James and John. The cup of suffering that the disciples must drink with Jesus is not offered as a winsome challenge, but as a harsh reality that gets in the way of human dreams. And the pattern of life depicted in Jesus' sayings on servanthood is hardly the stuff to inspire Christian status seekers. To put it another way: The text resists any attempt to make the way of the cross something humanly appealing.

At the same time, the passage does provide a model to emulate, and has influenced the Christian community at two crucial points. One of these is a valuing of martyrdom as a possible outcome of faithfulness (cf. the references to Matthew 20 in the Anabaptist work, *Martyrs Mirror*). Along with other passages, the text presents martyrdom as a way of participating in Christ's suffering and subsequent glory.

A second point at which the text has played an important role is in advocating a servant lifestyle. In addition to providing a measuring stick with which to evaluate the church's own ministry, the text has contributed to an understanding of leaders in all realms of life as "public servants," as persons called to serve the good of the community. Whether in dying or in living, then, we find ourselves addressed in Jesus' reply to the sons of Zebedee.

Part 5

Jesus in Jerusalem

Matthew 21:1—25:46

PREVIEW

Earlier in the Gospel, there are several episodes in which Jesus *withdraws* from confrontation with his opponents (cf. 12:14-15; 14:13; 15:21). All that changes, however, in Matthew 21—25. Jesus is now in Jerusalem, the center of the Jewish world, where his opponents are concentrated and able to wield power. Here the impending confrontation between Jesus and Jewish officialdom can no longer be avoided. For Matthew, the issue at the heart of this confrontation is Jesus' messianic authority. The story of Jesus' entry into Jerusalem is itself told in such a way that the reader knows: Here is David's Son in David's city! The only question is whether Jerusalem will acknowledge his kingship.

Theoretically, the episodes that follow could tell a story of Jesus winning over his opponents and enjoying the acclamation of his community. We know already, however, from the passion predictions and other clues along the way, that this is *not* the way it will work out. The sharp conflict that was already apparent in Galilee only intensifies in Jerusalem, leading at last to Jesus' definitive judgment on Jerusalem in chapter 23. This judgment anticipates the final judgment of all the nations, portrayed in 25:31-46 at the conclusion of Jesus' fifth and final discourse in the Gospel. There the humble king rejected by Jerusalem reigns in glory in the age to come. To put it another way: God vindicates and establishes Jesus' messianic rule, and so has the final word in the confrontation in Jerusalem.

The narrative in which all of this transpires follows the contours of the story told in Mark 11—13 and can be viewed as an expanded edition of the Markan account. As we examine some of the components of the expanded story, we will discuss how and where Matthew has enriched the Markan material.

OUTLINE

Conflict and Confrontation, 21:1—23:39

21:1-17	David's Son in David's City
21:18—22:14	Stories of Rejection
22:15-46	Disputes With Jewish Leaders
23:1-39	A Bitter Public Farewell

Instruction on the Endtime, 24:1—25:46

24:1-35	How Will the End Come?
24:36—25:30	Living in Readiness
25:31-46	Jesus Judges the Nations

Matthew 21:1—23:39

Conflict and Confrontation

PREVIEW

The journey to Jerusalem chronicled in 16:21—20:34 at last reaches its destination in Matthew 21, setting the stage for the final events of Jesus' ministry to Israel. These events unfold within a narrative framework of two days and revolve around the temple. Day one features the colorful actions with which Jesus enters the city and preempts business as usual in the temple (21:1-17), while day two focuses on Jesus the storyteller, debater, and prophetic critic of Jerusalem (21:18—23:39).

At the beginning of the narrative, the words and gestures of the pilgrims accompanying Jesus create a mood of joy and hope. By the end of the narrative, however, sounds of praise have given way to sounds of woe and regret. Because Jerusalem is unwilling to receive the one who comes, the only song for its future is a song of lament.

In constructing chapters 21—23, Matthew has enlarged the parallel account in Mark 11—12 in a substantial way at two points: (1) He offers a trilogy of parables on Israel's rejection of the gospel, where Mark has only one (cf. Mark 12:1-12; Matt. 21:28—22:14). (2) He appends a sermon by Jesus in the temple to conclude the section, a sermon in which Jesus castigates the leaders of Israel in the harshest possible terms (cf. chapter 23). In addition, Matthew has incorporated new material into the unit that opens the section, the unit to which we now turn our attention.

David's Son in David's City

Matthew 21:1-17

PREVIEW

When the blind men in 20:29-34 hail Jesus as the Son of David, there is no longer any attempt to contain the news (cf. by contrast 9:30; 16:20). The time is at hand for a public manifestation of Jesus "in his kingly majesty and authority" (Sand: 411). This is precisely what we find in the account of Jesus' first day in Jerusalem in 21:1-17, an account built around two provocative episodes.

In the first episode (vv. 1-11; cf. Mark 11:1-11; Luke 19:28-40; John 12:12-19), Jesus enters the city in a manner that discloses his messianic authority. In the second (vv. 12-17; cf. Mark 11:15-19; Luke 19:45-48; John 2:13-22), he lays claim to the temple in Jerusalem, challenging those who have warped its purpose and demonstrating what a religious institution ought to be about.

The two parts of the narrative exhibit a number of parallel features, including symbolic actions, quotations from the OT to interpret what is happening (vv. 5, 13, 16), and the acclamation of Jesus with the cry: *Hosanna to the Son of David* (vv. 9, 15). As the cry itself suggests, messianic acclamation is an appropriate label for the form the story takes.

OUTLINE

A Royal Processional, 21:1-11

Reclaiming God's House, 21:12-17

EXPLANATORY NOTES

A Royal Processional 21:1-11

Jesus approaches Jerusalem by way of Bethphage, likely a village on the eastern slope of the Mount of Olives. So named because of the plentiful olive trees that grew there, the Mount of Olives lay directly to the east of Jerusalem, across the Kidron Valley. It was a hill with special significance for Jewish eschatology, a site linked with God's coming to restore Jerusalem (cf. Zech. 14:1-5). Even the geography of the story, therefore, supports the statement the narrative makes. (Note that Jesus will return to the Mount of Olives in Matt. 24 to give instruction on the endtime to his disciples.)

Verses 2-7 focus on Jesus' means of transportation in entering the city: He comes to Jerusalem riding on a donkey and its colt. Several features of the text call for comment here, among them the way the animals become a part of the story. Both the command Jesus gives and the response the command assumes suggest a mysterious sovereignty on Jesus' part, which the disciples acknowledge as they go and bring the animals. (Cf. the same phenomenon in the instructions on the Last Supper in 26:17-19.)

Equally noteworthy is the fulfillment quotation Matthew adds in verses 4-5 to interpret Jesus' action (cf. John 12:14-15). Taken from the LXX, the quotation combines parts of two OT passages: The opening phrase comes from Isaiah 62:11, while the words about a king mounted on a donkey are cited from Zechariah 9:9. Matthew's reading of the latter text may account for yet another feature of the story, namely, the reference to *two* animals (the other Gospels mention only one).

While the Hebrew text of Zechariah has only one animal in mind, described in parallel phrases as a donkey and as a colt, the LXX introduces the conjunction *and* between the two phrases, allowing a scribe to think of two different animals. Matthew apparently reasoned: If Zechariah prophesied of both a donkey and her colt, the one who fulfills that prophecy must in fact have used both in his entry into Jerusalem.

More important than the number of animals is the significance they assume against the backdrop of Zechariah 9:9-10 (cf. Gen. 49:11; Sasson: 72-73). First, the very act of riding into Jerusalem on a donkey would have had royal and messianic connotations for many of Matthew's contemporaries. Moreover, the use of a donkey rather than a mighty war-horse says something about the character of the Messiah's reign. A ruler who comes to Israel on a donkey symbolizes a humble reign of serving the common good, not a kingdom of violence and military conquest. For Matthew, then, the scene of Jesus entering Jerusalem on a donkey both proclaims Jesus to be the Messiah and conveys a picture of the servant role which defines his messiahship.

The sequel to Jesus' action is the response of the crowds accompanying him (vv. 8-9). In a gesture recalling the moment when Jehu was anointed king (cf. 2 Kings 9:13), some of the people spread their garments in front of Jesus. Others lay down a carpet of branches, reminding one of celebrations such as the Feast of Booths or Tabernacles, where branches were used in ritual processions (cf. Ps. 118:27; 1 Macc. 13:51; 2 Macc. 10:7).

The cry *Hosanna* also comes from a temple liturgy (cf. Ps. 118:25-26). Originally a plea for assistance meaning *save* or *help us*, the cry later became a more general shout of praise and jubilation. Here, on the lips of the crowd, *Hosanna* serves as a formula of acclamation, welcoming Jesus as the messianic ruler (*Son of David*) who comes in God's name. The fuller expression, *Hosanna in the highest heaven,* means in effect: *Let heaven itself join us in acclaiming him!*

Finally, in a piece of narration found only in Matthew (vv. 10-11), Jerusalem itself responds to Jesus' festive entry. With the same verb he uses elsewhere to describe a storm or earthquake (cf. 8:24; 24:7; 27:51-54; 28:2-4), Matthew tells us that *the whole city was thrown into an uproar* (GNB). The description recalls the scene in 2:3 when all Jerusalem was *troubled* by the news of Jesus' birth! So it is that the residents of the city ask: *Who is this?* The somewhat subdued answer identifies Jesus in terms of his Galilean roots (cf. 2:23; 4:12-16) and the prophetic role in which he will soon confront the city. It is an ominous answer, we will learn shortly, because Jerusalem has a reputation of *killing* God's prophets (23:37). To call Jesus a prophet, therefore, is to signal in advance the fate that awaits him.

Reclaiming God's House 21:12-17

The second episode, the so-called cleansing of the temple, immediately follows Jesus' triumphal entry into the city (in Mark's account it falls on the second day of Jesus' visit). As Jesus enters the temple, the outermost court of the temple known as the court of the Gentiles, he encounters a not unusual scene. Merchants are selling animals for use in offering sacrifices, and money changers are converting Greek and Roman money into the traditional coinage needed to pay the temple tax. From the vantage point of the priestly aristocracy, such activity was essential to the life of the temple. For Jesus, however, it signifies an institution that has forgotten its proper function, an institution in which the powerful are exploiting the poor in the name of religion.

Jesus' response, the text tells us, is to engage in a symbolic act that disrupts this commercial activity, an act that casts Jesus in the role of the messenger of God who comes to purify the temple (cf. Mal. 3:1-4; Zech. 14:21b). To support his action, Jesus cites two OT passages, Isaiah 56:7 and Jeremiah 7:11 (the latter part of an earlier prophetic protest in the temple!). One text defines the true purpose of the temple, while the other condemns those who use the temple to further their own economic interests.

To portray what *ought* to happen in God's *house,* Matthew adds the material we find in verses 14-16. Here as elsewhere in the Gospel, the story and the characters point ahead to the life of the church. The blind and lame, hitherto excluded from the temple because of their deformities (cf. 2 Sam. 5:6-8; 1QSa 2:5-7), find a welcome in the community that Jesus gathers, a community open to all. Jesus himself both receives and heals those who come, demonstrating the divine mercy that marks his mission to Israel (cf. 9:27; 11:2-5; 14:14; 15:30-31) and his presence in the church. Beholding this mercy, the children begin to chant the same cries of *Hosanna* heard earlier in the story (cf. v. 9) and function as a metaphor for childlike disciples who recognize and worship Jesus (cf. 18:3; 19:14).

The only feature that shatters this idyllic scene is the complaint of *the chief priests and the scribes* (vv. 15-16; cf. Luke 19:39-40), who represent the old order that Jesus is challenging. They are offended by what they see and hear. Jesus deflects their criticism, however, by interpreting the children's praise as a fulfillment of the psalmist's words in Psalm 8:2. (Note the question-and-answer format of verse 16, which resembles a rabbinic dispute.) In short, infants or *little ones* discern and rejoice in what they see in Jesus, as they have throughout the Gospel (cf. 11:25!), while the guardians of Israel fail to perceive what is happening.

The narrative ends in verse 17 with a reference to Jesus' departure from Jerusalem and short journey to the nearby village of Bethany to spend the night. At one level, the words *he left them* are simply a transitional phrase leading into this note on Jesus' itinerary. At another level, however, the words point to the fundamental break that is occurring between Jesus and Israel.

THE TEXT IN BIBLICAL CONTEXT

More than once in the biblical story, the Lord instructed the prophets of Israel to use parabolic actions to convey a message. Thus Jeremiah wore yokebars on his neck to dramatize the impending bondage of Judah under Babylon (cf. Jer. 27—28). Ezekiel paraded before the people with the luggage of a person ready to go into exile (Ezek. 12). And Hosea, in an action that was both vivid and traumatic, married a prostitute to symbolize God's relationship with unfaithful Israel

(Hos. 1). It is just this sort of parabolic communication that is going on in Matthew 21, when Jesus enters the city riding on a donkey, and when he drives out those doing business in the temple.

The latter action links the text with a number of biblical passages in which the temple and its leadership receive criticism. In the temple sermon of Jeremiah (cf. Jer. 7 and 26), the critique focuses on a temple piety that falsely assumes divine protection of God's house, even when injustice permeates Israel's life. Here, as in Matthew 21, it is assumed that the temple is an important symbol of the community's faith; the concern of the prophet is to protest abuse of that symbol.

A more radical question is whether the temple is a valid or appropriate institution in the first place. Such is the question that Stephen raises in Acts 7 (cf. especially vv. 44-50), drawing on traditions likewise rooted in the OT (cf. Isa. 66:1-2; 2 Sam. 7:4-7). The author of Hebrews offers a more mediating viewpoint, according to which the priests and sanctuaries of Israel foreshadow the real means of access to God provided by Christ. They were valid for a time, but now are superseded (cf. Heb. 9:1—10:25).

In the Gospels, the issue of the temple surfaces not only in the story of the text, but in *sayings* of Jesus about the *future* of the temple. One such saying occurs at the beginning of Jesus's discourse on the endtime (Matt. 24:1-2; Mark 13:1-2; Luke 21:5-6), where Jesus predicts that the temple will be reduced to rubble. Even more provocative is the saying attributed to Jesus by those testifying against him at his trial before the Sanhedrin (cf. Matt. 26:60-61; Mark 14:57-58).

Whatever its original form, that declaration speaks of both the destruction of the temple and Jesus' building of a new one. The author of the Fourth Gospel, in his usual creative manner, takes this saying and connects it to the cleansing of the temple (cf. John 2:13-22). According to John, Jesus himself is the true temple of God's presence (cf. John 1:14). It is this reality that gives Jesus authority to act as he does in the temple court. And this reality will be fully evident when the temple of Jesus' body is resurrected from death.

THE TEXT IN THE LIFE OF THE CHURCH

As Christians move through the weeks of Lent, joy begins to break through the somber mood of the season when Palm Sunday finally arrives. A hymn frequently sung on that occasion is one with lyrics that go back to Theodulph of Orleans in the ninth century:

All glory, laud, and honor to Thee, Redeemer, King,
To whom the lips of children made sweet hosannas ring!
The people of the Hebrews with palms before Thee went;
Our praise and prayer and anthems before Thee we present.

Thou art the King of Israel, Thou David's royal Son,
Who in the Lord's name comest, the King and blessed One!
To Thee, before Thy passion, they sang their hymns of praise;
To Thee, now high exalted, our melody we raise.

Songs such as this are obviously based on the story of Jesus' entry into Jerusalem (although the reference to palms comes from the parallel account in John 12:12-19 rather than from Matthew). And Palm Sunday celebrations enable that story to speak to us in a lively and engaging manner.

If the story of Jesus' royal entry inspires a festive mood, the story of his activity in the temple is more likely to evoke concern and jar our sensibilities. How are we to interpret the seemingly violent behavior of knocking over tables and driving merchants out of the temple? A few interpreters have taken these details to mean that Jesus is acting as a Zealot, and that the episode reported is part of a larger scenario of violent revolution. If this were the case, however, the incident most certainly would have led to intervention by the temple police, and of this we hear nothing in the text.

As suggested earlier, it is more likely that Jesus' action was symbolic or parabolic in character, not an attempt to overthrow the system by violence. Nevertheless, the incident clearly is one of protest, and that protest is unmistakably forceful. One of the questions the text raises for Jesus' community, therefore, is how *we* should address situations where the conduct of religious or political institutions contradicts God's purposes. Are there occasions when we too are called to engage in bold parabolic actions—to confront those in power with a biblical vision of a new order?

Stories of Rejection

Matthew 21:18—22:14

PREVIEW

We have already noted that Matthew's account of Jesus' public activity in Jerusalem is set within a narrative framework of two days. The second day begins to unfold in Matthew 21:18, as Jesus returns to Jerusalem from Bethany and heads again for the temple. While still en route, Matthew tells us, Jesus offers a preview of Israel's fate by causing a barren fig tree to wither on the spot (21:18-22; cf. Mark 11:12-14, 20-25). Here we behold yet another parabolic action on Jesus' part, this time in the context of a miracle story.

Proceeding to the temple, Jesus begins to teach, but is quickly met by a delegation of leaders who question him about his *authority* (21:23-27; cf. Mark 11:27-33). The discussion that takes place is cast in the form of a rabbinic dispute, in which Jesus relates his authority to that of John the Baptist. It is clear, however, that Jesus' opponents refuse to acknowledge this authority, and Jesus addresses their unbelief in the collection of parables that follows (21:28—22:14).

The first of these parables, found only in Matthew, is the parable of the two sons (21:28-32). In its present form, it highlights the rejection of John the Baptist by the religious leaders.

The second story is taken from Mark (21:33-46; cf. Mark 12:1-12; G. Thom. 65, 66) and is variously labeled the parable of the vineyard or parable of the wicked tenants. In this narrative, the climax comes with the rejection and murder of Jesus himself, who is depicted as the son of the vineyard's owner.

The third unhappy tale is the parable of the marriage feast (22:1-14), from a source that Luke used as well as Matthew (cf. Luke 14:15-24; G. Thom. 64). Here the saga of rejection expands to include the rebuff and mistreatment of Jesus' disciples.

What we have in this trilogy of parables, skillfully assembled by Matthew, is a three-panel portrayal of God's repeated but unsuccessful attempts to solicit a faithful response from Israel to the offer of the kingdom. The consequence, the stories stress, is that Israel itself will be rejected, and that others will receive what Israel has forfeited.

OUTLINE

A Tree Without Fruit, 21:18-22

By What Authority? 21:23-27

Saying No to God, 21:28-32

A Vineyard Without Fruit, 21:33-46

Who Will Eat at God's Table? 22:1-14

EXPLANATORY NOTES

A Tree Without Fruit 21:18-22

The so-called cursing of the fig tree is the only story of its kind in the Gospels. Here a miraculous act of Jesus (the effect of Jesus' word is instantaneous in Matthew's account) serves to judge rather than save, to destroy rather than heal (cf. Acts 13:9-11). Whatever the origin of this Markan story (some suggest a connection with the parable of the fig tree in Luke 13:6-9), it is charged with symbolic meaning.

The unfruitful fig tree that arouses Jesus' anger is in fact the people of God described by Jeremiah: "When I wanted to gather them, says the Lord, there are no grapes on the vine, nor figs on the fig tree, even the leaves are withered, and what I gave them has passed away from them" (Jer. 8:13; cf. Jer. 24:1-10; Hos. 9:10; Joel 1:7; Mic. 7:1). Jesus' action, then, signifies the judgment of God on a religious community that "is covered with the ostentatious foliage of external piety," but in which "truly obedient deeds, the fruit of religion, are lacking" (Meier, 1980:237).

A second level of meaning surfaces in Jesus' conversation with the disciples in verses 20-22 (cf. 17:20; G. Thom. 48, 106). Jesus' miracle is a sign not only of judgment, but of the power available to disciples through prayer (cf. 7:7-11; 18:19; John 14:13-14), prayer that expresses an unwavering confidence in God (cf. Luke 17:5-6). Up to now, the faith of Jesus' followers has been hesitant and shaky, *little faith* (cf. 14:31; 17:14-20). If that faith becomes firm and articulate, however, the disciples will be able to do even more amazing things than Jesus has just done.

By What Authority? 21:23-27

The dispute narrated in verses 23-27 pits Jesus against two groups of Jewish leaders, one with the power of office (*chief priests*), the other with representative authority (*elders of the people;* cf. Exod. 19:7; Isa. 3:14; Jer. 19:1). It is the same combination of opponents who shortly will plot Jesus' destruction (26:3-5) and condemn him to death after his arrest (26:57-68; 27:1-2). When these *authorities* question Jesus about his *authority*, they raise an issue that accompanies Jesus throughout the Gospel (cf. 7:28-29; 12:38; 16:13-15; 28:18): What are Jesus' credentials? Who or what authorizes him to act as he is now acting in the temple (cf. John 2:18)?

Instead of answering directly, Jesus resorts to a typical ploy in rabbinic argument. He poses a counterquestion that puts his questioners on the defensive, making his response contingent on theirs. *Tell me,* Jesus says, *whether John the Baptist operated on God's behalf or on his own behalf* (paraphrased). As the story indicates, Jesus' opponents realize that either answer they might give will put them at a disadvantage. Conceding defeat, they decline to answer Jesus' question and so exempt him from answering theirs.

At one level, the story simply reveals Jesus' adroitness in outmaneuvering his adversaries. The one who has true but unacknowledged authority cleverly bests those who seek to use their authority against him. At another level, the story does in fact answer the question the opponents raise. By asking the counterquestion he does, Jesus implies that divine authority undergirds both his ministry and John's. Like John, with his parabolic action of baptism in the Jordan (3:1-6), Jesus acts in the temple to signal the imminent advent of God's reign. To put it another way, the text invites *the reader* to answer the question in verse 23, to acknowledge Jesus as one sent by God to act in God's name.

Saying No to God 21:28-32

The parable of the two sons plays a pivotal role in the unit before us. From a narrative standpoint, it can be read as a continuation of the episode in verses 23-27. It rebukes the leaders for their failure to believe and act on the message of John the Baptist (cf. vv. 25b, 32). The parable, however, is not merely a postscript to what precedes it. As noted earlier, it introduces a series of parables on Israel's rejection of God's messengers, each of which adds a new dimension to the story.

What we have in the first parable is a brief story (vv. 28-31a), followed by a simple illustrative comment (v. 31b), followed in turn by a more complex explanation (v. 32). In the underlying Greek text, there is some confusion about the order in which the two sons appear. Some manuscripts begin with the son who says no to the father's command, others with the son who says yes.

Whichever form of the text is more original, the point of the story is fairly clear: It is the doing of a deed that counts, not merely promising to do it (cf. 7:21-23; 12:50; 23:3-4). Saying yes and doing yes would be the best. Yet rebels who *change* their mindset and act as God requires, truly fulfill God's intention. By contrast, those who piously profess to do God's will but fail to carry it out, end up in the wrong. Hence, we hear in verse 31b that outcasts such as tax collectors and prostitutes will enjoy life in God's reign, while esteemed leaders of the community are excluded. (The phrase *ahead of you* most likely implies a sense of separation rather than order of entry.)

With the explanation supplied in verse 32, the drama of Jesus' parable is linked even more explicitly to the story of God's covenant with Israel. From a traditional point of view, that story can be construed in terms of the faithful who agree to keep the covenant (work in the vineyard), and sinners who do not. That is the way the parable begins. The situation changes, however, when God appeals to Israel afresh through John the Baptist.

John came to Israel *in the way of righteousness* (a Semitic expression; cf. Prov. 8:20; 12:28), in the sense that his message and baptism disclosed a way for all Israel to become God's righteous community (cf. comments on 3:15). In the face of this challenge, something surprising happened: Former no-sayers *believed* John (they repented and were baptized), while former yes-sayers disregarded him (cf. Luke 7:29-30). Playing further with the language of the story, Matthew notes that even *after* the one-time no-sayers repented (cf. *later* in v. 29 and *after* in v. 32), the leaders who claimed to follow God's will refused to change their mind. They adamantly rejected God's appeal through John.

A Vineyard Without Fruit 21:33-46

The parable in verses 33-46 also unfolds in a vineyard, this time with vivid imagery. Though the immediate source of the story is Mark's Gospel (12:1-12), both the theme and language of the parable are indebted to the song of the vineyard in Isaiah 5:1-7 (cf. v. 33 and Isa. 5:2). From a sociocultural perspective, the story attests the hostility that frequently existed between tenant farmers and absentee landlords in the first century.

The interest of the Gospel writers in the story, however, is theological rather than sociological. Whatever its earliest form, the parable as it appears in both Mark and Matthew depicts Jesus as the Son of God sent to God's covenant people (the tenants), but who is violently rejected by those to whom the covenant (the vineyard) was entrusted. As a sequel to the preceding parable in verses 28-32, the story tells us that Jesus fared no better than John the Baptist.

Of special interest are some of the distinctive features in Matthew's retelling of the parable:

(1) The man who plants the vineyard is identified as a landowner (cf. 20:1-16, where God likewise appears as a landowner).

(2) The owner asks for *his fruit*, not just some of the fruit (cf. Mark 12:2), wording that alludes to God's total claim on Israel and an expectation of a full harvest of good works.

(3) The servants (*slaves*) sent to obtain the fruit are dispatched in two groups, which may refer to the so-called former and latter prophets of Israel. (On the fate of the prophets, cf. 23:29-37; 5:12; Jer. 7:25-26; 2 Chron. 24:19-21; Neh. 9:26.)

(4) The son of the owner is sent *last of all* (NIV; GNB; cf. Heb. 1:1-2), and the description of his fate corresponds to the sequence of events in Jesus' crucifixion: First he is cast out of the vineyard, then killed (cf. John 19:17-18; Heb. 13:12).

(5) Jesus invites his listeners to draw the conclusion to the tale in verses 40-41, in doing which they pronounce judgment on themselves.

(6) An explicit interpretation of the outcome of the story is provided in verse 43: The promise of God's reign that has heretofore been part of God's covenant with Israel will now be offered to a more worthy *people*, that is, to a people that responds to Jesus and his message (the church).

(7) There is a repeated emphasis on the need to produce and offer the *fruits* God requires (cf. vv. 41 and 43). Only a people that performs the deeds of justice and mercy expected by God will inherit the kingdom.

Further commentary on the story is given in the form of scriptural citations and allusions. Verse 42 comes from Psalm 118:22-23 (cf. Isa. 28:16), which appears to have been a widely used proof text in the early church (cf. Acts 4:11; 1 Pet. 2:7). Verse 44, missing in a few early manuscripts, draws on language from several OT passages (cf. Dan. 2:34-35, 44-45; Isa. 8:14-15). Some commentators regard this verse as original to Matthew's text, while others view it as a later addition based on a similar saying in Luke's version of the parable (cf. Luke 20:18). Together, verses 42-44 could be paraphrased as follows: *The Son of God who was rejected and put to death has become the exalted head of a new and faithful community. Those who oppose him destroy themselves in the process and stand under his devastating judgment.*

Before proceeding to the third parable of rejection, Matthew inserts a short piece of narration in verses 45-46. Here the reader is reminded that those whose authority Jesus challenges in the temple (21:12-17, 23) and whom he addresses and condemns in the stories (21:28-41), are first and foremost Israel's *leaders*. Perceiving this, the leaders would like to take immediate action against Jesus (cf. Mark 11:18: "They kept looking for a way to kill him"). For the time being, however, popular esteem of Jesus as a prophet (cf. 21:11) serves as a buffer to protect him.

Who Will Eat at God's Table? 22:1-14

The parable of the marriage feast and its parallel in Luke 14:15-24 share a number of common elements (cf G. Thom. 64). In each instance selected guests are invited to a great banquet, but for one reason or another reject the invitation. This angers the host of the feast, who then sends his servants (*slaves*) into the streets to invite alternate guests to come to the banquet. One way or another, the meal will proceed and the table will be full.

Once again, however, Matthew's version of Jesus' story contains a number of distinctive features. Here the feast is a *wedding* banquet hosted by a *king* on behalf of his *son* (v. 2). Repeated invitations are carried to the intended guests, who not only refuse to attend but inexplicably abuse the king's couriers and even kill some of them (vv. 3-6, the same fate experienced by the landowner's servants in 21:34-36). Responding in kind, the king sends an army to destroy those invited along with their city (v. 7).

The search for new guests takes the king's servants to *the main streets,* roads leading away from the city to the world beyond (vv. 8-9), and attracts a huge but mixed crowd (v. 10). This paves the way for the scene with the embarrassed guest who lacks proper attire (vv. 11-13), and whose dismissal reads suspiciously like a sentence of final judgment (cf. 8:12; 13:42; 25:30; Wisd. of Sol. 17:1-2). Concluding the story is a terse proverblike saying that says in effect: Invitation does not guarantee participation (cf. 2 Esd. 8:3, 41; Matt. 7:13-14).

As the opening words of the text indicate, the kingdom in this story is *God's* kingdom, and the story told amounts to a historical allegory on God's offer of life in the kingdom. The wedding feast symbolizes the joy and festivity of the age to come (cf. Isa. 25:6-8; Matt. 25:1-10; Rev. 19:7-9; 1 Enoch 62:14; 2 Bar. 29:4-8). The invitation to come to the feast is reminiscent of the call of Wisdom (Prov. 9:1-6), while the two groups of servants who carry the word to Israel represent the prophets of old and Jesus' own disciples (cf. Jer. 7:25; Matt. 10:5-7, 40-42; 21:34-36; 23:34; Luke 11:49). The burning of the city (likely an allusion to the destruction of Jerusalem in A.D. 70) and the pronouncement of the original guests as unworthy, signify God's judgment on Israel for rejecting God's offer and God's messengers.

The command to *go therefore* in verse 9 anticipates the great commission in 28:19 and alludes to the mission to the Gentiles, which attracts *both good and bad* (cf. 13:47-50), true and false disciples. In turn, the *wedding garment* symbolizes the righteousness with which true disciples are clothed (cf. Isa. 61:10; Rom. 13:14; Col. 3:10, 12-14; Rev. 19:8), without which one cannot inhabit God's kingdom (Matt. 5:20).

According to Matthew, then, there are two ways persons can lose the opportunity to eat at God's table. One way is to snub the invitation (vv. 1-8). The other is to take the invitation for granted and fail to live as those who truly hunger for God's righteousness (vv. 9-14). Either way, the loss is incalculable.

THE TEXT IN BIBLICAL CONTEXT

When Israel rejects God, does God reject Israel? The question is one that keeps coming up in the biblical story—and so poignantly in the book of Hosea. As Hosea writes of God's own struggle with the question, he pulls us first one direction and then the other. The answer sounds both clear and conclusive when God declares: "Woe to them, for they have strayed from me! Destruction to them, for they have rebelled against me!" (7:13). Israel's doom appears sealed when God announces: "I will destroy you, O Israel. . . . Compassion is hidden from my eyes" (13:9, 14).

Alongside pronouncements such as these, however, we find words that communicate a quite different sentiment: "How can I give you up, Ephraim? How can I hand you over, O Israel? . . . My heart recoils within me; my compassion grows warm and tender. I will not execute my fierce anger" (11:8-9). Instead, God promises, "I will heal their disloyalty" (14:4).

In the NT, the two poles of this quandary are represented by Matthew on one hand and Paul on the other. The three parables we have just examined lambaste Israel and the leaders who shape its course in no uncertain terms: Israel has failed to produce the fruit God seeks, has violently rejected God's messengers, and has spurned the offer to feast in God's kingdom. As a result, Matthew tells us, God has turned away from Israel and begun gathering a new covenant people (21:43; cf. commentary on 16:1-20). Individual descendants of Abraham may find their way into this people, but Israel as a nation has ceased to be the heir and steward of God's reign.

In Romans 9—11, we find a more hopeful assessment of Israel's destiny in God's design. Paul is just as clear as Matthew that Israel has stumbled and opposed God's will. He likens Israel's condition to branches severed from a tree. Even so, when Paul asks rhetorically whether God has rejected his people, he exclaims: "By no means!" (11:1). Arguing that God's special relationship with Israel is irrevocable (11:28-29), Paul holds out the hope that *all Israel* will yet receive the gospel, and that Israel and the Gentiles will be coheirs of God's future (11:11-12, 25-27).

If Matthew and Paul diverge in their assessment of *Israel's* prospects, they fully agree that Israel's plight leaves no room for *Gentile* arrogance. Do not boast, Paul urges his Gentile readers, for it is only by God's mercy that you now belong to God's people, and only as you stand fast in faith will you continue as such (Rom. 11:18-22). Matthew makes the same point when he stresses the importance of producing fruit and wearing a wedding garment. Only as members of Jesus' community exhibit the same righteousness God sought from Israel will they enjoy life in God's kingdom.

THE TEXT IN THE LIFE OF THE CHURCH

As with Jesus' parables generally, the imagery and themes of the three parables of rejection have fascinated the church. One particular point of fascination has been the wedding garment in 22:11-12. Since God would hardly base eternal judgment on standards of social etiquette, what does this garment represent? The answers proposed by interpreters include faith, love, the sacraments, endtime salvation, fulfillment of the law, and deeds of righteousness. Confronting some of the proposals current in his own time, Calvin offers the following helpful counsel and perspective:

> There is no point in arguing about the marriage garment. . . . All Christ wants to say here is that we are called by the Lord under the condition that we be renewed in our spirits into His image, and therefore, if we are to remain always in His house, the old man with all his blemishes is to be cast off and we are to practice the new life so that our appearance (*habitus*) may correspond to our honourable calling. (1972, 2:109)

Yet another point at which the stories of the text have engaged interpreters is their unrelenting critique of Israel. Taken at face value, the stories convey a wholly negative picture of Israel and Jewish leaders, a picture that easily leads to stereotypical views of Jews as enemies of God. Where such stereotypes prevail (and examples abound in older sermons and commentaries on the text), we conclude at best that Judaism is a dead-end street. At least two considerations, however, call that conclusion in question:

(1) The harsh picture of Israel in the text is likely colored by tensions between church and synagogue in Matthew's world. (2) As noted above, Matthew's voice is one of many biblical voices that speak to the question of Israel's destiny, and the conversation we hear has an unfinished character.

However faithful or unfaithful first-century Israel may have been, we must be open to the possibility that the Jewish community no less than the Christian community has a continuing role in God's purposes. The most appropriate way for the church to use the stories in the text is thus not to judge the Jews, but to underscore the importance of faithful response to God's invitation in our own covenant history.

Disputes with Jewish Leaders

Matthew 22:15-46

PREVIEW

In the preceding unit, we found Jesus on the offensive against the leaders of Israel. Recoiling from this verbal assault, these same leaders begin to take action of their own in the episodes that follow. They put a series of questions to Jesus, hoping to trip him up at one point or another and discredit his teaching authority.

One of the encounters involves the Sadducees, the party of the priestly and lay nobility of Jerusalem. The other three feature the Pharisees as Jesus' antagonists, the predecessors of the rabbis with whom Matthew and his own community are in tension. Drawn from Mark's account of the same four conversations (Mark 12:13-37; cf. G. Thom. 100), the unit is framed with language that echoes Psalm 2. There too "the rulers take counsel together, against the Lord and his anointed" (Ps. 2:2; cf. Matt. 22:15, 34, 41), but clearly lose the contest with God and God's son (Ps. 2:4-12; cf. Matt. 22:41-46).

Sometimes the episodes of this unit are labeled conflict or controversy stories, stories such as those in 9:1-17 and 12:1-50. Unlike those accounts, however, the material in 22:15-46 does not revolve around provocative incidents in Jesus' ministry but around issues debated at great length in first-century Judaism. The episodes are thus more properly defined as *teaching disputes*.

Matthew's purpose in presenting these various disputes is likely twofold: (1) They reveal how Jesus answers his opponents in a way that fully vindicates his teaching authority. (2) The answers Jesus gives provide guidelines for his followers as they deal with related issues in their own faith and life.

OUTLINE

Caesar's or God's? 22:15-22

God of the Living, 22:23-33

The Greatest Commandment, 22:34-40

Whence Comes the Messiah? 22:41-46

EXPLANATORY NOTES

Caesar's or God's? 22:15-22

Eager to *entrap* Jesus (the verb derives from a word for a trap or snare used in hunting), the Pharisees decide to confront him with a delicate political question. This may account for the inclusion of Herodians, supporters of Herod's rule and sensitive to Rome, in the delegation sent to pose the issue.

It is clearly Pharisees we hear speaking, however, in the drawn-out flattery in verse 16 that leads up to the question. The phrases they use to describe Jesus are correct; he does indeed expound God's will truly, and does not let the barometer of popular opinion shape his speeches. Yet they by no means revere Jesus. They are operating out of malice and deceit, as Jesus perceives at once (v. 18).

Nevertheless, the question they raise in verse 17 is significant: Is it lawful to pay taxes to a foreign ruler? Is it in keeping with the Torah and our heritage? The tax in question was the Roman head tax or poll tax introduced in Judea in A.D. 6, which every inhabitant from age 12 (or 14) to 65 was required to pay. Paid with a silver denarius, it represented a day's wages for a laborer.

It was not the amount, however, but rather the principle of subjection to Rome that aroused antagonism to the tax. Adding to the resentment was the fact that the coin used to pay the tax was stamped with a likeness of Tiberias Caesar, along with an inscription honoring him as the venerable son of the divine emperor Augustus (cf. vv. 19-21a). Like others, the Pharisees found the tax distasteful, but reluctantly supported paying it.

In responding to the question, Jesus once again makes a clever countermove. First, he forces his questioners to reveal their own commitments. He asks to see the coin used to pay the tax, and behold, *they* have the emperor's money in their possession! Second, he states his position in such a way as to avoid a simple yes-or-no answer. In so doing, he escapes the trap of either (1) endorsing Rome's sovereignty and alienating the people, or (2) rejecting Rome's sovereignty and inviting arrest as an insurrectionist.

The substance of Jesus' answer, *Pay Caesar what is Caesar's and God what is God's,* could be paraphrased as follows: *Insofar as we live and participate in the civic order, there are civic obligations to fulfill. Our ultimate obligation, however, which sets boundaries and limits to all other obligations, is faithfulness to God, the ruler of all creation.* Whether impressed or simply confounded (cf. v. 22), Jesus' adversaries sense that he has somehow thrown the ball back into their court, and opt to take a time out.

God of the Living 22:23-33

Does individual life end with death, as many OT passages seem to assume (cf. Pss. 6:5; 49:10-12; 88:4-5), or will there be a resurrection of the dead? The question aroused considerable discussion in Jewish circles (cf. Acts 23:6-8; Eccles. 3:19-21; Wisd. of Sol. 2:1ff.; 1 Enoch 102:6ff.; Sanh. 10:1), with the Sadducees arguing against belief in a resurrection. Among the arguments the Sadducees cited was that the belief is not taught in the Torah, the only Scripture which they recognized as authoritative.

In the dispute before us, however, the Sadducees come at the question from a different angle: They present Jesus with a hypothetical case that mocks belief in resurrection by making it appear ludicrous. In the humorous story they spin, based on the practice of levirate marriage taught in the Torah (cf. Deut. 25:5-6; Gen. 38:8), a woman ends up married in sequence to each of seven brothers in the course of her life. Now then, the Sadducees ask, if they all are resurrected, in whose bed will the hapless woman sleep? It is clearly a story meant to evoke laughter.

By giving Jesus an apparently unsolvable puzzle, the Sadducees hope to demonstrate their superiority as theologians. Jesus, however, is more than equal to the challenge and offers a twofold rebuttal. First, he disputes the premise on which the puzzle rests, namely, that life in the age to come is simply an extension of life as we know it now. On the contrary, Jesus says, the power of God that makes resurrection possible will fashion a new world in which marriage arrangements no longer play a part. The Sadducees have too earthbound a view of God's possibilities.

Second, Jesus cites a text from the part of the Scriptures the Sadducees accept as evidence *for* the resurrection (Exod. 3:6; cf. 4 Macc. 7:19; 16:25). He stresses the present tense of God's word to Moses, "I *am* the God of Abraham." On that basis Jesus argues that those whom God calls, he maintains in an unbroken covenant relationship that death cannot destroy, and that resurrection will fully renew.

Listening in on all this, the crowds sense the same voice of authority they heard in Jesus' Sermon on the Mount. Once again, they are *astounded* (v. 33; cf. 7:28-29).

The Greatest Commandment 22:34-40

According to rabbinic tradition dating from the second century, the Torah contains no fewer than 613 laws (365 prohibitions and 248 commands). Already in Jesus' day, Jewish teachers were wrestling with the question of how all these commandments relate to each other, and whether the totality of them can be derived from one or more basic commandments.

The text reflects this ongoing discussion when the lawyer (scribe) mentioned in verse 35 asks Jesus: *Which commandment in the law is the greatest?* In the parallel account in Mark 12:28-34 (cf. Luke 10:25-28), a friendly two-way conversation ensues, in which Jesus and the scribe each commend the other for insights expressed. In Matthew, however, the tone is adversarial (the lawyer seeks to *test* Jesus), and Jesus alone speaks to the question. The answer Jesus gives in verses 37-40 has three noteworthy features:

(1) It identifies the *greatest and first commandment* as the command found in Deuteronomy 6:5 to love God with one's whole self. As in the LXX, the third phrase reads *with all your mind* instead of *with all your might* (the original Hebrew wording).

(2) It identifies a second norm, the commandment in Leviticus 19:18 to love our neighbors as we love ourselves, as a commandment *like* (or of like significance with) the first. Such a coupling of

these two passages has no parallel in the first century, although the Jewish philosopher Philo speaks in more general terms of the fundamental importance of reverence for God and human kindness.

(3) It states explicitly that everything in *the law and the prophets* hangs or hinges on these two commandments. Picking up the earlier discussion of the law in 5:17-20 (cf. 7:12), Matthew tells us here that the multitude of laws in Scripture are valid *inasmuch as* and *insofar as* they embody Jesus' central injunction to love God and neighbor.

Whence Comes the Messiah? 22:41-46

While the Pharisees are still assembled as a group (cf. vv. 41, 34), Jesus takes the initiative and launches the fourth dispute with a question of his own: *Whence comes the Messiah?* Speculation about the Messiah ran rampant in Jesus' day, and the dispute here both picks up this discussion and addresses it from the perspective of early Christian Christology. In Mark's account (Mark 12:35-37), the episode consists of a monologue by Jesus. In Matthew, a conversation flows back and forth between Jesus and the Pharisees:

Double-question by Jesus (42a)
    Answer by Pharisees (42b)
Second double-question by Jesus (43-45)
    Silence (46)

The answer the Pharisees give to Jesus' first question represents mainstream Jewish faith at the time: The Messiah will be a descendant (*son*) of David, who will triumph over Israel's enemies and rule even more mightily than David did (cf. Isa. 11:1ff.; Jer. 23:5; Ezek. 34:23; Ps. 89:20ff.; Ps. Sol. 17:23f.). Pushing the discussion further with his second question, Jesus quotes and comments on Psalm 110:1, a favorite proof text in the early church (cf. Acts 2:34; 1 Cor. 15:25; Heb. 1:3). Originally an enthronement text in which a liturgist is speaking to an ancient king, the psalm is here understood as a passage in which David is speaking to the future Messiah of Israel. From this perspective, the first *Lord* in the words quoted refers to God (Yahweh), the second *Lord* to the Messiah. Jesus' argument then runs as follows: *If David calls the Messiah his Lord, does this not imply that the Messiah is more than a mere human descendant of David?*

For Matthew, the correct answer is that the Messiah certainly is David's son (cf. 1:1-17), but even more important, *God's son* (cf. 1:18-25). The reader of the Gospel knows and sees this, but the

Pharisees do not; much less do they recognize that this son of God is Jesus. Like the Sadducees before them, therefore (v. 34), the Pharisees are reduced to silence (v. 46). And Jesus emerges from the whole series of disputes as one who teaches with incontestable power and wisdom.

THE TEXT IN BIBLICAL CONTEXT

In each of Jesus' disputes with the Pharisees and Sadducees, the topics addressed deal with recurring issues in the biblical story. Here we will look at the way two of those topics link up with the larger story, the topics of paying taxes and loving God and neighbor.

As already noted, the dispute over paying taxes to Rome raises the broader question of the allegiance God's people may or should give to the powers that govern. Not surprisingly, the biblical writers do not offer a single uniform answer to the question. In some instances, Scripture assumes a positive relationship between God and government, in which the state acts on God's behalf to create a just order and thereby prevent chaos from destroying human society (cf. Rom. 13:1-7; 1 Pet. 2:13-17; 1 Tim. 2:1-2). Where this is the case, the people of God are urged to be subject to the state, pray for its rulers, and fulfill civic duties such as payment of taxes.

In other instances, however, Scripture depicts God and government on a collision course. Such is the case in the book of Revelation, where the authority of Rome that Paul gladly recognized has become beastly and perverse (cf. Rev. 13). When rulers oppose God's purposes, resistance to their demands is imperative (cf. Acts 5:27-29; Dan. 1—3), and treason can become an act of faith (cf. Exod. 2:15-21; Jer. 26). In short, the policies Caesar pursues determine the extent to which God's people give Caesar what he demands.

The dispute over the greatest commandment is not unrelated to the preceding issue. It asks directly: What is the primary obligation of God's people? In our comments above, we observed that Jesus formulates a hitherto unparalleled answer to the question when he links Deuteronomy 6:5 and Leviticus 19:18 in his response. It is also true, however, that the inseparability of love for God and love for neighbor is not a "new" teaching, but one assumed throughout Scripture. Thus the prophet Micah writes: "What does the Lord require of you, but to do justice, and to love kindness, and to walk humbly with your God?" (Mic. 6:8).

Earlier still, the Decalogue itself combines injunctions that tell us how to love God on the one hand (Exod. 20:1-11) and our fellow humans on the other (Exod. 20:12-17). The convergence of piety and compassion that Jesus emphasized was thus already central to Israel's life—and it remains central in Jesus' own community. The author of 1 John speaks for other voices as well when he argues: "Those who say, 'I love God,' and hate their brothers or sisters, are liars; for those who do not love a brother or sister whom they have seen, cannot love God whom they have not seen" (1 John 4:20; cf. Rom. 12:1, 9-21; 13:8-10).

THE TEXT IN THE LIFE OF THE CHURCH

What does it mean to *give Caesar what is Caesar's and God what is God's*? The most prevalent approach to Jesus' statement from early times has been to assume that he is neatly dividing life into spiritual matters on one hand and civic or worldly matters on the other. In this case, Jesus is telling us to obey God in the spiritual realm and obey human rulers in the political realm (cf. Justin Martyr, *First Apology* 17; Calvin, 1972, 3:26-27). Like other citizens, then, believers always pay their taxes, support the established order, and (in most traditions) agree to fight their nation's wars.

The problem with this interpretation is that it effectively denies the sovereignty of God over *every* realm of life, political and spiritual. As suggested above, the more likely force of Jesus' statement is to invite us to decide political questions such as paying taxes in the context of our fundamental commitment to *seek first the kingdom of God.* Where the policies of the state contribute to greater peace and justice, thus reflecting God's own agenda, supporting the state is right and proper. Where the policies of the state, however, protect the powerful, destroy the weak, and threaten life itself, must we not in fact selectively say no to the state in order to say yes to God? To paraphrase Ecclesiastes: There is a time for civil obedience, and there is a time for civil disobedience (cf. Acts 5:29).

Jesus' response to the question of the greatest commandment would appear to be less ambiguous than his response to the tax question. Even so, it has engendered vigorous discussion in the Christian community. In what way is the command to love neighbor like or equivalent to the command to love God? Among the possible answers, at least four are noteworthy:

(1) Jesus is simply placing love for God and love for neighbor side by side as important twin obligations.

(2) Jesus is equating love of God with love of neighbor. To love the neighbor fully discharges our obligation to love God.

(3) Jesus is making a this-implies-that statement: If we truly love God, love of neighbor will surely follow.

(4) Jesus is telling us that love of neighbor is the field of action where we embody or demonstrate love of God.

The fourth statement most adequately catches up the nuances of Jesus' reply, to which Luther was well-attuned when he wrote:

> The love that I have toward God is the same love that directs itself toward the neighbor. . . . God says: Human one, I am too high for you, you cannot grasp me. But I have given myself to you in your neighbor. Love this one, the neighbor, my handiwork; then you are loving me. (767, 756)

A Bitter Public Farewell

Matthew 23:1-39

PREVIEW

In a work of art, shadows and contrasts frequently play an important role. Against the backdrop of dark and sinister tones, light and the subjects it illuminates stand out all the more. Such is the role that the caustic sermon in Matthew 23 plays in the literary art of the First Gospel. Here, in a setting that recalls the stinging temple sermon by the prophet Jeremiah (cf. Jer. 7; 26), Jesus depicts and denounces the dark conduct of his opponents. As he does so, he creates a powerful foil for the description of righteous disciples in another sermon—the Sermon on the Mount in chapter 5—7. To put it another way: The *woes* Jesus pronounces in the temple prompt the reader to recall the Beatitudes he pronounces on the mount in Galilee, and to ponder the two sharply contrasting destinies.

The episode in the Markan narrative that provides a launching point for the sermon in Matthew 23 is Jesus' warning about the scribes in Mark 12:38-40 (cf. 23:6-7). What Mark treats with a few verses, Matthew develops at length with material drawn from various sources. In addition to the initial episode, the saying in 23:11 comes from Mark (cf. Mark 9:34-35; 10:43). We also find material that may derive from Matthew's own community (cf. 23:1-5, 8-10), as well as prophetic and wisdom sayings from the common source of Matthew and Luke noted elsewhere (cf. Luke 11:37-52; 13:34-35; 14:11; G. Thom. 39, 89, 102).

The speech or sermon Matthew constructs from this diverse material divides into three parts, each beginning with a formula addressing a certain group in Jesus' audience. In the first segment, addressed to the crowds and disciples, Jesus talks about scribes and Pharisees in the third person (vv. 1-12). In the second segment, Jesus speaks directly to the scribes and Pharisees, delivering seven *woe* sayings that create a crescendo effect as they build in intensity (vv. 13-36). In the third and final segment, Jesus addresses all Jerusalem with an oracle lamenting its failure to respond to his mission and the desolation that will soon befall the city (vv. 37-39).

For Matthew and his readers, the sermon before us serves a dual purpose: (1) It creates a dramatic finale to Jesus' authoritative teaching in the temple, in which Jesus rebukes his opponents as fiercely as they have rebuked him. It raises the pitch of conflict in the narrative to the highest possible level.

(2) Its picture of Jesus' adversaries mirrors the church's adversaries in Matthew's day, inviting the church to differentiate itself from those adversaries. At one level, the discrediting of leadership on the other side is a move to create or justify social distance between synagogue and church. At a more profound level, Matthew is admonishing his community to examine its lifestyle, saying in effect: Don't let this happen to you!

OUTLINE

Wanted—A New Model, 23:1-12

Woe to You, Hypocrites, 23:13-36

Lament for a Lost City, 23:37-39

EXPLANATORY NOTES

Wanted—A New Model 23:1-12

In his opening statement, Jesus refers to those who *sit on Moses' seat* (v. 2). The decorative stone seat or bench at the front of synagogues of a later era was in fact called Moses' seat, and it is possible that this was already the custom in Matthew's time. In any case, the phrase attests the Jewish conviction that those who taught in the synagogue taught with authority deriving from Moses himself (cf. Aboth 1:1). Here the occupants of this teaching chair are identified as *the scribes and the Pharisees,* which reflects the situation in Judaism after the fall of Jerusalem in A.D. 70.

What is surprising in Jesus' statement is his counsel to practice and observe what the scribes and Pharisees teach (v. 3a). Earlier in the narrative, we found Jesus rejecting the teaching these leaders have to offer (cf. 15:1-20; 16:5-12). How shall we resolve this tension? The best solution is to read the first half of verse 3 not as a blanket endorsement of scribal tradition, but as a concessive statement that paves the way for what follows: *Insofar as the scribes and Pharisees transmit God's Torah, pay attention—but by no means copy the way they carry out their calling!*

Verses 4-7 paint a picture of the scribes and Pharisees that tells the reader *why* these leaders provide poor models. First, they make the fulfillment of God's will a burdensome affair, in which only the religious elite can hope to succeed (v. 4; cf. Acts 15:10). They prescribe rule after rule to regulate daily life, with little or no compassion for people who have trouble carrying out these prescriptions. Unlike the *easy* yoke Jesus invites would-be disciples to assume (cf. 11:28-30), the yoke the scribes and Pharisees impose is harsh and heavy.

Second, these leaders flaunt their religiosity in public to gain the plaudits of all who see them (cf. the earlier critique of such behavior in 6:1-8). Some illustrations of this perversion of piety include wearing attire with conspicuously overdone religious symbols (v. 5; cf. Exod. 13:9; Deut. 11:18; Num. 15:37-39), claiming seats reserved for the high and mighty at public gatherings (v. 6; cf. Luke 14:7-11), and coveting honorific titles (v. 7). It was customary in the Orient for persons of lesser rank to greet or salute those of greater rank with such titles, and the scribes and Pharisees want to get their share of this sort of recognition.

In *Jesus'* community, we hear in verses 8-10, the quest for titles that elevate leaders over others has no place. The church is to be an egalitarian community of sisters and brothers, not an organization resembling a pyramid. Three specific titles are enumerated in the text. *Rabbi* (v. 8, literally *my great one*) is the title verse 7 tells us was especially prized by scribes and Pharisees. Originally a form of address used to greet a variety of respected figures, *rabbi* eventually acquired the more technical meaning of an ordained Jewish scholar/teacher.

Father (v. 9) was not an official title in Jewish circles, so far as we know. However, a prophet in ancient Israel was sometimes addressed as "my father" (cf. 2 Kings 2:12; 6:21; 13:14), and both the patriarchs and teachers could be described as "fathers" of Israel (cf.

Sirach 44, and the title of the Mishnah tractate Aboth, Fathers).

Instructor (v. 10) translates a word from the Greek philosophic tradition and conveys a meaning similar to the Jewish title *rabbi*. The extent to which Matthew's community was employing honorific titles for its leaders remains uncertain. In any case, Matthew reminds his readers that God alone deserves respect as a "father figure," and that Christ alone has the status of an exalted teacher.

Verses 11-12 put the issue of titles in theological context with the help of two shorter sayings of Jesus. The first (v. 11) echoes earlier discussions in the Gospel about greatness (cf. 18:1-4; 20:26-27). The second (v. 12) picks up a longstanding emphasis in Israel's faith, that God humbles the proud and exalts the humble (cf. Ezek. 21:26; Job 22:29; Prov. 29:23; Isa. 2:17). Together the sayings make the point that greatness in Jesus' community is achieved not by lording it *over* others, but by self-humbling service *to* others.

Woe to You, Hypocrites 23:13-36

Pronouncements of woe abound in the biblical writings, sometimes as single sayings (cf. Num. 21:29; Isa. 31:1-3; Matt. 11:21-22), sometimes coupled with similar sayings in a series such as we find in this text (cf. Isa. 5:8-30; Hab. 2:6-19; Luke 6:24-26). As a literary form, a pronouncement of woe typically includes the introduction *woe to you*, a phrase naming those addressed, a description of the conduct or behavior which spells disaster, and an announcement of the judgment that will result.

Here the announcement of judgment to come is suspended till the end of the series and the lament that follows (cf. vv. 36, 37-39). In terms of mood or tone, the words *woe to you* express both dismay and indignation, sometimes accompanied by a sense of grief over what lies ahead. (See additional comments on woe-sayings in the preview to 11:20-30.)

The *seven* woes Jesus pronounces in verses 13-36 (v. 14 is a later addition to the text and is not included in the count) address the scribes and Pharisees in all but one instance as *hypocrites*. In each case, the term refers to a glaring discrepancy between the respectable public image these leaders convey and the dismal reality or substance of what they do or fail to do. It is this phenomenon that makes the scribes and Pharisees *blind guides* (cf. vv. 16, 17, 19, 24; 15:14). They are leaders who can't see well enough to guide others and who therefore will lead others to destruction rather than to life. Concrete cases of the discrepancy between appearance and reality are cited in the individual pronouncements, which we diagram as follows:

Pronouncement	Appearance	Reality
Verse 13	Leaders appear to be spiritual guides who lead others to life (cf. 23:2; Rom. 2:17-20).	Leaders in fact block access to kingdom by heavy burdens they impose and by opposing Jesus' mission.
Verse 15	Leaders appear to win others to faith in God of Israel by their vigorous proselytism.	Leaders in fact convert others to their own ways, which result in destruction, not life.
Verses 16-22	Leaders appear to be masters of discernment as they distinguish between types of oaths.	Leaders in fact, by their subtle reasoning, obscure the way every oath implicates God and therefore binds one.
Verses 23-24	Leaders appear to have superpiety, tithing not only essentials (grain, oil, wine; cf. Deut. 14:22-23), but even optional garden herbs.	Leaders in fact major in the minor, neglecting the Torah's concern for justice, mercy, and trust (cf. Mic. 6:8; Matt. 12:1-14).
Verses 25-26	Leaders appear to be scrupulous in every way in obeying law, washing outside as well as inside of eating utensils.	Leaders in fact fail to cleanse the interior that matters most, the interior of their own selves (cf. 15:1-20).

Verses 27-28	Leaders appear to be righteous role models, attractive to all who behold them.	Leaders in fact have a surface righteousness, like the whitewash put on Palestinian tombs each spring, masking death and decay within.
Verses 29-36	Leaders appear to align themselves with God's prophets, building tombs in memory of earlier messengers of God.	Leaders in fact align themselves with their forebears who killed the prophets, persecuting Jesus' messengers.

In the seventh and final pronouncement, the core saying in verses 29-31 is expanded through several wisdom sayings in the verses that follow. With bitter irony, Jesus urges his opponents to finish (*fill up*) the course which their forebears initiated and so reveal who they really are and the judgment they deserve (vv. 32-33; cf. 3:7; 12:34; 1 Thess. 2:14-16).

Jesus goes on then in verses 34-36 to define the setting in which this will occur, namely the sending of his own messengers to Israel in the roles assumed by God's servants of old (prophets, sages, scribes; cf. 10:40-41). In the parallel passage in Luke 11:49-51, Jesus refers to "the Wisdom of God" as the sender of prophets. In Matthew's rendition, Jesus speaks as one who himself embodies divine Wisdom when he says: I *send you prophets.*

Confronted by these envoys of Jesus, the Jewish leaders will perpetuate a pattern of violent opposition that has claimed the lives of God's servants throughout the biblical story, from the murder of Abel (Gen. 4:8) to the murder of *Zechariah son of Barachiah.* The Zechariah in view here is probably the priest Zechariah mentioned in 2 Chronicles 24:20-22, the last martyr to be named in the Hebrew Bible (which ends with 2 Chronicles). Confusion over the several Zechariahs who appear in the OT is evident elsewhere in Jewish and Christian tradition, and that appears to be the case in the text when Zechariah the martyr is mistakenly identified as *the son of Barachiah* (= the later prophet Zechariah; cf. Zech. 1:1). In any case, Jesus says, this record of bloodshed will come back to haunt those responsible as the Israel of Jesus' day (*this generation*) heads toward judgment.

Lament for a Lost City 23:37-39

The lament Jesus utters in verses 37-39 is linked to the preceding saying by its reference to the killing of prophets. Here Jerusalem, a holy city with an unholy history, is identified as the *place* where God's servants meet their doom (cf. Luke 13:33). For Matthew, Jerusalem represents a concentration of the power of evil that Jesus has confronted throughout his ministry to Israel, whose children he has tried to gather and protect as a hen does with her chicks.

The vivid metaphor in the text casts Jesus in a mothering role ascribed to God at several points in the OT story (cf. Isa. 31:5; Deut. 32:10-11; Pss. 17:8; 36:7; 91:1-4). Schweizer comments appropriately: "God does not simply require [persons] to come to him; he takes the initiative himself and desires to assemble those who are his own. This action of his has become flesh in Jesus" (444; cf. Calvin, 1972, 3:68-69).

But to no avail; the brood refuses to be gathered. Consequently, Jesus says, destruction will surely come. The words translated *your house* in verse 38 could refer to Israel as a whole, to Jerusalem, or even more specifically to the *temple* in Jerusalem (cf. the varied and sometimes overlapping meanings of *house* in Jer. 12:7; 26:6; 1 Enoch 89:50ff.; 2 Bar. 8:2). Given the symbolic departure from and comment on the temple that will soon follow (24:1-2), it is likely that Jesus' reference to a deserted house has the temple in mind. The judgment to befall the temple is characterized by the twin tragedies of God's withdrawal from the sanctuary (that is the loss of God's protective presence) and the desolation that will come at the hands of Israel's enemies (cf. 1 Kings 9:7-8; Jer. 12:7; 22:5; Tob. 14:4).

Anticipating both his departure from the temple and his imminent death, Jesus announces in verse 39 that the lives of his hearers will be void of his presence (= God's presence) *from this point on* (NRSV: *again*). This absence will prevail until that time when Jesus comes in judgment (cf. 26:64), and all history joins in the acclamation of the pilgrims in 21:9: *Blessed is the one who comes in the name of the Lord.* Some find here a glimmer of future hope for Israel, such as we find in Romans 11:25-32. More likely, however, Matthew's intent is to tell us that the condition for seeing and knowing Jesus is one that Jerusalem will fail to meet until it is too late.

THE TEXT IN BIBLICAL CONTEXT

A strand of Jewish faith and thought that contributed to early Christian faith in a major way is that of *Wisdom*. Personified as God's partner in creation and history (cf. Prov. 8:1-31; Sir. 24; Wisd. of Sol. 7:22-30), the figure of Wisdom provided a helpful model for thinking about Jesus' role as a divine agent. Among the clearer instances of this indebtedness to Wisdom material by the NT writers are the prologue to the Fourth Gospel and its picture of the *Logos* (Word) seeking a place to dwell (John 1:1-18) and the celebration of Christ's cosmic role in Colossians 1:15-20.

The point at which Matthew draws on wisdom themes is the relationship of Wisdom to the law and the prophets (cf. earlier comments on 7:13-29; 11:16-19; and 11:22-30). As a personification of God's self-revelation, Wisdom found expression in the Torah and sent prophets to declare God's word. Now, according to Matthew, Wisdom is personally present in Jesus, who both redefines the Torah and sends out his own disciples as new messengers of Wisdom (cf. 23:34).

A second point at which Matthew 23 connects with the larger biblical tradition is its harsh criticism of the leaders of Israel. This is by no means the first instance of such material in the Gospel (cf. comments on 6:1-18; 15:1-20; and 21:28—22:14), but it is clearly the most devastating. Denunciation of those who act contrary to God's purposes fills many a page in Scripture, and not surprisingly, some of the sharpest words are directed against the leadership.

One thinks of Jeremiah's and Ezekiel's condemnation of rulers who fail to shepherd God's flock (Jer. 22:13-23; 23:1-8; Ezek. 34), or of the repeated prophetic criticism of prophets and priests who abuse their calling (cf. Jer. 5:30-31; 23:9-40; Hos. 4:4-6; Mic. 3:5-8; Rom. 2:17ff.). When Jesus utters his woes and lament in the temple, therefore, he speaks as a long line of God's servants before him have spoken. Presupposed in the words of both Jesus and his predecessors is the conviction that God takes his covenant with the people very seriously—and will hold accountable those to whom the people look for counsel and direction.

THE TEXT IN THE LIFE OF THE CHURCH

A danger in canonizing and reading sacred texts that lambaste a group other than ourselves is that we assume we are called to join in the chorus of criticism. In the history of the church, this danger has proven to be more than hypothetical. Matthew's critique of Israel and its leaders has fueled century after century of Christian anti-Semitism, sometimes expressed in words and deeds even more harsh than those in the text. *[Anti-Semitism, p. 417.]*

Overlooked in this pathetic misuse of the text are two basic facts: (1) the bitter tone of chapter 23 derives in part from the mutual hostility between synagogue and church in Matthew's day. (2) Both Jesus and Matthew voice their indictment as self-criticism of a people to whom they also belong, not as slander from outside. As Matthew himself suggests to his disciples in 23:8-12, the right way to use Jesus' critique is as *a resource for self-examination by the church*.

One specific issue on which the text suggests such self-examination might focus is the question of how we define roles and relationships in the church. Some have speculated that Matthew's polemic against titles is directed against hierarchical tendencies at work in Syrian Christianity, such as are illustrated soon after Matthew's time in the statements of Ignatius of Antioch on the authority of the bishop (cf. Meier, 1980:265). In any case, the subsequent history of the church is one in which father-figures abound, to whom others defer with a host of lofty titles (father, elder, reverend, etc.). The text itself clearly challenges such a development.

As Elizabeth Schüssler-Fiorenza aptly comments on the passage: "The new kinship of the discipleship of equals does not admit of 'fathers' " and so rules out "the patriarchal power and esteem invested in them" (150; cf. 149-152). Significantly, it is the Gospel that most frequently depicts *God* as Father and King that most radically undercuts hierarchical relationships among God's people, pointing us instead to a lifestyle of mutuality.

Matthew 24:1—25:46

Instruction on the Endtime

PREVIEW

Chapters 24—25 present the fifth and final major discourse of Jesus in Matthew's Gospel. In the formula that marks the conclusion of the discourse, wording that varies slightly from that used in previous formulas confirms that Jesus' teaching ministry with his disciples is now ending. *When Jesus had finished saying* all *these things. . .* (26:1; cf. 7:28-29; 11:1). Echoed in the language is wording from an earlier address in the biblical story, the farewell message of Moses on the plains of Moab: "And when Moses had finished reciting all these words to all Israel. . ." (Deut. 32:45). The striking parallel supports the view that the discourse in chapters 24-25 constitutes a testament of Jesus, a private farewell address to his disciples that forms a sequel to the public farewell in chapter 23.

Like the sermon in chapters 5—7, the address in 24—25 is delivered from a hill or mountain. Here the setting is the Mount of Olives to the east of Jerusalem (v. 3), a site sometimes associated with endtime expectation. It is an appropriate location, since the discourse focuses on questions about the endtime, and in fact is often labeled the eschatological discourse.

The three primary topics addressed include Jesus' coming and the events that precede it (24:1-35), the need for believers to live in watchfulness or readiness as they await the end (24:36—25:30), and the final judgment over which Jesus will preside when he comes (25:31-46). Apocalyptic in form and flavor, the sayings before us depict the present age as one in which history is convulsing ever more violently as the end nears. In the midst of such turmoil, Jesus' disciples are encouraged to remain both expectant and patient, seizing troubled times as opportunities for witness and faithfulness.

As is his method in each of the discourses, so here also Matthew assembles material from a variety of sources. The anchor piece that Matthew uses to frame and launch the discourse is the so-called "little apocalypse" from Mark 13. We will proceed now to see how Matthew draws on Mark's material in 24:1-35.

How Will the End Come?

Matthew 24:1-35

PREVIEW

Few texts in the Gospels state their topic more clearly at the outset than does the passage at hand. *Tell us,* the disciples ask Jesus in 24:3, after he has announced the impending destruction of the temple, *when will this be, and what will be the sign of your coming and of the end of the age?* (cf. 2 Esd. 4:33; 6:7). As noted above, Matthew's primary source for both the question and the answer that follows is Mark 13. The Markan text in turn may draw on an earlier apocalyptic tract, one that related Jesus' message to a crisis such as Caligula's threat to set up his image in the temple (A.D. 40), or the beginnings of the Jewish-Roman war (A.D. 66-70).

Whatever its lineage, the material presented in 24:1-35 offers a picture of the traumatic process by which the endtime takes shape. Following the brief transitional narrative and conversation in verses 1-3, Jesus gives an overview in verses 4-14 of the tumultuous events ahead that will characterize the period between his departure and his coming. The section that follows in verses 15-28 does not describe events that come after those already indicated, but rather focuses in more closely on the difficult times predicted in 24:9-14. In verses 29-31, Jesus finally answers the question concerning *the sign* of his coming and depicts the awesome drama that brings the present age to a close. The unit concludes, then, in verses 32-35 with sayings assuring Matthew's readers that Jesus' triumphant advent is both imminent and certain.

OUTLINE

Setting the Stage, 24:1-3

All This Must Yet Happen, 24:4-14

A Great Tribulation, 24:15-28

The Sign of the Son of Man, 24:29-31

Near and Sure, 24:32-35

EXPLANATORY NOTES

Setting the Stage 24:1-3

The departure of Jesus from the temple noted in 24:1 is doubly significant for the unfolding story. First, it marks the shift from a public setting to one suited for private instruction of the disciples (cf. *privately*, v. 3). Second, it symbolizes the abandonment of the sanctuary predicted in 23:38-39. With the words of the latter saying still in mind, the reader is not surprised when Jesus counters the disciples' comment on the impressive architecture of the temple (one of the achievements of Herod the Great) with yet another prediction (24:2, paraphrased): *This monumental structure will be totally demolished!*

The new prediction leads naturally to the inquiry the disciples make in verse 3. (Note that Jesus is *sitting* as his followers come to him, the customary posture for a Jewish teacher; cf. 5:1-2). More clearly than in Mark 13:4, the double question here distinguishes two separate topics or issues:

3a: *When will* this *be (*the destruction of the temple)?

3b: *What will be the sign of your coming and of the end of the age?*

The *form* of the question anticipates a point that will emerge in Jesus' answer: While the destruction of the temple is part of the turmoil that *precedes* the end, an interval of time separates the two.

Another noteworthy facet of the question in 24:3 is the way it highlights *Jesus' coming* as central to the endtime drama. Of the four Gospel writers, Matthew alone uses the word translated *coming* (Greek: *parousia*; cf. vv. 27, 37, 39), a term that denotes presence or an act of becoming present. In the culture of the day, the term was sometimes used to designate the visit of a king or emperor or the appearance of a hidden deity. Its various connotations made it well-suited for use by the early church to refer to Jesus' triumphant advent in the endtime (cf. 1 Thess. 4:15; Jas. 5:7-8; 1 John 2:28).

The phrase *end of the age* is a construction peculiar to Matthew (cf. 13:39, 40, 49; 28:20), but expresses the common apocalyptic view that the present evil age will end dramatically, to be succeeded by a new era in which God's reign is fully established (cf. Dan. 11:35; 12:4, 11; Heb. 9:26).

All This Must Yet Happen 24:4-14

Jesus' answer to the question of verse 3 begins with a warning not to be deceived by self-proclaimed deliverers who announce the arrival of the end prematurely. Before the end can come, Jesus says, a number of things *must take place* (v. 6), and even these are but the beginning of the painful process (likened to childbearing) that will eventually usher in the age to come (v. 8; cf. Rom. 8:22f.). Only after the church has undergone a period of intense distress or tribulation (vv. 9ff.), and has fulfilled its mission to preach the good news of God's reign *throughout the world,* will the end come (v. 14).

The preliminary events named in verses 6-7 include both conflicts in the social order (wars and uprisings) and chaos in creation itself (famines and earthquakes). Matthew's readers would have had little difficulty thinking of specific disasters that matched this list, events such as the Jewish-Roman war, or the earthquake that destroyed Pompeii, or the famine during the reign of the emperor Claudius (cf. Acts 11:28).

Whatever allusions the text makes to happenings in the first century, it clearly develops themes that appear elsewhere in Jewish writings, particularly in apocalyptic texts. Thus 2 Esdras 13:31 speaks of the violence of the last times when people "make war against one another, city against city, place against place, people against people, and kingdom against kingdom" (cf. Isa. 19:2; 2 Chron. 15:6; 1 Enoch 99:4; 2 Esd. 6:22; 2 Bar. 70:8; Rev. 6:1-8). Stressed repeatedly in this material is the conviction that such happenings, painful as they may be, are part of a larger plan or design by which God will fulfill the divine purpose for history. It is in this sense that these events, sometimes called the messianic woes, *must take place* (cf. Dan. 2:28; Rev. 1:1; Matt. 18:7).

In the tribulation that follows the woes or birthpangs (vv. 9-12), the church will suffer at the hands of outsiders and insiders alike. The *nations* to whom Jesus' disciples proclaim the gospel (v. 14; cf.

28:19; Rev. 14:6) will react with hatred and persecute Jesus' witnesses (v. 9; note the striking inclusion formed by *all [the] nations* in verses 9 and 14, and cf. 10:18, 22a; John 15:18-21). Even more tragic, is the distress that will arise from *within* the Christian community. As the nations *hate* and *hand over* believers, so believers will do to one another (the same key verbs are used in verse 9 and verse 10).

Other marks of this time when *many will fall away* (or stumble; the verb used is *skandalizō*; cf. *stumbling block* in 18:5-10) include deception by false prophets (cf. 7:15ff.) and a growing moral indifference (NRSV: *lawlessness,* from the Greek *anomia*). The *cold* church depicted here lacks passion for love of either God or neighbor (cf. Rev. 2:4; 2 Tim. 3:1-5). The picture, however, is not totally bleak. Some believers will endure until the end arrives, and these will enjoy life in God's reign (v. 13; cf. 10:22b; Rev. 2:9-11).

A Great Tribulation 24:15-28

As suggested above, the sayings in verses 15-28 most likely do not introduce a new sequence of events, but rather give the reader a close-up shot of some of the events already enumerated. The close-up begins with a reference to a traumatic episode in Judea, described in verse 15 as *the desolating sacrilege,* a detestable violation of something sacred that evokes horror and dismay. Lest his readers be in doubt about how to interpret the obscure reference, Matthew points them to some passages ascribed to *the prophet Daniel* (cf. Dan. 9:27; 11:31; 12:11; 2 Thess. 2:4).

Here is one of many instances where OT texts with a specific meaning in their own time are viewed as finding a new fulfillment in the experience of the early church. We know from the Maccabean writings that the desolating sacrilege to which the book of Daniel referred was the repulsive act of the Syrian ruler Antiochus Epiphanes. In 168 B.C. he had an image of the god Zeus Olympios erected on the altar of burnt offering in the temple in Jerusalem and decreed that pagan sacrifices be offered on the altar (1 Macc. 1:41-59).

For Matthew, however, the words from Daniel fittingly describe a much more recent desolating sacrilege in *the holy place* (cf. Acts 6:13; 2 Macc. 8:17). The desecration that Matthew has in mind is that which the temple and all Jerusalem underwent at the hands of their Roman conquerors in A.D. 70!

The instructions for flight in verses 16-20 presuppose the chaos of that moment in Jewish history, a time when Jewish-Christians were still concerned about traditional Jewish sabbath customs (cf. v. 20). Matthew preserves this material not because of an interest in social history, however, but because he views the turmoil of A.D. 66-70 as the prototype or forerunner of even *greater* tribulation to come (vv. 21-22). Matthew probably sees his community as living in the midst of the tribulation of which he speaks, the duration and ultimate intensity of which only God knows. Like other biblical writers before him, Matthew describes this time of distress as unparalleled in human history (cf. Dan. 12:1; Joel 2:2), a period that no one could endure if God did not intervene in time.

It is in crisis times such as these that *false messiahs and false prophets will arise* (vv. 23ff.; cf. vv. 5, 11), with impressive credentials (cf. 7:22-23; Deut. 13:1-3; Rev. 13:11-18). What makes their appeal all the stronger is that they come in Christ's name (v. 5), from within the church. Some may set up shop in the wilderness, the traditional site for launching liberation movements (Exod. 3:1-12; Acts 5:36-37; 21:38), while others may fit the model of a hidden Messiah (*in the inner rooms*; cf. John 7:27).

From a literary perspective, it is fascinating to see how Matthew organizes a series of *Look* (Greek: *idou*) statements in verses 23-26. Warning his disciples about false appeals to *look* for deliverers (vv. 23, 26; cf. Mark 13:21; Luke 17:20-23), Jesus gives his own emphatic *look* statement in verse 25: *Take note, I have told you beforehand.* According to Jesus' words in verses 27-28, there will be no need for guesswork when the Son of Man really appears. It will be as obvious as "a horizontal lightning bolt . . . illuminating the whole earth, east to west, at the same moment" (Schweizer: 454). And it will be as certain as the presence of a carcass when one sees vultures circling (v. 28; cf. Luke 17:37).

The Sign of the Son of Man 24:29-31

Up to this point, Jesus has been clarifying the shape of things to come *before* the end. A shift occurs in verse 29, where Jesus at last begins talking about the final drama that will bring an end to the time of tribulation. Symbolic of the fact that God is about to refashion all creation, the heavenly bodies cease to radiate or rule life (v. 29; cf. Isa. 13:10; 34:4; Joel 2:2, 10; 2 Esd. 5:4). As their glory wanes, the glory and power of the Son of Man who comes *on the clouds of heaven* is all the more apparent (v. 30; cf. 16:28; 26:64; Dan. 7:13-14).

For those of *the tribes of the earth* who have rejected Jesus and his messengers, his sudden appearance prompts mourning (note how Matthew draws on language from Zech. 12:10 here, and cf. also Rev. 1:7). It is a time of joy, however, for *the elect from the four winds* (believers from every corner of the earth) who have accepted Jesus' message (v. 31; cf. 8:11; 13:41-43; Deut. 30:3-4).

In the midst of this picturesque description, Jesus speaks of the *sign* about which the disciples inquired, *the sign of the Son of Man* which will appear *in heaven* (v. 30a). But to what is Jesus referring? One of the earliest (though less likely) interpretations of the allusion is the sign of the cross. More recently, commentators have proposed that the sign consists of a counterpart to the blaring trumpet mentioned in verse 31, either a military standard or ensign (cf. Isa. 18:3; Jer. 4:21; 6:1; 51:27) or a great display of light. Still others argue that the sign is Jesus himself, and that we should translate the words in question: *The sign which is the Son of Man.* One way or another, Jesus is telling his disciples: You will know it when you see it!

Near and Sure 24:32-35

Unlike most trees in Palestine, the fig tree sheds its leaves each year. When new leaves appear, they signal the imminent approach of summer. Jesus uses this simple comparison to respond to the disciples' concern about the *when* of the endtime (cf. 2 Esd. 8:63—9:2). When Jesus' followers see *all these things* (v. 33), the panorama of events described in verses 4-28, they will know that the Son of Man (*he*) will soon make his grand arrival. (The pronoun translated *he* in the NRSV could also be translated *it* as in the NIV, meaning the consummation of this age.)

The further statement in verse 34 that *all these things* will transpire during *this generation* has proved problematic to later readers. Some have tried to circumvent the problem by interpreting *generation* to mean the people of Israel rather than a generation in chronological terms. Elsewhere in the First Gospel, however, *this generation* consistently refers to Jesus' contemporaries (cf. 11:16; 12:38-42), and that is probably the case here. From his own standpoint in time, Matthew thus understands: Jesus promises things to happen before the end; these have already been fulfilled, and we are living in the final stage of the birthing process (24:8) that will usher in the age to come (cf. Luke 21:31-32, "The kingdom of God is near . . .").

As verse 34 attests the *nearness* of Jesus' *parousia*, verse 35 attests its *certainty*. Everything in the old order will come to an end, including heaven and earth (cf. 5:18; 2 Pet. 3:10). Jesus' teaching, however, is the authoritative word that inaugurates the new order and so will not be superseded (cf. Isa. 40:8). When Jesus speaks of God's endtime triumph, his disciples can place complete confidence in his word.

THE TEXT IN BIBLICAL CONTEXT

In the introduction to chapters 24—25, we noted that this material is apocalyptic in form and flavor. Apocalyptic texts began to flourish in Israel in the postexilic period and include such specimens as Daniel, Joel, Zechariah 9—14, 1 Enoch, 2 Esdras, and similar works (cf. Isa. 24—27; 34—35; 65—66; Ezek. 38—48). Characteristic of apocalyptic thinking is the view that the present era of history is hopelessly in the grip of evil, that deliverance from this oppressive situation will not occur through the normal flow of things, and that a cataclysmic intervention by God is required to transform history and creation and usher in a new age.

Texts expressing this viewpoint abound in symbolic discourse, sometimes with poetic images whose meaning is fairly obvious, sometimes with obscure codelike language that requires interpretation. While the only full-fledged apocalypse in the NT is the book of Revelation, apocalyptic thinking played a major role in shaping the faith of the early church, as is apparent from the text before us.

Central to the apocalyptic faith of the early church was its expectation of the endtime coming or *parousia* of Jesus Christ. In what is likely the earliest NT document, Paul writes of "the coming of the Lord," who "with a cry of command, with the archangel's call and with the sound of God's trumpet will descend from heaven" (1 Thess. 4:15-16). Numerous texts echo this theme, including, of course, the eschatological discourse in the first three Gospels (cf. Mark 13; Luke 21:7-36; also 1 Cor. 15:23; 2 Thess. 2:8; James 5:7-8; Heb. 9:28; 2 Pet. 3:4, 12; 1 John 2: 28).

Theologically, affirmations of Jesus' endtime advent relate to the wider biblical drama at several points: (1) They recast in Christian form the OT expectation of Yahweh's coming to take charge of history in a new and decisive fashion (cf. Isa. 40:10; Mic. 1:2-3; Mal. 3:1-2). (2) They assert that Jesus will be instrumental in the future consummation of the kingdom of God, even as he was instrumental in inaugurating the kingdom in his mission to Israel. (3) They articulate a sequel or corollary to faith in Jesus' resurrection: As Jesus was exalted by God in his resurrection, so he will act as the exalted Lord at the end (cf. 1 Cor. 15:20-28).

THE TEXT IN THE LIFE OF THE CHURCH

The church's response to apocalyptic texts and the hope they express has taken a variety of forms. In some quarters, individuals or groups have taken such texts both literally and enthusiastically, assembling them like pieces of a jigsaw puzzle and constructing elaborate charts and timetables. In other circles, concern for the end of history has been replaced by concern for the end of each individual's life (death), and the apocalyptic vision of a new era has been equated with heaven above. Still other Christians have spiritualized apocalyptic language, conceiving judgment and resurrection as events that happen in our encounter with God here and now (cf. the tendencies in this direction in texts such as John 5:24; 11:25-26).

Beyond the church, apocalyptic pictures of an age to come have contributed to the Marxist vision of a new society, understood as a new order. This is to be inaugurated through human revolution within history, however, rather than through divine intervention.

While each of these approaches to apocalyptic texts is creative in its own way, each also distorts or limits the vision that Matthew and others were attempting to convey. In that vision: (1) We see God's determination to redeem history and creation, not simply provide a personal escape route from the evil that currently grips history. (2) There is a realistic sense of the continuing tension between the salvation that can be realized now and that which is not yet within our reach. (3) God invites humans to participate in the drama of the dawning kingdom. But because it is *God's* kingdom that is coming, neither religious zealots nor political revolutionaries control its coming. Such a vision provides the people of God with a wholistic approach to the present *and* the future, and challenges them to live accordingly.

Living in Readiness

Matthew 24:36—25:30

PREVIEW

As the first unit of Jesus' eschatological discourse ends, the reader knows that Jesus' coming is imminent. To use a current idiom, it feels so close one can almost taste it. But that is not the whole story. According to the sayings in 24:36—25:30, the interval between Jesus' departure and his return may be longer or shorter than expected. The timetable for the close of the age remains in God's hands, beyond human calculation.

Against such a backdrop, the unit before us addresses the question of how Jesus' community is to conduct itself as it awaits his coming. Jan Lambrecht sums up the answer the text provides when he writes: "Because the time of the return is unknown *and* near, and the parousia will occur unexpectedly *and* shortly, the only suitable attitude is one of *vigilance*" (1972:326, italics mine). To cite the language of the text itself, believers are to *keep awake* and *be ready* (cf. 24:42, 44; 25:10, 13). Vigilance or readiness is the proper ethical response to the eschatological situation in which Jesus' followers find themselves.

Matthew introduces this theme with the collage of brief pronouncements and comparisons we find in 24:36-44, assembled from several sources and settings (cf. Mark 13:32-37; Luke 12:39-40; 17:26-35; G. Thom. 21, 103). The sayings here clearly establish the need to be ready for an event that comes unexpectedly. To illustrate what readiness means, Matthew proceeds to narrate a series of three parables.

The story of the faithful or unfaithful servant in 24:45-51 has a Lukan parallel (cf. Luke 12:42-46) and defines readiness in terms of proper care for a master's household. In the parable of the wise and foolish maidens in 25:1-13, a story peculiar to Matthew but with certain elements found elsewhere (cf. Luke 12:35-36; 13:25-27), readiness is depicted as having adequate provisions. The so-called parable of the talents that concludes the trilogy in 25:14-30 is actually another account of faithful and unfaithful servants (*slaves*), based on the same story that Luke uses in Luke 19:11-27. This time the mark of readiness is the resourcefulness the servants show in handling the assets entrusted to them.

OUTLINE

Watch and Be Ready, 24:36-44

Care for the Household, 24:45-51

Stock Ample Provisions, 25:1-13

Be Resourceful Stewards, 25:14-30

EXPLANATORY NOTES

Watch and Be Ready 24:36-44

The forceful statement in verse 36 on the unknown day and hour of Jesus' coming is echoed in both verse 42 (*you do not know on what day*) and verse 44 (*at an unexpected* hour). Sounding a note we hear in other texts as well (cf. 2 Esd. 4:52; 2 Bar. 21:8; Acts 1:7; 1 Thess. 5:1), the saying underscores the gulf between our limited comprehension of God's plans and God's own foreknowledge of the outcome of history.

What is especially striking is the assertion that not even God's official couriers (*the angels*) nor the confidante who knows God more intimately than anyone else (*the Son*; cf. 11:27) is privy to this information. Some early copyists apparently were troubled by the implied limitation of Jesus' knowledge and so deleted the words *nor the Son* from their manuscripts! For Matthew, however, the strong language makes an important point: If Jesus himself must simply trust God to act at the appropriate time, prepared at all times for what God has in store, so also must Jesus' community.

The sayings that follow in verses 37-44 all depict situations in which a lack of readiness or vigilance spells disaster for persons when an unexpected trauma befalls them. Such was the case with the carefree contemporaries of Noah, engrossed in the pursuit of everyday life when the flood literally took them by storm! (vv. 37-39; cf. Gen. 6—8; 2 Pet. 2:5). Such is the case with a homeowner who is asleep at night, blissfully unaware that a thief has entered unannounced and is burglarizing his belongings (vv. 43-44; cf. 1 Thess. 5:2-4; Rev. 3:3; 16:15). And such will be the case at the end as pairs of men and women labor at their customary tasks of farming and milling, when God's own harvest operation suddenly commences and separates the prepared from the unprepared (vv. 40-42; cf. 13:36-43).

These assorted pictures and comparisons support the summons to vigilance in verses 42 and 44. Only if suitably prepared will Jesus' followers be able to welcome his sudden coming and the judgment it brings.

Care for the Household 24:45-51

The first of the three stories Matthew uses to illustrate readiness (or the lack of it) revolves around a master-servant relationship. Like Joseph in Potiphar's house in Egypt (Gen. 39:4), a servant is set over his master's household, with an assignment to see that everyone is fed properly. The words of the assignment recall the description of God as earth's food-supplier in Pss. 104:27 and 145:15! Two contrasting scenarios then follow, depicting radically different ways servants may carry out their charge and the outcome of each.

In the one case, the servant proves to be faithful (reliable) and wise (prudent), doing exactly as instructed. The reward for such a servant when the owner returns is a promotion involving still greater authority. In the other case, however, the servant forgets both his servant-status and his assignment, abusing the household and carousing with wild companions. Such a servant, characterized as *wicked,* faces the gory fate of dismemberment when his master returns (cf. 1 Sam. 15:33; Dan. 2:5).

For Matthew, the parable tells a story of life in *Jesus*' household, with a particular focus on the way servant-leaders in the church carry out their calling (cf. 1 Cor. 3:5-9; 4:1-2; 1 Pet. 5:1-5; 1 Tim. 3:2-3, 8, 14-15; Titus 1:7-9). Church leaders are called to nurture Jesus' community, and the faithfulness with which they discharge this calling determines their readiness for Jesus' coming. The acclamation of the faithful servant in the story as *blessed* connotes both divine approval and good fortune (that is, an important place in God's reign).

The punishment of the wicked servant by dismemberment likely functions as hyperbole for being cut off from life in God's reign (cf. Ps. 37:22, 28; 1QS 2:16-17). Confirming this is the reference in verse 51 to the servant's common destiny with those who have rejected Jesus, *the hypocrites* of chapter 23 and elsewhere (cf. 8:12; 22:13; 25:30).

Especially noteworthy in the story is the allusion to the *delayed* return of the master (v. 48), a theme present in the parables that follow as well (cf. 25:5, 19). The recurrence of this motif suggests that Matthew's community and other Christian groups were struggling with the so-called delay of the *parousia*: Jesus had not returned in glory as soon as the earliest believers had expected (cf. 2 Pet. 3:3-4). Part of Matthew's agenda, then, in chapters 24—25 is to make the case that vigilance is appropriate and necessary in spite of the delay. Since *the master of that slave will come on a day when he does not expect him and at an hour that he does not know* (v. 50), it is all the more important to be ready.

Stock Ample Provisions 25:1-13

The parable of the ten *bridesmaids* (Greek: *parthenoi*, which can also be translated *virgins*) begins with a plot summary in verse 1, which is then elaborated in the verses that follow. As the text indicates, the setting for the story is a wedding celebration, a topic of other sayings in the Gospel as well (cf. 9:14-15; 22:1-14). Note that the story is introduced explicitly as a parable about God's kingdom: When God's reign takes shape at the end, the plot of *that* story will be comparable to the plot of the wedding story before us.

Our knowledge of wedding customs in first-century Palestine is rather limited. It would appear, however, that the action in the story unfolds near or at the bridegroom's house. The wedding festivities are well underway and moving toward the dramatic moment when a party of friends or attendants (the bridesmaids) greets the bridegroom and escorts him in a nighttime procession to the entrance of his home. (Whether the bride accompanies the bridegroom or has arrived earlier is not clear.) The lamps or torches the young women carry (v. 8 seems to imply lamps) both provide light and enliven the processional.

Somewhat mysteriously, the arrival of the bridegroom is delayed, leading to the crisis that shapes the outcome of the plot. Having failed to bring enough oil, five of the bridesmaids hurry off to make a late-night purchase at a village shop—but return too late and find themselves barred from the wedding banquet. Meanwhile, the five prepared bridesmaids meet the bridegroom as planned and enjoy the party in his home.

However realistic or unrealistic from a historical standpoint, the story is rich with allegorical meaning. For Matthew and his readers, Jesus is the bridegroom whose coming is delayed (cf. 9:15; 22:1), eagerly but wearily awaited by his community (the sleeping maidens). To be ready for his coming, believers must be as lamps well supplied with the oil of good works, a light for all to see (cf. 5:14-16; 13:43; Dan. 12:3; Num. R. 7:19). Those thus prepared by following Jesus' teaching prove themselves to be *wise,* while those unprepared prove themselves to be *foolish* (cf. 25:2-4; 7:24-27!). For the latter, the story indicates, desperate last-minute maneuvers will lead nowhere (cf. *Lord, lord* in 25:11 and 7:21-23!). Thus the parable ends in verse 13 with another urgent appeal to *keep awake,* to be *ready.*

Be Resourceful Stewards 25:14-30

The parable of the *talents* entrusted to a man's servants (*slaves*) thrusts the reader into the world of commerce and banking. Although not stated explicitly, the master of the three servants is apparently a wealthy merchant, whose business takes him on the journey mentioned in verse 14. Like any good capitalist, he doesn't want his assets lying dormant while he is gone, and so turns them over to the three servants to invest or use in trade. The funds placed in their trust represent a sizable sum of money. As noted earlier (cf. 18:23-35), the talent was the largest unit of currency in the Hellenistic world. A single talent was equivalent to fifteen years of wages for a laborer!

The action in the story moves quickly from the opening scene (vv. 14-15). There is a brief report on the ways the three servants handle the assets at their disposal (vv. 16-18), then a much longer account of the reckoning that takes place when the master returns (vv. 19-30). For dramatic effect, the scenes where the master settles accounts with the first and second servants parallel each other exactly (cf. vv. 20-21 and 22-23). In each case, the servant reports a doubling of the entrusted assets, and in each case the master pronounces the servant *trustworthy* and enlarges his sphere of responsibility.

The third encounter, however, described in great detail (vv. 24-30), breaks the pattern of the first two in striking fashion. Here the servant maligns the master to excuse his timid decision to opt for security rather than creative investment. To be sure, burying a deposit in the ground was a common strategy in that era to avoid liability in the event of theft. The master, however, is not impressed. After criticizing the servant's laziness and lack of imagination, he redistributes the unused assets and dismisses the servant in no uncertain terms.

For the reader of the Gospel, it is obvious that this is yet another story illustrating readiness for Jesus' coming. The opening words in verse 14 (*For it is as if*) connect the parable with the *keep awake* saying in verse 13 and with the kingdom story that precedes it. Further, the talk about servants recalls the earlier servant story in 24:45-51.

As noted above, the understanding of readiness lifted up in the parable of the talents is that of resourceful stewardship—on the part of both leaders and the wider membership of the church. To each one in his community Jesus (or God) has entrusted a generous gift (remember the value of the talent!) to be used and multiplied. It is possible to construe this as the basic gift of life as Jesus' disciple (cf. the pearl of great price and hidden treasure in 13:44-46). Or it may be differing special gifts and callings (cf. v. 15, *to each according to his ability*; and Rom. 12:3-8). In any case, the plot of the story reveals that willingness to risk and develop God's gift is a critical component of readiness. Eduard Schweizer puts it well in his comment on the enigmatic statement in verse 29 (cf. 13:12; Luke 8:18; G. Thom. 41):

> Where God's gift has already borne fruit, God gives in superabundance; where it has remained fruitless, it is lost completely. This means that God's gift can never be passively possessed; it is like a muscle: It must be worked and stretched or it withers. (472)

THE TEXT IN BIBLICAL CONTEXT

In the book of Habakkuk, a prophet surveys the evil and violence that afflict his times—and asks why God is so slow to correct the situation: "O Lord, how long shall I cry for help, and you will not listen? . . . Why do you make me see wrong-doing and look at trouble?" (Hab. 1:2-3). The answer God eventually gives the prophet counsels continuing trust in spite of the apparent delay: "There is still a vision for the appointed time; it speaks of the end, and does not lie. If it seems to tarry, wait for it; it will surely come, it will not delay. . . . The righteous live by their faith" (Hab. 2:3-4).

The theme of *delay* that surfaces in the parables of 24:36—25:30 is thus an ancient theme, not a new one. What is new is the way it is linked to the particular agenda of Jesus' coming. Early in the life of the church, concern over Jesus' delayed appearance focused on the fear that believers who died prior to the *parousia* would miss out on the chance to experience the new era. That is apparently the issue Paul addresses in 1 Thessalonians (4:13-18).

A more radical questioning of the delay lies behind the statements we find in 2 Peter: "In the last days scoffers will come, scoffing and indulging their own lusts and saying, 'Where is the promise of his coming? For ever since our ancestors died, all things continue as they were from the beginning of creation' " (2 Pet. 3:3-4). In his response to such questioning, the author argues in verses 8-13 that God's apparent slowness in fact represents a merciful extension of the time for witness and repentance, and that believers need to maintain their readiness for the sudden coming of "the day of the Lord." Both the concern and the response are similar to what we find in the sayings of this Matthean passage.

THE TEXT IN THE LIFE OF THE CHURCH

In the ongoing centuries since the NT was written, the delay of the *parousia* has continued to generate both anxiety and discussion. For some, the phenomenon of delay has only served to heighten the intensity of expectation: "If Jesus didn't come yesterday, he is all the more likely to come today or tomorrow." For others, the fact that an event announced as imminent in the first century has not yet occurred has led to a "back-burner" eschatology: "God will doubtless end the world someday, but how does that affect my life now?" For still others, talk about Jesus' coming is labeled as a product of Jewish-Christian apocalyptic circles—and then dismissed as irrelevant to present-day faith.

Together with Matthew, we need to search for a way of appropriating early Christian faith in Jesus' coming that is more constructive that any of the alternatives cited. We need as a church to live out of the same confidence in God's eschatological triumph that undergirded earlier believers, even though the form of our expectation may differ from theirs. Eduard Schweizer points us in the right direction when he comments on the text as follows:

> When Jesus calls on his disciples to keep watch, he is calling on them to take the reality of God so seriously that they can come to terms with its sudden appearance at any moment within their lives, precisely because they know that this reality will one day come unboundedly in the kingdom of God. (468)

In the history of interpretation, the parable in 25:14-30 has been invoked for more mundane purposes than preparation for the *parousia.* The so-called parable of the talents frequently turns up as a text for stewardship sermons, in which hearers are urged to dedicate their "talents" to the work of the Lord. While this type of exposition treats the *talents* in the parable too simplistically, it is not wholly misguided. The text does in fact tell a story about stewards, inviting the reader to raise the question: Am I playing my part as a faithful steward of the reign of God which shapes our calling as God's household? When we respond to that question, the answer we give will have something to do with stewardship in the local church.

Jesus Judges the Nations

Matthew 25:31-46

PREVIEW

With the disciples thoroughly drilled on the need to be ready (24:36—25:30), Matthew is prepared to resume the portrayal of the end introduced in 24:29-31. There we learned that when Jesus appears in glory, *all the tribes of the earth will mourn* (24:30). The reason they mourn is that they know Jesus' coming spells *judgment.* In the unit before us, which concludes the eschatological discourse, we find an elaborate and provocative picture of that judgment, with *all the nations* present and accounted for.

The material the text presents, found only in Matthew's Gospel, is sometimes called the "parable" of the sheep and the goats. Such a designation is based on a brief parabolic saying in verses 32-33, where the process of judgment is compared to separating a flock into two groups. Quickly, however, this imagery gives way to a description of the scene of judgment itself. The unit is thus more accurately labeled an apocalyptic vision of judgment, akin to the judgment scenes depicted in the Similitudes of Enoch (cf. 1 Enoch 38; 62).

At several different levels, the judgment scene in 25:31-46 involves a *final* judgment: It is final in terms of the narrative of the Gospel, the finale to which the many earlier allusions to judgment point. It is final in the way that it marks the end of the age and renders God's decisive verdict on all human history. And it is final in the sense of the finality of the two contrasting destinies for humankind announced by the One who judges.

OUTLINE

Gathered and Separated, 25:31-33

Come, You Blessed, 25:34-40

Depart, You Accursed, 25:41-46

EXPLANATORY NOTES

Gathered and Separated 25:31-33

As the heading for these verses indicates, Matthew portrays the final judgment as an act of *gathering* and *separating.* Those gathered encompass *panta ta ethnē*, which can be translated either *all the Gentiles* or *all the nations.* The latter translation is better suited to express the all-inclusive character of the judgment in view. Since the good news is to be preached to every people or nation (24:14; 28:19), all humankind will be held accountable at the end of the age.

The verb for *gather* was commonly used to describe the herding of animals and fits well with the flock metaphor in the scene of separation that follows. It is unclear from the vocabulary in verse 32 whether the division of the flock is into sheep and goats (goats prefer the warmth of an enclosed area at night) or into ewes and rams. In any case, the text draws on similar parabolic imagery in Ezekiel 34:17-22 to depict the separation into two groups that judgment implies. One group is placed at the judge's right hand (the place of favor), the other group at the left (a place of lesser favor or disfavor).

The overarching picture of a gathering of the nations for judgment is found in several OT passages (cf. Joel 3:1-12; Zech. 14:2-5; Isa. 66:18). In these texts, it is God who acts as the ruler of history and executes the role of judge. In Matthew 25, however, it is *the Son of Man* (= Jesus) who comes, reigns, and carries out divine judgment. The imagery of an exalted figure in human form derives from the book of Daniel (cf. Dan. 7:13-14; 1 Enoch 62:2, 5) and is reflected in a number of *Son of Man* sayings in the First Gospel (cf. 13:41-42; 16:27; 19:28; 24:30-31; 26:64). According to Matthew, the rejected *human one* who proclaimed the gospel of the kingdom to Israel, will appear at the end as the exalted judge of all the nations.

Come, You Blessed 25:34-40

The title *king* is used sparingly for Jesus in the Gospels, doubtless because of its political connotations (cf. Mark 15:2-32; John 1:49; 18:33-38). In Matthew and elsewhere, however, it is clear that Jesus is destined to rule on God's behalf in the endtime (cf. 2:1-12; 16:28; 21:5; 25:34; Rev. 17:14; 19:16). Accordingly, Jesus speaks as *the king* in verses 34-46, turning first to the group on his right whom he labels *blessed.* They are so named because they are about to receive the gift promised earlier in the Beatitudes (5:3-12). As Israel was given an inheritance in the promised land, so the blessed in the endtime inherit a place in the promised kingdom!

The distinguishing characteristic of the blessed that qualifies them for life in God's reign is that they are *righteous* (v. 37), which is defined in terms of the six works of mercy catalogued in verses 35-36: They have fed the hungry, given drink to the thirsty, welcomed the stranger, clothed the naked, visited the sick, and cared for the imprisoned. The deeds cited all exemplify hospitality toward those in need, and all are mentioned in Jewish literature as deeds that commend a person in God's sight (cf. Isa. 58:7; Ezek. 18:7; Job 22:6-7; Sir. 7:35; Tob. 4:16; T. Jos. 1:6; 2 Enoch 9—10; Midr. Ps. 118).

The surprise that the righteous ones register in verses 37-39 is not that they are being credited with such deeds, but that the recipient of their works of mercy was the exalted king himself! "How so?" they ask. In a Jewish midrash on Deuteronomy 15:9, God tells the people of Israel: "My children, when you have given food to the poor, I account it as though you had given food to me" (cf. also Prov. 19:17; Heb. 13:2-3). Along similar lines, Jesus responds to the blessed with the familiar words of 25:40: *As you did it to one of the least of these who are members of my family, you did it to me.*

The crux of interpretation for the passage is the identity of *the least of these.* In the exposition of the text to which we are most accustomed, *the least of these* are defined as the poor and needy of the world, whoever they happen to be. There is considerable evidence in the First Gospel, however, that Matthew has a much more specific group of poor and needy persons in mind:

(1) The phrase *least of these* recalls passages in which Jesus refers to his *disciples* as *little ones* (10:42; 18:6, 10).

(2) In the only other texts where Jesus speaks of his *family members* or *brothers,* the term describes *disciples* of Jesus who do God's will (12:46-50; 23:8-9).

(3) Jesus announces in the mission discourse in chapter 10 that those who receive his *disciples* receive him (10:40), and that those who offer a drink to disciples who thirst will be rewarded (10:42).

(4) It is with his *disciples* that Jesus promises to be present in the world until the end of the age (28:20; cf. 18:20).

For Matthew, then, the conversation Jesus has with all the nations in the final judgment focuses on the way humankind has responded to Jesus in the person of his *disciples*, from the greatest to *the least of these.* The scene is anticipated in Matthew 10, where the topic is Israel's response to the mission of the twelve (cf. 10:11-15, 40-42). Now the setting is a cosmic one, presupposing the response of all the peoples of earth to the universal mission of the disciples described in 28:18-20 (cf. 24:14). As this mission unfolds, Jesus visits the world through his disciple-messengers, who find themselves in hardship and need as they move from place to place. The *blessed* are those who have opened themselves to Jesus by welcoming his messengers and offering hospitality. The *accursed* are those who have rejected Jesus by rejecting his messengers and denying them hospitality.

Depart, You Accursed 25:41-46

The dialogue in verses 41-45 between Jesus and the group at his left is structurally parallel to the dialogue recorded in verses 34-40.

Among the common features which we find are these:

(1) Formal words of address (cf. *Come, you that are blessed* in verse 34 and *You that are accursed, depart from me* in verse 41).

(2) Commands consigning the two groups to their respective destinies, which have already been *prepared* (vv. 34 and 41).

(3) Descriptions of the works of mercy that the two groups did or did not perform (vv. 35-36 and 42-43).

(4) Expressions of surprise over Jesus' assertion that he has been among his hearers as someone in need (vv. 37-39 and 44).

(5) Replies by Jesus beginning with the solemn formula, *Truly, I tell you . . .* (vv. 40 and 45).

Although the *form* of the two sections of dialogue is identical, the verdict given in verses 41-45 contrasts sharply with that in verses 34-40. Having failed to welcome Jesus in the person of his messengers, the addressees here are forever banished from his presence (cf. 7:23). The place to which they are sent is a fiery lake designed to consume and destroy all that is evil (cf. 5:22; 13:42, 50; Rev. 14:10; 20:10).

On any reading, the metaphor is a grim one. Note, however, that Matthew's language carefully avoids any suggestion that God has predestined a part of humankind for such a fate. While the kingdom has been *prepared for God's people* (v. 34), the lake of fire has been *prepared for the devil and his associates* (v. 41). It is only by their own choosing that some humans may share the dire future of the forces of evil that oppose God's purposes.

The saying in verse 46 that concludes the account of the last judgment sums up the destinies of the blessed and the accursed, but in reverse order. The resulting pattern of the larger narrative is thus chiastic:

a. Commendation of the blessed (34-40)
  b. Condemnation of the accursed (41-45)
  b'. Destiny of the accursed (46a)
a'. Destiny of the blessed (46b)

Hearing language that echoes Daniel 12:2 (cf. John 5:28-29), the reader learns that the lot of those condemned by the King is *eternal punishment,* while the lot of those who found favor with the King is *eternal life.* It is uncertain whether *eternal punishment* implies ceaseless torment, annihilation, or simply total and irreversible separation from God. *Eternal life*, on the other hand, clearly refers to life with Jesus and his community in the new age God creates, a life in which all of God's promises will be fulfilled, and a life that evil and death can never destroy. On this note Matthew chooses to conclude the text, thereby accenting the destiny he hopes his readers will attain.

THE TEXT IN BIBLICAL CONTEXT

As the vivid scene of Matthew 25:31-46 illustrates, a theme regularly associated with Jesus' coming is that of *judgment*. Thus James describes the One who is to come as "the Judge . . . standing at the doors" (James 5:9). The author of 2 Thessalonians speaks of the repayment for evil deeds that will occur "when the Lord Jesus is revealed from heaven" (2 Thess. 1:5-10). And the visions of Revelation are replete with judgment scenes, including the final judgment before the "great white throne" (Rev. 20:11-15; cf. 11:15-18).

The situation is similar in the OT and in other Jewish writings, where God's presence or coming leads to judgment for both Israel and foreign nations (cf. Ps. 50:1-6; Isa. 59:15-19; Joel 3; Zeph. 3:8; Mal. 3:5-6; 1 Enoch 38, 62). Underlying Jewish and Christian texts alike are the assumptions that God holds humankind accountable for its conduct, and that God will act to rectify the situation when humankind acts contrary to the divine purpose.

At least two features, however, distinguish early Christian predictions of judgment from similar sayings in Israel. In the NT:

(1) The arena of human action which attracts God's closest scrutiny is no longer the political drama of Israel among the nations, but the drama of faith and unfaith as people respond to Jesus and the salvation he brings.

(2) Jesus himself occupies center stage in the final judgment, whether as a key witness in the proceedings (cf. Luke 12:8-9) or as the actual agent of divine judgment (as in Matt. 25:31ff.).

THE TEXT IN THE LIFE OF THE CHURCH

The judgment scene in Matthew 25:31-46 has not suffered from neglect. It has inspired works of art such as Michelangelo's famed *Last Judgment* in the Sistine Chapel in Rome. It has inspired stories such as Leo Tolstoy's classic tale of Martin the cobbler, "Where Love Is, There God Is." And it has inspired Christian ministries of compassion for the hungry and oppressed, including both denominational programs and cooperative ventures such as Bread For the World, Church World Service, and World Vision. (For a testimony to its impact on the piety of one believers church body, see the sixteen-stanza poem by Alexander Mack, Jr., found in Durnbaugh, 1967:579-582.)

More recently, however, the concept of a final judgment has been seriously questioned. In some instances, the questions concern the way judgment texts are sometimes used—to induce fear as a means of prompting conversion or ensuring conformity to a group's norms. In other instances, the questions focus on whether the image of God or Jesus as *judge* remains valid. To put it another way: Are the cross and the court compatible metaphors?

The overarching answer of the NT to questions such as these is that *God's cosmic objective is to redeem and restore,* not condemn and destroy. That is what the cross is all about, and that is what the mission of the Christian community is all about.

At the same time, the biblical writers presuppose that the outcome of the story of God and humankind hinges not only on God's intention, but on human decision and response as well. History is not simply a playground, where God says at last, "It was only a game," but an arena of moral accountability, where life choices really matter (cf. Meier, 1980:305-306). The dark side of this reality is the possibility that some will remain stubbornly resistant to God's reign, unwilling to live within its grace and demands, unwilling to seek justice and practice mercy. That is what stories of final judgment are all about.

In the story of the king's judgment in Matthew 25, at least two issues call for further attention. One is the question of where the *church* finds itself in the story. If we stay with the interpreation suggested in the preceding pages, we will be inclined to say that the church is Jesus' needy brothers and sisters. Like the early disciples, we as Christians represent and embody Jesus in the world. But are we really in a position to give that answer? Insofar as we find ourselves in the role of Jesus' homeless, wandering disciples, afflicted and in need as we serve as Jesus' emissaries, we may claim the identity of *the least of these.* Such was the claim of Brethren and Mennonites in 1775 when they presented a joint petition to the Pennsylvania General Assembly regarding their peace stance (cf. Durnbaugh, 1967:362-365), and there are occasions today when the designation still fits. One thinks of volunteers who live and work with the poor of Latin America to protest injustice and to build communities of hope.

More often than not, however, the church as we know it in Western culture more nearly resembles *the nations* to whom Jesus' messengers are sent. We are settled communities who must decide how *we* will receive Jesus. From that vantage point, the all-important question to ask ourselves is this: Have we welcomed the radical witness of those disciples who in Jesus' name challenge our usual preoccupations? When worldly powers afflict them, have we stood alongside them in love and solidarity and active care for the needy? *Truly, I tell you, just as you did it to one of the least of these who are members of my family, you did it to me.*

A broader issue to address is the popular interpretation of 25:31-46 as a story about serving human need wherever it is found. Here Jesus' brothers and sisters are identified as the hungry and poor of the world, and Christians (along with others) are called to minister to them. It is this approach to the text that has spawned the worldwide programs of service and compassion mentioned above. How shall we evaluate this use of Matthew's story? From an exegetical standpoint, it represents a misreading of the text. Matthew's own agenda in the story is how the world receives and responds to Jesus, not how Christians respond to the world. At the same time, Matthew might not be unhappy with the new frame of reference we have given to his story. Elsewhere in his Gospel, he includes an episode that underscores love of neighbor as the place we show our love for God (22:34-40; cf. 5:43-48). The view that we find and serve God where we find and serve human need thus fits with Matthew's faith—and echoes other biblical voices (cf. Heb. 13:2-3; Gen. 18:1-15). To put it another way: If we use the text at hand as an appeal to God's people to show compassion to all in need, we are going beyond the immediate story, but not beyond the biblical story!

Part 6

Jesus' Death and Resurrection

Matthew 26:1—28:20

PREVIEW

As do each of the Gospels, Matthew's story of Jesus culminates in a dramatic account of Jesus' death and resurrection. The part of this drama that presents the crucifixion and the events immediately preceding it (chaps. 26—27) is commonly labeled the passion narrative (passion = suffering). Among the vignettes it comprises are Jesus' Last Supper with his disciples, incidents of betrayal and denial, several hearings or trials, and the crucifixion scene itself. The consensus of most scholars is that the passion narrative was one of the first composite accounts about Jesus to be assembled and used in the early church, a kind of protogospel.

Concluding the narrative is a brief report of Jesus' burial. At first glance, the report appears to be a mere footnote to the tragedy of the crucifixion, a device that will enable the reader to leave the story. In fact, however, it sets the stage for a surprising sequel to Jesus' passion—the discovery of the empty tomb and Jesus' appearance as the risen Lord. Here at last it becomes clear that the divine power at work in Jesus has not been defeated. Exalted by God, Jesus is now in a position to continue his mission on a global scale through his community.

The core of Matthew's story of Jesus' death and resurrection comes from Mark (cf. Mark 14-16). Indeed, Mark is likely Matthew's sole *written* source at this point. Matthew has, however, enriched the Markan narrative in various ways. He has incorporated oral traditions from his community such as those concerning the fate of Judas (27:3-10). He has enhanced and reshaped accounts such as Jesus' trial before Pilate (27:11-26). And he has so constructed the report of Jesus' reunion with the disciples following the resurrection that it gathers up a number of key themes of the Gospel (cf. 28:16-20). The end result is a story that moves from episode to episode so naturally that it is difficult to detect major breaks or divisions. There are, nevertheless, five groups of episodes that hang together as literary units.

OUTLINE

Prelude to Passion, 26:1-16

A Farewell Gathering, 26:17-46

In the Hour of Trial, 26:47—27:10

A Crucified King, 27:11-56

From Death to Life, 27:57—28:20

Prelude to Passion

Matthew 26:1-16

PREVIEW

In labeling the unit that launches the passion narrative, writers commonly use words such as prelude, prologue, or overture. Categories such as these describe the unit well. Themes are introduced in 26:1-16 that will be developed more fully in the units that follow. And the narrated events set in motion the plot that will lead to Jesus' death.

Based on Mark 14:1-11, Matthew's prelude to passion exhibits an a b a' pattern in which the primary story is interrupted by a second story and then later resumed. (See Mark 5:21-43/Matthew 9:18-26 for a similar use of this technique.) We may thus diagram the structure of the text as follows:

a. Plotting against Jesus commences in a gathering of chief priests and elders.

b. Woman anoints Jesus with oil at Bethany, a friendly and loving act in the midst of hostility.

a'. Plotting against Jesus resumes with Judas' offer to deliver Jesus to the chief priests.

OUTLINE

Consigned to Death, 26:1-5

Anointed for Burial, 26:6-13

Marked for Betrayal, 26:14-16

EXPLANATORY NOTES

Consigned to Death 26:1-5

When Jesus concludes the discourse of chapters 24—25 (see the comments on 26:1 in the introduction to the discourse), he himself makes the transition to the narrative ahead: He offers yet another prediction of his impending death (v. 2), similar to those in 16:21; 17:22-23; and 20:17-19. Here the pronouncement links Jesus' death with Passover, a feast that coincided with the seven-day Festival of Unleavened Bread commemorating Israel's rescue from slavery in Egypt (cf. Exod. 12:1-28). Passover fell on the fifteenth of the lunar month Nisan (March/April), and that is the probable date of Jesus' crucifixion as well. The purpose of the pronouncement, of course, is not to satisfy the curiosity of the historian. Instead, it prompts the reader to ponder Jesus' death as a type of Passover event.

By placing Jesus' prediction of his death at the outset of the narrative, Matthew makes it clear that Jesus is no helpless victim, taken by surprise. He knows what is about to transpire even as (or before) the leaders begin plotting his demise. In fact, he acts as "the agent who guides the events of the passion instead of just enduring them" (Meier, 1980:309; cf. the similar portrayal of Jesus in the passion narrative of the Fourth Gospel). As a result, the hostile gathering described in verses 3-5 becomes an event in which Jesus' opponents unwittingly fulfill his word.

Matthew depicts this gathering as a special session of the Sanhedrin convened by Caiaphas, who held the office of high priest from A.D. 18 to A.D. 36 (cf. John 11:49), with *the chief priests and the elders of the people* as coconspirators. (cf. the collusion of the same two groups in the challenge to Jesus' authority in 21:23ff.). According to the text, the session ends on a note of unrelieved tension: The conspirators want to arrest Jesus while he is in town for Passover. But how can they do so without inciting a riot among Jesus' supporters? Not until verses 14-16 will a solution present itself.

Anointed for Burial 26:6-13

All four of the Gospels contain a story about a woman who anoints Jesus (cf. Mark 14:3-9; Luke 7:36-50; John 12:1-8). Except for Luke's account, which possibly reflects a different episode, the story is located in a home where Jesus is lodging in Bethany (cf. 21:17). According to Matthew and Mark, the owner of the home is a certain *Simon the leper,* whose name recalls another leper healed by Jesus earlier in the narrative (8:1-4).

The woman herself, introduced without a name, is one of several characters in the Gospel who stand outside the circle of the twelve, but who honor Jesus with gestures or words appropriate for disciples. Indeed, the woman is sensitive to Jesus' needs in a way that eludes the disciples! Jesus therefore needs to defend the woman's action in verses 10-12, alluding as he does so to Deuteronomy 15:11. The point Jesus makes is not that poverty is predestined, nor that his community should ignore the poor. Instead, he argues that this particular act of extravagant love is proper at this particular point in the story in light of what lies ahead.

Whatever the woman's own perception of her deed, Jesus interprets her action as a preburial rite. The use of oils and spices to prepare a corpse for burial was a customary act of Jewish piety. Here, however, the body being anointed is still certainly alive, and the rite is being performed in anticipation of death. A possible second level of meaning in the story focuses on the pouring of oil on Jesus' head. Such was the practice in the coronation of kings in ancient Israel (cf. 1 Sam. 16:12-13), and Matthew may see the woman's action as confirming Jesus' destiny as God's anointed ruler. In any case, the woman's deed is described as one that will be recounted when *this good news* is preached. The phrase *this good news* refers to the message about God's kingdom, particularly as this reign takes shape in the drama of Jesus' passion. By her action, the woman has made herself part of this drama—and will be remembered accordingly.

Marked for Betrayal 26:14-16

In verses 14-16, Matthew returns to the unresolved question of verses 3-5: How can Jesus be arrested without causing a public uproar? The answer is that a member of Jesus' own inner circle will betray him, and that member is Judas Iscariot (cf. 10:4). Judas makes four appearances in Matthew's passion narrative: here in a visit to the chief priests, at the last supper (26:20-25), at the place of betrayal (26:47-56), and finally in a scene of remorse (27:3-10).

The reason(s) behind Judas' decision to betray Jesus remain obscure. In his own attempt to reconstruct a motive, Matthew presents the dialogue in verse 15 suggesting that Judas is governed by greed: *What will you* give me *if I betray him to you?* Such a question suggests a person whose *treasure* is in the wrong place, who has not yet learned that it is impossible to serve both God and wealth (cf. 6:19-24; 19:16-24).

The *thirty pieces of silver* paid to Judas for his assistance figure prominently in the account of Judas' remorse and suicide. From a narrative standpoint, then, the amount is mentioned here as a detail that will be important later. Even before we get to the later episode, however, the reference to the thirty coins is significant. It recalls a passage in Zechariah 11:12 where a good shepherd is paid the slave wages of thirty shekels (cf. Exod. 21:32), which he tosses back into the temple treasury. Through this allusion, Matthew achieves two things: (1) He reminds us that the drama of Jesus' passion is unfolding along biblical lines. (2) He informs us that the sum of money for which Jesus is betrayed is a trivial amount, a further indicator that Judas has lost his sense of priorities.

From that moment, the text tells us, Judas was looking for an opportunity to make his move. It is the same phrase used earlier in the Gospel to announce a major turning point in the story (cf. 4:17; 16:21). From now on, it is not a question of *whether* Jesus will be taken by his enemies, but only *where* and *how*.

THE TEXT IN BIBLICAL CONTEXT

The passion narrative that begins in 26:1 hardly comes as a surprise. To the contrary, Matthew has carefully prepared the reader for the violent outcome of Jesus' mission. Long before the gathering of the chief priests described in 26:3-5, a similarly ominous gathering with some of the same players is reported at the time of Jesus' birth (2:3-6). Already at that time Jesus is marked for destruction and spared only by God's providential intervention (2:13-23).

This early preview of things to come is reinforced as the narrative develops: Jesus' predecessor is imprisoned and beheaded (14:1-12), hostility mounts between Jesus and Israel's leaders (cf. 12:14; 21:45-46), and Jesus himself predicts his eventual execution in Jerusalem (16:21; 20:17-19; 21:33-41). Caught up in this narrative pattern, the reader knows that human and divine forces will somehow converge to bring Jesus to the cross.

This convergence of divine and human is what in fact happens in 26:1-16 and beyond. In the foreground we find human players such as Judas and the chief priests, guided by evil, hostile intentions as they plot Jesus' death. In the background, however, is the purposeful shaping of history by God, which can encompass even human evil in the divine design for redemption. The text picks up both levels of action in the ambiguous passive voice of verse 2, when Jesus announces that *the Son of Man will be handed over to be crucified* (see comments on 17:22-23, and cf. also 26:24).

As Matthew develops this understanding of the interplay of human evil and divine good, he is informed by the biblical narrative that precedes him. A particular story that comes to mind is that of Joseph. The cruel treatment he endured at the hands of his brothers ultimately serves God's purpose to save Joseph's people from famine: "Even though you intended to do harm to me," Joseph says to his brothers, "God intended it for good, in order to preserve a numerous people" (Gen. 50:20). For Matthew, and for the NT as a whole, that is precisely what takes place as Jesus moves through the ordeal of the cross.

THE TEXT IN THE LIFE OF THE CHURCH

As the drama of Jesus' passion takes shape, the spotlight shifts back and forth between the central character (Jesus) and others who move on and off stage. Not surprisingly, the church's use of the text has frequently focused on the portrayals of the various characters and the dialogue that surrounds their appearances. A case in point is the scene with the woman who anoints Jesus, who has been identified with one or another of the Marys in the Gospels from early times on (cf. John 12:3). More recently, the woman has assumed importance as one of a number of female actors in the story of Jesus whose roles and voices help to balance our typical reading of the Gospels from a male perspective.

Even more fascinating than the woman herself has been the conversation in which the disciples protest and Jesus defends the woman's deed. At times the words about always having the poor with us have been cited to support the view that poverty in the world cannot be eliminated. At other times the woman's deed has been held up to justify extravagance or luxury in the church (= Christ's body). Interpretations such as these are dubious, to say the least.

The real issue the anointing at Bethany raises is that of being able to respond to Christ in the right way at the right time. Alongside our usual, everyday expressions of commitment, there are special occasions when devotion to Christ will elicit actions that are spontaneous, uncalculated, even outlandish. And who knows? In our own cultural context, the object of such extravagant love on Christ's behalf might be none other than the poor!

If the woman at Bethany has attracted interest as a model of love and devotion, Judas Iscariot has received still greater attention as a model of betrayal. The fact that the NT provides few clues to explain Judas' action has led to various speculations. As noted earlier, the text itself moves in the direction of attributing the act to a serious character flaw (cf. also John 12:6). Many subsequent writers pursue this line with relish, portraying Judas as the classic villain (cf. Calvin, 1972, 3:125-126).

In recent times, interpreters have asked whether Judas might have acted out of more complex motives. Might Judas have been trying to force Jesus' hand, to get him to raise an army or call on *legions of angels* (26:53) to free Israel from Roman rule? Was Judas disillusioned, betraying Jesus because he believed that Jesus had betrayed the hopes people had placed in him? Did Judas perhaps come to share the view of the chief priests that Jesus was a false prophet?

Whether one or another of these explanations is historically correct, we cannot say. What is clear is that the figure of Judas presented in the text represents a tragic possibility for disciples in every age, the possibility of betrayal. To be close to Jesus is to have the perilous opportunity either to further Jesus' mission or to subvert it.

A Farewell Gathering

Matthew 26:17-46

PREVIEW

The second unit of Matthew's passion narrative consists of several scenes in which Jesus is together with his disciples for the last time. Throughout this section, the centerpiece of which is a farewell meal, the mood is one of saying goodbye and letting go. Jesus here confronts the way death will sever old ties and struggles to accept the script of suffering before him. A further indicator that Matthew views the various scenes as belonging together is the literary inclusion formed by verses 18 and 45: When Jesus announces at the end of the unit that *the hour is at hand,* his words echo a similar pronouncement at the outset: *My time is near.* The two phrases bracket the unit and define the context in which the various episodes unfold.

The material Matthew presents in this section comes from Mark 14:12-42, which includes the same sequence of events: Preparation for Passover, a table conversation about betrayal, the Last Supper itself (including Jesus' words about the bread and cup), a prediction of abandonment and denial, and Jesus' prayers in Gethsemane. Each of these episodes contains memorable pronouncements by Jesus, some of which appear in the outline below.

OUTLINE

I Will Keep the Passover, 26:17-19

One of You Will Betray Me, 26:20-25

This Is My Body, 26:26-29

This Night You Will Deny Me, 26:30-35

Your Will Be Done, 26:36-46

EXPLANATORY NOTES

I Will Keep the Passover 26:17-19

The text places the episode before us on *the first day of Unleavened Bread.* Technically, the festival would not have started until the sundown when Thursday the fourteenth of Nisan ended and Friday the fifteenth of Nisan began. Here the language is used somewhat loosely to encompass the daytime hours on Thursday, when persons prepared for the occasion.

These preparations included the disposal of all leavened bread, the baking of unleavened bread, and the slaughter of a Passover lamb. In the Fourth Gospel, the author follows a chronology of events in which Jesus is *crucified* on the day of preparation (cf. John 19:14-30). In Matthew, however (as in Mark and Luke), Jesus and his disciples prepare and eat a Passover meal, and Jesus is not crucified until the following morning or afternoon.

When the disciples approach Jesus in verse 17, the question foremost on their minds is finding a suitable place for the Passover. Jesus replies in a manner that recalls his instructions to the disciples in 21:1-3 as he neared Jerusalem: *Go into the village . . . and immediately you will find. . . .* Here the command reads: *Go into the city to a certain man and say. . . .* In each case Jesus speaks with a kind of sovereignty, knowing that all will be cared for, and the disciples need only to act on his word.

Noteworthy in the message this time is the pronouncement mentioned above: *My time is near.* The saying has an apocalyptic ring, in which *time* (Greek: *kairos*) refers to a critical moment in God's design to inaugurate the age to come. According to Matthew, Jesus' death and resurrection is just such a critical moment, and that moment has now arrived (cf. John 12:23; 16:32).

One of You Will Betray Me 26:20-25

As the curtain goes up on the second scene, we find Jesus and the twelve *reclining at the table* (NIV), ready to celebrate Passover. Jesus abruptly changes the mood from gladness to gloom by announcing that his soon-to-be-betrayer is a member of the dinner party. Dismayed at the news, the disciples take turns asking the question: *It isn't I, is it? Surely you don't mean me, do you?*

The answer Jesus gives in verse 23 leaves the disciples hanging, for every one of them has dipped their bread into the same common dish. The saying does not identify a specific individual, but simply underscores the fact that betrayal will come by someone close to Jesus, someone at the supper. As Jesus' reply continues in verse 24, he accents the horrendous culpability his betrayer bears (cf. 27:3-4), even though this event will become part of God's script for redemption (*The Son of Man goes* as it is written . . .).

Finally, the conversation narrows to a private exchange between Judas and Jesus found only in the First Gospel. As did the others, Judas poses the question: *Surely not I?* Whereas the others addressed Jesus as *Lord,* however, Judas calls him *Rabbi* (v. 25; cf. 26:49), the title an outsider or enemy might use. It is a sign that Judas is distancing himself from the circle of faith. Knowing full well that Judas is playing a game, Jesus answers with an ambiguous reply he will use again later in the narrative (26:64; 27:11): *You have said so.* It is a way of saying yes without saying yes, making the questioner assume responsibility for the answer. To Judas, then, Jesus says in effect: *You know the answer to that one!*

This Is My Body 26:26-29

Tabletalk continues in scene three of the unit as Jesus, according to Jewish practice, takes bread and wine, and blesses and thanks God for them. Then he redefines their significance and invites the disciples to partake. In the setting of the text, this moment in the story is usually labeled "the Last Supper." In the setting of the church, when the ritual of bread and cup is reenacted, the event is called the Lord's Supper, communion, or eucharist. The latter name derives from the Greek verb *eucharisteō*, *giving thanks*, which is used in verse 27.

Frequently the words of Jesus cited in the text are referred to as the "words of institution." Thus they are viewed as instructions that *institute* the celebration of the Lord's Supper in the life of Jesus' community. We may safely assume that the text was in fact read this way in the early church, and two minor additions Matthew makes to Mark's account may reflect liturgical usage of Jesus' words: Matthew adds the word *eat* after *take* in the statement about the bread, and he includes an instruction to *drink* from the cup.

Within the boundaries of the Gospel story, the most natural way to view what Jesus does at the Last Supper is as *parabolic action*, which Jesus interprets through the words he speaks. The breaking and distributing of the bread acts out what Jesus is doing with his body/self for the sake of others. The pouring and offering of the cup acts out the way Jesus' lifeblood will be sacrificed for the sake of others. It is in this sense that Jesus proclaims *this is my body* and *this is my blood.*

In the case of the cup, the interpretation is longer, and Matthew extends it even further with the addition of the phrase *for the forgiveness of sins* (v. 28; cf. 1:21; Rev. 1:5). The words *for many* reflect language used to describe the role of the suffering servant in Isaiah 53 (cf. 53:10-12), with *many* denoting the numberless multitudes for whom one individual acts.

Blood of the covenant alludes to the blood ceremony by which the covenant at Sinai was established (cf. Exod. 24:8; Zech. 9:11), and the identification of the covenant with *Jesus'* blood suggests a new or altered covenant (cf. Jer. 31:31; Luke 22:20; Rom. 3:25). According to Matthew, the covenant made at Sinai is "renewed and embodied in Jesus himself. He becomes the living blood bond between God and God's people" (Senior, 1985b:67).

By *eating* the bread and *drinking* the cup, the disciples will signify their desire to be part of this living blood bond. They will be acting out their own parable in response to the action Jesus initiated. All of this,

Jesus tells us in verse 29, anticipates that moment when the fellowship of the Last Supper is renewed and fulfilled at the endtime table of God's kingdom (cf. 22:1-14; Rev. 19:9; Isa. 25:5-8).

This Night You Will Deny Me 26:30-35

It was customary to conclude the Passover by singing Psalms 114—118, a collection of praise psalms called the Hallel (= praise). The text alludes to this custom in verse 30, where the action shifts from the supper table to the Mount of Olives. Once again Jesus introduces a discordant note into a normally festive event, this time with a prediction of abandonment and denial. *You will all become deserters,* Jesus says, using a verb that connotes taking offense or stumbling over something (cf. 11:6; 13:57; 15:12). For a time, Jesus' impending ordeal will be too much for his followers to deal with; they will dissociate themselves from him and run the other way.

This too is "according to the book," and the specific text Jesus cites is Zechariah 13:7, where the prophecy goes on to describe the scattered sheep as "little ones" (cf. Matt. 18:6-9). Through God's power, Jesus as shepherd will triumph over death and regather his scattered flock when he rejoins them in Galilee (cf. 28:7, 10, 16). As Donald Senior observes, what the text depicts is a passion experience of Jesus' community that corresponds to his own (Senior, 1985b:72). Both are governed by the motif of death and resurrection.

Peter, true to form, will have none of this. Having earlier refused to accept the fact that Jesus would suffer (16:21-23), he is now equally adamant that he will stick with Jesus through it all. Whatever others do, *I will never desert you.* No matter what the cost, *I will not deny you.* As Jesus knows, however, Peter's courage will not match his rhetoric. Before daybreak (when the cock crows), Peter will in fact deny Jesus, not just once but three times. That is to say, his denial will be total.

Your Will Be Done 26:36-46

Gethsemane, which means *oil press,* was presumably a grove of olive trees on the western slope of the Mount of Olives (cf. "garden," John 18:1). It is there that the final scene of the unit transpires. Echoing Abraham's words to his servants in Genesis 22:5 (where another sacrifice was about to occur), Jesus asks the disciples to sit/stay while he goes *over there* to pray.

No less than Abraham, Jesus is faced with an overwhelming assignment, one in which he must yield himself as the sacrifice. Knowing what lies before him, he wants support as he prays, and the disciples he chooses to accompany him are the same three present at his transfiguration (17:1-13). It is to them that Jesus confides his deepest feelings: *My soul is overwhelmed with sorrow, to the point of death* (v. 38, NIV). The words come primarily from Psalm 42:6 (cf. also Jon. 4:9), a psalm of lament which fits the situation and provides a backdrop for Jesus' prayers.

The prayers themselves are clearly numbered (cf. vv. 42, 44), supplying an overarching structure for the episode. For two of the three prayers, words of Jesus are quoted in which he asks to be spared from drinking the *cup,* meaning the cup of suffering (vv. 39 and 42; cf. 20:22-23; 26:27-28). Jesus is no would-be martyr, eager to give up his life. Nevertheless, even as he prays for other options, he expresses his commitment to subordinate his desires to God's design (cf. 6:10). On moving to the second prayer, we detect a certain progression in the way Jesus articulates this commitment. In the first instance, he prays somewhat optimistically: *If it is possible, let this cup pass from me.* In the second, he seems to know that he will not find a way out: *If this* cannot pass unless *I drink it, your will be done.*

In between the three petitions Jesus makes, there are interludes in which he returns to his three companions and finds them sleeping (vv. 40, 43). They have proved unable to fulfill Jesus' request to keep watch with him in an hour of crisis (v. 38b). The language of watching or keeping awake is highly metaphorical, suggesting the need for God's servants to be prepared for the traumatic events by which the kingdom comes (cf. 24:42-43; 25:13; 1 Thess. 5:1-11; 1 Pet. 5:8). To put it another way: The ordeal of impending suffering that Jesus confronts at Gethsemane is but the first of a series of eschatological crises calling for readiness on the part of his community.

Thus Jesus elaborates on his command to watch in verse 41, urging prayerful vigilance in order to remain faithful when faith is tested. In contrasting spirit and flesh, Jesus is not speaking of a dualism of soul and body. Instead, he is describing "two opposing tendencies struggling for domination within the one body-person" (Senior, 1985b:81). We are to watch and pray, then, so that the fleshly tendency to evil and weakness does not gain the upper hand, jeopardizing our commitments as persons of faith.

As the scene concludes (vv. 45-46), the three disciples are still groggy from sleep, anything but ready. The crisis of Jesus' passion will leave them totally disoriented, as he has already predicted. Jesus himself, however, is fully ready, for he has followed his own counsel to watch and pray. Taking charge once again, he tells the disciples that it is time to go forth and meet what is coming. The hour of betrayal has arrived (cf. v. 18), and so has the betrayer.

THE TEXT IN BIBLICAL CONTEXT

Only twenty years had elapsed since Jesus' death, when Paul wrote to the church at Corinth: "For I received from the Lord what I also handed on to you, that the Lord Jesus on the night when he was betrayed took a loaf of bread, and when he had given thanks, he broke it and said 'This is my body that is for you. Do this in remembrance of me' " (1 Cor. 11:23-24; cf. also vv. 25-26).

This reference to the Last Supper is all the more striking when one notes how seldom Paul cites the story of Jesus in his letters. It is obviously a tradition that is bedrock material for the life of the church. Confirming this fact is the presence of a Last Supper account in all four Gospels, although in the supper story the Fourth Gospel curiously substitutes the story of foot washing for the episode of the bread and cup (cf. John 13:1-17).

More intriguing than simply tabulating the NT references to the Last Supper is observing how it enters into the theological reflection of certain authors. In 1 Corinthians, Paul speaks of the Lord's Supper both as a rite of remembrance and anticipation (11:26) and as an experience through which we participate in Christ or enjoy communion with Christ (10:14-22). The latter text goes on to stress that believers must choose between the table of the Lord and sacred meals honoring other deities; participation in both would amount to idolatry.

In the Fourth Gospel, the bread-talk missing at the Last Supper surfaces in a more developed form in the discourse on the bread of life in John 6. There, following the feeding of the five thousand, Jesus describes himself in eucharistic terms: "I am the living bread that came down from heaven. Whoever eats of this bread will live forever; and the bread that I will give for the life of the world is my flesh" (6:51).

To listen to language like this is to perceive how the church's worship both grows out of and breaks with the worship of Israel. The backdrop to the Last Supper is clearly the drama of the exodus as commemorated at Passover. Now, however, a new act of deliverance has occurred; a new covenant has been established; and a new festival is in order. Christ is "our paschal lamb" (1 Cor. 5:7), and Christ is the bread from heaven that replaces manna (John 6:48-50). To put it another way: It is in Christ's death and resurrection that the church finds the ritual center for its life.

THE TEXT IN THE LIFE OF THE CHURCH

Of all the texts in the NT, few if any have left their imprint on the life of the church more visibly than the accounts of the Last Supper. From earliest days on, Christian communities were adapting the tradition attested in Matthew for their own celebration of the Lord's Supper. How frequently the celebration occurred, and whether it was attached to or separate from the fellowship or *agapē* meals of the community, are questions still disputed. What is certain is that a service of the bread and cup came to occupy a central place in the liturgy of the early catholic church—and in most subsequent Christian traditions as well.

Sadly, the same text has also been the source of bitter controversy. Much of the controversy has revolved around the so-called words of institution. What did Jesus mean when he said, *This is my body* and *This is my blood*? What does or doesn't happen when we make similar pronouncements as a part of the eucharist?

According to one stream of tradition, the words of institution effect a change in the bread and wine, such that the elements themselves in some way become Christ's body and blood. (The technical term for the change in the elements is *transubstantiation*.) At the other end of the spectrum is the Radical Protestant view, whose proponents may speak of the bread and wine as "only symbols." Here the bread and wine are viewed like pictures in a book, as figures that simply illustrate a reality that lies outside of or beyond the eucharist. Eucharist is observed in this case as a rite of remembrance ordained by Jesus (an ordinance), but not as a sacrament of communion.

Somewhere between the Catholic and Radical Protestant views of eucharist is the tradition that speaks of the "real presence" of Christ in the Lord's Supper. As the term implies, those adhering to this view believe that Christ makes himself present to the communicant in and through the bread and cup as the elements are partaken. How this happens remains a mystery of faith.

In the Anabaptist tradition, many voices echo the Radical Protestant view described above (cf. Klaassen: 190ff.; Eller). Menno Simons, however, speaks of the Lord's Supper in a way that moves beyond this view, using the vocabulary of sacrament and mystery as well as that of sign (Klaassen: 208-210; Menno Simons: 142-151). For Menno, the Lord's Supper is at one and the same time an act of remembrance, an act of unity among the members who eat together, and *an act of communion*.

A contemporary Anabaptist theology of the Lord's Supper might begin with the premise that Christ is sacramentally present at all times *in his community* (cf. Matt. 1:23; 18:20; 28:20). Because this is so, the community can and does *commune* with Christ when it reenacts the parabolic drama of the Last Supper in its eucharistic gatherings. For some churches, the richness of the drama is enhanced as eucharist is combined with other features of the Last Supper such as a fellowship meal, foot washing, or both. With or without this fuller script, something powerful happens when we partake of the Lord's Supper. We not only remember, but are renewed within the loving bond with God and with one another that Jesus established through his death and resurrection.

Whatever tradition we hold concerning eucharist, it is critical that we open ourselves to the power of the story it acts out. The Lord's Supper is not merely a rite of the church, for us to guard or cherish. It is a portrayal of Love giving itself in death to redeem the *world*. To *eat* the bread and *drink* the cup, then, is not only a matter of replenishing ourselves. It is a declaration of solidarity with Christ on behalf of all who yearn for God's deliverance.

In the Hour of Trial

Matthew 26:47—27:10

PREVIEW

When the hour of arrest finally comes, how do Jesus and those around him conduct themselves? The unit before us lets us visualize the answer through a series of episodes that begins with Judas' betrayal and ends with Judas' suicide. As illustrated below, these episodes evolve in a chiastic pattern:

a. Judas betrays Jesus' life
    b. Jesus accused by his enemies
        c. Peter denies Jesus
    b'. Jesus condemned by his enemies
a'. Judas takes his own life

All but one of the five episodes come from the Markan narrative (cf. Mark 14:43—15:1), the exception being the report of Judas' remorse and death. The latter seems to be based on an oral tradition known to Matthew, a tradition that took different forms in the church's memory (cf. another version in Acts 1:15-20).

OUTLINE

Betrayed with a Kiss, 26:47-56

Faithful Under Fire, 26:57-68

Denial Under Duress, 26:69-75

Decision for Death, 27:1-2

Consequences of Betrayal, 27:3-10

EXPLANATORY NOTES

Betrayed with a Kiss 26:47-56

The spectacle that unfolds in verses 47-56 is both ludicrous and tragic. It is ludicrous in that the arrest party descends on Jesus like a group of commandos on a search-and-destroy mission (cf. v. 55). It is tragic in that this militant crowd is led by *one of the twelve,* namely Judas. The kiss with which Judas identifies Jesus was a customary sign of honor for greeting a rabbi (which is once again the title Judas uses to address Jesus; cf. 26:25). Here though the gesture is more akin to the kiss of Joab in 2 Samuel 20:8-10, who plunged a sword into Amasa as he reached out to embrace him! When Jesus calls Judas *Friend,* therefore, the tone is clearly ironic (cf. 20:13; 22:12), and the elliptical phrase that follows expresses Jesus' awareness of and consent to what is about to happen: *Do what you are here to do* (the Greek text reads literally, *For what you are here*).

The arrest then proceeds, but not without incident. As in Mark's account, someone draws a sword and slices off the ear of the high priest's slave. Matthew, however, portrays the incident, not as a random act of violence on the part of the crowd, but as an act of defense by one of Jesus' followers (cf. John 18:10, where the follower is further identified as Peter). This sets the stage for the sayings in verses 52-54, in which Jesus declines such defense, sayings found only in

Matthew's version of the story. As others have observed, the sayings offer three reasons for Jesus' rejection of armed defense:

(1) Violence is a strategy that ultimately destroys those who adopt it (v. 52, a proverb-like saying that may hint at Rome's crushing of the Jewish rebellion in A.D. 70; cf. Revelation 13:10; Jeremiah 15:2).

(2) If Jesus wanted military assistance for his mission, he could have countless divine warriors at his side in an instant (v. 53, where *twelve legions* equals a fighting force of 72,000 combatants!)

(3) Defense of Jesus would in fact prevent him from fulfilling the Scriptures that call him to the cross (v. 54).

As the scene concludes, Jesus chides his captors for making their move in the secrecy of the night (v. 55), then reiterates the theme that this ugly undertaking will nevertheless fulfill *the scriptures of the prophets* (v. 56). The emphasis on the prophets is characteristic of the First Gospel. Matthew underscores the prophetic dimension of Scripture at several points (cf. 5:17; 11:13; 13:35), and he turns to the prophets time and again for the fulfillment quotations that abound in his narrative (cf. 1:22-23; 4:15-16; 21:4-5).

Faithful Under Fire 26:57-68

With Jesus in custody, and with the disciples in flight (cf. v. 56b), the action shifts from Gethsemane to the palace of Caiaphas, the high priest. There Jesus will undergo a hearing conducted by Jewish authorities. Before he reports on this hearing, Matthew alerts the reader to Peter's presence as an observer in the courtyard (v. 58). This sets the stage for the episode in verses 69-75.

Viewed historically, Jesus' examination by Jewish authorities raises several issues. Data such as the location (the high priest's residence) and the hour (a meeting by night) suggests a hearing by a select group or special judicial arm of the council (Sanhedrin). Matthew and Mark, however, depict the event as a hearing by *the whole council* (v. 59), in which the chief priests, elders, and scribes are all present.

Whatever the scope of the hearing, we know that the council did not have the final authority to carry out capital sentences. The purpose the hearing serves, then, is that of gathering data to buttress the case that the authorities will make before Pilate. Hence, the text tells us, the council sought *false testimony against Jesus.* They were looking for testimony to incriminate Jesus, whether credible or not.

The only charge on which two witnesses can agree (Jewish law required the evidence of at least two witnesses to condemn a person to death; cf. Deut. 17:6) is the saying attributed to Jesus in verse 61: *I am able to destroy the temple of God and to build it in three days.* Nowhere in Matthew's Gospel does Jesus make such a pronouncement (the closest parallel is John 2:19; cf. G. Thom. 71). Jesus does, however, assert his authority over the temple (21:12-16; cf. also 12:6), and predicts the destruction of the temple (24:2; 23:38).

Further, Matthew sees Jesus' death and resurrection as inaugurating a new reality that replaces the institutions of Israel (cf. 27:51-54). The testimony of the two witnesses is thus not labeled false, even though it is maliciously motivated. For the high priest, the testimony is pertinent insofar as talk about erecting a new temple might imply messianic claims (cf. Targum to Isa. 53:5). Consequently, he pushes Jesus to respond to his accusers (v. 62), and getting nowhere, confronts Jesus with a direct question about his messiahship (v. 63).

Caiaphas' question is noteworthy in at least two respects: (1) It is cast in the language of Peter's confession of faith in 16:16. (2) It admonishes Jesus to answer under oath (cf. 1 Kings 22:16). Consistent with his opposition to oaths (cf. 5:33-37), Jesus answers the question indirectly: *You have said so* (v. 64a; cf. 26:25). Jesus says in effect: *You have made my confession for me!*

Jesus goes on then to make his own statement about his relationship to his accusers (v. 64b), a statement resembling other Son of Man sayings in the Gospel (cf. 16:27-28; 19:28; 24:29-31) drawing on imagery from Psalm 110:1 and Daniel 7:13-14. A paraphrase of Jesus' words might read: *The one you are judging now will meet you later as your exalted judge from heaven!* It is this claim that evokes the outburst described in verses 65-66, in which Jesus is charged with the capital offense of blasphemy (cf. Lev. 24:16). This the high priest certifies by the symbolic gesture of tearing his robes (cf. Sanh. 7:5). Following is a scene of mockery (vv. 67-68), a counterpart to the later mocking of Jesus by Roman soldiers (27:27-31). A final decision on Jesus' fate is not yet reached, however. It is suspended while the spotlight shifts to another scene to one side of the center stage.

Denial Under Duress 26:69-75

The scene with Peter in Caiaphas' courtyard is presented as a subplot that unfolds during the same time that Jesus' hearing is going on. Such a juxtaposition of scenes invites the reader to contrast the calm and courageous witness Jesus bears with the sorry way Peter conducts himself. The form of the episode is a series of three statements to Peter by others in the courtyard tying him to Jesus and the disciples. Each challenge evokes a protest from Peter denying any connection.

Moreover, Peter's denial-statements build in intensity. In his reply to the first servant girl (vv. 69-70), Peter attempts to evade the issue: *I do not know what you are talking about.* In his reply to the second servant girl (vv. 71-72), Peter takes an *oath* to support his disclaimer (acting more like an outsider than a disciple; cf. 5:34). Finally, when he is pressed by a whole group of bystanders who recognize his distinctive Galilean accent (vv. 73-74), he invokes a curse to underscore his denial of any ties with Jesus. (It is unclear whether Peter invokes this curse on himself or on Jesus; cf. 1 Cor. 12:3.)

Already in the first exchange, Matthew tells us that Peter's denial of Jesus was *before all of them* (v. 70). The wording here picks up the language of the mission discourse, where Jesus contrasts those who acknowledge him *before others* and those who deny him *before others* (10:32-33; cf. 5:16). For the moment at least, Peter stands with those whose faith wilts and withers in a time of testing. As the scene ends (v. 75), the crowing of the rooster reminds Peter and the reader of Jesus' fateful prediction earlier that night (26:34). It is a reminder that moves Peter to bitter weeping, a response that suggests both a crushing awareness of failure and a sense of repentance that can lead beyond failure.

Decision for Death 27:1-2

While Peter weeps, Matthew directs our attention back to Jesus' hearing. There, after the night session, the members of the council take formal action at daybreak. They *came to the decision to put Jesus to death* (NIV) and *handed him over* to Pilate to carry out their wishes. Earlier in the narrative, one of the predictions of Jesus' passion informed us that *the Son of Man will be handed over to the chief priests and scribes, and they will condemn him to death; then they will hand him over to the Gentiles* (20:18-19). All that has now come to pass, Matthew tells us.

Consequences of Betrayal 27:3-10

The episode of betrayal with which the unit began finds its sequel in a dismal report of how the betrayer ends his life. According to verse 3, Judas has stayed close enough to the proceedings that he can *see* the outcome, and he is *seized with remorse* (NIV) when he realizes the miscarriage of justice to which he is a party. (The word translated *repented* in the NRSV is not the usual NT word for repentance, which implies radical conversion, but rather a term that suggests *feeling* differently than before, such as feelings of regret or remorse.)

Judas' remorse leads him to try to undo his pact with the chief priests. It is a futile course, however, for the cynical authorities have no interest in either Judas' guilt (cf. Deut. 27:25) or in Jesus' innocence. And so, with no apparent way out, Judas succumbs to despair and hangs himself (cf. 2 Sam. 17:23 for an OT incident that parallels the story of Judas).

As indicated earlier, a report of Judas' violent death appears in both Matthew and Acts, and both accounts connect this event to a field called the *Field of Blood.* The accounts differ, however, as to how it all transpires. According to Acts, Judas himself buys the field, and the field acquires its name as a result of a gory accident in which *Judas'* blood splatters the field (Acts 1:18-19). In Matthew, on the other hand (cf. vv. 6-8), where Judas dies by hanging, the priests buy the field with the *blood money* Judas returned to them, and it is that factor which accounts for the name *Field of Blood.*

Whatever the exact course of events, the memory of Judas' demise reconstructed by Matthew fits well in his narrative. At one level, it confirms the picture of Israel's leaders as hypocrites (cf. 15:1ff.; 23:13ff.). While the leaders have no compunction about condemning *innocent blood,* they become quite scrupulous about the proper disposition of the *blood money* paid to achieve their end (v. 6; cf. Deut. 22:19).

At another level, the story further links the events of Jesus' passion to *the scriptures of the prophets.* It contains details that also appear together in both Zechariah and Jeremiah (cf. Zech. 11:12-13; Jer. 18:2-3; 19:1-13; 32:6-9), details such as the pieces of silver, potter, field, and burial ground. For Matthew, these verbal parallels are more than coincidences; rather, they signify that the story of Judas fulfills ancient prophecies. Thus Matthew ends the account with a composite fulfillment quotation drawn from these passages (vv. 9-10), inviting readers to discover the connections for themselves.

THE TEXT IN BIBLICAL CONTEXT

As Matthew tells the story in the unit before us, he does so in a manner that allows several sharp profiles to emerge. One is the profile of

Judas, a picture of both duplicity and despair. A second profile is that of Peter, whose failure of faith in Caiaphas' courtyard stands over against his discerning confession of faith at Caesarea Philippi. The most carefully developed profile, however, is that of Jesus himself as we behold him in the midst of his arrest and hearing. The contours of that profile are noteworthy in at least two respects.

First, the Jesus we observe here acts in a manner congruent with his own teaching earlier in the Gospel. Having challenged his disciples to risk losing *their* lives for the sake of his mission (16:24-28), he himself does not turn and run to save *his* life. Instead, he submits willingly to his destiny of suffering. Having taught his listeners to love their enemies and to refrain from violent acts of retaliation (5:38-48), he himself forswears the option of violence when it is offered during his arrest. Having urged his followers not to be anxious when they face hostile authorities, but to bear faithful testimony (10:16-39), he himself maintains composure and displays courage in the witness he gives before the council. In other words, Jesus exemplifies the correspondence between word and deed that is so important in Matthew's Gospel.

Second, the Jesus we observe here embodies the experiences attributed to God's suffering, righteous servants in the OT story. Like them, he is accused falsely: "False witnesses have risen against me, and they are breathing out violence" (Ps. 27:12; cf. Matt. 26:60; Pss. 35:11; 37:32). Like them, he stands silent before his accusers: "Like a lamb that is led to the slaughter, and like a sheep that before its shearers is silent, so he did not open his mouth" (Isa. 53:7; cf. Matt. 26:63; Pss. 38:14; 39:9). Like them, he is subjected to cruel mockery: "I gave my back to those who struck me, and my cheeks to those who pulled out the beard; I did not hide my face from insult and spitting" (Isa. 50:6; cf. Matt. 26:67-68; 27:30).

Still other points of correspondence will appear later in the narrative of the crucifixion (cf. 27:32-50 and Ps. 22). For Matthew, the passion of Jesus is a story in which earlier cries of suffering in the biblical drama take flesh anew in powerful and climactic fashion. To put it another way: *It is in Jesus that Israel's vocation as God's suffering, righteous servant is finally fulfilled.*

THE TEXT IN THE LIFE OF THE CHURCH

The three profiles presented in the text have all played a significant role in the subsequent teaching of the church. Judas' portrayal, not unlike that of Benedict Arnold in the history of the United States, has become a paradigm of betrayal (cf. TLC for 26:1-16). In a similar manner, Peter's denial is lifted up repeatedly as an example of how even pillars of faith can collapse and crumble. Like the later picture of Ananias and Sapphira in Acts 5, the negative models of Judas and Peter have been used to admonish the faithful: "Don't let this happen to you."

Quite different in character is the profile of Jesus, in which the church has found positive clues for its own vocation from earliest times. Of the various facets of this profile, none has proved more intriguing than the stance Jesus takes regarding violence in 26:52: *Put your sword back into its place; for all who take the sword will perish by the sword.* It is likely that this saying had the conduct of Jesus' community in mind from the outset, perhaps as counsel to refrain from joining in popular rebellions.

Whatever its original scope, the saying has been interpreted in widely differing ways in the centuries that followed. Many, like Calvin, have limited its applicability to situations where individuals take the law into their hands and act violently to rectify matters (1972, 3:159-160). From this perspective, the saying does not rule out participation in war and violent punishment of offenders ordained by governing powers. Even a few Anabaptist voices support this understanding of the text (cf. Balthasar Hubmaier in Klaassen: 271-272).

In most believers church circles, however, the prevailing view sees Jesus' saying as forbidding any use of violence by Jesus' followers: "We teach and acknowledge no other sword, nor tumult in the kingdom or church of Christ, than the sharp sword of the Spirit, God's Word. . . . The civil sword we leave to those to whom it is committed. Let everyone be careful lest he transgress in the matter of the sword, lest he perish with the sword. Matt. 26:52" (Menno Simons: 200). Along similar lines, the 1785 Annual Meeting of the Church of the Brethren responded to issues growing out of the American Revolutionary War as follows:

> We do not understand . . . that we can give ourselves up to do violence, or that we should submit to the higher powers in such a manner as to make ourselves their instruments to shed men's blood. . . . Our loving Saviour, though innocent, was attacked in a murderous manner . . . and Peter was quick and ready to draw his sword according to the legal justice of God. . . . But what says the Saviour: "Put your sword back into its place, for all who take the sword will perish by the sword." (Durnbaugh, 1967:356)

In our own situation, Jesus' saying clearly undergirds a commitment to nonviolence on the part of the church—but it goes beyond that. As noted earlier, Jesus' call to renounce the sword is based on a proverbial observation about the way violence breeds violence in the world. Violence is not only inappropriate for the vocation of Jesus' community, but a destructive course for the human family as a whole. The saying, therefore, provides a basis from which the church can invite both its own membership and society at large to look for alternatives to violence in addressing social issues.

A Crucified King

Matthew 27:11-56

PREVIEW

In the two preceding units of the passion narrative, the action first revolves around Jesus and his disciples (26:17-46), then around Jesus and his Jewish captors (26:47—27:10). Now, with the prisoner turned over to Pilate, the story shifts to Jesus' fate at the hands of the Gentiles. He will be tried by a Roman governor, mocked by Gentile soldiers, and crucified by these same soldiers. Bracketing the unit are a question and a confession, both of which deal with Jesus' identity. At the outset Pilate asks his prisoner: *Are you the King of the Jews?* The surprising confession that the Roman centurion and his cohorts make near the end of the unit affirms that Jesus is this and more: *Truly this man was God's Son.* For this part of the story, Matthew draws on the account in Mark 15:2-41, which he adapts and expands at several points along the way.

OUTLINE

What Shall I Do with Jesus? 27:11-26

Hail, King of the Jews, 27:27-31

Jesus on the Cross, 27:32-44

Truly This Was God's Son, 27:45-54

Faithful to the End, 27:55-56

EXPLANATORY NOTES

What Shall I Do with Jesus? 27:11-26

As Pilate interrogates Jesus, the proceedings turn on the charge that Jesus purports to be *the King of the Jews.* The title, which plays a key role throughout the unit (cf. vv. 30, 37), is formulated from the vantage point of a non-Jew or outsider (cf. 2:1-2). A Jew would be more inclined to speak of *the King of Israel* (the expression we find in v. 42). What the title alleges is that Jesus is a messianic pretender, a threat to Rome and to Pilate's rule on behalf of Rome.

When Pilate asks Jesus if the title fits, Jesus responds with the same ambivalent expression he has used twice earlier in the story: *You say so* (cf. *You have said so* in 26:25, 64). It is a reply in which the reader who knows the story of the magi (2:1-12) will hear a positive answer. At the same time, it avoids *saying* yes to the bristling political overtones of the title. Therefore, Jesus' accusers continue to press their case. Neither to them nor to Pilate, however, does Jesus have anything else to say. Instead, he maintains the silence already noted (cf. 26:62-63; Ps. 39:1b, 9; Isa. 53:7).

Sensing that the motives of Jesus' accusers are less than honorable, but not wanting to incur their ill will, Pilate opts to let the crowd make his decision for him. Further influencing his course of action is some advice from his wife peculiar to Matthew's account, confirming Jesus' innocence and urging the governor not to get entangled. (Note that once again, as in the infancy narrative, God advises persons through their dreams; cf. 1:20; 2:12, 13, 19).

The strategy Pilate pursues involves an otherwise unknown custom of releasing a Jewish prisoner of the people's choosing at Passover. In the case at hand, the choice Pilate offers is between two prisoners named Jesus—Jesus Barabbas and Jesus Christ! The story implies that Pilate hopes the crowd will choose the one called Messiah rather than the *notorious* Barabbas, and thereby relieve him from ruling on Jesus' guilt or innocence. Not so, however. The text portrays the crowds as fully under the sway of the leaders who seek to destroy Jesus. As a result, the crowd demands amnesty for Barabbas and crucifixion for Jesus.

Concluding the trial scene is Pilate's gesture of washing his hands to absolve himself of responsibility for killing the innocent. It is a strange twist to the story, since the rite described is based on an OT practice rather than Roman judicial custom (cf. Deut. 21:1-9). What is strange from a historical perspective, however, creates rich irony from a literary and religious standpoint. The pagan Pilate acts like a good Israelite to separate himself from a deed that violates covenant justice, while the people of the covenant eagerly embrace responsibility for this deed: *His blood be on us and on our children* (v. 25).

Note how the text portrays this declaration as an outcry of *the people as a whole*. According to Matthew, it is Israel acting corporately that seeks Jesus' death and invites the consequences it will bring. In so doing, it continues to live out of the script of its forebears who shed the innocent blood of the prophets (cf. Jer. 26:15; Matt. 21:33-44; 23:29-32). How to use and interpret a text like this is a matter we will take up later. Meanwhile, the story itself moves on, and Pilate yields to the wishes of the crowd, consigning Jesus to death.

Hail, King of the Jews 27:27-31

After Jesus is subjected to the harsh flogging that typically preceded a crucifixion (v. 26), he undergoes yet another preliminary ordeal. He is mocked by Pilate's soldiers, just as earlier he had been mocked by members of the Sanhedrin (26:67-68). The place where this episode unfolds is the praetorium, the residence of Pilate during his brief stays in Jerusalem. (Normally the Roman governor resided at Caesarea.) At full strength, the battalion of Syrian and other auxiliary troops at Pilate's disposal would number 600 or more. Here *the whole cohort* that makes sport of Jesus likely is considerably smaller.

As described by Matthew, the act of mocking proceeds in two stages. First, the soldiers engage in a parody of Jesus' alleged kingship (vv. 28-29). The scarlet robe they place on him was likely a red soldier's tunic. Together with the crown of thorns (as royal diadem) and reed (as royal scepter), the robe adorns Jesus as a vassal king. Likewise, when the soldiers pay mock homage and utter *Hail, King of the Jews,* their words mimic "Ave Caesar," used to hail the emperor.

For the soldiers, all of this is sheer jesting, and cruel jesting at that. Unwittingly, however, the soldiers are proclaiming the lordship of Jesus that the reader knows is his true destiny. The second stage of the mocking consists of the physical abuse noted in verse 30 (cf. again Isa. 50:6). At last the soldiers tire of their game, reclothe Jesus in his own garments, and lead him away to his death.

Jesus on the Cross 27:32-44

Crucifixion, by all accounts, was a barbarous and extremely painful means of execution. Its victims included various despised elements of society, such as slaves, bandits, and those condemned for sedition. Indeed, such is the company Jesus shares when he is crucified (see v. 38). The potential is here, then, for a gory melodrama, which thankfully the Gospel writers choose not to present.

Marked by brevity and reserve, the report of Jesus' crucifixion begins by noting the assistance he needed in carrying the horizontal bar of the cross (the upright beam would already have been in place). The destination, we are told, was called Skullplace, whether because the terrain of the site resembled a skull, or simply because the site was a place of death. It is there, in any case, that Jesus is hoisted on the cross, after he declines the slightly narcotic drink often offered to a prisoner.

In customary fashion, Jesus' clothes are divided among his executioners, and a placard erected proclaiming his offense. With Jesus himself labeled as a would-be *King*, the two robbers or insurrectionists at either side appear as royal attendants of his pitiful court. The episode ends, at last, with yet another scene of mockery, in which three successive groups of people deride Jesus—first some bypassers, then the religious leaders, and finally the two robbers.

Though brief in scope, the report Matthew gives is rich with biblical allusions. More specifically, the language used reflects the language of the Psalms at several points. Note the parallels below:

(1) The drink given to Jesus (v. 34): "They gave me poison (LXX: gall) for food, and for my thirst they gave me vinegar to drink" (Ps. 69:21).

(2) Casting lots for Jesus' clothes (v. 35): "They divide my clothes among themselves, and for my clothing they cast lots" (Ps. 22:18).

(3) The mocking of Jesus (vv. 39-44): "All who see me mock at me, they make mouths at me, they shake their heads" (Ps. 22:7).

(4) The taunt of the leaders (v. 43): "Commit your cause to the Lord; let him deliver—let him rescue the one in whom he delights!" (Ps. 22:8; cf. Wisd. of Sol. 2:17-20!).

Together these allusions reinforce the picture of Jesus as God's suffering, righteous servant.

No less noteworthy is the theological irony that abounds in the account. Thus the placard asserting Jesus' offensive claim to kingship is meant to discredit him. For Matthew, however, who adds the words *This is Jesus* to the inscription (cf. Mark 15:26), the placard publicly proclaims that Jesus is God's anointed ruler.

A similar phenomenon occurs in the mocking of Jesus. When Jesus does not respond to the challenge to save himself and come down from the cross, it would appear at first glance that he has failed. What the mockers do not see, however, is that their challenge is setting up a sequel to the story in 4:1-11 (cf. also 16:1), a sequel that some have called the last temptation of Christ. From this perspective, the fact that Jesus does not come down from the cross is hardly evidence of failure. Instead, it is a sign of faithfulness to his calling. The reader knows, then, that the leaders are in for a big surprise when they unknowingly cite Scripture to make their taunt *let God deliver him.* Indeed, that is precisely what God is about to do.

Truly This Was God's Son 27:45-54

Confirmation that God will act comes quickly. According to verse 45, the heavens respond to the crucifixion by shrouding the earth in darkness, a sign of either divine grief or divine displeasure (cf. Amos 8:9; Exod. 10:22). The darkness lasts, we are told, from 12:00 noon to 3:00 p.m., presumably the hour when Jesus' death finally occurs.

As that hour nears, two things happen that further connect the story with the Psalms. Citing Psalm 22:1, Jesus cries out a prayer that declares his trust in God even as he feels abandoned by God: *My God, my God, why have you forsaken me?* It is a prayer that does not gloss over the chasm between suffering and shalom that humans experience as God's absence. In spite of that, however, Jesus *prays*, hoping that God will yet come to his aid (cf. Ps. 22:19-24).

Hearing the Aramaic word Jesus uses for *my God, Eli*, some bystanders mistakenly assume that he is calling for Elijah to return to earth and offer help (cf. comments on 17:9-13). This in turn leads one of the bystanders to offer Jesus a drink of diluted vinegar to sustain him till Elijah arrives (cf. Ps. 69:21b), while others adopt a wait-and-see attitude. There is no further waiting, however. Crying out a final time (cf. Ps. 22:2, 5), Jesus yields his life in death to the One who called him to this vocation.

Immediately thereafter, several cataclysmic events occur, "cosmic signs of God's answer to the prayer of Jesus" (Senior, 1985b:141). They are events which herald that a new world is now taking shape proleptically in the midst of the old, inaugurated by Jesus' death. Among the three signs Matthew lists is one also reported by Mark (Mark 15:38), the tearing of the temple curtain (v. 51a). The curtain mentioned is probably the veil that separated the most sacred area of the temple, the holy of holies, from the rest of the sanctuary (cf. Exod. 26:31-35). Its rending signifies both God's judgment on the temple (cf. 21:12-13) and the advent of an era of unrestricted access to God's mercy (cf. 21:14-16; Heb. 10:19-20).

Meanwhile, Matthew tells us, the ground below confirms that something earthshaking is underway (v. 51b; cf. also 28:2). Earthquakes and the splitting of rocks are regularly associated with God's coming in the biblical story (cf. Judg. 5:4; 1 Kings 19:11; Ps. 68:8) and so become a sign of God's endtime activity as well (cf. Joel 3:14-17; 2 Esd. 9:2-3; Matt. 24:7-8). The final item in Matthew's list builds on the motif of quaking ground and leaves no doubt that a new age is beginning to emerge (vv. 52-53): Tombs are opened, prophets and other ancient servants of God are resurrected, and the former dead make surprise visits to the living. (But only, Matthew adds, at risk of getting ahead of his story, *after* Jesus himself is raised!)

Here the events and the language used to portray them reflect Ezekiel's promise of a day when God would open the graves of his people and raise them to new life (cf. Ezek. 37:11-14; Dan. 12:1-2). Originally a prophecy of fresh hope for Israel after exile, Ezekiel's vision sparked hope among later readers in an endtime resurrection of the dead and a reconstitution of God's people. This, the text implies, is what is beginning to happen in and through Jesus' death.

Earlier in the narrative, we were told that the detail of soldiers who executed Jesus *kept watch over him* (v. 36). They are still *keeping watch* when the earthquake occurs (v. 54) and are awestruck by *what took place.* Not just the centurion (as in Mark 15:39), but the whole guard unit confesses: *Truly this man was God's Son.* To put it another way, the Gentile soldiers confess what the Jewish spectators and leaders mocked just a short time ago (vv. 39-43). All of this points forward to the creation of a new community of disciples gathered from *all nations* (28:18), and may echo Psalm 22 yet one more time (cf. 22:27-28).

Faithful to the End 27:55-56

Verses 55-56 comprise a postscript to the unit. They inform us of one additional group of observers who witness the crucifixion, a sizable number of *women* who *followed Jesus* on his journey to Jerusalem. Chief among these women, only three of whom are named, is Mary Magdalene (cf. Luke 8:2). Unlike the twelve, the women have not fled the area, but loyally stand by and look on *from a distance* (Ps. 38:11). They have supplied Jesus' needs before and are ready to attend to his needs again. Shortly they will get their chance and become witnesses to Jesus' resurrection as well. Their cameo appearance here sets the stage for what is to come.

THE TEXT IN BIBLICAL CONTEXT

The two focal points of the unit we have just examined are Jesus' *trial* by Pilate and his *crucifixion* at Golgotha. In each instance, the text connects both with the story of Israel that precedes it and the story of the church to follow. Jesus' trial recalls the ordeal of the prophet Jeremiah, whose death was sought by the religious leaders, but who was defended by "the officials" (cf. Jer. 26:7-24; especially vv. 8, 16). In Jesus' case, Pilate plays the role of the governmental advocate (and even more so in the parallel accounts of Luke and John), albeit with no success.

Even more significant is the way Jesus' trial before Pilate, together with his hearing before the council, foreshadows court appearances of his followers. Disciples get what their teacher gets, Matthew tells us (10:24-25), and this includes being *dragged before governors and kings because of me, as a testimony to them and the Gentiles* (10:18). In Luke's two-volume work (Luke and Acts), subjection to hearings and trials is one of a series of parallels the author highlights between the experience of Jesus and that of his witnesses. Examples of these parallel trial situations include appearances of Peter and John and of Stephen before the authorities in Jerusalem (Acts 4:1-22; 5:17-42; 6:8—7:60) and numerous instances of Paul testifying before Jewish and Roman officials (Acts 18:12-17; 22:30—23:10; 25:6-12; 25:23—26:32).

With regard to the *crucifixion*, the OT backdrop for Jesus' death has already been documented. He suffers and dies as the righteous servant of God depicted in Psalms and Isaiah. What merits further attention here is the way the crucifixion shapes the vocabulary and thought of the early church. The NT writers not only uplift the centrality of Jesus' death, but use "cross-talk" in a variety of ways to ex press their message. Thus the Fourth Gospel speaks of Jesus' being "lifted up" in his death, a metaphor with double meaning that refers to crucifixion and exaltation as one and the same event (cf. John 12:23-33).

Paul describes his preaching of the gospel to the Galatians as a public portrayal of Christ crucified (Gal. 3:1), to believe in whom is to be "crucified with Christ" (Gal. 2:19). Elsewhere Paul argues that the cross and the shame it signifies provide a paradigm of the life of faith, in which God's strength manifests itself precisely in human weakness (1 Cor. 1:18-31). Other texts that speak of the cross in relation to *our* calling include the Gospel passages on taking up one's cross and following Jesus (cf. Mark 8:34-35). Passages in Hebrews and 1 Peter call us also to bear abuse "outside the city" or "camp" and emulate the endurance Jesus modeled on the cross (cf. Heb. 13:12-13; 12:1-2; 1 Pet. 2:18-25). In these and other ways, the language of faith in the NT reveals its indebtedness to the story of Golgotha.

THE TEXT IN THE LIFE OF THE CHURCH

How fully the church of the second and third centuries took over the "cross-talk" of the NT is unclear. Early Christian archaeology suggests that the cross may *not* have been a primary symbol during this period. From the fourth century on, however, a piety of the cross becomes increasingly prominent in the life of the church. Two well-known forms of this piety that date originally from the Middle Ages are passion plays and the Stations of the Cross. The latter involves a commemoration of fourteen incidents in Jesus' passion, beginning with his condemnation in Pilate's house and concluding with his entombment. Customarily this is done with a series of pictures or carvings, though Holy Week pilgrims to Jerusalem can move through the stations in a more literal fashion.

More familiar forms of piety shaped by the text include Good Friday services (often based on Jesus' words from the cross as found in the various Gospels) and numerous hymns about the cross sung during Lent and at other times. Some titles that come readily to mind include "Beneath the Cross of Jesus," "In the Cross of Christ I Glory," and "When I Survey the Wondrous Cross."

Not all the ways the text has influenced Christian history have been laudable, however. An element in the text that has played a devastating role is the moment in Jesus' trial when the people of Israel gathered there cry out: *His blood be on us and on our children.* Frequently these words have been interpreted as a statement of collective guilt that applies to all Jews in all times—and so used to justify persecution of Jews as an accursed people. This clearly represents a tragic misuse of the text.

For Matthew, *our children* refers to the immediate descendants of those who take responsibility for Jesus' death, and the guilt incurred is judged once and for all in the destruction of Jerusalem in A.D. 70 (cf. 23:34-39). Moreover, these words must be viewed in the context of the hostility between church and synagogue in Matthew's day; each side tended to depict the other in the worst possible light.

For us, the critical question that the cry of the people raises, is not who killed Jesus. Instead, it is a question of where we find *ourselves* corporately guilty for violent acts of injustice in the world. If we pursue that question far enough, we will have little interest in condemning the Jews. *[Anti-Semitism, p. 417.]*

From Death to Life

Matthew 27:57—28:20

PREVIEW

The final unit of Matthew's Gospel tells of Jesus' burial and resurrection. As noted earlier, the burial episode can be viewed from two perspectives. On one hand, it marks the conclusion to the passion narrative, the story of Jesus' suffering. On the other hand, it lays a foundation for a new story, the discovery of an *empty* tomb, which in turn signals the possibility of seeing One who has been raised from death.

Burial and resurrection traditions are already linked in Mark's Gospel, and they are even more intricately intertwined in Matthew. This is evident in the chiastic structure of the unit, as delineated below (see France, 1985:402):

a. Jesus dead and buried
    b. Setting of the guard
        c. Empty tomb and risen Lord
    b'. Report of the guard
a'. Jesus alive and sovereign

The materials Matthew uses to construct this narrative are diverse in form and origin. From Mark's Gospel comes the core of the burial and empty tomb accounts (27:57-61 and 28:1-10; cf. Mark 15:42—16:8), which Matthew adapts at several points. The accounts of the setting of the guard (27:62-66) and report of the guard (28:11-15) likely reflect oral tradition from Matthew's community. With this material Matthew adds the latest installment to an ongoing dispute between Jews and Christians over why Jesus' tomb was empty.

For the final episode in 28:16-20, Matthew draws on some earlier report of Jesus' appearance to the disciples after his resurrection. It is unclear, however, whether this earlier tradition was oral or written (none of the appearance stories in the other Gospels fully parallels

Matthew's). What *is* clear is that 28:16-20 serves both as a resurrection story and as a conclusion to the Gospel as a whole.

OUTLINE

A Decent Burial, 27:57-61

Guarding the Grave, 27:62-66

Raised from the Dead, 28:1-10

Unwelcome News, 28:11-15

Discipling the Nations, 28:16-20

EXPLANATORY NOTES

A Decent Burial 27:57-61

In the first century, the executed did not normally receive what we call a decent burial. Their bodies were either left to decay above ground or dumped into a public grave. The Gospels report, however, that Jesus was spared this indignity. A man named Joseph, from a town in northern Judea, seeks and obtains permission from Pilate to bury Jesus before sundown in accord with Jewish tradition. Appearing here for the first time in the narrative, Joseph is identified by Mark as a member of the Sanhedrin who shared Jesus' hope in the kingdom of God (Mark 15:43). Matthew omits this information, choosing instead to describe Joseph as a rich disciple of Jesus (27:57).

This statement takes us by surprise, since the Gospel elsewhere portrays the wealthy as poor prospects for disciples (cf. 19:23ff.)! In addition, only the twelve have been characterized as disciples thus far in the story. Whatever the explanation, it is clear that Joseph *acts like* a disciple, providing a sequel to the action of the woman who anointed Jesus at Bethany (26:6-13).

The tomb which Joseph as a rich man has at his disposal was one of many such tombs carved in the cavernous rocky terrain around Jerusalem, perhaps with several chambers for various family members. Because it has not yet been used, it is called a *new tomb.* It is there that Jesus' body is placed, wrapped in *a clean linen cloth* to avoid the shame of being buried naked. In typical fashion, then, a stone is rolled in front of the opening to secure the tomb and block entry.

Note that no service of interment accompanies the burial. Joseph carries out his deed of love and respect in private. It does not go unobserved, however. Two of the same women who witnessed Jesus' crucifixion witness his burial as well (cf. vv. 55-56, 61). They have begun their vigil of grief, a vigil that will put them at the right place at the right time on Easter morning (cf. 28:1).

Guarding the Grave 27:62-66

The episode related in verses 62-66 falls on the Sabbath (Saturday), though the text tells us that in a roundabout way. It speaks of the day which is *after* the day when people *prepared* for the Sabbath (cf. Mark 15:42). The events that unfold on this day build on the burial-narrative in verses 57-61. Since Pilate has taken the liberty to release Jesus' body for burial, the Jewish leaders ask Pilate to make sure that Jesus *stays* buried.

According to the NRSV, Pilate tells the chief priests in verse 65 to use their own police for this purpose (*You have a guard*). It is probable, however, that Pilate's response should be translated: *Take a guard* (NIV, NRSV footnote). That is, Pilate assigns a unit from his own troops to carry out the leaders' request (cf. 28:14, which implies that the soldiers report to Pilate). Tight security prevails then as the stone at the tomb is sealed (cf. Dan. 6:17), and the guard takes up a vigil quite different from that of the women.

The setting of the guard serves at least two purposes in the narrative. First, it launches a preemptive strike against the later charge that Jesus' disciples stole his body from the tomb (cf. v. 64; 28:13-15). If the tomb is securely guarded by Pilate's soldiers, theft of the body is unthinkable. Second, the incident creates a dramatic backdrop for what will soon follow. It symbolizes a last effort by worldly powers to prevent God's reign from challenging their own. Even Pilate, however, drops a hint that this effort will not succeed. *Make the tomb as secure as you can,* he tells the religious leaders, *as secure as you know how.* And so they do. But it will not be secure enough to keep Jesus in the grip of death.

Raised from the Dead 28:1-10

As do each of the Gospels, Matthew begins his Easter story by reporting the discovery that Jesus' tomb is empty. The time reference in the Greek text of 28:1 *could* imply that the discovery occurred late Saturday evening, as the Sabbath was ending. It is more likely, however, that the NRSV renders the sense of the text correctly, and that the story told has an early dawn setting (cf. Mark 16:2).

Central to the story are the women who come to the tomb, hear the message that Jesus has been raised, and thus become the first witnesses to the resurrection. While this core of the story is common to all three of the synoptic Gospels, Matthew's version of the episode contains a number of distinctive features:

(1) Only two women go to the tomb, the two Marys who earlier witnessed the crucifixion and burial. Further, they go not to anoint Jesus (the sealed tomb would prevent that), but simply *to see the tomb*. Presumably they plan to resume their vigil of mourning.

(2) The mysterious young man in a white robe in Mark 16:5 becomes the *angel of the Lord*, whose appearance here corresponds to earlier visits mentioned in the birth and infancy stories (cf. 1:20, 24; 2:13, 19). Portrayed with vivid images from the book of Daniel (10:6; 7:9-10), this divine messenger rolls the stone away in the women's presence before he delivers his message.

(3) The visit of the angel unleashes a powerful earthquake. Like the previous earthquake at the crucifixion (cf. 27:51-54), this one confirms that an old order is breaking up and a new one dawning. The earthquake is not itself what frees Jesus from the tomb, but rather serves as a sign that *God* has raised Jesus (cf. 12:38-40).

(4) The guards introduced in the prior episode witness the signlike events along with the women (neither group sees the resurrection itself). Unlike the women, the guards remain terrified, reluctant witnesses.

(5) When the women leave the sepulcher, they do so not only with fear, but with *great joy*. Moreover, they do not keep silent, as is the case in Mark's account (Mark 16:8), but instead carry out the command to tell the good news to the disciples.

(6) Before the women find the disciples, Jesus himself appears to the women (vv. 9-10). Only Matthew records this appearance, although the Fourth Gospel reports a private reunion between Jesus and Mary Magdalene (John 20:1-18). The upshot of this addition to the story is that the women are not only the first to *hear* that Jesus is raised, but also the first to *see* the risen Lord.

Brief as it is, the report of Jesus' appearance to the women makes several important points (cf. Meier, 1980:364). First, the resurrection of Jesus has a bodily dimension. The women are able to *take hold* of Jesus' feet. Second, the resurrection renews the family relationship of

Jesus and his disciples. Jesus speaks of a reunion with *my brothers.* Third, Galilee is named again as the place where this reunion will occur. The reason Jesus chooses Galilee will become apparent shortly (cf. 28:16-20; 26:32). Finally, the One who names us his sisters and brothers is also our Lord. He is One whom the women *worship* when he meets and greets them.

Unwelcome News 28:11-15

While the women rush to tell Jesus' disciples the good news, the soldiers leave the tomb to make their own report to the chief priests. For the latter, the report of the signs at the sepulcher does not lead to joy or faith. Instead, it prompts still further devious plotting. The meeting of the Sanhedrin described in verses 12-14 recalls the anxious assembly of Herod and the religious leaders on the occasion of Jesus' birth (2:3-4), as well as the meeting of Jewish leaders that planned Jesus' death (26:3-5). Once again money plays a role in the conspiracy (cf. 26:14-16; 28:12), as the leaders bribe the soldiers to cover up the truth with a false story.

The script the chief priests propose is not particularly ingenious. After all, how could *sleeping* soldiers witness anything, whether a miracle or a theft? If failure on guard duty was a capital offense (cf. Acts 12:19), how would the council *satisfy* the governor? From Matthew's standpoint, the incongruity of the script only serves to underscore the false witness of those who deny the resurrection.

The final verse of the episode tells us why Matthew included the material on the guards in his story of the resurrection. As Justin Martyr confirms in his *Dialogue with Trypho*, a Jew (ca. A.D. 150), one of the earliest Jewish responses to the Christian story of the empty tomb was to argue that the disciples stole Jesus' body and then asserted that Jesus had risen from the dead. We noted above how the account of the setting of the guard attempts to preempt that argument. The presence of Roman soldiers makes theft impossible.

If the tomb is guarded, however, a new question arises: How did the rumor start that Jesus' body was stolen? It is this question that the text answers with the bribery of the soldiers in 28:11-15. Whatever our judgment on the historicity of this material, it clearly is effective as a dramatic statement. The false testimony of the bribed soldiers contrasts sharply with the joyous witness of the two women.

Discipling the Nations 28:16-20

The promised reunion of Jesus with his disciples in Galilee is the episode with which Matthew concludes his Gospel. Lingering only a moment to describe the setting, he moves quickly to the pregnant words of the risen Jesus in verses 18-20. The latter consist of three distinct statements: a declaration of authority (v. 18), a formula of commissioning (vv. 19-20a), and a word of assurance (v. 20b).

In an attempt to identify the form of Matthew's account, scholars have compared it to enthronement texts (cf. Phil. 2:5-11; Dan. 7:13-14), to OT stories of calling and commissioning (cf. Exod. 3), and to certain patterns of divine speech in the Bible (cf. Gen. 46:3-4). Some of the parallels cited are quite striking (see comments below). No one of the suggested prototypes, however, corresponds fully to what we find in the text. The latter is best viewed as a resurrection story that draws freely on a number of OT traditions, to show how Jesus' resurrection fits into and fulfills God's activity in Israel's story.

The narration in verses 16-17 tells us that the Gospel story ends where it began—in *Galilee* (cf. 4:12-16; 2:19-23). Jesus and the disciples are not simply coming home, however. Galilee signifies hope for the Gentiles (4:15-16), the wider family of nations to whom the disciples will soon be sent (v. 19).

Since Judas is gone, it is only *eleven* disciples who go to a specific (*the*) but unnamed *mountain* to meet Jesus. The location recalls earlier peaks in the story, such as the mountain in the temptation story (4:8-10), the mountain of the first discourse (5:1ff.), and the mount of transfiguration (17:1-8). Like those mountains, this one signifies Jesus' authority to gather and teach the endtime people of God (v. 18; cf. comments on the mountain in 5:1).

When the moment of reunion finally occurs, the experience evokes two reactions. As did the magi at Jesus' birth (2:11), the disciples worship Jesus. Some, however, even as they worship, do so with the same hesitant or little faith that has characterized the disciples throughout the Gospel. They *doubt* (cf. 14:28-33; 17:20-21). It will take the reassuring *word* of Jesus in the verses that follow to fortify them for their calling.

The declaration of authority in verse 18 is framed in language reminiscent of two OT passages. In the final verse of the final book of the Hebrew Scriptures, the Persian king Cyrus proclaims: "The Lord, the God of heaven, has given me all the kingdoms of the earth" (2 Chron. 36:23). The second passage is found in the visions of Daniel, where a human figure appears before God's throne, and "to him was given dominion and glory and kingship, that all peoples, nations, and languages should serve him" (Dan. 7:14). The cosmic authority of which these texts speak is the authority God has granted to Jesus by raising him from death.

Earlier in the story, Satan sought to entice Jesus by promising him such authority (4:8-9). Now Jesus has that authority by the will of God, a foretaste of the dominion he will exercise in the endtime (cf. 19:28; 25:31ff.). *With* this authority, he is in a position to issue the commission that follows.

The *great commission* in verses 19-20a expands the directives for mission found in chapter 10. There Jesus commanded the disciples to restrict their mission to Israel. Now that restriction is lifted. It is God's design that the church Jesus promised to build (16:18-19) be a universal community, comprising persons from *all nations.* The main verb in the Greek text of the great commission is *mathēteuō, make disciples.* Jesus instructs the eleven, his disciples thus far, to expand the circle, to invite others to join them in following Jesus.

The other three verbs in the text are participles that connect with the main verb. Given this structure, we might paraphrase verses 19-20a as follows: *As you go forth, call people everywhere to become disciples, which will involve both baptizing them into God's community and summoning them to embody my teaching in their lives.* Note that baptism, the rite of incorporation, is described in trinitarian terms. We are baptized *in the name of* (and thereby enter into a new allegiance with) a God we know as Father, Son, and Holy Spirit.

As disciples pursue their mission, they do so with the assurance Jesus offers in 20b: *I am with you always.* It is the promise that God gave to Jacob in Genesis 46:3-4, to Moses in Exodus 3:12, and to the exiles in Isaiah 43:1-7. Now Jesus speaks as God speaks. To put it another way: The One who is named God-with-us at the outset of the Gospel (1:23) promises that he will continue to be God-with-us in his community. (Note how 28:20b and 1:23 thus form a literary inclusion.) Earlier, Jesus indicated that he would be with his disciples when they assembled in his name (18:20). Here he assures us that he will accompany us in our going out as well, until the day dawns when his now hidden presence becomes visible in glory.

THE TEXT IN BIBLICAL CONTEXT

In a letter to the house churches at Corinth, the apostle Paul writes: "I handed on to you as of first importance what I in turn had received:

that Christ died for our sins in accordance with the scriptures, and that he was buried, and that he was raised on the third day in accordance with the scriptures, and that he appeared to Cephas, then to the twelve" (1 Cor. 15:3-5).

The summary of faith that Paul recites makes it clear that the resurrection of Jesus is no peripheral matter. It is central to the proclamation of the early church. It vindicates Jesus' mission and establishes his lordship (Rom. 1:4; Acts 2:32-36). It is the first installment of God's transformation of all creation (1 Cor. 15:20-28), in which we ourselves begin to participate through God's Spirit (Rom. 8:11; 2 Cor. 5:17; Col. 2:12). Further, it gives us reason to hope that we too shall be resurrected and so encourages us in suffering (1 Pet. 1:3-9).

The Gospel accounts of the empty tomb and of Jesus' appearances tell us in story form how this resurrection faith originated. They describe how one gets from the seeming defeat and despair of Good Friday to the Easter confidence so evident in the early church. To the dismay of many readers, the stories differ considerably in detail (cf. Mark 16:1-8; Matt. 28:1-20; Luke 24; John 20:1—21:23), leaving the curious with a number of questions: How many women went to the tomb, and what exactly did they discover? Did they or didn't they report to the disciples? To whom did Jesus first appear? And did his reunion with the disciples take place in Galilee or Jerusalem? In spite of the variations, the Gospel stories agree that the story of Jesus does not end with his death. Instead, Jesus as the resurrected one continues to carry out the mission he inaugurated in Israel.

Thus the stories of Jesus' appearances include commissioning episodes like Matthew 28:18-20, in which the disciples receive a new or expanded mandate for mission. The book of Acts begins, as the Gospel of Luke ends, with a commissioning scene that echoes the theme of universality we find in Matthew: "But you will receive power when the Holy Spirit has come upon you; and you will be my witnesses in Jerusalem, in all Judea and Samaria, and to the ends of the earth" (Acts 1:8; cf. Luke 24:46-49).

In the Fourth Gospel, the commissioning statement is brief (John 20:21-23), but alludes to a much fuller statement of the church's mission to the world found in Jesus' high-priestly prayer in John 17 (see especially John 17:18). Finally, there is the autobiographical testimony of Paul concerning Jesus' belated appearance to him. God was pleased "to reveal his Son to me," Paul writes, "so that I might proclaim him among the Gentiles" (Gal. 1:16; cf. 1 Cor. 15:8-11; Acts 26:12-18).

Precisely at this point, as resurrection stories speak of a mission to the world, they pick up and refocus a theme that runs through the larger biblical story: While God chooses one people to act on his behalf, God's ultimate concern is with all the peoples of the earth. We hear this message in the short story of Jonah. It takes a whale of an effort on God's part to broaden the horizons of a reluctant prophet and convince him to do mass evangelism in the pagan city of Nineveh.

We hear the same message as God speaks to a community of exiles about their mission: "It is too light a thing that you should be my servant to raise up the tribes of Jacob and to restore the survivors of Israel; I will give you as a light to the nations, that my salvation may reach to the end of the earth" (Isa. 49:6). Indeed, we hear that message already at the outset of Israel's saga, as God declares a promise to Abraham: "I will bless you, and make your name great, so that you will be a blessing . . . and in you all the families of the earth shall be blessed" (Gen. 12:2-3). It is this universal calling that Jesus entrusts to his disciples in the great commission.

THE TEXT IN THE LIFE OF THE CHURCH

The drama that unfolds at the tomb in Matthew 28:1-10 has shaped Christian worship in powerful ways. Nowhere is this more evident than in the all-night liturgy of the Orthodox Church that comes to a joyous climax on Easter morning. On a lesser scale, the Easter sunrise services familiar to many of us also attempt to recreate the story of the text. We sing of the vain efforts of earthly powers to seal the grave, and we join with the angel of the Lord in proclaiming: "Christ the Lord is risen today!" By the central place we assign Easter in the church year, we affirm that we too are a community of the resurrection, one with those who first heralded the good news.

Now as then, however, the Easter story evokes a wide range of reactions and responses. For some, the retelling of the story may elicit the same mixture of skepticism and awe ascribed to the disciples in the text. Did Jesus in fact appear to his disciples, breaking into their experience in strange and unexpected ways? Or were the disciples simply "seeing things," projecting their wishes onto the screen of their vision? The element of surprise that the stories report supports the testimony of the NT that resurrection faith was God's gift, not human projection. Nonetheless, the stories of the empty tomb and of Jesus' appearances offer us signs rather than proof. They invite us to believe, and thereby to discover for ourselves the reality of the resurrection. They cannot, however, compel that faith.

For those who *have* believed, the great commission in 20:19-20a has proved a very influential text. First, it has contributed significantly to the theology and practice of baptism in the church. By anchoring baptism in a command of the risen Lord, it made this rite an indispensable ordinance of Jesus' community. By framing that command in trinitarian language, it helped the pattern of a threefold baptismal action to prevail over the earlier practice of baptism in Jesus' name only (cf. Acts 2:38). And by linking baptism with *discipleship*, it provided support for Anabaptists and later groups arguing for believers baptism.

Second, the great commission and related texts have propelled the church to understand itself as a *community in mission*. Jesuits, Anabaptists, and Pietists alike took their cues from the text, as did the great missionary movement of the nineteenth and early twentieth centuries. To be sure, not everything done in the name of the Great Commission inspires admiration. At times the missionary enterprise has been all too closely linked to the colonial ambitions of one nation or another.

Matthew points us in a different direction. To disciple the nations is not a matter of control and dependency, or of one people imposing its culture on another. It is instead a matter of inviting the world to discover and claim for itself the promise of life in God's reign, that life which we have begun to enjoy through the power of the resurrected Lord. Understood in this way, the great commission continues to commission us.

Outline of Matthew

Part 1: JESUS' ORIGINS AND CALLING
Matthew 1:1—4:16

Jesus' Family History	**1:1-17**
Heading	1:1
From Abraham to David	1:2-6a
From David to the Exile	1:6b-11
From the Exile to Jesus	1:12-16
Summary	1:17
Jesus' Birth and Infancy	**1:18—2:23**
A Child Conceived by the Spirit	1:18-25
Joseph's Dilemma	1:18-19
The Angel's Message	1:20-21
A Supporting Prophecy	1:22-23
Joseph's Response	1:24-25
A Child Acclaimed as King	2:1-12
The Magi Seek a New King	2:1-2
Herod Confers with His Advisers	2:3-6
Herod Confers with the Magi	2:7-8
The Magi Find a New King	2:9-12
A Child Delivered from Destruction	2:13-23
The Flight to Egypt	2:13-15

- An Office Call 9:9
- Grace at Table 9:10-13
- New Calls for New 9:14-17

Mighty Works, Cycle 3 9:18-34
- Double Deliverance 9:18-26
- Faith and Sight 9:27-31
- Like Nothing Else 9:32-34

Jesus Commissions His Disciples 9:35—10:42

Laborers for the Harvest 9:35—10:4
- Help Wanted 9:35-38
- Position Filled 10:1-4

The Mission of the Twelve 10:5-15
- Restricted to Israel 10:5-6
- Rules for the Road 10:7-10
- Reception and Rejection 10:11-15

The Cost of Discipleship 10:16-42
- Faith on Trial 10:16-23
- A Common Fate 10:24-25
- Fearless Witness 10:26-33
- A Price to Pay 10:34-39
- Channels of Grace 10:40-42

Part 3: ISRAEL RESPONDS TO JESUS
Matthew 11:1—16:20

Faith and Unfaith, Part 1 11:1—12:50

John the Baptist and Jesus 11:1-19
- Who Is Jesus? 11:1-6
- Who Is John? 11:7-15
- How Were They Received? 11:16-19

Who Receives Wisdom? 11:20-30
- A Pronouncement of Woe 11:20-24
- A Promise of Blessing 11:25-30

Jesus and the Sabbath 12:1-21
- Hunger on the Sabbath 12-1-8
- Healing on the Sabbath 12:9-14
- A Low-Profile Messiah 12:15-21

By What Power? 12:22-37

Part 4: JESUS' FINAL JOURNEY
Matthew 16:21—20:34

Suffering and Glory	**16:21—17:21**
The Way of the Cross	16:21-28
Destined to Suffer	16:21-23
Losing and Finding Life	16:24-28
A Glimpse of Glory	17:1-13
The Glory of the Son	17:1-8
Jesus and Elijah	17:9-13
A Crisis of Faith	17:14-21
Jesus Challenges Unfaith	17:14-18
Jesus Counsels His Disciples	17:19-21
Life in Jesus' Community	**17:22—18:35**
Freedom and Submission	17:22-27
Submission to Death	17:22-23
Submission to the Tax	17:24-27
A Community of Caring	18:1-14
The Disciple as Child	18:1-4
Don't Make Others Stumble	18:5-9
Care for the Little Ones	18:10-14
Dealing With Brokenness	18:15-35
When Sin Occurs	18:15-20
Seventy Times Seven	18:21-22
Be Merciful to One Another	18:23-35
Demands of Discipleship	**19:1—20:34**
Marriage and Children	19:1-15
From Galilee to Judea	19:1-2
When Two Become One	19:3-9
Called to Singleness	19:10-12
Let the Children Come	19:13-15
Giving and Getting	19:16—20:16
Too High a Price?	19:16-22
Compensation Beyond Measure	19:23-30
The Goodness of God	20:1-16
Status or Servanthood	20:17-34
En Route to Suffering	20:17-19
The Way of the Servant	20:20-28
The Gift of Sight	20:29-34

Part 5: JESUS IN JERUSALEM
Matthew 21:1—25:46

Conflict and Confrontation	**21:1—23:39**
David's Son in David's City	21:1-17
A Royal Processional	21:1-11
Reclaiming God's House	21:12-17
Stories of Rejection	21:18—22:14
A Tree Without Fruit	21:18-22
By What Authority	21:23-27
Saying No to God	21:28-32
A Vineyard Without Fruit	21:33-46
Who Will Eat at God's Table?	22:1-14
Disputes with Jewish Leaders	22:15-46
Caesar's or God's?	22:15-22
God of the Living	22:23-33
The Greatest Commandment	22:34-40
Whence Comes the Messiah?	22:41-46
A Bitter Public Farewell	23:1-39
Wanted—A New Model	23:1-12
Woe to You, Hypocrites	23:13-36
Lament for a Lost City	23:37-39
Instruction on the Endtime	**24:1—25:46**
How Will the End Come?	24:1-35
Setting the Stage	24:1-3
All This Must Yet Happen	24:4-14
A Great Tribulation	24:15-28
The Sign of the Son of Man	24:29-31
Near and Sure	24:32-35
Living in Readiness	24:36—25:30
Watch and Be Ready	24:36-44
Care for the Household	24:45-51
Stock Ample Provisions	25:1-13
Be Resourceful Stewards	25:14-30
Jesus Judges the Nations	25:31-46
Gathered and Separated	25:31-33
Come, You Blessed	25:34-40
Depart, You Accursed	25:41-46

Part 6: JESUS' DEATH AND RESURRECTION

Matthew 26:1—28:20

Prelude to Passion	**26:1-16**
Consigned to Death	26:1-5
Anointed for Burial	26:6-13
Marked for Betrayal	26:14-16
A Farewell Gathering	**26:17-46**
I Will Keep the Passover	26:17-19
One of You Will Betray Me	26:20-25
This Is My Body	26:26-29
This Night You Will Deny Me	26:30-35
Your Will Be Done	26:36-46
In the Hour of Trial	**26:47—27:10**
Betrayed with a Kiss	26:47-56
Faithful Under Fire	26:57-68
Denial Under Duress	26:69-75
Decision for Death	27:1-2
Consequences of Betrayal	27:3-10
A Crucified King	**27:11-56**
What Shall I Do with Jesus?	27:11-26
Hail, King of the Jews	27:27-31
Jesus on the Cross	27:32-44
Truly This Was God's Son	27:45-54
Faithful to the End	27:55-56
From Death to Life	**27:57—28:20**
A Decent Burial	27:57-61
Guarding the Grave	27:62-66
Raised from the Dead	28:1-10
Unwelcome News	28:11-15
Discipling the Nations	28:16-20

Glossary and Essays

OUTLINE

Abbreviations/Citations
Anti-Semitism
Apocalyptic
Apocrypha
Chiastic
Christ/Christology
Dead Sea Scrolls
Epiphany
Eschatology
Essenes
Exile
Gentile
Gospel
Inclusio/Inclusion
Jewish Groups and Parties
Jewish Writings
Matthew, Distinctive Themes
Matthew, Literary Characteristics
Matthew's Sources
Messiah
Midrash
Mishnah
Postexilic
Qumran
Septuagint
Synoptic
Talmud
Targum
Theophany
Torah
Wisdom

ABBREVIATIONS/CITATIONS In addition to books from the Bible, the abbreviations for which are familiar to most readers, a number of other ancient texts are cited in the commentary. Below is a key to these citations, as well as to other abbreviations used in the commentary. After most items a number appears in parentheses, indicating one of the following categories of writings:

1 = Old Testament Apocrypha
2 = Jewish Pseudepigrapha
3 = Dead Sea Scrolls
4 = Rabbinic Text from the Mishnah
5 = Rabbinic Text from the Talmud
6 = Rabbinic Midrash
7 = Early Christian Writings

For further information on the various categories of Jewish literature, see the essay "Jewish Writings."

Aboth	Aboth or Pirqe Aboth (4)
Acts of Thomas	Acts of Thomas (7)
Ass. Mos.	Assumption or Testament of Moses (2)
Barn.	Letter of Barnabas (7)
2 Bar.	Second or Syriac Apocalypse of Baruch (2)
Ber.	Berakoth (4)
bBer.	Berakoth (5)
bShab.	Shabbath (5)
CD	Damascus Document (3)
1 Clem.	First Letter of Clement (7)
Did.	Didache or Teaching of the Twelve Apostles (7)
1 Enoch	First or Ethiopic Apocalypse of Enoch (2)
2 Enoch	Second or Slavonic Apocalypse of Enoch (2)
2 Esd.	Second Esdras (1)
Exod. R.	Exodus Rabba (6)
G. Eb.	Gospel of the Ebionites (7)
G. Naz.	Gospel of the Nazaraeans (7)
G. Thom.	Gospel of Thomas (7)
GNB	Good News Bible
JB	Jerusalem Bible
Jub.	Jubilees (2)
Kalla	Kalla (5)
KJV	King James or Authorized Version
Lev. R.	Leviticus Rabba (6)
L. Adam	Life of Adam and Eve (2)
LXX	Septuagint (Greek translation of OT)
1 Macc.	First Maccabees (1)
2 Macc.	Second Maccabees (1)
4 Macc.	Fourth Maccabees (1/2)
Mek. Exod.	Mekilta on Exodus (6)
Midr.	Midrash (6), followed by name of OT book
NAB	New American Bible
NASB	New American Standard Bible
NEB	New English Bible
NIV	New International Version
NJB	New Jerusalem Bible
NKJV	New King James Version
NRSV	New Revised Standard Version
NT	New Testament
Num. R.	Numbers Rabba (6)
OT	Old Testament

Pesah.	Pesahim (4)
Ps. Sol.	Psalms of Solomon (2)
1QH	Thanksgiving Hymns or Hymn Scroll (3)
1QM	War Scroll (3)
1QpHab	Habbakuk Commentary (3)
1QS	Manual of Discipline (3)
1QSa	Rule of the Congregation (3)
REB	Revised English Bible
RSV	Revised Standard Version
Sanh.	Sanhedrin (4)
Shab.	Shabbath (4)
Shek.	Shekalim (4)
Sib. Ora.	Sibylline Oracles (2)
Sir.	Sirach or Ecclesiasticus (1)
Sota	Sota(h) (4)
T. Abr.	Testament of Abraham (2)
T. Asher	Testaments of the Twelve Patriarchs, Asher (2)
T. Iss.	Testaments of the Twelve Patriarchs, Issachar (2)
T. Jos.	Testaments of the Twelve Patriarchs, Joseph (2)
T. Jud.	Testaments of the Twelve Patriarchs, Judah (2)
T. Levi	Testaments of the Twelve Patriarchs, Levi (2)
T. Zeb.	Testaments of the Twelve Patriarchs, Zebulon (2)
TBC	The Text in Biblical Context
TLC	The Text in the Life of the Church
Tob.	Tobit (1)
Wisd. of Sol.	Wisdom of Solomon (1)
Yoma	Yoma (4)
Yoma Bar.	Yoma, Baraitha (5)

ANTI-SEMITISM Anti-Semitism is the technical term for hostility toward Jews, whether ethnic, sociocultural, or religious in character. Already widespread in the ancient Greco-Roman world, anti-Semitism has been a recurring and often violent phenomenon throughout the Christian era. The most traumatic expression of anti-Semitism in modern times was the Holocaust, or the Shoah, in which millions of Jews perished as a result of the policies of Hitler's Third Reich. In more subtle forms, anti-Semitism continues to affect the way many Christians feel and think about the Jewish community.

According to some critics, the NT itself fosters anti-Semitism by the way it portrays Jewish leaders and Jewish religion. Along with the Fourth Gospel, Matthew's Gospel is frequently singled out as particularly troublesome. Harsh language abounds in references to Jewish leaders, including epithets such as hypocrites, vipers, blind guides (cf. 15:6; 23:13-28). The same leaders are accused of perpetrating a bloody heritage of murdering God's servants (23:29-36). As the plot of the Gospel develops, the picture of Israel becomes increasingly one of unbelief. The climax comes in the trial of Jesus when the crowds cry out *his blood be on us and our children* (27:25). The consequence, according to Matthew, is that God abandons Israel's holy place (23:38) and takes the kingdom away from Israel (21:43).

It is clear that material such as this has the *potential* to incite anti-Jewish feelings. But is Matthew in fact pursuing an anti-Semitic agenda? Several considerations prompt us to say no: (1) Matthew views the story he tells as a *fulfillment* of God's promises to Israel, not as a negation of Israel's story.

(2) Matthew depicts the new community that responds to Jesus as followers of Israel's Messiah and obedient to Israel's Torah. (3) The critique of Judaism which pervades the Gospel is primarily a critique of a religious establishment, not of an ethnic group. (4) Matthew carries on his debate with Judaism as a *Jewish*-Christian, reflecting the pain and pathos of one who stands within Jewish tradition, not the prejudice of an outsider. (5) Matthew lets the reader know that the criteria with which he judges Israel apply to the church as well, discouraging any attempt to assume a stance of religious superiority.

Having said all that, it remains true that an uncritical use of texts from Matthew can lead to a distorted view of Judaism and contribute unwittingly to anti-Semitism. How can preachers and teachers guard against that? Among other things, we can keep calling attention to the way conflict between the church and synagogue in Matthew's day colored his picture of Judaism. In addition, we can lift up ancient and contemporary materials that show Jewish tradition as vital and constructive—to offset texts that portray Judaism in a negative light. Further, we can use Matthew's critique of Jewish leaders and tradition as a generic critique that applies to all religious institutions, including our own, rather than as a means to vilify one particular people. Finally, we can engage in dialogue with Jewish brothers and sisters, a dialogue in which we may discover that God is indeed working through their history as well as through our own. (For further comment, cf. TBC and TLC on 21:18—22:14; TLC on 23:1-39; and TLC on 27:11-56).

APOCALYPTIC An *apocalypse* is a writing that purports to *reveal* (Greek: *apokaluptō*) how God will soon intervene to end the present evil age and usher in a new age. The related adjective *apocalyptic* can be used to refer to such literature, or to a way of thinking about history and the endtime characteristic of such literature, or to groups and movements that embrace that way of thinking. See TBC and TLC on 24:1-35 for a fuller discussion of apocalyptic thinking and apocalyptic texts.

APOCRYPHA See essay on *Jewish Writings.*

CHIASTIC See *Matthew, Literary Characteristics.*

CHRIST/CHRISTOLOGY The word *Christ* comes from the Greek *Christos*, meaning *anointed one.* In literature from the NT era, *Christos* regularly refers to the Messiah (Hebrew: *Mašiaḥ*), an anointed ruler like King David able to deliver Israel from bondage and rule with strength and justice. Such is the case where *Christos* appears in the Gospels (cf. Matt. 1:1; 11:2), and where the vocation of Messiah is ascribed to Jesus (albeit somewhat cautiously). In the context of the early church, *Christos* soon came to be used not only to designate Jesus as the Messiah, but as a part of Jesus' proper name. Thus the letters of Paul and Christian writings ever since abound with references to *Jesus Christ*.

Narrowly defined, the word *Christology* would refer only to teaching about the Messiah. Most often, however, Christology serves as an umbrella word that covers all the terms and concepts used to define who Jesus is and his role in God's design. With that broader definition in mind, what can we say about *Matthew's* Christology? What Christological themes or categories stand out in the First Gospel?

For Matthew, *Jesus is God with us, to inaugurate God's reign, speak and act with God's power, and create a community that lives in a right relationship with God*. Matthew's Christology can thus be labeled a *narrative* Christology, a Christology shaped first and foremost by the story of what God was doing in and through Jesus of Nazareth. Along the way, Matthew uses a number of titles for Jesus that have an earlier history in Jewish tradition, titles such as Messiah, Lord, Servant, Son of David, and Son of God. He also takes over an expression found in his sources, in which Jesus refers to himself as the Son of Man. When such categories appear, however, they cannot be interpreted simply in terms of what they meant in earlier Jewish contexts. Rather, the story Matthew tells redefines old categories and fills them with new meaning. A case in point is the title Messiah, which no longer refers to someone who saves and rules by political conquest, but to one who mediates the mercy and power of God that heals human brokenness.

Of the various titles and motifs at his disposal, two that Matthew highlights to express his understanding of Jesus are (1) the Son of God and (2) the Wisdom of God. According to Matthew, Jesus enjoys a unique relationship with God from the moment of his conception by the Spirit (1:18-23). This is confirmed in the story that follows by epiphanies in which God attests Jesus' sonship (cf. 3:17; 17:5), by episode after episode in which Jesus acts with divine authority (cf. 7:29; 9:6), by the familial intimacy with God which Jesus exhibits in naming God as Father (cf. 7:21; 11:25), and by the open confession of Jesus as God's Son at strategic junctures in the narrative (cf. 16:16; 27:54). As God's Son, Jesus knows God as no one else does—and so is able to reveal God's purpose and will to his followers (cf. 11:27).

To put it another way, Jesus as God's Son is able to speak as divine Wisdom, the Wisdom of God that has been making God's ways known to Israel from the very beginning. Thus Jesus can subordinate the word of Moses to his own word (5:21-22), his deeds can be described as the deeds of Wisdom (11:19), he can invite persons to come to himself to discover Wisdom (11:28-30), and he can speak as Wisdom speaks of sending out God's messengers (23:34; cf. Luke 11:49).

In these and other ways, Matthew's story prepares us for the ringing announcement at the end of the Gospel: *All authority in heaven and on earth has been entrusted to* the risen Jesus (28:18). The one who came as God-with-us to inaugurate God's reign in Israel is now powerfully at work as God-with-us to extend that reign—to create a people of God drawn from every tribe and nation. (For further comment on Matthew's Christology, cf. TBC and TLC on 1:18-25; 2:1-12; 7:13-29; 11:20-30; and 17:1-13.)

DEAD SEA SCROLLS See *Jewish Writings*.

EPIPHANY An *epiphany* is an event in which the presence and power of the Divine is manifested in some tangible way. Among the subtypes of epiphanies are *theophany* (a manifestation of God), *Christophany* (a disclosure of Christ's divine status), and *angelophany* (an appearance of one or more angels as divine messengers). The word epiphany is best known to most Christians as the name of a feast day in the Christian year. It is associated in the Eastern church with the revelation of Jesus as God's Son at his baptism, but in the Western church with the disclosure of Christ's glory to the Gentile magi. Matthew's story reports a number of epiphanies, most of which are Christophanies. In addition to the revelatory events accompanying Jesus' baptism, epiphanies take place when Jesus calms a storm at sea, when he walks on water, when he is transfigured on a mountain, when he dies on the cross, and when he appears to his followers as their resurrected Lord.

ESCHATOLOGY Derived from the Greek term *eschatos*, which means *last* or *final, eschatology* refers to the last things or final events in God's relationship with history and creation. Put more simply, eschatology is teaching about the *endtime*. In the centuries immediately preceding the Christian story, Jewish hope became increasingly an eschatological hope. Yearnings for a life rich with God's justice and shalom (peace, wholeness, well-being) focused more and more on a future act of divine deliverance rather than on blessing that could be expected in the present course of history. In *apocalyptic* eschatology, this hope in God's future intervention becomes even more pronounced. Only when God destroys the present evil age and creates a wholly new age will the ancient promises be fulfilled.

Matthew tells the story of Jesus against the backdrop of apocalyptic eschatology. When Jesus speaks of the kingdom of heaven or kingdom of God, he is talking about God's endtime reign. He is talking about God acting to reclaim and refashion every aspect of life. What is strikingly new in Jesus' proclamation, however, is that this endtime rule of God is no longer viewed as something still only on the drawing board. Instead, it is underway in the present time, enabling persons to hear God's final word, receive God's endtime mercy, and become God's endtime people. Although the end is not yet, the power of God that will eventually transform creation is already at work through Jesus and his disciples. See also TBC and TLC on 4:17-25.

ESSENES See *Jewish Groups and Parties.*

EXILE In the biblical story, the *exile* refers to the deportation of several thousand citizens of Judah to Babylonia (cf. Matt. 1:11-12), following the defeat of Judah by the armies of King Nebuchadnezzar early in the sixth century B.C. A few decades later, in 539 B.C., an edict by a new world conqueror, Cyrus of Persia, enabled Jewish and other exiles to return to their homelands. Although those exiled represented only a small percentage of the total population of Judah, they included many of its most prominent leaders, political and religious. Not surprisingly, then, the experience of the exile and finally deliverance from exile became permanently etched in Israel's corporate memory. Because the exile constituted a major break in the biblical story, radically altering the form of Israel's life, scholars frequently refer to events and figures prior to the exile as *pre*exilic, and to those following the exile as *post*exilic.

GENTILE The word *Gentile* comes from the Latin *gens* (people, nation) and means a non-Jew. In the NT, the plural *Gentiles* translates the Greek *ethnē*, which can also mean *nations.* The distinction between Jews and Gentiles is reflected in numerous NT texts and mirrors a mutually felt separateness in the ancient world. From the Jewish perspective, Israel as a nation had a calling that set it apart from other nations. Further, the people who inhabited these other nations were viewed as alien because of their worship of false gods and their generally looser sexual conduct. While Jew and Gentile could not avoid dealing with each other in the course of everyday life, the Jewish community sought to maintain symbolic boundaries through the rite of circumcision, special dietary laws, and other practices. In the Gospel of Matthew, the boundary between Jew and Gentile becomes apparent in the way Jesus restricts his mission and that of his disciples to Jewish territory. Throughout the story, however, there are hints that Gentiles will eventually share in God's kingdom. And at the end of the Gospel, Jesus lifts the earlier restriction and commissions his apostles to make disciples of *all* nations, to create a community to which Gentiles as well as Jews may belong.

GOSPEL Both the word *gospel* (Anglo-Saxon: *godspel*) and the Greek term *euangelion* which it translates mean *good news.* In the early church, *good news* referred either to Jesus' own preaching or to preaching about Jesus. Matthew, for example, speaks of Jesus proclaiming the good news of the kingdom (4:23). Paul, on the other hand, speaks of the gospel which he and other apostles preach, the good news of what God has done to save us through Jesus Christ (cf. Rom. 1:16; 15:19; 1 Cor. 15:1-2). Only later, in the second century of the Christian era, did *gospel* become a designation for a literary document about Jesus, such as the Gospel According to Matthew. The author of Mark probably contributed to this development by the use of *euangelion* to describe his subject matter in the opening line of his work (Mark 1:1).

A much-debated question among NT scholars is how to classify the books now called Gospels in terms of genre or type of literature. Do the Gospels represent a new literary genre, or do they belong to some existing classification? The prevailing view today is that the Gospels comprise a subtype of the genre of biography in the Greco-Roman world. To put it another way: Mark and his successors were influenced by familiar models of biographical and historical writing as they endeavored to recount Jesus' words and deeds in the form of a structured prose narrative (cf. Aune: 17-76). At the same time, the category of biography does not wholly catch up what the Gospel writers were about. The story the Gospels tell is one in which a *biographical* interest in Jesus is subordinated to a *theological* interest in what God is doing through Jesus and his community.

INCLUSIO/INCLUSION See *Matthew, Literary Characteristics.*

JEWISH GROUPS AND PARTIES In the aftermath of the Maccabean revolt in the second century B.C., several groups emerged within Judaism that continued to be part of the religious landscape of the NT era. These included the *Sadducees*, the *Essenes*, and the *Pharisees*. Our knowledge of these groups is based largely on references in three sources—the NT, rabbinic texts, and the Jewish historian Josephus. For the Essenes, the Dead Sea Scrolls provide yet additional valuable data.

The *Sadducees* appear in our sources as a party of priestly and lay aristocrats. Recognizing only the written Torah as binding, they contested the living tradition of the Pharisees and others. Early on the Sadducees lent their support to the moves by the Hasmonean or Maccabean family to take over the office of high priest. Others, however, reacted differently to this development. For the *Hasidim* or pious ones who had earlier joined with the Maccabees to purify Israel's holy place (1 Macc. 2:42, *Hasideans*), the Hasmonean high priests represented a new kind of defilement.

The group known as *Essenes* came from these disenchanted *Hasidim*. Separating themselves from mainstream Jewish society, the Essenes formed communities where they could practice a more disciplined religious life. This included strict observance of priestly rituals of purity. The best-known Essene enclave was the Qumran community by the Dead Sea, the writings from which exhibit both a rich piety and a fervent eschatological hope.

Like the Essenes, the *Pharisees* derived from the *Hasidim* and sought to practice their Jewish faith in a disciplined and visible manner. Instead of abandoning existing institutions, however, or withdrawing from society, the Pharisees attempted to apply the Torah to every facet of Jewish life. Largely a lay movement, the Pharisees laid the foundation for rabbinic Judaism, and the oral tradition of the Pharisees is now contained in the Mishnah.

While the Pharisees saw themselves as a renewal movement, the Gospels portray them in a different light. In spite of the fact that there were broad areas of common ground between Jesus and the Pharisees, the Gospel writers are sharply critical of this group. In Matthew the Pharisees appear in the forefront of Jewish opposition to Jesus and his summons to a new righteousness. They are depicted as hypocrites, who make a pretense of being righteous while failing to attend to deeper issues of justice and mercy. Their oral law is criticized as burdensome, and as sometimes contrary to the word of God in Scripture.

In evaluating this negative picture of the Pharisees, two considerations are important. On one hand, it is true that a religious group can become so preoccupied with adherence to a particular program of piety that on the whole it ends up thwarting rather than furthering true renewal. This likely was the case with some segments of the Pharisaic movement in the NT era, and to this extent the critique Matthew and others offer is valid. On the other hand, it is also true that groups locked in controversy frequently caricature their opponents with demeaning stereotypes. Wholesale criticism of Pharisees in the Gospels represents just such a stereotype, one that Christians today must refuse to perpetuate.

A fourth group, one that emerged later than the Sadducees, Essenes, and Pharisees, is that of the *Zealots* (cf. Luke 6:15). In the tradition of Phinehas (Num. 25) and the Maccabees (1 Macc. 2:23-28), they were *zealous* for God's law and ready to kill the Gentile oppressor. What we know for sure about the Zealots is that they played a leading role in the Jewish revolt against Rome in A.D. 66-70. For deeply religious reasons, the Zealots were committed to overthrowing the yoke of Roman rule. It is not certain whether the Zealots existed as a distinct party as early as the time of Jesus. Most scholars today think not, arguing that such political unrest as did exist in the early decades of the first century had not yet crystallized into a unified movement (Merkel: 979-982).

JEWISH WRITINGS A number of Jewish writings are cited in the commentary, writings that shed light on or offer parallels to the language and thought world of Matthew. Many of these writings are part of the Hebrew Scriptures or OT, which Matthew often cites according to the Greek translation known as the *Septuagint*. In addition to those books regarded as canonical by all Jews and Christians, the Septuagint also includes more than a dozen writings from the late OT period which we call the *Apocrypha* (hidden works). These additional writings, books like the Wisdom of Solomon, Sirach, and 1 and 2 Maccabees, played a significant role in Greek-speaking Jewish communities and were also part of the early church's Bible.

Beyond those documents which assumed scriptural status, there is a vast body of Jewish writings from the period 200 B.C. to A.D. 200 known as the

Pseudepigrapha. So called because many of its works falsely claim authorship by ancient biblical figures such as Moses or Enoch, the Pseudepigrapha includes apocalyptic works, testaments, legendary expansions of OT stories, wisdom texts, and poetic material. Further writings from the intertestamental period are contained in the *Dead Sea Scrolls*, produced by the Essene community at Qumran. Among the Dead Sea documents we find biblical writings, commentaries on those writings, liturgical texts, apocalyptic texts, and works setting forth guidelines for the life of the community.

As well as writing *new* works, the Jewish community invested considerable energy into expounding old texts, and this too resulted eventually in a massive body of literature. Playing a key role in this enterprise were the persons the Bible refers to as *scribes*, those who devoted themselves to the study, transmission, interpretation, and teaching of Scripture. While scribes did not necessarily belong to a particular party in Judaism, most of the scribes we hear about in the Gospels have links to the Pharisees. They are thus the forerunners of the rabbinic teachers of Matthew's day and later.

Among the texts which emerged from scribal reflection on the OT are the *Targums*. The Targums are Aramaic paraphrases of the Hebrew text, which thus interpret the biblical material in the process of translating it. More elaborate exegesis and interpretation of the biblical text goes by the name of *Midrash*. There are numerous volumes of midrashic commentary on the Hebrew Scriptures, often referred to by the plural form *Midrashim*.

For the Pharisees, the focus of biblical interpretation was developing *oral law* applying the written Torah to all facets of everyday life. Mark 7:3 calls this "the tradition of the elders." A major and authoritative *written* compilation of these legal traditions is found in the *Mishnah*, which was produced around A.D. 200. The Mishnah contains 63 tractates, which are roughly equivalent in length to the books of the Bible. Rabbinic teachers continued to develop the materials in the Mishnah, and their extensive additional commentary appears together with the Mishnah in the *Talmud*. The Babylonian Talmud contains the work of rabbis in Babylon, while the Palestinian Talmud is the product of Jewish scholars in Palestine. To learn more about Jewish writings outside the OT, see the works by Nickelsburg and Perelmutter noted in the Bibliography.

MATTHEW, DISTINCTIVE THEMES Scholars of an earlier generation often delighted in summarizing the major doctrines or ideas of a given biblical book. Underlying such an exercise was the assumption that the primary aim of biblical authors was to communicate certain truths to their readers. That is a dubious assumption, however, especially in the case of the Gospels. Like the other evangelists, Matthew is concerned first and foremost to tell a *story*, and this story cannot be reduced to a list of moral or spiritual concepts. Nevertheless, the narrative Matthew constructs does develop a number of distinctive or characteristic themes. The paragraphs that follow attempt to highlight some of these themes, introducing each with a related phrase from the Gospel.

(1) *The kingdom of heaven has come near* (4:17). The all-encompassing, overarching theme of the First Gospel is the advent of God's reign or rule. While each of the Gospels has kingdom sayings, no one introduces the topic more frequently or develops it more fully than Matthew. The good news that Jesus brings is characterized as good news *of the kingdom* (cf. 4:23; 9:35; 24:14). The blessing promised to the righteous in the Beatitudes is life in the kingdom (cf. 5:3, 10). The great majority of Jesus' parables are introduced as

stories about the kingdom (cf. 13:24; 18:23; 20:1; 22:1; 25:1). As depicted by Matthew, God's reign is both future and present. Not until Jesus' coming at the end will God's reign be fully established on a cosmic scale. Already, however, that reign is taking hold of history, contending with the forces of evil and creating a new order in the midst of the old (cf. TBC and TLC on 4:17-25).

(2) *They shall name him Emmanuel* (1:23). As noted above in the entry on Christology, Matthew views Jesus as nothing less than God-with-us. The same God who acted powerfully in Israel's story in days of old is now at work again in the person of Jesus. That is why Jesus can announce that the kingdom has come near in his mission. That is why Jesus is able to save people from sin and offer them forgiveness. That is why Jesus is able to redefine the Torah given to Israel at Sinai. That is why Jesus is able to calm a turbulent sea or to walk on the water. That is why Jesus is able to feed Israel in the wilderness. That is why human powers cannot confine him to his grave. And that is why his disciples worship him as God's Son and their Lord.

(3) *I have come not to abolish but to fulfill* (5:17). The mission Jesus undertakes in Matthew's story evokes conflict and opposition. Jesus sets his word over and against some of both Jewish traditions and biblical injunctions. He delivers stinging indictments of Israel's leaders. In spite of this, Matthew argues that Jesus and his program by no means annul the heritage of Israel. Instead, Jesus comes to *fulfill* Israel's story. He relives or reenacts key moments of that saga in the events of his life and mission. He teaches and acts in ways foretold in prophetic oracles. He points his hearers to the will of God that underlies the Torah. And he forms a community committed to carry out Israel's calling in faithful covenant with Israel's God (cf. TBC and TLC on 5:17-48).

(4) *Blessed are those who hunger and thirst for righteousness* (5:6). According to Matthew, *righteousness* is central to the agenda of both John the Baptist and Jesus (cf. 3:15; 5:6; 5:20; 6:33; 21:32). The meaning this term carries in the First Gospel is that of a right relationship with God. As such, righteousness is both a gift and a goal. It is a *gift* in the sense that God's advent in Jesus opens up the possibility of a right relationship. Jesus enables us so to see and hear, that living within God's will and purpose is now within reach. In claiming this gift, however, we do not yet fully possess it. A right relationship with God is a *goal* we must continually seek, an ongoing quest. It is precisely those who keep moving *toward* that end who will find it *in* the end.

(5) *Take my yoke upon you, and learn from me* (11:29). The calling and forming of disciples is at the heart of the program Jesus pursues in Matthew's narrative. The first account of Jesus' public activity tells of an invitation to specific persons to *follow me* (4:18-22), and subsequent accounts relate other call episodes (8:18-22; 9:9). Those who become disciples receive Jesus' instruction (cf. 5:1-2; 18:1ff.) and come to understand his message in a way that eludes the crowds (cf. 11:25-27; 13:10-17, 36ff.). In spite of the fact that the faith of the disciples sometimes falters (cf. 14:31; 17:20), the reader knows that disciples enjoy a special relationship with Jesus. It comes as good news, then, at the end of the Gospel, when the reader discovers that the circle of discipleship is not limited to the twelve. Jesus invites all to become his disciples. And through his sayings as assembled in the Gospel, later followers can continue to learn from the divine Wisdom present in Jesus.

(6) *I will build my church* (16:18). For Matthew, the goal of Jesus' mission as God-with-us is not simply to touch many individuals. Rather, Jesus seeks

to create a righteous *community*, a community that serves as a light to the world (5:14-16). This was Israel's calling among the nations (cf. Isa. 42:6-7), and Jesus' mission begins as an appeal to all Israel. As the story proceeds, however, and Israel at large rejects Jesus' summons, Jesus announces that he will reconstitute the people of God on a new foundation. He will build *his* community, the messianic community of God's kingdom, on those he has called as his disciples (16:18-19). This community, Matthew tells us, knows itself to be the family of God (cf. 23:8-10; 12:49-50), enjoys God's protection when evil powers assail it (16:18), and can order its life with divine authority because Jesus is present in its midst (18:18-20; 16:19).

(7) *Go therefore and make disciples* (28:19). The story Matthew tells is a story of mission, a story in which coming and sending shape the plot. Jesus is aware that he himself *comes* to Israel as one sent by God (cf. 9:13; 10:34, 40; 11:19; 15:24; 20:28), and he sends out co-workers to extend and complete his mission (cf. 10:5ff., 16ff.; 23:34; 28:18-20). In its earliest stages, this missionary venture is restricted to *the lost sheep of the house of Israel* (10:5-6; 15:24). The disciples receive an expanded assignment, however, at the conclusion of the story. As emissaries of the resurrected Jesus, they are dispatched on a mission to all the peoples of the world (28:19-20; cf. 5:13-16; 24:14). The community that Jesus forms, therefore, does not live for itself alone. To be the church is to be in mission, inviting the world to receive the good news of God's reign.

MATTHEW, LITERARY CHARACTERISTICS The overall statement that best describes Matthew's literary artistry is that he *knits things together with great skill and great care*. Among the techniques he uses to achieve this end, the following are noteworthy:

(1) *Numerical arrangements*. In both smaller and larger units, Matthew lists or arranges items according to numerical patterns—groups of three, groups of seven, etc. Thus the genealogy in 1:2-17 contains three groups of fourteen generations each. Sayings of Jesus are organized into five major discourses. Both the Beatitudes in 5:3-10 and the parables in chapter 13 contain two groups of four. Three parables of rejection are told in 21:28—22:14. Seven woes are pronounced against the scribes and Pharisees in chapter 23. Other examples abound.

(2) *Thematic groupings*. As Matthew draws on his sources, he frequently groups related material to address a particular topic at greater length. This is especially evident in the five major discourses. Thus the various sayings in chapter 10 develop the theme of mission, those in chapter 13 comment on the kingdom of heaven, and those in chapters 24—25 deal with endtime judgment. The same interest in thematic composition is evident in the collections of miracle stories in chapters 8—9, in the controversy stories of chapter 12, and in the critique of Jewish leaders in chapter 23.

(3) *Repetition*. Again and again in his composition, Matthew repeats certain words and phrases. Repetition underscores key motifs, reinforces the memory, and assists the reader in making important connections. One of the most significant uses of this technique is known as *inclusio* or inclusion. Here a phrase opening a section of material is repeated or restated in similar form at the end, thus *enclosing* the unit (cf. 5:1-2 and 7:28-29; 5:17 and 7:12; 4:23 and 9:35; 1:23 and 28:20). Another type of repetition consists of formulas such as those used to introduce fulfillment quotations (cf. 1:22; 12:17) or to conclude discourses (cf. 7:28; 11:1). Still other examples include paral-

lelism such as we find in the Beatitudes (cf. 5:3-10) and use of verbal echoes to link earlier and later material (cf. 3:2 and 4:17; 3:7 and 23:33; 5:48 and 19:21; 10:22 and 24:9).

(4) *Chiasmus*. Chiasmus is the technical term for an inverted sequence of parallel literary elements. Instead of *a a' b b'*, the items are arranged in the order *a b b' a'*. A clear example of a chiastic pattern is the quotation of Isaiah 6:10 in Matthew 13:15:

a. This people's *heart* has grown dull,
b. Their *ears* are hard of hearing,
c. They have shut their *eyes*,
c'. That they may not look with their *eyes*,
b'. And listen with their *ears*,
a'. And understand with their *heart*.

Other microexamples of chiasmus in Matthew include 1:1, 17; 7:6; 11:17-19; and 23:16-22. On a larger scale, Matthew sometimes follows a chiastic pattern in arranging the components of an entire literary unit (cf. Preview to 26:47—27:10 and to 27:57—28:20).

(5) *Comparison and contrast*. Yet another technique Matthew uses to structure his material is contrasting *this* with *that*. Sometimes the contrasts occur in back-to-back vignettes. Note, for example, how 11:20-30 contrasts judgment on Israel's cities with the *rest* promised to disciples, or how 26:57-75 contrasts Jesus' confession with Peter's denial. In other instances, the contrasting items are more widely separated in the text, but no less apparent. Thus the woes addressed to opponents in 23:13-36 stand over against the Beatitudes spoken to disciples in 5:3-11. And the depiction of Galilee as a land of promise and hope (cf. 4:15-16; 28:7, 10) stands over against descriptions of Jerusalem as a place of unbelief and violence (cf. 2:3; 21:10; 23:37). Contrasts such as these help to develop the plot of conflict that shapes Matthew's story (cf. Kingsbury, 1988:3-9).

(6) *Foreshadowing*. A common device in plot construction is the introduction of episodes early in a narrative which anticipate later developments. Matthew uses this device quite effectively. Thus the anxious consultation of religious leaders in Jerusalem at the time of Jesus' birth foreshadows the conspiracy of leaders seeking Jesus' death in the passion narrative (cf. 2:3-4; 26:3-5). The worship of the infant Jesus by the magi anticipates the worship of the risen Jesus by the disciples (cf. 2:2, 11; 28:16-17). Satan's offer of worldwide dominion to Jesus in the temptation narrative looks ahead to God's delegation of such authority to Jesus at the end of the story (cf. 4:8-9; 28:18). And the commissioning of the disciples for a mission to Israel foreshadows the later commissioning of the disciples to go to all nations (cf. 10:5ff.; 28:19-20).

MATTHEW'S SOURCES A great deal of scholarly study of the Gospels in the nineteenth and twentieth centuries can be characterized as an attempt to answer two questions: (1) Why do the Gospels *agree* where they agree? (2) Why do the Gospels *differ* where they differ? According to most scholars, part of the answer to the first question is *common sources*: The Gospel writers used each other's work and/or additional common materials. The writer of Luke implies as much in the preface to his narrative (cf. Luke 1:1-4), and there is good reason to believe that Matthew likewise drew on earlier sources.

The points of agreement which suggest common sources consist of two basic types. First, there are passages where *all three* synoptic Gospels (Matthew, Mark, Luke) agree in terms of common material, common order, and/or common wording. For example, compare Matthew 21:1-27; Mark 11:1-33; and Luke 19:28—20:8. Where differences occur in this so-called triple tradition, Mark seems to be the common element. Rarely do Matthew and Luke agree with each other against Mark. Further, there are numerous instances where it is easy to understand why Matthew or Luke might have edited Mark's version, but difficult to argue why Mark would have altered Matthew's or Luke's version. For these and other reasons, most scholars hold that Mark is the earliest of the synoptic Gospels, and that both Matthew and Luke used some edition of Mark as one of their sources.

Second, there are passages where Matthew and Luke have common material that is not found in Mark. For example, compare Matthew 4:1-11 and Luke 4:1-13; Matthew 5:1-48 and Luke 6:17-36; Matthew 11:1-19 and Luke 7:18-35. We might explain these parallels by Matthew's use of Luke or Luke's use of Matthew. However, neither Matthew nor Luke seem to be aware of the other's stories of Jesus' birth. Consequently, the majority of scholars explain the material Matthew and Luke have in common on the basis of a source outside the Gospels to which both had access, a source which has since disappeared. The designation usually given to this hypothetical source is *Q*, which is the first letter of the German word for source (*Quelle*). In the opinion of many writers, *Q* was more of an open-ended collection of material (oral and/or written) than a document with a fixed text, and it is likely that Matthew and Luke drew on different editions of *Q*.

The proposal for Gospel sources sketched above is commonly known as the Two-Source theory of Gospel origins (cf. diagram). To be sure, there are questions it does not address, such as where Matthew obtained material not found in either Mark or Q, or how the somewhat independent tradition found in the Fourth Gospel relates to the synoptic tradition. As far as it goes, however, the Two-Source theory provides a plausible account of Gospel parallels and a constructive foundation for further analysis of the Gospels. The commentary on Matthew in the preceding pages assumes and builds on this theory, while avoiding reference to the somewhat arcane symbol *Q*.

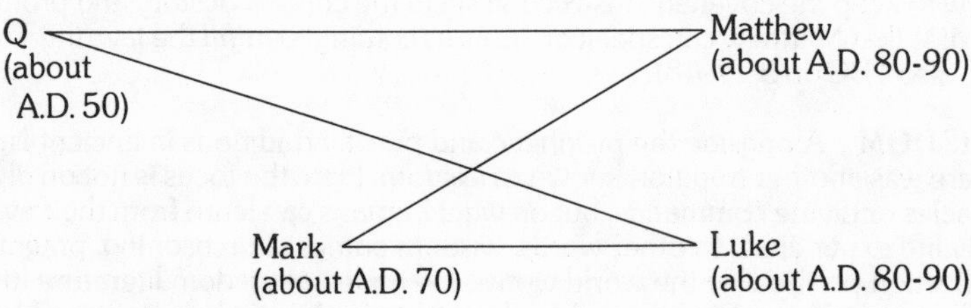

MESSIAH See *Christ/Christology*.

MIDRASH See *Jewish Writings*.

MISHNAH See *Jewish Writings*.

POSTEXILIC See *Exile.*

QUMRAN Khirbet Qumran is the name for the ruins of an Essene (see "Jewish Groups and Parties") community located near the northwest corner of the Dead Sea. The so-called Dead Sea Scrolls produced by this community were discovered in nearby caves.

SEPTUAGINT See *Jewish Writings.*

SYNOPTIC The adjective *synoptic* suggests seeing something from the same vantage point. Matthew, Mark, and Luke are frequently called the *synoptic Gospels* (or simply the Synoptics) because they give us similar pictures of Jesus' ministry and teaching. Related expressions include *synoptic tradition* and *synoptic problem*. *Synoptic tradition* refers to the common body of sayings and stories on which the synoptic Gospels draw. The *synoptic problem* is the question of how to explain the agreements between these Gospels (cf. *Matthew's Sources*).

TALMUD See *Jewish Writings.*

TARGUM See *Jewish Writings.*

THEOPHANY See *Epiphany.*

TORAH The Hebrew word *Torah* means *teaching* or *instruction*. Used originally to refer to specific instances of instruction in Israel's story (cf. Exod. 13:9; 18:16; Num. 19:2; Deut. 17:8-11; Josh. 1:7-8; Jer. 6:19), Torah later became a technical term referring to the Pentateuch. It is also used in a broader sense to refer to the totality of Jewish teaching, both written and oral. Because Israel's Torah abounds in commandments and statutes, both ethical and ritual, the word *law* is frequently used as synonymous with Torah. The understanding of Torah as law is already apparent in the LXX, where Torah is translated as *nomos* (*law*), and the NT builds on this understanding. However, Israel's Torah is more than legal codes. It is God's instruction to Israel on how to keep the covenant, instruction set in the context of story and promise. So it is that Matthew can speak of Jesus as coming to *fulfill* the law, the Torah (cf. also TBC on 5:17-48).

WISDOM Alongside the prophetic and priestly traditions in ancient Israel, there was another tradition known as *wisdom*. Here the focus is not on divine oracles or divine commands, but on what humans can learn from their everyday life experience. In other words, wisdom comes via reasoning, pragmatic reflection on the way the world works. Examples of wisdom literature in the OT include Proverbs, Job, and Ecclesiastes. As the wisdom tradition developed, some writers began to relate wisdom more closely to Israel's faith and story. Wisdom came to be viewed not merely as the object of human searching, but as a product or expression of God's self-revelation in history and creation. We see the shift in the differing ways Lady Wisdom functions in various texts. In some cases, the personification of wisdom as a woman who calls persons to gain understanding is simply a literary device (cf. Prov. 1:20ff.; 9:1ff.). In texts such as those found in Sirach and the Wisdom of Solomon, however, personified wisdom speaks as a divine agent, the Wisdom of God (cf. Sir.

24:1ff.; Wisd. of Sol. 7:22ff.; Prov. 8:22-31). For the study of Matthew, familiarity with the wisdom tradition is important in two respects: (1) A number of sayings ascribed to Jesus fit within this tradition (for example, Matt. 6:19-34). (2) Matthew views Jesus as one who embodies divine Wisdom, and as thus able to speak for God in all that he teaches (cf. 11:25-30, and also TBC on 7:13-29).

Abila
Damascus
ABILENE
Sidon
Zarephath
Mt. Hermon
N
W
E
S
SYRIA
Tyre
Caesarea Philippi
PHOENICIA
GALILEE
Ptolemais
Chorazin
Bethsaida
Capernaum
Mt. Carmel
Magadan
Sea of Galilee
Cana
Tiberias
Nazareth
Mt. Tabor
Gadara
Nain
DECAPOLIS
Mediterranean Sea
Caesarea
Salim
Aenon
Jordan River
Gerasa
Samaria
Mt. Ebal
SAMARIA
Sychar
Mt. Gerizim
Joppa
+Arimathea
PEREA
Ephraim
Jericho
+Bethany
Emmaus
Azotus
Jerusalem
Qumran
JUDEA
Bethany
Ascalon
Bethlehem
Dead Sea
Machaerus
Gaza
Hebron
IDUMEA
NABATEA
Palestine in New Testament Times
Map by Paula Johnson, Merrill R. Miller, and Jan Gleysteen
+ Means city has uncertain location

The New Testament
World
Map by Paula Johnson, Merrill R. Miller, and Jan Gleysteen
+ Means uncertain location
BLACK SEA
ADRIATIC SEA
AEGEAN SEA
MEDITERRANEAN SEA
ITALY
Rome
Puteoli
Neapolis
SICILY
Rhegium
Syracuse
MELITA
MELITENE
ILLYRICUM
OR
DALMATIA
MOESIA
THRACE
MACEDONIA
Philippi
Neapolis
Amphipolis
Apollonia
Thessalonica
Beroea
SAMO-
THRACE
ACHAIA
Nicopolis
Athens
Corinth
Cenchreae
Mysia
Troas
Assos
Mitylene
Pergamum
Thyatira
Sardis
Philadelphia
Hierapolis
Colossae
Laodicea
Smyrna
SAMOS
Ephesus
Miletus
Trogyllium
PATMOS
COS
Cos
Cnidus
Rhodes
RHODES
CRETE
Phoenix
Fair Havens
Salmone
CAUDA
CLAUDA
ASIA
BITHYNIA and PONTUS
GALATIA
Pessinus
Ancyra
Tavium
CAPPADOCIA
Phrygia
Pisidia
Antioch
Iconium
Lystra
Derbe
Lycaonia
Cilician Gates
LYCIA
PAMPHYLIA
Patara
Myra
Perga
Attalia
CILICIA
TRACHEA
Tarsus
CILICIA and SYRIA
Seleucia
Antioch
CYPRUS
Salamis
Paphos
Sidon
Damascus
Tyre
Ptolemais
Caesarea
Joppa
Jerusalem
Gaza
Cyrene
LIBYA
Alexandria
EGYPT
N
S
E
W

Bibliography

Achtemeier, Paul J., ed.
1985 *Harper's Bible Dictionary*. San Francisco: Harper & Row, Publishers.

Albright, W. F., and C. S. Mann
1971 *Matthew* (The Anchor Bible). Garden City, N.Y.: Doubleday & Company, Inc.

Allen, Willoughby C.
1912 *A Critical and Exegetical Commentary on the Gospel According to S. Matthew* (International Critical Commentary). Edinburgh: T. & T. Clark Limited.

Allison, Dale C.
1987 "The Structure of the Sermon on the Mount." *Journal of Biblical Literature* 106:423-445.

Augsburger, Myron S.
1982 *Matthew* (The Communicator's Commentary Series). Waco, Texas: Word Books.

Augustine of Hippo
1956 *Sermons on Selected Lessons of the New Testament* (Nicene and Post-Nicene Fathers of the Christian Church, vol. 6). Grand Rapids, Mich.: Willliam B. Eerdmans Publishing Company.

Aune, David E.
1987 *The New Testament in Its Literary Environment*. Philadelphia: The Westminster Press.

Bacon, Benjamin
1930 *Studies in Matthew*. New York: Holt.

Barrett, C. K.
1987 *The New Testament Background: Selected Documents*, rev. ed. San Francisco: Harper & Row, Publishers.

Bauer, David R.
1988 *The Structure of Matthew's Gospel: A Study in Literary Design*. Sheffield, Great Britian: Sheffield Academic Press.

Bauman, Clarence
1985 *The Sermon on the Mount: The Modern Quest for Its Meaning*. Macon, Ga.: Mercer University Press.

Beare, Frank W.
1981 *The Gospel According to Matthew*. San Francisco: Harper & Row, Publishers.

Beasley-Murray, G. R.
1986 *Jesus and the Kingdom of God*. Grand Rapids, Mich.: William B. Eerdmans Publishing Company.

Betz, Hans Dieter
1985 *Essays on the Sermon on the Mount*. Philadelphia: Fortress Press.

Bonhoeffer, Dietrich
1959 *The Cost of Discipleship*, 2nd ed. New York: Macmillan Company.

Bornkamm, Günther, Gerhard Barth, and Heinz Joachim Held
1963 *Tradition and Interpretation in Matthew*. Philadelphia: The Westminster Press.

Braght, Thieleman Janszoon van
1950 *Martyrs Mirror*. Scottdale, Pa.: Herald Press.

Brown, Raymond E.
1977 *The Birth of the Messiah*. Garden City, N.Y.: Doubleday & Company, Inc.

Brown, Raymond E., Karl P. Donfried, and John Reumann
1973 *Peter in the New Testament*. Minneapolis, Minn.: Augsburg Publishing House.

Brown, Raymond E., and John P. Meier
1983 *Antioch and Rome: New Testament Cradles of Catholic Christianity*. New York: Paulist Press.

Brown, Schuyler
1979 "The Matthean Apocalypse." *Journal for the Study of the New Testament* 4:2-27.
1980 "The Matthean Community and the Gentile Mission." *Novum Testamentum* 22:193-221.

Burnett, Fred W.
1979 *The Testament of Jesus-Sophia: A Redaction-Critical Study of the Eschatological Discourse in Matthew*. Washington, D.C.: University Press of America.

Calvin, John
1960 *Institutes of the Christian Religion* (Library of Christian Classics, vols. 20-21). Philadelphia: The Westminster Press.
1972 *A Harmony of the Gospels: Matthew, Mark and Luke* (Calvin's New Testament Commentaries, vols. 1-3). Grand Rapids, Mich.: William B. Eerdmans Publishing Company.

Charlesworth, James H., ed.
1983 *The Old Testament Pseudepigrapha*, 2 vols. Garden City, N.Y.: Doubleday & Company, Inc.

Chilton, Bruce, and J. I. H. McDonald
1987 *Jesus and the Ethics of the Kingdom*. Grand Rapids, Mich.: William B. Eerdmans Publishing Company.

Chrysostom, John
1956 *Homilies on the Gospel of Saint Matthew* (Nicene and Post-Nicene Fathers of the Christian Church, vol. 10). Grand Rapids, Mich.: William B. Eerdmans Publishing Company.

Clement of Alexandria
1956 *Who Is the Rich Man That Shall Be Saved*? (The Ante-Nicene Fathers, vol. 2). Grand Rapids, Mich.: William B. Eerdmans Publishing Company.

Combrink, H. J. B.
1983 "The Structure of the Gospel of Matthew as Narrative." *Tyndale Bulletin* 34:61-90.

Cope, O. Lamar
1969 "Matthew 25:31-46—The Sheep and the Goats Reinterpreted." *Novum Testamentum* 11:32-44.
1976 *Matthew: A Scribe Trained for the Kingdom of Heaven*. Washington, D.C.: Catholic Biblical Association of America.

Crosby, Michael H.
1988 *House of Disciples: Church, Economics, and Justice in Matthew*. Maryknoll, N.Y.: Orbis Books.

Crossan, John Dominic
1973 *In Parables: The Challenge of the Historical Jesus*. New York: Harper & Row, Publishers.

Davies, W. D.
1963 *The Setting of the Sermon on the Mount*. Cambridge, Great Britian: Cambridge University Press.

Davies, W. D., and Dale C. Allison
1988 *A Critical and Exegetical Commentary on the Gospel According to Saint Matthew*, vol. 1 (International Critical Commentary, new series). Edinburgh: T. & T. Clark Limited.

Deutsch, Celia
1987 *Hidden Wisdom and the Easy Yoke: Wisdom, Torah, and Discipleship in Matthew*. Sheffield, Great Britian: Sheffield Academic Press.

Dodd, C. H.
1961 *The Parables of the Kingdom*, rev. ed. New York: Charles Scribner's Sons.

Donahue, John R.
1988 *The Gospel in Parable: Metaphor, Narrative, and Theology in the Synoptic Gospels*. Philadelphia: Fortress Press.

Donaldson, Terence L.
1985 *Jesus on the Mountain: A Study in Matthean Theology*. Sheffield, Great Britian: Sheffield Academic Press.

Driver, John
1980 *Kingdom Citizens*. Scottdale, Pa.: Herald Press.

Drury, John
1985 *The Parables in the Gospels: History and Allegory*. New York: Crossroad Publishing Company.

Durnbaugh, Donald F.
1958 *European Origins of the Brethren*. Elgin, Ill.: Brethren Press.
1967 *The Brethren in Colonial America*. Elgin, Ill.: Brethren Press.
1968 *The Believers' Church. The History and Character of Radical Protestantism*. New York: The Macmillan Company; 1985 ed., Scottdale, Pa.: Herald Press.

Edwards, Richard A.
1985 *Matthew's Story of Jesus*. Philadelphia: Fortress Press.
1985 "Uncertain Faith: Matthew's Portrait of the Disciples." *Discipleship in the New Testament*. Edited by F. F. Segovia. Philadelphia: Fortress Press.

Eller, Vernard
1971 "Beliefs." *Church of the Brethren Past and Present*. Edited by Donald F. Durnbaugh. Elgin, Ill.: Brethren Press.

Ellis, Peter F.
1974 *Matthew: His Mind and His Message*. Collegeville, Minn.: The Liturgical Press.

Filson, Floyd V.
1960 *The Gospel According to St. Matthew* (Harper's New Testament Commentaries). New York: Harper & Row, Publishers.

Fiorenza, Elisabeth Schüssler
1983 *In Memory of Her: A Feminist Theological Reconstruction of Christian Origins*. New York: Crossroad Publishing Company.

France, Richard T.
1985 *The Gospel According to Matthew: An Introduction and Commentary* (Tyndale New Testament Commentaries). Grand Rapids, Mich.: William B. Eerdmans Publishing Company.
1989 *Matthew: Evangelist and Teacher*. Grand Rapids, Mich.: Zondervan Publishing House.

Frankemölle, Hubert
1974 *Jahwebund und Kirche Christi: Studien zur Form- und Traditionsgeschichte des "Evangeliums" nach Matthäus*. Münster: Aschendorff.

Freyne, Sean
1988 *Galilee, Jesus, and the Gospels: Literary Approaches and Historical Investigations*. Philadelphia: Fortress Press.

Fuller, Reginald H.
1963 *Interpreting the Miracles*. London: SCM Press.

Funk, Robert W.
1985 *New Gospel Parallels*, vol. 1. Philadelphia: Fortress Press.

Garland, David E.
1979 *The Intention of Matthew 23*. Leiden: E. J. Brill.

Gerhardsson, Birger
1966 *The Testing of God's Son*. Lund: C. W. K. Gleerup.
1979 *The Mighty Acts of Jesus According to Matthew*. Lund: C. W. K. Gleerup.

Gish, Arthur G.
1979 *Living in Christian Community*. Scottdale, Pa.: Herald Press.

Gnilka, Joachim
1978-79 *Das Evangelium nach Markus*, 2 vols. (Evangelisch-Katholischer Kommentar zum Neuen Testament, 2/1 and 2/2). Neukirchen-Vluyn: Neukirchener Verlag; and Zürich, Einsiedeln, Köln: Benziger Verlag.
1986-88 *Das Matthäusevangelium*, 2 vols. (Herders Theologischer Kommentar zum Neuen Testament). Freiburg, Basel, Wien: Herder.

Goulder, M. D.
1974 *Midrash and Lection in Matthew*. London: S. P. C. K.

Gray, Sherman W.
1989 *The Least of My Brothers; Matthew 25:31-46: A History of Interpretation*. Atlanta: Scholars Press.
Guelich, Robert A.
1982 *The Sermon on the Mount: A Foundation for Understanding.* Waco, Texas: Word Books.
Gundry, Robert H.
1967 *The Use of the Old Testament in St. Matthew's Gospel.* Leiden: E. J. Brill.
1982 *Matthew. A Commentary on His Literary and Theological Art.* Grand Rapids, Mich.: William B. Eerdmans Publishing Company.
Hagner, Donald A.
1985 "Apocalyptic Motifs in the Gospel of Matthew." *Horizons in Biblical Theology* 7:53-82.
Hare, Douglas R. A.
1967 *The Theme of Jewish Persecution of Christians in the Gospel According to St. Matthew.* Cambridge, Great Britian: Cambridge University Press.
Harner, Philip B.
1975 *Understanding the Lord's Prayer*. Philadelphia: Fortress Press.
Hauerwas, Stanley
1983 *The Peaceable Kingdom: A Primer in Christian Ethics.* Notre Dame, Ind.: University of Notre Dame Press.
Hendrickx, Herman
1984 *The Infancy Narratives*. London: Geoffrey Chapman.
1984 *The Passion Narratives of the Synoptic Gospels*. London: Geoffrey Chapman.
1984 *The Resurrection Narratives of the Synoptic Gospels*. London: Geoffrey Chapman.
1984 *The Sermon on the Mount*. London: Geoffrey Chapman.
1986 *The Parables of Jesus*. London: Geoffrey Chapman.
1987 *The Miracle Stories of the Synoptic Gospels*. London: Geoffrey Chapman.
Hengel, Martin
1974 *Property and Riches in the Early Church*. Philadelphia: Fortress Press.
1981 *The Charismatic Leader and His Followers*. New York: Crossroad Publishing Company.
Hill, David
1972 *The Gospel of Matthew* (New Century Bible). London: Oliphants.
Horsley, Richard
1987 *Jesus and the Spiral of Violence. Popular Jewish Resistance in Roman Palestine*. San Francisco: Harper & Row, Publishers.
Hubbard, B. J.
1974 *The Matthean Redaction of a Primitive Apostolic Commissioning: An Exegesis of Matthew 28:16-20*. Missoula, Mont.: Scholars Press.
Hummel, Reinhart
1963 *Die Auseinandersetzung zwischen Kirche und Judentum im Matthäusevangelium*. Munich: Chr. Kaiser.
Interpretation
1987 Vol. 41, no. 2 (special issue on Sermon on the Mount).

Jeremias, Joachim
1963 *The Parables of Jesus*, rev. ed. New York: Charles Scribner's Sons.
Jeschke, Marlin
1988 *Discipling in the Church: Recovering a Ministry of the Gospel*, 3rd ed. Scottdale, Pa.: Herald Press.
Johnson, Marshall D.
1969 *The Purpose of the Biblical Genealogies*. Cambridge, Great Britian: Cambridge University Press.
Jonge, Marinus de
1988 *Christology in Context: The Earliest Christian Response to Jesus*. Philadelphia: The Westminster Press.
Kennedy, George A.
1984 *New Testament Interpretation Through Rhetorical Criticism*. Chapel Hill, N.C.: University of North Carolina Press.
Kierkegaard, Søren
1948 *The Gospel of Suffering*. Minneapolis, Minn.: Augsburg Publishing House.
1961 *Christian Discourses*. New York: Oxford University Press.
Kingsbury, Jack Dean
1969 *The Parables of Jesus in Matthew 13*. London: S. P. C. K.
1975 *Matthew: Structure, Christology, Kingdom*. Philadelphia: Fortress Press.
1978 "Observations on the Miracle Stories of Matthew 8—9." *Catholic Biblical Quarterly* 40:559-573.
1979 "The Figure of Peter in Matthew's Gospel as a Theological Problem." *Journal of Biblical Literature* 98:67-83.
1984 "The Figure of Jesus in Matthew's Story: A Literary-Critical Probe." *Journal for the Study of the New Testament* 21:3-36.
1986 *Matthew*, 2nd ed. (Proclamation Commentaries). Philadelphia: Fortress Press.
1988 *Matthew As Story*, 2nd ed. Philadelphia: Fortress Press.
Kissinger, Warren S.
1975 *The Sermon on the Mount: A History of Interpretation and Bibliography*. Metuchen, N.J.: Scarecrow Press, Inc.
1979 *The Parables of Jesus. A History of Interpretation and Bibliography*. Metuchen, N.J.: The Scarecrow Press, Inc.
Klaassen, Walter, ed.
1981 *Anabaptism in Outline: Selected Primary Sources*. Scottdale, Pa.: Herald Press.
Klassen, William
1966 *The Forgiving Community*. Philadelphia: The Westminster Press.
Koenig, John
1979 *Jews and Christians in Dialogue: New Testament Foundations*. Philadelphia: The Westminster Press.
Küng, Hans
1976 *The Church*. Garden City, N.Y.: Doubleday & Company, Inc.
Künzel, Georg
1978 *Studien zum Gemeindeverständnis des Matthäus-Evangeliums*. Stuttgart: Calwer Verlag.
Ladd, George Eldon
1964 *Jesus and the Kingdom*. New York: Harper & Row, Publishers.

Lambrecht, Jan
1972 "The Parousia Discourse: Composition and Content in Mt. XXIV-XXV." *L'Évangile selon Matthieu. Rédaction et Théologie*. Edited by M. Didier. Gembloux: Duculot.
1985 *The Sermon on the Mount: Proclamation and Exhortation*. Wilmington, Del.: Michael Glazier, Inc.

Lange, Joachim, ed.
1980 *Das Matthäus-Evangelium*. Darmstadt: Wissenschaftliche Buchgesellschaft.

LaVerdiere, Eugene A., and William G. Thompson
1976 "New Testament Communities in Transition: A Study of Matthew and Luke." *Theological Studies* 37:567-597.

Liechty, Daniel
1988 *Andreas Fischer and the Sabbatarian Anabaptists*. Scottdale, Pa.: Herald Press.

Lindars, Barnabas
1983 *Jesus Son of Man*. Grand Rapids, Mich.: William B. Eerdmans Publishing Company.

Lohfink, Gerhard
1984 *Jesus and Community*. Philadelphia: Fortress Press.

Luther, Martin
1960 *D. Martin Luther's Evangelien-Auslegung*, Zweiter Teil. Edited by Erwin Mülhaupt. Göttingen: Vandenhoeck & Ruprecht.

Luz, Ulrich
1989 *Matthew 1—7: A Commentary* (Evangelisch-Katholischer Kommentar zum Neuen Testament, 1/1). Minneapolis: Augsburg Fortress.

Macmullen, Ramsay
1984 *Christianizing the Roman Empire*. New Haven, Conn.: Yale University Press.

M'Neile, Alan Hugh
1915 *The Gospel According to St. Matthew*. London: Macmillan & Co. Ltd.

Matera, Frank J.
1986 *Passion Narratives and Gospel Theologies: Interpreting the Synoptics Through Their Passion Stories*. New York: Paulist Press.
1986 "The Plot of Matthew's Gospel." *Catholic Biblical Quarterly* 49:233-253.

Mays, James Luther, ed.
1981 *Interpreting the Gospels*. Philadelphia: Fortress Press.

McArthur, Harvey K.
1960 *Understanding the Sermon on the Mount*. New York: Harper & Brothers, Publishers.

Meier, John P.
1976 *Law and History in Matthew's Gospel*. Rome: Biblical Institute Press.
1979 *The Vision of Matthew: Christ, Church, and Morality in the First Gospel*. New York: Paulist Press.
1980 *Matthew* (New Testament Message). Wilmington, Del.: Michael Glazier, Inc.

Menno Simons
1956 *The Complete Writings of Menno Simons, c. 1496-1561*. Scottdale, Pa.: Herald Press.

Merkel, H.
1976 "Zealot" in *The Interpreter's Dictionary of the Bible,* Suppl. Vol.: 979-982. Nashville, Tenn.: Abingdon.

Minear, Paul S.
1982 *Matthew, the Teacher's Gospel.* New York: The Pilgrim Press.

Mohrlang, Roger
1984 *Matthew and Paul: A Comparison of Ethical Perspectives.* Cambridge, Great Britian: Cambridge University Press.

Moltmann, Jürgen
1977 *The Church in the Power of the Spirit.* New York: Harper & Row, Publishers.

Montague, George T.
1989 *Companion God: A Cross-Cultural Commentary on the Gospel of Matthew.* New York: Paulist Press.

Mounce, Robert H.
1985 *Matthew: A Good News Commentary.* New York: Harper & Row, Publishers.

Neusner, Jacob
1975 *First Century Judaism in Crisis.* Nashville, Tenn.: Abingdon Press.

Newman, Barclay M., and Philip C. Stine
1988 *A Translator's Handbook on the Gospel of Matthew.* London, New York, Stuttgart: United Bible Societies.

Neyrey, Jerome H.
1985 *Christ Is Community: The Christologies of the New Testament.* Wilmington, Del.: Michael Glazier, Inc.

Nickelsburg, George W. E.
1981 *Jewish Literature Between the Bible and the Mishnah: A Historical and Literary Introduction.* Philadelphia: Fortress Press.

Nolan, Brian M.
1979 *The Royal Son of God: The Christology of Matthew 1—2 in the Setting of the Gospel.* Göttingen: Vandenhoeck & Ruprecht.

Oden, Thomas C.
1978 *Parables of Kierkegaard.* Princeton, N.J.: Princeton University Press.

Patte, Daniel
1987 *The Gospel According to Matthew: A Structural Commentary on Matthew's Faith.* Philadelphia: Fortress Press.

Perelmutter, Hayim Goren
1989 *Siblings: Rabbinic Judaism and Early Christianity at Their Beginnings.* New York: Paulist Press.

Perrin, Norman
1976 *Jesus and the Language of the Kingdom.* Philadelphia: Fortress Press.

Przybylski, Benno
1980 *Righteousness in Matthew and His World of Thought.* Cambridge, Great Britian: Cambridge University Press.

Reumann, John
1982 *"Righteousness" in the New Testament.* Philadelphia: Fortress Press.

Richard, Earl
1988 *Jesus One and Many: The Christological Concept of New Testament Authors.* Wilmington, Del.: Michael Glazier, Inc.

Richardson, Cyril C.
1953 *Early Christian Fathers* (Library of Christian Classics, vol. 1). Philadelphia: The Westminster Press.
Ridderbos, Herman N.
1987 *Matthew* (Bible Student's Commentary). Grand Rapids, Mich.: Zondervan Publishing House.
Rohde, Joachim
1968 *Rediscovering the Teaching of the Evangelists*. Philadelphia: The Westminster Press.
Sand, Alexander
1986 *Das Evangelium nach Matthäus* (Regensburger Neues Testament). Regensburg: Verlag Friedrich Pustet.
Sasson, J. M.
1976 "Ass" in *The Interpreter's Dictionary of the Bible,* Suppl. Vol.: 72-73. Nashville, Tenn.: Abingdon.
Schnackenburg, Rudolf
1963 *God's Rule and Kingdom*. New York: Herder and Herder.
1985-87 *Matthäusevangelium 1,1—16,20;* and *Matthäusevangelium 16,21—28,20* (Die Neue Echter Bibel Kommentar zum Neuen Testament). Würzburg: Echter Verlag.
Schweizer, Eduard
1975 *The Good News According to Matthew*. Atlanta: John Knox Press.
Senior, Donald
1977 *Invitation to Matthew*. Garden City, N.Y.: Doubleday & Company, Inc.
1983 *What Are They Saying About Matthew*? New York: Paulist Press.
1985a "Healing As Boundary-Breaking: The Cross-Cultural Impulse of Early Christianity." Unpublished paper.
1985b *The Passion of Jesus in the Gospel of Matthew*. Wilmington, Del.: Michael Glazier, Inc.
Senior, Donald, and Carroll Stuhlmueller
1983 *The Biblical Foundations for Mission*. Maryknoll, N.Y.: Orbis Books.
Shuler, Philip L.
1982 *A Genre for the Gospels: The Biographical Character of Matthew*. Philadelphia: Fortress Press.
Simons, Menno
See *Menno Simons*.
Smith, Robert H.
1983 *Easter Gospels: The Resurrection of Jesus According to the Four Evangelists*. Minneapolis, Minn.: Augsburg Publishing House.
1989 *Matthew* (Augsburg Commentary on the New Testament). Minneapolis, Minn.: Augsburg Publishing House.
Snodgrass, Klyne
1988 "Matthew and the Law." *Society of Biblical Literature 1988 Seminar Papers*. Atlanta: Scholars Press.
Snyder, Graydon F., and Kenneth M. Shaffer, Jr.
1976 *Texts in Transit*. Elgin, Ill.: Brethren Press.
Stanton, Graham, ed.
1983 *The Interpretation of Matthew*. Philadelphia: Fortress Press.
1984 "The Origin and Purpose of Matthew's Gospel: Matthean

Scholarship from 1945 to 1980." *Aufstieg und Niedergang der römischen Welt*, II.25.3. Edited by Wolfgang Haase. Berlin: Walter de Gruyter & Co.

Stegner, William R.
1989 *Narrative Theology in Early Jewish Christianity*. Philadelphia: Westminster/John Knox.

Stendahl, Krister
1962 "Matthew." *Peake's Commentary on the Bible*. Edited by Matthew Black and H. H. Rowley. London: Thomas Nelson and Sons.
1968 *The School of St. Matthew*, rev. ed. Philadelphia: Fortress Press.

Strecker, Georg
1988 *The Sermon on the Mount: An Exegetical Commentary*. Nashville, Tenn.: Abingdon Press.

Suggs, M. Jack
1970 *Wisdom, Christology, and Law in Matthew's Gospel*. Cambridge, Mass.: Harvard University Press.

Talbert, Charles H.
1977 *What Is a Gospel? The Genre of the Canonical Gospels*. Philadelphia: Fortress Press.

Tannehill, Robert C.
1975 *The Sword of His Mouth*. Philadelphia: Fortress Press.

Theissen, Gerd
1978 *Sociology of Early Palestinian Christianity*. Philadelphia: Fortress Press.
1983 *Miracle Stories of the Early Christian Tradition*. Philadelphia: Fortress Press.

Thompson, Marianne M.
1982 "The Structure of Matthew: An Examination of Two Approaches." *Studia Biblical et Theologica* 12:195-238.

Thompson, William G.
1970 *Matthew's Advice to a Divided Community: Mt. 17:22—18:35*. Rome: Biblical Institute Press.
1974 "An Historical Perspective in the Gospel of Matthew." *Journal of Biblical Literature* 93:243-262.
1989 *Matthew's Story: Good News for Uncertain Times*. New York: Paulist Press.

Tilborg, S. Van
1972 *The Jewish Leaders in Matthew*. Leiden: E. J. Brill.

Trilling, Wolfgang
1964 *Das wahre Israel: Studien zur Theologie des Matthäus-Evangeliums*. Munich: Kösel Verlag.

Vermes, Geza
1968 *The Dead Sea Scrolls in English*. New York: Penguin Books.

Viviano, Benedict T.
1990 "The Gospel According to Matthew." *The New Jerome Biblical Commentary*. Edited by Raymond E. Brown, Joseph A. Fitzmyer, and Roland E. Murphy. Englewood Cliffs, N.J.: Prentice-Hall.

Waetjen, Herman C.
1976 *The Origin and Destiny of Humanness: An Interpretation of the Gospel According to Matthew*. San Rafael, Calif.: Omega Books.

Weaver, Dorothy Jean
1990 *Matthew's Missionary Discourse: A Literary Critical Analysis*. Sheffield, Great Britian: Sheffield Academic Press.

Weber, Hans-Ruedi
1979 *Jesus and the Children: Biblical Resources for Study and Preaching*. Geneva: World Council of Churches.

Wilkins, Michael J.
1988 *The Concept of Disciple in Matthew's Gospel*. Leiden: E. J. Brill.

Williams, George H., and Angel M. Mergal
1957 *Spiritual and Anabaptist Writings* (Library of Christian Classics, vol. 25). Philadelphia: The Westminster Press.

Wink, Walter
1968 *John the Baptist in the Gospel Tradition*. Cambridge, Great Britian: Cambridge University Press.
1988 "Jesus' Third Way." *Society of Biblical Literature 1988 Seminar Papers*. Edited by David J. Lull. Atlanta: Scholars Press.

Yoder, John Howard
1972 *The Politics of Jesus*. Grand Rapids, Mich.: William B. Eerdmans Publishing Company.
1983 *What Would You Do?* Scottdale, Pa.: Herald Press.

Yoder, Perry B.
1982 *From Word to Life*. Scottdale, Pa.: Herald Press.

Recommended Resources For Personal and Group Study

Augsburger, Myron S. *Matthew* (The Communicator's Commentary Series). Waco, Texas: Word Books, 1982. Exposition by a well-known communicator in the Anabaptist tradition.

Bornkamm, Günther, Gerhard Barth, and Heinz Joachim Held. *Tradition and Interpretation in Matthew*. Philadelphia: Westminister Press, 1963. Scholarly study of Matthew's approach to law, miracles, and other topics.

Brown, Raymond E. *The Birth of the Messiah*. Garden City, N.Y: Doubleday & Company, Inc., 1977. A comprehensive commentary on the infancy narratives of Matthew and Luke.

Davies, W. D., and Dale C. Allison. *A Critical and Exegetical Commentary on the Gospel According to Saint Matthew*, vol. 1 (International Critical Commentary, new series). Edinburgh: T. & T. Clark Limited, 1988. An impressive scholarly commentary covering Matthew 1—7. Volumes 2 and 3 will follow later.

France, Richard T. *The Gospel According to Matthew: An Introduction and Commentary* (Tyndale New Testament Commentaries). Grand Rapids, Mich.: William B. Eerdmans Publishing Company, 1985. A well-done evangelical commentary for the general reader.

Guelich, Robert A. *The Sermon on the Mount: A Foundation for Understanding*. Waco, Texas: Word Books, 1982. A solid, scholarly commentary on Matthew 5—7, combining exegesis with theological reflection on the Sermon.

Gundry, Robert H. *Matthew: A Commentary on His Literary and Theological Art*. Grand Rapids, Mich: William B. Eerdmans Publishing Company, 1982. A bold, detailed, and sometimes erratic analysis of Matthew's work as editor.

Kingsbury, Jack D. *Matthew As Story*. 2d ed. Philadelphia: Fortress Press, 1988. Kingsbury is one of the most prolific and informed contemporary interpreters of Matthew. This work provides an excellent introduction to the Gospel as narrative.

Lambrecht, Jan. *The Sermon on the Mount. Proclamation and Exhortation*. Wilmington, Del.: Michael Glazier, Inc., 1985. A readable introduction to the Sermon and its message.

Luz, Ulrich. *Matthew 1—7: A Commentary*. Minneapolis: Augsburg Fortress, 1989. A scholarly work translated from a European series, combining critical analysis with ecumenical reflection on the influence and interpretation of Matthean texts in the history of the church. Two additional volumes will follow.

Meier, John P. *Matthew* (New Testament Message). Wilmington, Del.: Michael Glazier, Inc., 1980. A stimulating popular commentary in a Roman Catholic series, attentive to Matthew's theological agenda and editorial tendencies.

Schweizer, Eduard. *The Good News According to Matthew*. Atlanta: John Knox Press, 1975. Translated from a series aimed at German-speaking pastors and teachers, this commentary focuses on the way Matthew adapts and shapes earlier Gospel tradition.

Senior, Donald. *The Passion of Jesus in the Gospel of Matthew*. Wilmington, Del.: Michael Glazier, Inc., 1985. A readable and stimulating analysis of the final chapters of the Gospel and how they relate to Matthew's overall agenda.

Senior, Donald. *What Are They Saying About Matthew*? New York: Paulist Press, 1983. A review of recent study of Matthew, concisely and simply written for the lay reader.

Stanton, Graham H., ed. *The Interpretation of Matthew*. Philadelphia: Fortress Press, 1983. A collection of key essays that have contributed to current scholarly understanding of Matthew.

Thompson, William G. *Matthew's Story: Good News for Uncertain Times*. New York: Paulist Press, 1989. An excellent resource for personal or small group study of Matthew.

The Author

Richard B. Gardner is a teacher and writer who effectively bridges the worlds of scholarly study of Scripture and Bible study in the local church. An ordained minister of the Church of the Brethren, he has prepared Bible study curriculum and led seminars and workshops both for his own denomination and for the larger church.

Gardner is an associate professor of New Testament at Bethany Theological Seminary in Oak Brook, Illinois. In addition to his teaching responsibilities, he directs several cooperatively sponsored programs of field-based ministry education for the Church of the Brethren.

From 1974 to 1988, Gardner served in several capacities with the parish ministries staff of the Church of the Brethren General Board. These included editing the quarterly *A Guide for Biblical Studies*, developing the church membership series *A People of Promise*, contributing to the development of the Foundation Series, curriculum design with the interdenominational Committee on the Uniform Series, and launching the program Education for a Shared Ministry. Prior to his denominational staff assignments, Gardner pastored two Church of the Brethren congregations in northern Ohio, 1971-74: the Paradise and Wooster Christ churches.

Among the author's published materials are numerous contributions to curriculum resources, including the *International Lesson Annual, New Ventures in Bible Study* and *A Guide for Biblical Studies*. He has also written for the periodicals *Messenger* and *Brethren Life and Thought* and contributed articles to the *Brethren*

Encyclopedia. He currently serves as president of the Brethren Journal Association and is a member of the Society of Biblical Literature and the Chicago Society of Biblical Research.

Gardner did his doctoral work at the University of Würzburg in Germany, where he received the D.Theol. degree *summa cum laude* in 1973. He received his M.Div. degree *magna cum laude* from Bethany Theological Seminary in 1965 and a B.A. *magna cum laude* from Juniata College, Huntingdon, Pennsylvania in 1962. He has also done graduate study in New Testament theology at Fuller Theological Seminary in Pasadena, California.

Born in Johnstown, Pennsylvania, the author currently resides in Winfield, Illinois. He is married to Carol Jean West Gardner, and both are active members of Christ Church of the Brethren in Carol Stream, Illinois.